Praise for *The Other Man in Me*

Neurosis may be defined as the suffering that arises from our splitting off aspects our of psyche (soul). By that standard, all of us suffer—all of us have parts of our personality that lie unknown to us. Shalley's *The Other Man in Me* is a very insightful, articulate, and courageous exploration of the Other that he discovered within himself. His willingness to face the reality, the complexity, and the summons of his soul serves as a challenge to all of us to bear the risk and the gift of looking within, and dialoguing with what comes to meet us.

— James Hollis, Ph.D., Jungian analyst and bestselling author of sixteen books, including *Finding Meaning in the Second Half of Life* and *Living Between Worlds: Finding Personal Resilience in Changing Times*

Sheldon Shalley offers us an extraordinary archetypal journey through human sexuality and, ultimately, human life itself. This provocative, challenging, and healing narrative illuminates the pain and joy of life coming to know itself.

— K. Brynolf Lyon, Ph.D., LMHC, Lois and Dale Bright Professor of Christian Ministries, and co-author of *How to Lead in Church*

A fascinating account of one man's passage to unify matter and spirit, body and identity, biology and social commitment through the arduous effort of intense inner psychological work.

— J. Gary Sparks, author of *At the Heart of Matter*

The Other Man in Me is a story of one man's courage in encountering and integrating his Inner Man, one that was lost along the way in the confusion of his attraction to the same sex, learning that it was so much more than just a physical attraction. It's a fascinating journey that he has detailed and will serve as a guide for any man that has found himself conflicted with his attraction to other men. Mr. Shalley's writing is both clear and emotionally evocative while simultaneously providing a unique psychological perspective. Highly recommended for any man wanting to explore his sexuality in depth."

— Dr. Steven Farmer, author of *Earth Magic* and *Healing Ancestral Karma*

Sheldon invites his readers deep into his internal world that is alive with dreams, associations, and characters. There he discovers his feminine and masculine sides, which are attempting to find balance and harmony. It is a disturbing, enchanting adventure into one man's struggle to understand his sexuality and what lies beneath its surface.

— Pat Hedegard, psychoanalyst and national faculty, International Psychotherapy Institute

This book is courageous. It is the result of a journey of struggle and discovery as one man uncovers the multiple selves that inhabit his soul. Culture's strictures force each of us to hide portions of ourselves in the shadows of our identity. Some never discover the rich secrets that can expand and enrich our lives. Sheldon has. And he has invited those secrets into the light and shared them with us that we too might know ourselves more fully and live more freely.

— Dan Moseley, Ph.D., professor emeritus at Christian Theological Seminary

A personal story that has a general resonance. I applaud Sheldon's journey of discovery into the hidden story in his sexual attraction and his courage to tell it.

— Greg Ellis, M.D., author of *Re-Membering Frankenstein: Healing the Monster in Every Man*

The Other Man in Me follows the courageous journey of one man in his quest to claim and understand his "two-spirit" soul. Growing up in a family with traditional and conservative values, Shalley had to find meaning to his same-sex attractions and an understanding of the "other man" living in his soul. Shalley provides hope and a path toward reconciliation and healing for those stuck in the painful conflicts between their inner and outer lives.

— Jackie Montrie, mental health counselor and marriage and family therapist

A transformational understanding of human sexuality.

— James Shalley, Psy.D., director of Associates in Family Care

THE OTHER MAN IN ME

Erotic Longing, Lust and Love: **The Soul Calling**

A Journey of Discovery into the Hidden Story in Sexual Attraction

SHELDON SHALLEY

ISBN: 978-1-09833-498-7 (Paperback)
ISBN: 978-1-09833-499-4 (Ebook)

First printing edition 2020

Art by Sheldon Shalley
Editing by Anne Dillon, NY Book Editors
Cover Design by Christy Collins and BookBaby
Author Photo by Matthew Doudt Photography

Printed and Bound in the United States of American

Published by BookBaby
Pennsauken, NJ 08110
www.BookBaby.com

Visit www.sheldonshalley.com

DEDICATIONS

To my wife, Betty, whose enduring love engendered the capacity to expand the container of our relationship so that this journey into the depths of my soul was possible. As such, she became a co-creator of the man who emerged from this journey.

To all who seek to understand the other in them.

DISCLAIMER

This book deals with a man's journey to understand his same-sex attractions. While I have taken great care to ensure that the subject matter is dealt with in a compassionate and respectful manner, keeping it within the symbolic and psychological framework of his therapy, it may be troubling for some readers. Discretion is advised.

At times acquaintances, friends, and family members appear in the dreams that are discussed in this book. In most cases I have changed their names to protect their privacy. Anything said about them are solely the dreamer's associations and projections and is not meant in any way to reflect their actual lives.

The content of this book is for information purposes only and is not intended to diagnose, treat, cure, or prevent any condition or disease. You understand that this book is not intended as a substitute for consultation with a licensed professional. Please consult with your own physician, mental health specialist, or spiritual advisor for matters related to emotional health, mental health, or spiritual concerns. The use of this book implies your acceptance of this disclaimer.

To keep the price of this book reasonable, my art is printed in black and white. To view my paintings in full color, visit My Gallery at www.artbyshalley.com.

TABLE OF CONTENTS

INTRODUCTION:

Homosexuality and the Soul's Longing

> " . . . When a man comes across something that intrigues him, even though to others it may seem dull and inert, a mere stone, he should suspect that this stone contains for him a spirit. If that spirit calls to him he ought to go and rescue it from its stony prison and make for it a more worthy body, whether in his eyes it seems a precious stone or whether it is a stone of stumbling—a point at issue—which also contains a spirit that will not let him rest in peace until he has redeemed it from its despised condition."
>
> —Mary Esther Harding, *Psychic Energy*

Behind all forms of sexuality is the great longing to find some way to experience the unity of oneness with the Other. Ultimately that "Other" is the "Other" in us as our own soul and all that lies hidden there repressed, shunned, and ignored. In their attempts to be known, these hidden places often get projected onto others. Whatever our sexual orientation may be, at its core is a longing for our own soul and the desire to bring into existence that which lies buried there. Thus, all sexuality, including homosexuality, can be understood as one of the many ways the soul expresses itself. All attraction is a longing of the soul. To understand the hidden meaning in the attraction is to bring a level of understanding and consciousness to the experience, which shifts one from living under its spell as "fate" would have it, to living with it in a conscious relationship.

There are times when living out one's sexual desires and attractions in the outer world is too demanding, not feasible, and may not be appropriate, such as in the case of sexual compulsions. In such situations a person's libido needs to be expressed elsewhere, often internally. Carl Jung suggested that when a person turns his desire away from outer things, his libido turns inward and he reaches the place of the soul.[1] Turning libido inward opens a man to the possibility of discovering the spiritual meaning of his desires and finding a new life plan.[2]

Where does that inward journey lead? Where does it end? The answer is unknown until one day you realize you are home. Somewhere deep inside you resonate with what you have discovered, who you have become. You recognize that you have found your truth. There is no need to defend it. Other points of view do not diminish it. You can allow others their judgments without judging. You are home! You have come to understand that those desires and attractions were symbols of the soul's longing to live its unlived life, not yet understood. That life, unconscious, dormant in your soul, *becomes* your life. In this I am suggesting that the life that you find was what you were longing for all along—the intent and spiritual purpose behind the sexual desires and attractions you experienced.

I was born into an evangelical minister's home. I was also born with the proclivity for same-sex attractions. I say "born" because current brain research indicates that biology plays a part in sexual

---

1 Jung, *Collected Works 14*, 443.

2 Main, *Childhood Re-imagined*, 35.

attraction.[3] Of course, I didn't know that when I was growing up. As my life unfolded, I discovered that while I was attracted to certain women, I was also attracted to certain men. These two worlds—my same-sex attractions and my religious training that believed homosexuality was a "sin"—would eventually collide.

This collision would lead me into a deep, soul-searching journey of self-discovery and to an understanding that sexual attraction—same-sex attraction—isn't just about sex. It isn't just about erotic feelings for another man. While it is that, it is also more than that.

---

3 Psychology and science have multiple theories on the origins of or the reasons for male homosexuality. Dutch physician and neurobiologist Dick Swaab says "[c] urrent evidence indicates that sexual differentiation of the human brain occurs during fetal and neonatal development and programs our gender identity—our feeling of being male or female and our sexual orientation as hetero-, homo-, or bisexual" (Sexual Orientation and its Basis in Brain Structure and Function, Proceedings of the National Academy of Sciences, PNAC, vol. 105, no. 30 Dick F. Swaab, 10273–10274). Brain research over the past decade has brought to light differences in brain responses between gay and straight men to various stimuli. Certain brain studies show evidence for structural and functional brain differences related to gender and sexual orientation, while other studies have shown that the brains of gay and straight men respond differently to human pheromones (Savic, I, H. Berglund, P. Lindström), (2005). Brain response to putative pheromones in homosexual men. (Proc Natl Acad Sci USA, 102:7356–7361). While these studies do not prove that our brains are hard-wired for sexual orientation, it does indicate that biology may play a part in one's sexual proclivities. Whether our brains determine our sexual preferences and behaviors or whether our sexual behaviors change the brain's structure and response is still undetermined. I think that sexual orientation in all its wide range of expressions is a complicated process that is a response to both nature and nurture. However, current research is providing evidence of a biological influence. I intentionally chose to use the words "born gay or at the very least bisexual" because I believe that current research suggests that we are born with the "markers" (biological and psychological) that both push us and pull us toward those experiences that will bring to birth the nature of our individual souls. Coagulated by Craig Chalquist, M.S., Ph.D., author of *Terrapsychology: Reengaging the Soul of Place* (Spring Journal Books, 2007).

Freud's discovery of the unconscious changed the world forever. For the first time we came to understand that phenomena outside of conscious awareness influences our beliefs, our thoughts, our feelings, and our behaviors, and therefore how we see the world and how we perceive reality. Jung's discovery of the collective unconscious with its archetypes altered our world even further. Not only did the unconscious influence reality, it organized it according to certain universal patterns, acting like a magnet attracting various and relevant experiences that influenced us to live out their emotional and behavioral stories.

Einstein's famous discovery that E=MC2 or energy equals mass plus light squared, set in motion a series of scientific experiments that concluded, in the language of quantum physics, that at the most basic level everything is energy. Both the physical plane of matter and the more abstract plane of the mind are energy. Therefore, our thoughts, our emotions, our fantasies, and our behaviors are expressions of energy, each vibrating with information that attracts to it those experiences that match its energy.

Sexuality and spirituality can thus be understood as expressions of energy. Sexuality does not exclude spirituality, nor does spirituality exclude sexuality.[4] Rather, they represent two aspects of a person's total energy flow. Sexuality and spirituality are one energy. The flow in one direction is complementary to, and dependent upon, the flow from the opposite direction.[5] This means that the spiritual life of each person is an inner, private exploration in which each individual is trying to understand the meaning and purpose of his or her life in his or her own terms. Inevitably, as sexuality and spirituality become increasingly

---

4 Jung, *Collected Works 14*, 443.

5 Moore, *Sexuality and Spirituality*, 20.

recognized as interdependent and complementary forces, the fulfilling of this purpose includes an exploration of one's sexual life.[6]

If everything is energy, and if sexuality and spirituality are two aspects of one energy flow—each complementary and dependent on the other—then homosexuality and same-sex attraction can also be understood to have a spiritual purpose. By spiritual purpose I mean the intent of homosexuality as an interplay of energy within the individual to provide a healing to the soul—a reconciliation of a split between the "outer-man" or "ego-self" and some "inner-man" or "unconscious self" that longs to live and of which a man may be completely unaware.

From an energetic point of view, same-sex attractions, fantasies, and behaviors are fundamental and meaningful patterns of energy that play at creation and development. They are archetypal in the sense that they express the call of a basic power in the depths of the soul that is essentially of a spiritual or sacred nature.[7] These images and sexual acts carry a certain mystery, a certain sense of awe, a certain power that grabs the soul. The experience, whether in fantasy or acted out, can be so powerful that it is capable of lifting one outside of oneself into some transcendent place.

With the explosion of gay rights, same-sex marriage, and increasing numbers of people "coming out" and proclaiming their sexual orientation, there is the potential for a split in our thinking. We are either gay or straight. If we have same-sex attractions can we be in a traditional marriage or a heterosexual relationship without being judged as somehow going against our "true nature"? Is there a place for the homosexual or bisexual man within the context of a traditional marriage or heterosexual relationship? Could same-sex attractions be

6 Ibid., 19.

7 Whitmont, *Return of the Goddess*, 259.

about something else altogether; some other longing of the soul that takes the form of same-sex desires, fantasies, and attractions?

I applaud the advances we are making in tearing down the prejudices against gay, lesbian, bisexual, and transgender people. However, I wonder about those countless individuals who are married and have chosen to remain married or in a heterosexual relationship or other living circumstances and struggle with being gay or bisexual, or having same-sex desires and attractions, silently suffering in the recesses of their souls. Many men are afraid to face their same-sex desires and attractions, repressing them, hiding them, living in quiet desperation, often feeling confused and at odds with themselves, wondering about the meaning of it all. Like me, they want acceptance and understanding. They want a way to live with these longings that is congruent with their soul's deepest needs and works within the context of their individual lives.

If you are a gay or bisexual man who is happy with the life you are living, you have found your path. This book may not be for you. This book is for:

- the gay, bisexual, and straight men who wrestle with same-sex desires, fantasies, and attractions, and perhaps even wrestle with the idea of having some same-sex encounters but are caught in conflicting priorities;
- the man who for one reason or another is unable to leave his circumstances—perhaps his wife and family, a partner, his religion or other values—to embrace a same-sex relationship in the outer world;
- the man who has some sense that there may be something else at the core of his same-sex attractions. (Maybe it isn't just about sex and the need for a physical man.);

- the man who is caught between the pull of two passions—two spirits—one to embrace the feminine and the other to embrace the masculine;
- the man who needs to find a way to live with his same-sex attractions that is congruent with his soul's purpose and deepest longings;
- the partners and family members who need to understand the struggle and travail of their loved ones.

The challenge is how to hold the tensions of these "conflicts of the soul," these seemingly contradictory paths, while making sense of them. The task is to find meaning in it all so that one can live one's life with compassion and honesty, being true to the deeper nature and longing within.

In the case of same-sex attraction, this may be the call of an ancient man, a memory living in the depths of the soul of a time when the masculine was a companion of the earth, one with her, living as a spirit in nature instead of personifying a masculine image living in the heavens.

While the ideas in this book may have application to other forms of sexual attraction, this book is about male same-sex attraction as I have come to understand it in my life. I propose that there are many forms of homosexuality and the reasons for same-sex attractions are as varied as the people who experience them. Same-sex attraction has its own meaning peculiar to the individual and psycho-spiritual development depends on becoming conscious of that meaning.[8]

In my opinion, sexual attraction—what arouses one person and what arouses another—is a highly complicated phenomenon with multiple contributors. On one hand, sex is simply a biological drive,

---

8 Hopcke, "Jung's Attitudes toward Homosexuality," 154–161.

a physical arousal produced through the combination of endocrine, neuronal, and molecular mechanisms that wants to fulfill itself. The object of desire may be secondary. It can be an unknown man in a men's room or public park who you do not know and whom you will never see again. It can be someone you meet online for mutual masturbation or any number of other scenarios.

At another level, sexual attraction is fueled by loving feelings, longings for a connection with the object of one's affection.

At a third level, sexual attraction can be understood as symbolic. Our fantasies, our attractions, and even our behaviors mirror parts of us, telling a story of our own individual mythology. By mythology I do not mean falsehood, but rather images as symbols that bring a level of understanding to our attractions, which cannot be known simply through the image or our own personal history. For example, a man's penis in the act of receiving oral sex isn't just his penis, but a symbol for some part of him that longs to be validated, honored, brought to life, perhaps even worshipped. The symbolic meaning is truer than the act of oral sex because it acknowledges a reality that could not otherwise be expressed.[9] It is this point of view that begins to hint to us that sexual attractions in all their forms and behaviors can have spiritual meaning and intent.

I believe that sometimes life provides a conflict of priorities that force us to discover our soul's longing and purpose. It is in the process of finding the source of these "soul conflicts" that we discover a deeper meaning—why we are here and what we are to do. As such, I believe that these "soul conflicts" have a spiritual purpose. That spiritual purpose is to lead us to that part of us that transcends ego needs, that transcends our personal history, that transcends our family and ancestral

---

9 Christensen, *C. S. Lewis on Scripture*, 76–77.

patterns, that transcends our beliefs, even what we might hold valuable. It connects us to the Divine Spark within us that longs to fulfill its destiny.

Spiritual meaning is born when sexual fantasies, attractions, and behaviors are recognized as symbols of energy patterns at work within the individual. When we recognize that images are the mediating world between the physical and the spiritual, between the mind and the body, between spirit and matter, between the inner and the outer, we discover a pathway to the individual meaning of our individual lives. The spiritual goal of the energy that expresses itself as same-sex desires, attractions, and behaviors may be understood as an innate potential that seeks correspondence in the outer world. Whether a man lives this experience out in a same-sex relationship or as an inner experience is a matter of his particular soul's destiny and personal choice.

My own personal experience and the experience of the hundreds of people I have worked with over the past twenty-nine years as a clinical social worker and psychotherapist have taught me that there are as many soul conflicts as there are individuals. But all these soul conflicts seem to have something in common. The conflict is between the life one is living and the life one longs to live. It is a split between the outer and inner lives—a split between ego and soul. For me this split, this conflict of soul priorities, manifested as a conflict between my life as a husband, father, musician, church leader, and well-respected man of my community, and my secret same-sex desires, attractions, and fantasies. This conflict ultimately resulted in cursory sexual encounters with men in men's restrooms—wherever I could find them.

Was I gay, straight, or bisexual, or none of the above? At the time I wondered, should I leave my marriage and my life as I knew it and embrace a gay lifestyle? Was that my journey? And how was I to reconcile these seemingly opposing worlds? How could I make sense of it all? How do I resolve what emerged as conflicting needs of my soul?

I kept a detailed journal of my dreams, fantasies, conflicts, and inner struggles for most of my life. This book is the result of my journey back through the pages of those journals—a looking back at that life forty years later. In the rearview mirror I see more clearly how the life vibrating in the depths of my soul was actually guiding me often through my same-sex attractions to discover and embody the "other man" living there.

If we understand that sexual desires, fantasies, and attractions may be interpreted as symbolic expressions of the soul, cries of the spirit vibrating with information that long for recognition and life, then we can consciously make constructive choices about them. For if we fall under their spell unconsciously, we are at risk of unwittingly living them out in destructive and compulsive behaviors that may wreak havoc on our lives and our families. By discovering their hidden meanings we can make decisions about how to live with them in a way that is congruent with our soul's needs and the individual meaning of our desires and fantasies without necessarily living them out physically in sexual relationships or denying them.

I dream that

> *I go out to the parsonage where my pastor, an evangelical minister, used to live. I enter the back door. The house has been all remodeled. In the first room a repair man is doing some kind of work. He leaves. I walk on through the house. I notice it has been re-carpeted—everywhere except the family room, which has been tiled with a mosaic tile. I don't think anybody is at home, so I walk on through the house. I open the door to a room. It is a bedroom. There is a boy sleeping*

> *in the bed; he is completely covered. I am surprised to find someone in the house. I didn't think they had any young children. I leave quietly so as not to wake him and have him find me in the house.* (Journal, 11-5-83)

As I meditated on this dream, I felt compelled to go back into the dream and interact with its images.

> *I open the door to the bedroom. I go in and sit down on the bed. I pull the blanket back. I see a fair, young blond boy. He becomes a large wolf, now a large green snake. Yet still he is the boy.*
>
> *Sheldon: "Who are you, little boy?"*
>
> *Boy: "I am the little boy who is still hiding, covered up in the parsonage, afraid to accept his instincts, afraid to embrace life and relationship, the little boy that stays hidden and wrapped up in the rules and morals of the parsonage, in bed covered with a blanket of fear. You must take me with you. Me, with all my instincts, drives, needs. I am your younger brother, your other self, your primitive self, the part of you that desires the masculine. Please free me from the parsonage bedroom. Please remove the blanket that keeps me hidden. Please embrace me. Please love me! Please free me!"*
>
> *I take his hand, a combination now of the little boy, the wolf, and the big green snake, and lift him into my arms and carry him from the bedroom to the outside. As I do this, the wine-colored shag carpet becomes flames of fire and burn the house down. As the boy and I walk off down the road, I walk straight ahead, knowing that the smoke of the burned down house is billowing up into the sky.*

> *I walk on. I sense the charred remains. Suddenly the little boy is walking by my side. How I love him. As we walk, I feel like a little child—helpless, vulnerable, and wondering, now what do I do?*
>
> *Suddenly the little boy becomes white, like a spirit or ghost. He enters into me. We are now a man in a long white robe, like a wise man, a spirit being, much like the image of Christ. He is us, and yet we are still there on the road watching. He is heading south. We stand watching, holding hands. It is like we are transparent or spirits ourselves. We walk off to the right into a green field. As we walk things pass through us. The field is green and there are flowers.* (Journal, 11-5-83)

Five nights later, I dream "I am told by a voice that the little boy that I freed from the former parsonage is my homosexual self and that the healing of the homosexual is in freeing him from the parsonage." (Journal, 11-10-83)

The dream says, "The healing of the homosexual self is freeing him from the parsonage." At first glance the word *healing* conjures up thoughts of "something wrong that needs to be fixed," some "flaw" that needs to be changed or cured, a "sin" that needs to be confessed and redeemed, or some "evil" from which one needs to be set free. While the word *heal* can be defined in such ways, the word *heal* also means "to repair or reconcile," "to heal the rift between," "to become whole or sound," "to mend," "to restore." It also literally means "to make whole."

I discovered that freeing my homosexual self from the parsonage, from the "age of the parson" in which I was raised, *was* about healing. But it wasn't about fixing something that was wrong, sick, or a "sin."

It was about restoration, reconciliation, and healing the rift between me and other parts of myself. It was a story about the soul's longing to become whole, to embrace the pieces that had been repressed or that had not yet made it into consciousness at all. It was a story about finding the soul's path, the individual meaning of an individual life. Ultimately it was the healing of the mind-body split in me, the split between the forbidden and the acceptable, the split between spirit and matter, between the "ego-self" and the "unconscious Other." For me the drive behind my same-sex attraction was the longing for a man buried deep within my soul, a re-connection to an ancient memory of a man that, as previously stated, used to roam the earth, the man connected to the Divine in nature. It was a return to the Green Man, an archetypal masculine that is one with nature, a divine intelligence, a divine light, a wisdom and consciousness that exists in matter that both protects and reveals its spirit—its light—whether that matter is a stone, a tree, an animal, an organ in the body, or the earth herself. This was a story of the discovery of the spirit in the "matter" of same-sex desires, fantasies, and attractions and its path to the soul—to that *spark of the divine* that lives in each of us as our unique individual life. To the extent that any man is cut off from aspects of the masculine that are his to embody, this archetypal masculine will erupt from the unconscious in a multitude of ways, including same-sex fantasies and attractions.

Chapter 1, "The Call of the Masculine" tells the story of the entrance of same-sex attractions into my life and the call of the masculine as an archetypal force to be reckoned with.

Chapter 2, "The Call of the Soul" identifies the emergence of my soul's conflicts and the soul's response to my same-sex attractions as a call to seek "the treasure hard to find."

Chapter 3, "The Call of the Dreams," details my confrontation with the unconscious and the discovery that deep within us lives an unknown land. This is a land with its own laws and its own plans and purposes populated with characters playing out sometimes tempestuous relationships in the depths of our souls. These archetypal forces and images live in the very depths of us and long for recognition, for communion, for expression, and a way to get into life. They make their appearances in our dreams. By engaging them they help us find our soul's path and to write our own destinies.

Chapter 4, "Meeting the Shadow," tells of the return of what we have repressed and the challenge of embracing and integrating into consciousness what we have pushed away into the darkness of the unconscious in order to live the life we are living.

Chapter 5, "Honoring the Witch," is my confrontation with the feminine in me and her perspective on my life.

In Chapter 6, "The Emerging Self," the Divine Masculine makes his appearance as Phallos and the inner Christ. This chapter details my increasing awareness that my same-sex attractions were really about leaving my life as I knew it and embracing this "Other" in me.

Chapter 7, "The Call of the Swan Maiden," tells of the response of the unconscious to my desire to return to a homosexual relationship and details more clearly the meaning and purpose of my homosexuality and same-sex attractions.

Chapter 8, "Manifestations of the Self in Male Same-Sex Behaviors," suggests the symbolic and spiritual meanings in male same-sex oral sex, anal sex, and masturbation.

Chapter 9, "Looking in the Mirror," continues to clarify that what I am seeking in my same-sex attractions, fantasies, and longings is really about what is longing to come into consciousness in me—the discovery of another man living in my soul, the shaman and the Earth

Masculine. This is a consciousness that recognizes that the Divine Masculine isn't some God living up in the heavens ruling over the earth and the feminine but a divine spirit vibrating in the very nature of the earth and matter, one with her as co-equal and co-creator.

In Chapter 10, "Same-Sex Attractions and the Interplay of the Masculine and Feminine," I show how my same-sex attractions played out in my own inner masculine and feminine relationship. I suggest that our masculine and feminine energies play out their inner relationships in our external lives, whether they be between a man and a woman, between a man and a man, or between a woman and another woman.

Chapter 11, "Caught in an Archetypal Tale," further clarifies the conflict that emerged between that part of me that was feeling same-sex attractions on the one hand, and the man of the church and the parsonage on the other. I then detail how I forged a path forward from there.

Chapter 12, "Same-Sex Attractions and the Hero's Journey" is the culmination of ten years of inner work and learning to listen to the voice of this other man living in my soul. In it, I discuss my decision to leave the safety of my life as I knew it, that of a respected high school teacher, and to embrace what Joseph Campbell calls the "hero's journey"—the journey of individuation to discover one's individual life. This decision would come to mean more than just leaving teaching and the town where my family and I had lived for twenty-plus years. It was about leaving an ideology, leaving a belief system, leaving a particular world view and discovering the one living in my soul—the one that was more authentic and congruent with my own individual self.

Chapter 13, "Archetypal Implications in Same-Sex Dreams, Fantasies, and Behaviors" tells how this journey continued to reveal itself through my paintings. Images that appeared in these paintings became guides that introduced me to unconscious parts of myself. I came to see that behind my same-sex attractions was the expression of the Green Man, the archetypal masculine who I mentioned above. His appearance in my life became the impulse for my journey into shamanism, with its emphasis on Spirit as well as its emphasis on matter and Spirit in nature. This was my attempt to heal the mind-body split in me and to free myself from the masculine image of the evangelical parsonage.

Chapter 14, "The Music Begins," tells of the emergence of a Divine Masculine spirit different from the one I'd been raised with. This masculine spirit was one with nature, a consort and companion of the Earth Mother and the Goddess of ancient times, a reunion of spirit and matter. I came to look at objects, people, and even the events of my life as sacred and as having some spiritual or transcendent purpose and meaning—as music in my soul.

In Chapter 15, "Return to Eden and the Soul's Next Manifestation," I discuss how my dreams and my art introduced me to my soul's next manifestation and put me more firmly on the shamanic path.

Chapter 16, "The Matter of the Heart and the Heart of Matter," is my journey to resolve the spirit/matter, mind/body split by exploring the "imaginal sight" of the heart and its capacity to see the spirit that is vibrating in matter.

Chapter 17, "The Return of the Green Man," tells of the emergence of the archetype of the Green Man in my art, and his meaning.

Chapter 18, "Homosexuality and the Two-Spirit Archetype," discusses the role of the berdache, or two-spirit, in Native American and other indigenous cultures as a medicine man and shaman who serve as a "go-between," an entity between the masculine and the feminine, between matter and spirit.

Chapter 19, "The Rest of the Story," tells the impact of my journey on my family.

In the Appendix I describe the characteristics of my parents and how their relationship to me and to each other influenced my psychic configuration to set up another masculine image in my soul that longed for expression.

While this journey into the depths of my own soul was influenced by Jungian psychology and my own analysis with Jungian analyst, Dean Frantz, I have chosen to describe these experiences as expressions of my own soul as I experienced and interacted with them, letting them speak for themselves. However, there are times when I have found it necessary to talk about my experiences within the framework of Jung's psychology. Anyone familiar with Jungian psychology will recognize this underlying bias by which I make sense of the soul's longing.

Consistently, the images that surfaced in my dreams in response to my desires to act on my same-sex desires indicated, as touched on earlier, that my attractions were about something else wanting to come to life in me. In my ongoing analysis, I drew from both personal and archetypal material presented in my dreams and spontaneous images arising in meditation and art. I also drew upon the meanings that I found in coincidences, serendipitous meetings, and synchronicities, and explored my own same-sex attractions and the same-sex motifs found in mythology and in certain customs and rituals of some primitive societies. In so doing, I have been able to tell a story of the discovery of the symbolic and spiritual meaning of my own homosexuality and same-sex attractions. These interpretations can open a man to deep places in his soul—places that can assist him in finding his way when faced with conflicts on how to live with same-sex desires in a manner that is congruent with his own established priorities and the meaning of his individual life. It some ways this book is the culmination of that same-sex longing.

Irrespective of how a man chooses to live his same-sex desires and attractions, whether that be in brief sexual encounters with other men, in a loving same-sex relationship or marriage, or as an inner relationship with the masculine within, I invite you to listen to the longings of an ancient man who longs for us to live in harmony with all that is.

CHAPTER ONE

The Call of the Masculine

Universal images of the masculine live in the depths of a man's soul. To the extent that a man is cut off from aspects of the masculine that are his to embody, they will erupt from the unconscious in multiple ways.

I first became aware of my own same-sex attractions the summer between my graduation from high school and my freshman year in college. I had various girlfriends throughout junior high and high school. While I had what seemed like a serious relationship with a girl during my senior year, that relationship ended after graduation. Shortly thereafter, I found myself visiting a men's restroom in a public park where I watched a man masturbate. He performed oral sex on me that day. Looking back at this event fifty years later I see more clearly the significance and unconscious purpose this event had for my life. For in that brief encounter with an unknown older man in a men's room in a public park, in nature itself, archetypal Phallos awakened from his slumbering in the far reaches of my unconscious and made himself known.

Although the description of this scene might seem voyeuristic and pornographic, I had indeed fallen under the spell of the archetypal Phallos. For years I lived under that spell as Phallos both pushed me and pulled me into other similar experiences in its attempt to connect me to this raw, chthonic masculinity. Eventually I would come to see more clearly how, up to that point, I had been a passive responder to the external cues of my life, complying with the rules of the parsonage, fitting into being the companion of the literal and symbolic mothers of the church and other institutions in my need to be accepted and loved. That was the safest way. For whenever I had attempted to assert myself by actions such as taking a shortcut through the neighbor's lawn, for instance, or expressing excitement about the pencils my dad got me for kindergarten, raising my hand to answer a question in school, fighting with a peer, or inserting my own creative style into my music, I had often been met with criticism. This frequently caused shame and embarrassment in me and made me feel somehow that my actions had been wrong or inappropriate in some way.

In the men's restroom with that older man, a stranger to me, for the first time I asserted myself with my own erected phallic member—my own phallic power, my own raw masculine self—and found that it was received, accepted, and validated. That felt good. Plus it was also exciting and scary, risky, and a breaking of the rules. Something came alive in me that set me on a journey to find other such experiences—men who would receive me, accept me, and validate me in my most basic, raw, intimate, secret masculinity, at the level of my soul.

Phallos himself had come alive in me, connecting me to some part of myself that had lain dormant, or if he had raised his head, had been immediately shamed and shut down except when he fit into the milieu of the parsonage's family dynamics. I would discover that men's rooms were places where I could find this raw masculine energy and feel connected to my own masculinity. I would leave such places feeling connected and empowered, somehow having the confidence and the courage to return to the demands and expectations of my rather passive response to my life. These connections gave me the strength to be the man I needed to be in the world in which I lived. It was as if I was a much better man after such encounters—less moody, less irritable, more creative, and more assertive—less under the spell of the feminine. Ironically, in my heterosexual relationship I took on the role of the man, of the masculine, the one who penetrates and takes. In my homosexual relationships I took on the role of the woman, of the feminine, the one who receives and takes in.

My sexual encounters with men seemed to connect me to another part of myself that empowered me to live my life. Of course, I didn't understand that in the early years. I simply lived out this desire unconsciously, caught in the instinctive urge of archetypal Phallos.

"Phallos is sacred to men as the manifestation of the inner self."[10] A phallic symbol does not mean the sexual organ itself but the libido. No matter how clearly the penis appears simply as a penis, it is more than that. It is always a symbol of the libido.[11] While the libido is popularly thought of as sex drive, libido also refers to psychic energy—energy as a force behind all psychological activity.[12] As such it is the creative power of our own soul[13] and includes the basic human conditions of creativity, connection with the "Other," and ecstasy. It also motivates the spiritual movement from ego to inner self.[14] Phallos, as a source of life and libido, is the creator and worker of miracles, and, as archaeological studies all over the world has shown, was worshipped everywhere,[15] from the Priapus, Orphic and Dionysiac cults of ancient Greece to the worship of Cybele and Attis in ancient Rome to the Shiva deity of India to the worship of Osiris in Egypt to mention a few.

---

10 Monick, *Castration and Male Rage*, 9.

11 Jung, *Collected Works 5*, par. 329.

12 Ibid., par. 194.

13 Ibid., par. 176.

14 Monick, *Castration and Male Rage*, 18.

15 Jung, *Collected Works 5*, par. 146.

The phallus works in darkness and creates a living being.[16] In the end, Phallos becomes the carrier of man's projection of the Divine in man, the source of life, libido, creativity, and the object of his own soul. In Eugene Monick's *Castration and Male Rage* the author points out "[t]he object of a man's touching is not simply his sexual organ per se."[17] Rather, the "touching is his means of establishing himself with himself,"[18] of reconnecting to the memory of the sacred masculine within him, archetypal Phallos, the place of "soul, soul-bearing and soul-ownership."[19]

After a long struggle with Phallos and his relationship to the feminine, I discovered another masculine image living in the depths of my soul, a masculine image different from the one that reigned in the parsonage. He wasn't bound by the rules and dogma of the evangelical minister's home in which I was raised, caught in Cartesian dualism that had split spirit and matter and had taken spirit out of nature, asserting that nature itself was inherently evil. Rather, he spoke of a wisdom in nature, of a belief "that Nature, including human nature, contains within itself a directing intelligence which is the source of all knowledge concerning the nature of a person's being and becoming."[20]

Phallos spoke of a time when the masculine was in a relationship with the earth and the feminine rather than in control of her. He spoke of a time when the masculine and feminine, the God and the Goddess, were two passionate lovers or fellow consorts ruling in harmony.[21] This male image demonstrated a different relationship with the world, a different relationship with the earth, a different relationship with my

---

16 Ibid., par. 180.

17 Monick, *Castration and Male Rage*, 18.

18 Ibid.

19 Ibid.

20 Stein, *Betrayal of the Soul*, xxxvii.

21

own soul, with my own body. He was the masculine consciousness of nature, and in fact was one with nature.

In the beginning of this journey he was the face of the unconscious itself. As my journey evolved, the images that flowed from the unconscious began to show me that true male power exists in its magical relationship with the feminine, not in a relationship to her or over her. I discovered that my own authenticity, my own sense of masculinity, my own sense of self came from the wisdom vibrating in the depths of my own soul. In stepping into that space, I discovered my self—a self that often took the form of a same sex attraction. I learned that I was projecting this man inside me onto a man out there in my search to find him in matter, in nature, in the body of another. It was my search to embody him—a memory of something that vibrated in my own soul.

> *As the music starts, the drums carry my back to a dream, a teenage boy in a thatched roof hut, being shot in the stomach by a man. As the music continues, I pull up into a fetal position on the floor. Slowly I begin to move, almost like I'm dancing. Like a ballet I dance with the music. Yet, it is like a birth, moving, expanding. A wolf comes and sits quietly to my left, observing, as if waiting. A cat appears, a jaguar perhaps. She moves. Then it is like I am the cat. I feel my movements, stretching, rolling, sitting. Yes. I am the cat!*
>
> *A tree appears. So strong. So large. I sit against it. Flashes of light appear. Dancing on. A gentle touch. A cough. I feel an opening as my body stretches up, up, and out from its former fetal position, back arching. The music finishes. The dance continues.* (Journal, Holotropic Breathwork Experience, 4-5-00)

Eight days following this experience, while driving to work, the following verse came to me almost complete in a matter of minutes.

Animal, Earth, and Tree

As the sun rises over the African jungle, a shot rings out.
Somewhere in a thatched roof grass hut a teenage boy lies dead.
The action of a white man come to save him from his pagan ways.
A gut-shot they call it, a bullet straight to the stomach.
A slow, agonizing, painful death.
As the blood slowly drains from the stomach wound
Freeing him from animal, earth, and tree
An intellectual shell remains.
Years pass . . . and somewhere in the far reaches
of his psychic past, a memory remains
A memory of animal, earth, and tree.
Slowly the blood, long encased in its earthen tomb, begins to stir
Flowing up, up and upward, back into the gut-shot wound.
And with it, Animal, Earth, and Tree.

I imagine it was the memory of that long-lost connection that was calling to me in the awakening of the same-sex attraction in a men's room in a public park on a summer afternoon in 1963. This memory stood in opposition to my then one-sided patriarchal masculine consciousness that saw the masculine as power and dominance over the feminine and nature. This consciousness that had taken spirit out of nature, had taken spirit out of matter, and had split the mind and the body.

This masculine consciousness rejected the sensual, rejected the body, rejected the sexual, rejected the earthy. It rejected even nature itself and saw the soul with all its rhythms and desires as something to be saved. I now understand that Phallos as symbol contained not only the masculine as a god up in heaven but an archetypal force that lives in and infuses matter and nature. This was the masculine that was one with the earth, one with the Goddess. It was he that was calling to me.

However, at the time I didn't know that. I confused Phallos with the phallus, the penis, and projected onto the object that longing for a connection to that deep unconscious masculine energy in me. In fact, I would venture to say that Phallos himself orchestrated this entire encounter in his longing to get into life.

This can be understood as an example of falling under the spell of an archetype. To the extent that one is unconscious of this, the archetype itself will direct a man's life and he will call this fate.[22] Of course and again, I didn't know that at the time. I only knew that something had been awakened in me, had been "turned on" so to speak. I now had an erotic desire for men.

After that initial encounter I visited public restrooms in search of sex with men, in search of Phallos. Having started in the summer of 1963, this continued until 1973. This search for Phallos, the sacred masculine as the Earth Masculine, the masculine spirit that lives in nature as a co-creator with the feminine, will weave itself through the following chapters.

In the fall of 1963, I attended a small Christian college. I was a shy and introverted guy. Dating and social interactions were somewhat awkward and difficult for me, even though I had dated in high school. During college I continued to think in terms of girlfriends and occasionally dated. It was during this time that I met and married my wife.

---

22 Jung, in Aion, CW 9ii, § 126

Still I continued to have a secret life, periodically going to public men's restrooms to meet men for sex.

I graduated from college and my wife and I moved to a small Midwestern town where I began teaching at the local high school and we attended a local church. I was active in many aspects of the church, serving as music director, board member, and teaching Sunday school, the model "Christian" husband, father, and church and community leader.

In 1970 I started a Master of Arts program at a state university. At the university I discovered that the men's rooms were full of men readily available for sex. My sexual encounters with other men increased during these years. Not only did sex with men increase, a conflict increased inside me, a conflict between the two lives I was leading. It was as if I was satisfying two separate needs, living as two separate people, living in two separate worlds. I found an increasing inner pressure to reveal my homosexuality and same-sex attractions, a growing need to "come out."

After graduating from the university, my access to sex with men was greatly diminished. Because of the growing conflict inside me and a growing sense that I needed to become more congruent with my religion and my loyalty and commitment to my wife and family, I stopped going to men's restrooms in search of sex. At the same time, I slowly came to realize that the image I presented to the world—the heterosexual man who was husband, father, teacher, musician, and spiritual leader—wasn't *all* of who I was. The part of me that was attracted to other men was certainly a part of me, a part that I needed to embrace.

As time went on, the weight of living two lives, living split energies, was becoming difficult to carry. Finally, the inner tension became too great, and I told my wife about my homosexual feelings and same-sex encounters. She, of course, was devastated. What did this mean for our relationship, for our marriage, for our children, for her? My wife and I were left to decide what we were going to do with our relationship. After much soul-searching we both agreed that we had something worth keeping and neither of us wanted to divorce. We decided to face this together and move forward with repairing and rebuilding our relationship and raising our children. We also agreed that if at any time this choice was not working for either one of us, we would revisit our decision at that time, and perhaps opt for a different outcome.

While there were times when my homosexual desires and attractions retreated, they would also resurface. It was only after coming out and the conflicts resulting from the collision of these two worlds that I discovered the need to understand my homosexuality, a need to make sense of my same-sex attractions, and to find the meaning in them. The masculine was calling.

During one of the very conflicted times, I had this dream:

> *Four blind or partially blind boys are riding on horses. Other adults and I are with them as guides. One horse becomes upset and knocks a boy to the ground. He seems dead. One of the adults gives CPR to the boy but cannot revive*
>
> *him. Another adult then begins to give this boy CPR and does revive him. We put him back on the horse and the same thing happens. I think,* "Why are we out horseback riding with blind boys? This is plain ridiculous. I'm going back home (to the small Indiana town where I live)."
>
> *I start back home, and a bull comes out of nowhere and starts chasing me. I run from it and jump a fence and go into a small barn. The bull leaves for a moment to reattack. I say, "I'm ready for you this time." The bull comes back and chases me. I climb a tree thinking I'll be safe, but to my surprise*

> *the bull climbs right up the tree after me. I remember being amazed that the bull could climb a tree. I shout at it to go away. It falls back down the tree.* (Journal, 1978)

Critical to understanding this dream is the meaning of the bull. Images in dreams are carriers of energy at play in an individual. These images often reveal messages from the soul. In general, animals in dreams represent instinctive forces we have lost touch with. The fact that animals appear so often in our dreams indicates the importance of discovering their meaning as dream symbols. They often point to a very important fact when they turn up in a dream, a fact that can almost always be understood by learning the dreamer's personal associations to the animal and by studying the animal as it has appeared in religion, mythology, and fairy tales throughout history.

Like indigenous people, Jung believed that the animal represented the "divine" aspect of the human psyche. Animals live in contact with a "secret" order within nature itself and, much more so than humans, are connected with the "absolute knowledge" of the unconscious. The animal lives according to its own inner laws beyond good and evil.[23] Therefore, when they appear in our dreams, they help us to transcend the dichotomies of good and bad or right and wrong as set by family systems and cultural institutions. They also help us transcend a society's standards, especially when those institutions and standards violate the rights of a group of people or deny the wisdom inherent in nature, including our own.

For me the bull was a large, powerful, intimidating, aggressive, and dangerous animal whose purpose was to fertilize the herd to produce offspring. On the personal level, the bull symbolizes the powerful,

---

23 Hannah, *Archetypal Symbolism of Animals,* viii.

aggressive, and intimidating—even dangerous and scary—masculine fertilizing and procreative energy in me. It represented a certain masculine energy that was chasing me and from which I was running. However, as an archetype and from its role in mythology and ancient religions, the bull is a more complex and ambivalent symbol. As such, its full meaning is beyond the scope of this book. Thus, I will highlight the meaning of the bull as it relates to my own story.

First the bull is a symbol of both the masculine and the feminine.[24] His male fertility, his fiery temperament, and his role as father of the herd make him the masculine principle in nature. The bull's crescent-shaped horns link him to moon worship and to the feminine. Throughout history, the bull was depicted as feminine as often as he was masculine and may be associated with either one.[25]

Second, the bull is a symbol of the Divine Masculine, being associated with multiple pre-Christian gods and goddesses. Archaeological research confirms the bull's association with the phallus and gives evidence of phallic-bull worship all across the ancient world, commencing in 6000 BCE and spreading across Europe, Africa, and Asia. Sometimes this horned phallic god took the form of a bull with human face, sometimes a human with a bull's head, sometimes a horned god holding his erected phallus, sometimes a phallus with a face. The evidence is clear that the principle manifestation of the male god took the form of a bull, confirming the bull's association with divinity and with the phallus, making him a symbol for Phallos, the Divine Masculine.[26]

Third, the bull as the masculine generative spirit in nature is the forerunner of the Green Man as the spirit of vegetation, of green and

---

24 Cooper, *Illustrated Encyclopaedia*, 26–27.

25 Cirlot, *Dictionary of Symbols*, 33–34.

26 Tucker, "Christ Story Bull Page."

growing things, and the masculine spirit in nature as a source of regeneration and life. The bull shows up in the Greek god Dionysus, the Roman god Bacchus, and the Egyptian god Osiris, all of whom are known as "bull-gods" and all of whom are ancestors of the Green Man. In this regard, the Green Man is the generative masculine power of Mother Earth and the Great Goddess. Herein he is her son, lover, and guardian—living in unity with her.[27] While it would be years before the Green Man would show up spontaneously in my paintings, the historical evidence suggests that this archetype was already present in the bull image chasing me in this dream. With his emphasis on relationship with Mother Earth, the Goddess, and Spirit in nature as an indwelling intelligence, it would be the Green Man who would lead me to shamanism and the inner shaman.

Fourth, the fact that the bull held such a prominent place in the religious practices of people the world over for over fifteen thousand years speaks to its archetypal presence. In this the bull vibrates in the collective unconscious, reminding us of a time when the spirit of the Divine Masculine inhabited nature and lived in harmony with the Earth, the Great Mother, the Great Goddess, and the Divine Feminine.

In Egypt the sacred black bull Apis was believed to be the incarnation of the creator and fertility god Ptah, along with creator and sky god Amon, and Osiris, the god of the dead. While Christianity was spreading through the Roman world, the cult of Mithras, a Persian sun-god, was being embraced and spread by Roman soldiers. According to this religion, Mithras had assisted in the creation of life on earth by taking a bull into a cave where he cut its throat. The first plants and animals then sprang from the bull's blood and semen and managed to populate the earth. Initiates into this cult were purified by the blood of

---

27 Anderson, *Green Man*, 21.

a bull, causing them to be symbolically reborn into eternal life. Mithras was also worshipped as a sun-bull.

Bulls are also symbols of the storm gods such as Adad, Thor, and Ishkur. The bull as a thunder or storm god is a symbol of fertility, creation, and the violence of nature, which cannot be tamed.

The bull as a male deity was also familiar to the Israelites given that many of their neighbors worshipped gods in this form. The Canaanite Baal, the Babylonian Hadad and Enlil, and the gods Bel and Eabani serve as examples.

In Hinduism, as in many religions, the bull symbolizes strength and fertility, especially fertility that is sparked or strengthened by fire, heat, the sun, and lightning. The Rig-Veda states that the heavenly bull Rudra fertilized the earth with his sperm. Agni, the god of fire, was called "the mighty bull" and the Hindu god Indra is also associated with the bull.

In Greco-Roman mythology, the bull was sacred to Aphrodite and Venus, to Dionysus and Bacchus, to Poseidon and Neptune, and to Zeus and Jupiter.

According to the research of Suzetta Tucker, author of "Christ Story Bull Page" bulls were sacrificial victims in many nations. The Israelites sacrificed bulls on many occasions, usually as tokens of repentance and reconciliation with God. Christians often view these sacrifices as a foreshadowing of the purifying sacrifice of Christ, which then became the path to repentance and reconciliation with God. According to Jungian psychology, bull sacrifices and bullfights are symbolic of acting out the desire to kill the beast within each of us.[28]

The presence of the bull in my dream suggested that this archetype was now rising up from its slumbering in my unconscious, to connect

---

28 Tucker, "Christ Story Bull Page."

me to this other aspect of the masculine. This view of the masculine was very different from the one that reigned in the parsonage—in the evangelical minister's home that saw sensuality, sexuality, the body, the feminine, and nature itself as somehow evil—something to be dominated and subjected to a patriarchal masculine living up in heaven. This would describe the attitude and beliefs of the parsonage from which, according to the "parsonage dream" presented in the introduction, I must free my homosexual self if I was to heal him.

Could it be that the energy chasing me in the form of a bull was some Earth Masculine, some masculine principle inhabiting nature? Was it that generative male procreative humid force of the chthonic masculine that was also a symbol of the life-giving, death-dealing, regenerating forces of the chthonic feminine? In analytical psychology, *chthonic* is the word used to describe the spirit of nature within, the unconscious earthly impulses of the soul. Although it can manifest as envy, lust, sensuality, deceit, and all those dark aspects of the unconscious—even the spirit of evil as in the sense of death and destruction—it also manifests in the positive, as a "spirit in nature" that creatively gives life to humans, things, and the world.[29] Was this other masculine calling to me? The presence of the bull in my dream suggested that the archetype of the masculine spirit as a divine intelligence in nature, at one with the feminine, was now rising up from its slumbering in my unconscious.

Again, I did not fully understand the meaning and implications of this dream. But as my journey evolved, this bull energy would appear time and time again in different forms and guises to suggest the meaning of my same-sex attractions, pushing and pulling me toward some yet unknown end.

---

29 Jung, *Man and His Symbols*, 267.

The bull with its masculine and feminine history and symbolism was an apt symbol for my own sexual ambivalence, my bisexuality. On one hand, the bull as a symbol of the chthonic masculine principle, the Earth Masculine, was pursuing me in its attempt to impregnate me with the masculine spirit that I longed for, symbolized by my homosexual desires. On the other hand, the bull as the chthonic feminine or the Great Mother/Goddess was that which Western psychology said I must overcome if I was to develop my masculine identity. Thus, the bull is that which slays and that which is to be slain. However, I would learn later that this bull energy wasn't to be slain but rather related to and integrated into a broader version of myself.

Applying the bull's dual nature to the then context of my life, the bull, besides representing my bisexuality and same-sex attractions, could also be said to represent the two choices chasing me—to remain in my current life, stay married, and serve the church (chasing the feminine), or to leave and pursue same-sex relationships (pursuing the masculine). While I had made the conscious choice to remain in my current life, symbolized in the dream by my decision to return to the small Midwestern town in which I lived, the dream showed that something else was happening in my unconscious. This dual nature wouldn't let me return home. Rather it *chased* me. When something is chasing us in a dream, it often means that we are running from something. What was I running from? In the dream the bull only stopped chasing me when I faced it. If I was to discover what was chasing me, I had to stop running. I had to face this masculine-feminine energy. I had to face the bull energy in me.

In the dream I was leading four blind boys on horses. This suggests that while I was attempting to guide or relate to my unconscious masculine instinct—symbolized by the four boys on horses—I was having difficulty. After the second boy fell off his horse, symbolizing my unsuccessful attempts to deal my unconscious masculine energies, I was ready to quit and go back to the small Midwestern town, which represented a return to the parsonage, the church—back to what was familiar, comfortable, and known.

However, at this point, the bull, this powerful, procreative masculine energy, prevented me from doing so by erupting from my unconscious. My attempt to escape this energy by climbing a tree didn't stop its pursuit. It was only when I faced the bull, confronting it, that it stopped. But the dream left me with a dilemma. While the bull was no longer chasing me, I was still "up a tree" and the bull was on the ground below. In order to get down I would have to face the bull energy in me. While that could symbolize the masculine, it could also mean that I had to face the "bull" in me as that which was not true. This included the lies, the false appearances, that which was not congruent with my deeper soul's truth. I had to face some internal instinctive force, symbolized by the bull, which I had lost touch with or, perhaps, which I had never been in touch with.

How was I to face the bull? What was I to do with the bull energy? If I took my cues from its archetypal pattern in mythology and in ancient religion, the bull was either worshipped or killed as a sacrifice to the gods and goddesses. That seemed to suggest that I either had to pursue same-sex relationships (worshipping bull-phallus) or sacrifice the bull (deny the same-sex attractions and return to the rule of the parsonage). However, my personal journey provided a third path. The bull energy was not to be worshipped in continuing compulsive same-sex encounters nor was he to be sacrificed. Rather the bull energy—this chthonic, archetypal masculine energy vibrating in my soul—was to be accepted, given compassion, and integrated into a more expanded and whole self, one that embraced the masculine as a spirit in nature, in my own nature, my own soul.

As stated previously, dream images are representations of energy at work in the unconscious as expressions of the soul that are longing for recognition and integration into life. To discover the meaning of this energy is a spiritual process—a way of getting at the spirit in the matter, a way of understanding the meaning of the energy at work in the image. Although this dream occurred two years prior to the dream where I was told that "healing the homosexual self was in freeing him from the parsonage," the unconscious was already revealing a story that was operating in the depths of my soul—a story that indicated that I couldn't return to the life of the parsonage represented by the bull interfering with the dreamer's decision to "go back to the small Midwestern town."

At the time of this dream I didn't know the significance of the bull. But I soon discovered that the bull as a companion of the goddess was a symbol of Phallos—that sacred masculine—but not as power *over* her but as one *with* her. Together they were working in the depths of my own soul at the creation of a new consciousness, one that already knew that the soul, like nature herself, contains within itself a directing intelligence—a divine light—that vibrates with all the information and knowledge of that soul's being and becoming, of that soul's destiny. Like the oak tree that knows how to become an oak, the soul knows how to become its unique individual self. This is an example of those archetypal forces swimming in the soup of the collective unconscious, seeking to bring about balance and the evolution of a person's consciousness. This dream showed that there was an aggressive, powerful, and potentially overpowering and destructive force operating in my unconscious that I needed to face. The unconscious masculine clearly was calling me.

Notes and Exercises

Parts of us become split off from consciousness. These parts retreat into the unconscious where they remain hidden until they break forth in some secret or forbidden action, make themselves known to us in a secret fantasy, or chase us in a dream. Here is a way to access those hidden aspects:

> *Think of something you did or continue to do that might be considered inappropriate, wrong, unacceptable, forbidden, or taboo in the life that you are living, something that is outside of your accepted view of yourself. Maybe it is something shaming or embarrassing that you try to forget or hide. Maybe it is something you wouldn't want anyone to know about, some secret life. Perhaps it has to do with sex. Maybe it is related to drugs or some other destructive or illegal behavior. Trust whatever comes to you.*
>
> *Ask yourself, "What part of me is that? Look at the object of your desire and ask, "What am I looking for? What part of me is that?" Think about what the characters or images in those events might represent or symbolize (fear, aggression, control, power, freedom, independence, acceptance, creativity, etc.). What are you longing for? What is trying to get into life?*
>
> *Now complete this sentence: "The Call of____________."*
>
> *Think of a fantasy that you engage in over and over. What is the longing in the fantasy? What is the attraction? What are you doing in the fantasy? What are others doing in the fantasy? Now think of those images as parts of you. What*

are your associations, your thoughts, and your feelings about these parts? What might they represent or symbolize in you?

Fill in the blank. "__________ is calling me."

Think of a dream where you are being chased. What is chasing you? What are you running from—not only in the dream, but in your life? Ask yourself what that might represent or symbolize.

Complete the following: "Running from __________."

As you reflect on your answers to these three exercises, what is trying to get your attention? What is trying to get into life? What is calling you?

CHAPTER TWO

The Call of the Soul

I dream that

> *I had a dream about homosexuality. I then dream that I dream several nights in a row and each dream is a continuation of the first dream, a continuing story, and each night adds an episode about homosexuality. I see the first dream again. Upon looking at this dream more closely I notice that the paper had been torn off and therefore the bottom of the paper curls under. I flatten the paper out and notice another line to the dream that I did not know was there. The line says, "a treasure hard to find."* (Journal, 1-18-84)

Hidden in the soul of a man is a life that longs to live. In the process of living our lives, that longing often gets buried under the demands of a job, the responsibilities of a relationship or a family, the beliefs of religion, the desires for success, and the tasks necessary for maintaining a life that a man judges must be his life to live. In other words, this man becomes burdened by a life that is in opposition to the life that longs to live. There are reasons, very practical, rational, understandable, and even good reasons to live the life he has chosen. He must stay in a job in order to pay his bills and to maintain his lifestyle. He made a commitment to his wife and children, and he takes his commitments seriously. His belief in God and serving God and others is important to him. He is looked up to in his profession and is a valued citizen in his community.

I call this life the "ego's life" or the "outer life." This is the "I" that I know myself to be. This is the life that I live in the outer world—the life I show my friends and coworkers, my neighbors, and even my family. This is the life that also maintains a particular image—a persona or mask—that I find necessary to present to the world.

For me this was the "I" that did all the "right things," the "I" that lived according to the rules of a responsible, God-fearing man raised in an evangelical minister's home. There was much that was good, right, and valuable in that minister's home. I learned the value of hard work in getting what I wanted. I learned to put God and others first. I learned the value of service. I learned to express my talents. I learned the world was a safe place. Most importantly I learned there is a spiritual reality that is just as real as the physical world.

I also learned that if you didn't obey the rules of that spiritual reality, or if you hurt other people, you got in trouble. All that I learned shaped me into a sensitive, introspective, spiritually oriented man who placed God, family, work, and service in high priority. There is usually much that is good and important about the ego-life that any man creates. The ego-life or outer-life only becomes a problem if a conflict emerges, if a certain unhappiness or dissatisfaction begins to surface. He finds himself irritable, depressed, or anxious, not wanting to do the things he used to enjoy. He finds himself turning to alcohol or drugs, sex, or some other compulsive or destructive behavior. He finds himself caught in spontaneous fantasies, daydreams, and other creations of the imagination. If he allows himself any reflection, he might discover that he is caught in a conflict of priorities, in conflicts of the soul. These symptoms might be the soul calling to him.

The word *soul* is an ambiguous term that has multiple meanings and uses. These meanings range from its use in psychology to refer to *psyche*, "the unconscious and inner world of an individual," to religion's use of *soul* as "the image of God in us." While the etymology of both *psyche* and *soul* are identical, *soul* carries a slightly different meaning. The soul doesn't see *just* us or the other persons who make up our inner world—it sees something more. It connects us to the Other who is the source of all things, the Absolute. As others have suggested, if the Absolute is the ocean, we as souls are drops in that ocean. If the Absolute is God, we are expressions of God. The soul is our divine essence. I define soul as the part of us that not only includes all that we are but also transcends who we know ourselves to be, the part of us that transcends our personal histories, transcends our family and ancestral patterns, and transcends our beliefs. It even transcends what we might hold to be valuable and true and connects us to the Divine Spark in us that longs to fulfill its destiny.

We can access our soul through prayer and meditation, through reflection, dreams, imagining, fantasy, shamanic journeying, and psychotherapy—any of the modes that recognize realities as primarily symbolic or metaphorical or spiritual or energetic—where imagination meets reality. We could say that the soul is the image-making process by which it connects us to its life. The soul's life is that which gives our lives meaning and purpose and fulfills the destiny and purpose of the Divine or the transcendent in us. It is the part of us that has always been and will always be, the eternal us.

As long as the external representation for an inner psychic experience is congruent with the internal and unconscious image, life goes well. But when the images emerging from the unconscious no longer mirror or match the external forms, a breakdown occurs, and a change or transformation is indicated and often required.

In the previous chapter, I stated that I ended my same-sex relationships and my wife and I had agreed to move forward with our relationship. It was late at night. My wife and I had just completed an intense and painful conversation regarding my same-sex attractions and the direction of our relationship. I walked through our home, into the bedrooms of each of our children, looking at them sleeping so innocently. I hoped they were unaware of the struggles of their parents, weighing a decision that could potentially change their lives forever.

I stood first at my son's bed, watching him sleeping, so peacefully. In my daughter's room, with the glow of the moon shining across her face, I stood there, tears running down my cheeks, examining and weighing the priorities of my soul. I couldn't imagine leaving my wife and breaking up our family, causing such pain. Whether one maintains that my ultimate decision was based on a weak ego or fear of family or public reactions, I somehow knew from somewhere deep inside me that divorce was not to be my soul's journey. I remember having the awareness that if I left my family and pursued a homosexual life, in the end I would come to know what I already somehow knew intuitively—that my same-sex attractions were not really about sex, not even about being straight or gay, but something else, some other longing of my soul.

At the time I had no idea what that meant, but in that moment, I became the carrier of what I refer to as "conflicts of the soul." As stated in the introduction, it's my belief that, in our lives, we can create scenarios wherein we are called in two different directions that are not compatible with each other. This is done for a reason: to help us discover who we really are and why we are on the planet. In exploring this conflict, we can determine our true longings and life purpose. As such, these conflicts are deeply spiritual, for it is in the discovery of the source of these "soul conflicts" that the deeper meaning of our lives is revealed. It leads us to our true and authentic Self, the Self that transcends ego needs and desires.

A few days after weighing these conflicts of my soul, I had the dream with which I began this chapter. Here it is again. I dream

> *I had a dream about homosexuality. I then dream that I dream several nights in a row and each dream is a continuation of the first dream, a continuing story and each night adds an episode about homosexuality. I see the first dream again. Upon looking at this dream more closely I notice that the paper had been torn off and therefore the bottom of the paper curls under. I flatten the paper out and notice another line to the dream that I did not know was there. The line says, "a treasure hard to find."* (Journal, 1-18-84)

This dream contained several levels. First, it referenced a dream from the past about homosexuality. Next, it referenced a current dream about homosexuality, and then it referenced future dreams about homosexuality. A dream-within-a-dream shifts the action from one entire "stage" to another, so that the first dream seems to have taken place upon a smaller stage that is contained within the larger stage of the next dream.[30] This dream-within-a-dream placed homosexuality within the larger context of the "treasure hard to find," suggesting there was some relationship between my homosexuality and this "treasure hard to find."

This was the hidden message that I had missed earlier in reference to my same-sex desires. Thus, began my journey to find this "treasure,"

---

30 Hall, *Jungian Dream Interpretation*, 89–90.

a long journey into the inner worlds of my same-sex desires and fantasies. It would twist and turn through dreams, synchronicities, and art, and eventually to a masculine image living in my soul.

I discovered that deep within me lived an unknown land—a land with its own characters, its own laws, and its own plans and purposes, populated with characters playing out sometimes tempestuous relationships in the depths of my soul—archetypal forces, images—living in the very depths of me that long for recognition, for communion, for expression—and for a way to get into life. By engaging them they invited me to find my soul's path and to write my own destiny. Their lives became my life. Thus, began my journey to find this "treasure hard to find."

The "treasure hard to find" is referred to in various religions and esoteric traditions as our central core, the divine inner Self, the *Atman* in Hindu religion, the inner Christ in Christianity, the divine principle that is inherent in the real self or soul of the individual. For me this "treasure hard to find" was some part of me that was hidden in the unconscious.[31]

When such symbols appear in our dreams they often point to the center of the total personality, the totality of the psyche as both conscious and unconscious, the Self.[32] The *Self* is the term Jung used to refer to our wholeness, the energy that is behind all psychological events. It expresses itself in our dreams. It is behind the synchronicities in our lives. It is that which guides and directs our path to wholeness and to the discovery of our unique individual life. The Self is an image of God, a representation of God as symbolized in the psyche. I refer to it as the Divine Spark in us that is ours and ours alone to discover. It is that unconscious Other, the unknown and unknowable partner

31 Jung, *Collected Works 5*, par. 569.

32 Ibid.

in us that longs to unite the split in us between the ego-self and the unconscious Other—the soul.

The Self often appears in dreams, visions, and art as impersonal images like a circle, mandala, crystal, or stone, or personally as a royal couple, a divine child, or some other symbol of divinity. Great spiritual teachers like Christ, Muhammad, and Buddha are also symbols of the Self.[33] These are all symbols of wholeness, unification, and reconciliation of opposing parts.[34] An encounter with the Self feels like a "religious experience" with God and leaves us feeling vitalized and enriched.

At the time I had little meaning of what that dream meant, except that somehow my homosexuality and same-sex attractions, the "treasure hard to find," and my soul were somehow related. I awoke early in the morning, just as dawn was breaking, reflecting on my life and the conflicts that had emerged over the past several months. I heard birds singing outside my bedroom window. I lay in bed thinking to myself, "*Birds don't worry about whether their song is good or bad or right or wrong or pretty or even wanted. They just sing their song. They just do what they are born to do.*" I remember thinking, "*I just want to do what I am born to do. I just want to sing my song.*"

I then fell back to sleep and had a dream. In the dream I saw two beautiful rings in brilliant colors of red, yellow, and blue, one within the other, spinning in the universe. This dream had a numinous quality that left me somehow changed, like I had been in the presence of something Divine. Jung speaks of the numinosum as an effect that seizes the human subject, independent of his will, which causes an alteration of consciousness with a force not unlike a religious experience.[35] The

33 Bolen, *The Gods in Everyman*, 21

34 Edinger, *The Aion Lectures*, 72.

35 Jung, *Collected Works 11,* par. 6.

dream had such an effect on me that I felt compelled to paint it. I called this painting *The Birth of the Self.* (See figure 1.)

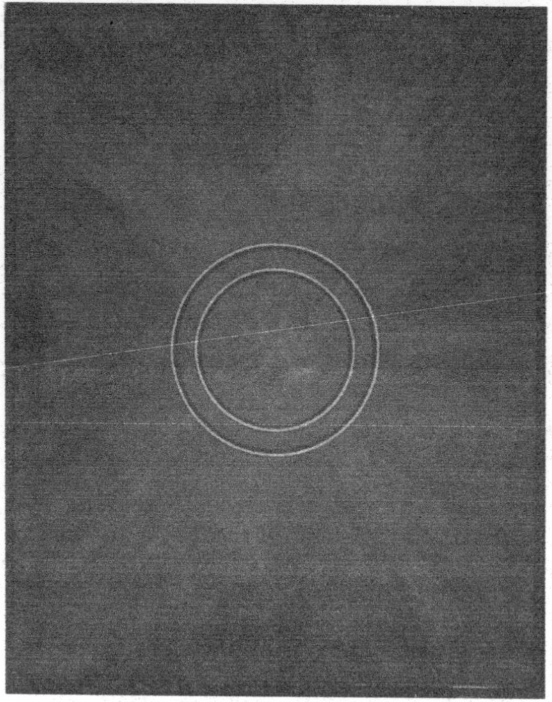

Figure 1. *The Birth of the Self*

Upon reflection, I now wonder if this powerful dream of the two rings was the universe's response to my soul's cry to sing its song. Before that, the birds as the song of nature herself had called to me. I remembered even earlier in my life, at the age of four or five, riding my tricycle early one morning and hearing the song of the mourning dove and feeling some strange attraction to it. Even today I can remember the moment I first heard the dove's song, where I was, the coolness of the morning air, the sound and the feeling, as if somewhere deep inside me there was a distant memory of that song.

My journey into shamanism and energy medicine has taught me that the practice of shamanism is a spiritual one that evolves from a perception that the world is alive, conscious, dynamic, interconnected, and responsive. The shaman enters altered states of consciousness and interacts with the spirit world in order to attend to, intervene, and transmit these transcendental energies into this world to bring healing and balance to an individual, a family, or the community.

In shamanism all animals and birds have a medicine that we can tap into. The dove has a wealth of lore and legend surrounding it, most of which is associated with the goddess, the feminine, and the maternal instinct, given its connection to water and the unconscious. The dove is the bringer of peace, love, and gentleness. It is a messenger of Spirit and aids in the communication between the physical and spiritual worlds. The mournful song of the dove speaks of the deepest parts of the soul and stirs our emotions and imagination. The dove's medicine is to remember the purity of the creative spirit at the soul level. The dove helps us follow our own soul's path.[36]

Renowned Jungian psychologist James Hillman proposed that we already hold the potential for the unique possibilities inside us, much like an acorn holds the pattern for an oak tree. This unique, individual energy of the soul becomes displayed throughout our lifetime and shows up in our calling and life's work when it is fully actualized. According to Hillman, events are not inevitable but bound to be expressed in some way dependent on the character of the soul of the individual.[37]

Various scientists and researchers have suggested the idea of energy fields that vibrate with information particular to that field. Hungarian philosopher of science, systems theorist, and prolific author

---

36 Andrews, *Animal-Speak,* 133–134.

37 Hillman, *Soul's Code, 191-213.*

Ervin László posits that consciousness is a field known as the quantum vacuum, or the Akashic field, and as such, is comprised of the history of the universe from the time of the Big Bang until today. This interconnecting cosmic field that exists at the roots of reality not only holds the record of all that has ever happened in life, it relates it to all that is yet to happen. According to the theory, the Akashic field helps a universe know how to become a universe, helps plants know how to be plants—and so forth and so on, conveying all the information of life itself, even perhaps helping a soul know how to live its life.[38]

English biologist and author Rupert Sheldrake has proposed the idea of the morphic or morphogenetic field. According to Sheldrake, the morphogenetic field is a field of information that operates autonomously; a database of information that allows people access to the information contained in programs within that particular field. In addition to providing a database of information, these fields serve to provide a mental form consisting of thoughts and images that are consistent with that field. For example, a cardiac field becomes heart tissue because the field contains all the information necessary to create heart tissue.

Sheldrake was the first to posit the existence of a learning field that instructs and informs the scientifically recognized ones. According to Sheldrake, a morphic field can be set up by the repetition of similar acts or thoughts. This explains why members of a family pass down certain behaviors and even emotions. A mother's anxiety might be carried to son or daughter via morphic fields rather than DNA. Morphic fields, being subtle in nature, are not limited to time or space. Sheldrake's philosophy also holds that past life memories could pass from lifetime to lifetime through a soul's morphic field. These memories would be

---

38 "What is the Akashic Field?" www.cjmartes.com/cjmartes_akashicfield.asp.

nonlocal in nature and therefore not anchored in the brain or a particular life.[39]

Renowned author and leading-edge thinker Will Taegel has proposed an eco-field. This is a region or space configuration of energy vibrating with information and meaning, underlying a specific location; it transmits that information between its various parts.[40] There are also archetypal fields of universal experiences that are believed to affect matter and behavior through the energy vibrating in the archetype.

We can no longer think in terms of human behavior being shaped in the end only by the individual or family but rather must take seriously the reality and influences of archetypal interactive dynamics.[41] The Luminous Energy Field (LEF) of shamanism holds that there is an aura of energy and light that surrounds us and informs our physical body. This energy field is believed to contain an archive of all of our personal and ancestral memories, which when activated, act like a blueprint containing instructions that compel us toward behaviors, relationships, and other experiences that mirror our emotional, psychological, and spiritual wounds.[42] Common to these various theories is the assertion that everything is energy and that energy vibrates with information and this information has an effect on us.

Could it be that my soul held a particular pattern that resonated with the energy field or medicine of the dove that awakened in me a path that would slowly unfold—pulling me toward it, toward my song, toward some longing in my soul as my calling and life's work? I understand now that the dream on "the treasure hard to find" was ushering in what would become my decision to choose an inner path, what Carl

39 Dale, *Subtle Body*, 145–146.

40 Taegel, *MotherTongue*, 75–86.

41 Whitmont, *Alchemy of Healing*, 58–59.

42 Villoldo, *Shaman, Healer, Sage*, 46.

Jung calls an inner adaptation as opposed to an outer adaptation—directing libido inward for the possibility of developing a new life.

What began as a bull chasing me would turn into a "treasure hard to find." The decision to answer the call to seek this treasure—the soul's longing and, according to the dream, the goal of my same-sex attractions—resulted in the discovery of a powerful force, an unconscious masculine energy and spirit living in me. It would lead me to the meaning of my same-sex attractions and their meaning for my life. The journey would require building a relationship between this masculine force and my ego-self, between him and the feminine in me, and between him and the outer worlds of my wife, my family, and the environment in which I lived as they played out their sometimes tempestuous relationships in the depths of my soul. The map for this journey would emerge through my dreams, my art, and various synchronicities, to become the guide of my journey. I would discover archetypal forces—images—living in me that longed for recognition, for communion, for expression, for love and acceptance. Their lives would become my life. The soul was calling.

Notes and Exercises

Life sometimes provides a conflict of priorities that force us to discover our soul's longing and purpose. In the process of finding the source of our soul conflict, we discover a deeper meaning to our lives—why we are here and what we are to do. This conflict is usually between the life we are living and a life that wants to live—a split between ego and soul, a split between our inner world and the outer world. This conflict will often act out in various ways—through sex addiction, marital affairs, drug addiction, workaholism, eating disorders and even depression and anxiety.

What are the conflicts in your life? Where are you split between being one way and wanting to be another way. Where are you caught between competing priorities? If money, need for security, family responsibilities, living up to expectations—your own or someone else's—was not an issue, what would you do? Where would you go? What would you change?

Where does your energy naturally want to go? What do you find yourself fantasizing about, thinking about, reading about, searching for on the internet, longing for? What obsessive thoughts, needs, or feelings are recurring to you that you can't get out of your mind? Where our energy spontaneously wants to go is often a hint about what wants to come alive in us. The task is to understand this energy—not only literally but symbolically. Does it represent some creative energy in you that longs expression? These wanderings of the mind are often the soul calling. What is calling you?

CHAPTER THREE

The Call of the Dreams

"The dream is the small hidden door in the deepest and most intimate sanctum of the soul . . ."

—Carl Jung

"Pay attention to your dreams for I will speak to you through them." It was January 1978, just a couple of months past my thirty-third birthday. The shy, introverted boy of my childhood had become a self-reflective, introspective, analytic young man seeking an inner life through the study of religion and philosophy. This included a daily practice of Bible reading, prayer, and meditation. By that point in my life, I had read the Hebrew Scriptures three times and the Christian scriptures fifteen times. In my reading, I discovered that the Bible spoke of a dynamic active power, one that could heal and transform lives and one that could even speak directly to man through dreams and visions.

I began to read other books, written by modern-day people who reported such experiences. What I read began to open my eyes to a new kind of God —one that spoke directly to man through dreams and other experiences of the unconscious. I began to expand my theology and to free my thinking to believe in the possibility of a powerful and personally accessible spiritual realm.

I often prayed and meditated, and it was on one of these occasions that I heard the following words from some place deep within me: "Pay attention to your dreams for I will speak to you through them." Not only was this an auditory experience, but it was also a *felt* experience. I knew that something had happened inside me. I didn't know what it was exactly, but I knew that I was somehow changed. I refer to this experience as "my transformation."

Although my understanding and interpretation of this event has expanded over the years, at the time I interpreted that event in the context of the stage of consciousness I was in at that time.[43] Influenced by my religious beliefs and my Judeo-Christian training I interpreted the "I" in that experience as God. *God* would be speaking to me through my dreams. While I had remembered an occasional dream from time to time, that night I began remembering multiple dreams most nights, and I remembered them with greater clarity, an experience that continued for many years and continues to some extent to this day. This experience connected me to a sense of something greater than myself and lifted me out of the pain and struggle of the past five years—the coming out to my wife and by this time to my extended family about my same-sex attractions and the ending of my same-sex relationships.

Around this same time, I came across references in my reading to Swiss psychiatrist Carl Jung and his assertion that dreams are a language through which the soul communicates to us. I began to read books on dreams and Jungian psychology, understanding and interpreting dreams, and Jung's approach to dreams. I also began to keep a dream journal, writing down my dreams in detail. But did God really speak through dreams?

---

43 Wilber, "Which Level of God Do You Believe In?"

Theories abound as to why we dream. We know that all people dream. But do these experiences of sleep we call dreams have value? Are they trying to tell us something? Do dreams serve some purpose? Can they be a source of inspiration, information, and even direction for our lives? Why *do* we dream?

Research on the neurophysiological states associated with dreaming shows that dreaming occurs every ninety minutes during a sleep state of rapid eye movement (REM). Since REM states occur in infants and in most animals where psychological factors are not a major consideration, scientists believe that dreams must serve some biological function.[44] In fact, if REM sleep is interrupted, REM sleep and dreaming increases, causing researchers to believe that REM sleep and dreaming is a way of processing information in a search for solutions to problems. Other researchers believe that dreaming is a function of the nervous system—to take in, process, and integrate new information.[45]

On the other hand, dreams have always been a major vehicle by which creative impulses emerge. Dreams regularly serve as a source of "artistic" inspiration. Robert Lewis Stevenson composed his masterpiece, *Dr. Jekyll and Mr. Hyde*, by transcribing and reworking events that had taken place in his dreams. Composers such as Mozart and Beethoven made extensive use of the music they had first heard in their dreams. Pop artist Billy Joel reports that much of his music he initially hears in his dreams. Samuel Taylor Coleridge composed the poem "Kubla Khan" by directly transcribing his dream inspiration. Mendeleyev sketched the first model of the periodic table—that staple of all introductory chemistry texts—after seeing the basic elements of the physical universe dispose themselves in relation to one another

---

44 Hall, *Jungian Dream Interpretation*, 22–23.

45 Greenberg and Pearlman, *An Integrated Approach to Dream Interpretation and Clinical Practice*, 294–295.

in an orderly and beautiful pattern in a dream. Niels Bohr sketched the formulation of his "quantum theory" from information given to him in a dream. Albert Einstein got the first inkling of the idea for his theory of relativity in a dream and said his entire scientific career was a meditation on that dream. Elias Howe, the inventor of the sewing machine, after having exhausted all conventional ideas about building a machine that could sew, got the idea of putting the hole in the point of a needle from a dream. I could go on and on, for history from ancient times to the present is full of examples of the creative impetus that dreams and dreaming may provide.

Besides the biological and creative functions of dreams, many religions both past and present recognize the value of dreams and even assert that God often speaks through dreams. A study of the Judeo-Christian tradition shows a clear and consistent theory about the use of dreams as a medium of revelation from God.[46]

But it isn't just scientists, artists, and the religious or spiritually adept who are rewarded with creative breakthroughs as a result of paying attention to their dreams. Just like the artists and the scientists who struggle for answers to their conflicts and receive insights and solutions in their dreams, all of us are involved in struggles. We may not be trying to invent something or write music. Instead we may be trying to find a way to work through a childhood trauma, make a decision about whether to take or leave a job, whether to enter therapy, leave a relationship, or break free from a longtime addiction. All of us prime the dream pump every time we ask ourselves honest questions about our most important life issues. Being ready and open to our dreams' healing and creative messages allows us to touch the deep parts of

---

46 Kelsey, *God, Dreams, and Revelation*, 17.

ourselves that not only stand in the way of our healing and growth, but also point the way to healing and wholeness.

Among the many things that a dream may be I have discovered that a dream is a spontaneous, self-portrait expressed in symbolic form of the actual situation in the unconscious.[47] The dream shows the situation—not as I conjecture it to be or want it to be—but as it really is.[48] It furnishes the unconscious material that has been triggered or activated by a conscious situation.

The dreams I have shared herewith thus far begin to provide a window into my same-sex attractions from the point of view of the unconscious and suggest a path forward. In the "bull dream" the unconscious showed a powerful energy chasing me. The bull with its association to both the masculine and the feminine becomes an apt symbol for my bisexuality and the carrier of the conflict between my heterosexual self and my homosexual self and between the masculine and feminine in me. As representative of the "bull-gods" of antiquity, the bull is a symbol of Phallos, the sacred masculine as an unconscious masculine energy in me. As an archetype, the bull is the procreative, fertilizing Divine Masculine spirit in nature, which works in union with the Divine Feminine, the Great Goddess, to bring forth a new consciousness. Taken as an object and a symbol of my internal world, the bull is the Divine Masculine energy living in my own soul, seeking to create and live its life in and through me—a powerful and dynamic power.

The "treasure hard to find" dream places homosexuality in the larger context of the soul's journey to find its unique and individual life. In the "parsonage dream" I am told the healing of the homosexual

---

47 Jung, *Dynamics and Structure of Psyche*, 253, 263.

48 Jung, *Collected Works 8*, par. 505.

self is in freeing him from the evangelical minister's home—from the milieu in which I was raised.

The next several chapters take you through a journey of significant dreams in which I discover the meaning behind my same-sex attractions as the call of the spirit within me to follow its path. I came to understand that the dreams, the synchronicities, and my soul's promptings were the voices of this Other in me that longed for life, this Other that often sought itself outside of me in another man. He was, in fact, a man living in me.

In the year following my "transformation experience" I ended my relationship with my male friend and closed the Christian bookstore that my wife and I owned and operated. Although there was some sadness around the loss of both these relationships, there was also relief. I could no longer carry the demands of these two worlds and the conflicts and stresses they caused both in my relationships with my wife and family and in my internal world. I was still living what I call "split energies." It was exhausting; I couldn't be fully present in either place. My relationship with my wife and family were becoming more important. After making the decision to end the relationship with my male friend and close the bookstore, I embraced more fully my life as husband and father. I also embraced more fully my roles of teacher in the local high school, and music director in the local church. This felt good. The tension of living two lives had been eliminated.

I continue to maintain that the three years my wife and I had the Christian bookstore were critical and important years. I often say that the bookstore, even though it eventually caused us to lose our house, saved our home. The financial demands and responsibilities of the store, along with my job as teacher, my growing loyalty and commitment to my wife and raising our children, as well as my commitment to serving the church, provided the external container for my life at that time. It served as a sort of grounding and external stability for our lives after the crisis of coming out to my wife and family regarding my same-sex attractions and affairs. I am grateful for these external realities that forced me to hold the tensions of those years for it is in holding the tensions of opposing forces that often results in the rising of something new.

As owner of the bookstore I had the responsibility of ordering and reviewing many books. Some of them were on the value of dreams and the importance of listening to one's dreams. Some even stated that God spoke to us through our dreams.

Ken Wilber's integral theory identifies several stages of consciousness and states that a person at any level of consciousness can have a spiritual experience, but that person will interpret that experience through the lens of the general stage he is at. That is, he will interpret it through the mental structures that he possesses or that have already emerged in his development. For example, Jean Gebser, a German born philosopher, linguist and poet, identified five major levels of development that humans go through—archaic, magic, mythic, mental, and integral. If we accept Gebser's levels as generally true then there is an archaic spirituality, a magic spirituality, a mythic spirituality, a mental spirituality, and an integral spirituality.

According to Wilber, "An archaic God sees divinity in any strong instinctual force. A magic God locates divine power in the human ego and its magical capacity to change the animistic world with rituals and spells. A mythic God is located not on this earth but in a heavenly paradise not of this world, entrance to which is gained by living according to the covenants and rules given by this God to his peoples. A mental God is a rational God, a demythologized Ground of Being that underlies all forms of existence. And an integral God is one that embraces all of the above."[49]

If human beings do indeed go through stages of psychological development, then their understanding of God or Goddess or Spirit will likewise undergo development. Honoring each and every stage as an equally crucial component of that development is an important part of any integral approach to spirituality.

To have an altered state or peak experience of divine light or interior luminosity such as hearing a voice say "listen to your dreams for I will speak to you through them" as a man raised in a fundamentalist evangelical church, I would tend to *interpret* that experience in terms of the mythic level of development and see this experience as the voice of the God as defined by my particular church and religious system, and project that experience onto the church. Paul Tillich was a German-American Christian existentialist philosopher and Lutheran theologian who suggested God is "the ground of being itself." To understand my experience now from an integral point of view that understands God as the ground of all being from which all things that exist emanate, including my own existence, then God is, as Tillich suggests, the ground of all being brooding below the varying symbols and traditions and does not minimize the original experience or my interpretation of that experience. It simply expands it to include God as the ground of all being in which we live and have our being, in fact, in which *all* life lives and has *its* being—no matter our inherited tradition, whatever that may be.[50]

A book by Herman Riffel called *Christian Maturity and the Spirit's Power* came across my desk. This book would change my life. It is interesting how one book coming into a person's life at a particular

---

49 Wilber, "Which Level of God Do You Believe In?"

50 "The Ground of All Being"– High Gravity Pt. 4 (Tillich).

time can have such a powerful impact. Riffel was a Christian author who discovered that dreams and listening to dreams were an important and valuable part of his journey. (He also frequently referred to Carl Jung and Jung's belief that God speaks to us through our dreams.)

At the same time that Riffel's book crossed my desk, a colleague had been putting books on Jung and dreams into my mailbox at school. One of the books was *The Kingdom Within* by John Sanford. Sanford was an Episcopalian minister who had also found dreams a valuable resource in his journey. And he was a Jungian analyst. In his book *The Kingdom Within* he interpreted the various biblical stories as symbolic of inner life experiences. This opened me up to the understanding of the "symbolic life."

Something deep within me resonated with these two books. Thus, began my journey into the study of dreams and eventually my own dreams.

Looking back, I see how the desire for a bookstore in the early 1970s—irrespective of my motivation at the time—was somehow a call from the soul to place me in a position where at some point in the future a book coming across my desk might invite me to listen to the promptings of my heart. Some might call this magical thinking. I call it the unfolding of some unconscious plan.

In 1981 my wife and I would have to sell our home in order to settle the debt that the bookstore had accumulated. In retrospect, the selling of our house was the beginning of the loosening of our roots and attachments to a life that wasn't mine to live. This all occurred at the same time I was beginning to struggle with my musical role at church, which included wearing the hats of church pianist, organist, and choir director. It again became a time of upheaval and uncertainty.

I had ended my cursory same-sex encounters some years prior to my transformation experience wherein I heard a voice telling me that

God would speak to me through my dreams. After this experience, as mentioned earlier, I had ended my relationship with my male friend. At this point, I settled into my life as high school teacher, husband, father, and church leader, given that my wife and I had decided to remain married and to work on our relationship and raise our children.

I had been involved with music beginning in childhood, playing various musical instruments and studying the piano from the age of eight. In college I continued to study piano and be involved in music, traveling with a gospel quartet. So, it was natural for me to continue to use my music as a means of self-expression and service to the local church. I had taken an active role in the church and in addition to the aforementioned roles as church pianist, organist, and choir director, I was also a board member, and Sunday School teacher.

At the same time, I continued my personal journey into recording and paying attention to my dreams and seeking God's wisdom for my life, not only through daily Bible reading and prayer, but also through my nightly dreams. The more I recorded my dreams and read books on dreams, the more I began to listen to them and to allow them to influence my life.

As I explored the various theories on the purposes and interpretations of dreams from the scientific perspective, as well as the psychological and spiritual, and as I discussed dreams and my growing belief of the importance of listening to dreams with my family and others within my circle of friends, I began to run into another conflict. On one hand I had had the personal experience telling me to listen to my dreams because God would be speaking to me through them, a position with which Carl Jung, John Sanford, Morton Kelsey, Herman Riffel, and others agreed with. On the other hand I was being told in other books written from a Christian or biblical point of view, and from certain authorities in my Christian world, that although God had spoken to people through dreams in the Bible, that era was over.

God no longer needed to speak to people through dreams because we now had the Bible as his word and direct revelation. For those within the Christian framework who did believe that dreams continued to have some purpose and meaning, the dreams had to be interpreted in ways that were congruent with the teachings of the Bible. In other words, the Bible was to be the final authority on the meaning of the dream, a statement that something deep inside me resisted.

Once again, I found myself living two lives. But this time it wasn't a secret life of sexual encounters with men, it was the secret life of my dreams and an inner life that was coming more and more into conflict with the external life that I was living as church leader and church music director. During this time, I had several dreams about houses in various stages of repair, remodel, and restoration. Houses in dreams often refer to the psyche or soul, and the condition of the house or what is happening in the house mirrors what is happening in one's inner world.

In the first "house dream"

> *My wife and I and another couple are tearing out walls in an old two-story house. The women are doing the work while the man and I are lying suspended horizontally in air. As I reach over and take his hand, he quotes something from Shakespeare. While I don't remember exactly what he says to me, I know that what he tells me means "What I am saying is the opposite of what I mean."* (Journal, date unknown)

This dream brings to my awareness several aspects of what is happening in the unconscious. For one, the feminine is doing all the work of remodeling or remolding the structure of my inner life, while the masculine is suspended in spiritual limbo as symbolized by the image of being suspended in air. This dream reflects the current state of my ego's position. I'm caught in indecision, in uncertainty, in ambivalence, in spiritual limbo. This dream can also be understood as showing my ego's spiritually inflated position as not having my feet on the ground. Not only does the dream show that the feminine in me was working hard at restructuring my life, it also showed that I was letting my wife carry the responsibility of repairing and rebuilding our relationship while I was involved in my spiritual exploration.

On one hand this was a sad and disturbing dream, which woke me up to the fact that I was not in touch with reality. However, I have discovered through the years that dreams are often paradoxical. What appears as a negative upon further exploration often reveals an underlying positive intent. Therefore, I have suspended a moral judgment of dreams as being either good or bad. For although this dream woke me up to the fact that I was not in touch with reality—I didn't have my feet on the ground—it *did* get me in touch with reality: "What I say is the opposite of what I mean." This was a sobering and unsettling dream. How was I saying the opposite of what I meant?

The feminine and the masculine can be understood as two modalities of the process of separating the ego from its containment in the unconscious matrix that contains all the potential aspects of the psyche. As such they become energetic forces operating in the depths our own souls, longing—as I have said before—for recognition, expression, and life. Thus, when a woman or a man or other feminine or masculine images or symbols appear in a dream or fantasy, that energy of the psyche has embodied itself in this representation so that we can see just what this energy is like and how it is manifesting at that moment in our lives and current situation. The energy shows itself in concrete form so we can see it and come to understand the nature of this energy as it is manifesting in our unconscious life.

When I reached over and took the hand of this other man, thereby getting in touch with this other masculine energy in me, he revealed my unconscious situation and the message of this dream by telling me that "What I say is the opposite of what I mean."

To say one thing and mean its opposite or to use words to express something different and opposite to their literal meaning is called irony. The ironic statement usually involves the explicit expression of one attitude or evaluation, but with indications that the speaker intends a very different, often opposite, attitude or evaluation.[51]

For example, I complain about the controlling behavior of a woman in my group of friends while failing to see my own controlling behavior, or I pride myself in my stated flexibility while feeling internally frustrated, even angry, when people disagree with me. To the extent that the ironic situation plays out unconsciously, that is, I am unaware of the contradiction between what I say and my feelings or behaviors, herein lies the shadow. The issue of the shadow is not about admitting faults; rather it is realizing that you are not as you appear—not to others, and not to yourself.[52]

The shadow contains those parts of us that for one reason or another we disown or wish to keep out of sight; qualities we would rather not see in ourselves, such as controlling behavior, jealousy, or deceitfulness. While the shadow is often seen as negative, it is often only negative because the characteristics are not valued by or are in opposition to one's current consciousness or view of oneself.

The shadow also contains valuable unrealized potentials. Either way this creates an opposite or an "opposing other," that which I would

---

51 Abrams and Harpham, *Glossary of Literary Terms.*

52 Zweig, Connie, and Abrams, eds., *Meeting the Shadow,* 156.

never want to be, or that which I can't imagine myself to be, or that which I long to be, but won't allow myself to be—the "not I." It is as if the unconscious is saying "I know that you may not see yourself this way, Sheldon, but what you say is the opposite of what you mean and who you really are. You present one image and live another." Since dreams show the inner truth and reality as it really is and not as I would like it to be,[53] the dream is bringing to consciousness some discrepancy in me—I am not as I appear or think I am.

Over the next several months I began to look at the discrepancies between what I said and how I felt, and between what I said and how I thought and behaved. This dream set the stage for the entrance of the shadow, that "other" in me that was the opposite of my "ego-self" or "outer self."

Notes and Exercises

Dreams can be understood as expressions of the soul, the language through which the soul speaks to us, revealing to us what lies hidden there. Dreams connect us to something greater than ourselves. We prime the dream pump every time we ask ourselves honest questions about our most important life issues. Being open to our dreams allows us to touch the deep parts of ourselves that not only stand in the way of our healing and growth, but also show the way out and connect us to our soul's path and even our destiny.

A great way to begin to listen to the wisdom of your soul is to keep a dream journey. Place a notebook by your bed and when you awaken from a dream, write it down before it sinks back into the unconscious and you lose its message. Then later, read the dream. Notice the characters in the

53 Jung, "Practical Use of Dream Analysis" in *Collected Works 16*, 304.

dream. Who are they? What comes to mind when you think about the images? What do you associate the images with? What do they represent to you? What parts of you might the symbolize? What is the dream trying to get you to pay attention to?

A great book that offers a practical step-by-step approach to dream work is *Inner Work: Using Dreams and Active Imagination for Personal Growth* by Robert Johnson.

CHAPTER FOUR

Meeting the Shadow

Several months later, I have the sixth and last house dream of this series. I dream

> *The house is complete. We are all moved in and everything is lovely, not royal as in some of the house dreams, but lovely. The house is up on a hill overlooking a lake. My wife and I are in the front area with all the windows. There is a generally good feeling. A man calls at the door. He is a dark, shadowy figure. I invite him to stay the night. He needs someplace to stay.* (Journal, 1-4-80)

As outlined in the introduction, this book is the story of my discovery of unconscious aspects living in my soul as revealed through my dreams and my journey to integrate them into my life as my soul's calling. This dream ushers in the shadow. The shadow refers to the dark, feared, unwanted, and often unknown parts of our personality, those qualities that could have become a part of us but didn't fit into the ideal image we had for ourselves or the image that others—such as our parents, society, peer group, or religious training—had for us. Thus these aspects became rejected and repressed.

As we develop, we tend to identify with those qualities that are acceptable in our family or in the environment in which we are raised and reject all those qualities that contradict or oppose this ideal self. However, these rejected qualities do not cease to exist but continue to live in the unconscious where they form a kind of secondary personality that some call the shadow. A man's shadow contains rejected masculine qualities and although we tend to think of these in negative terms, the shadow actually contains many vital qualities or "unlived life" that, if related to in appropriate ways, enhance one's life.[54]

I had this dream in January of 1980, two years to the month of my "transformation" experience wherein I was told to listen to my dreams for "God would be speaking to me through them." In these two years, my transformation experience had left me with a greater sense of the power available through God and a certain boldness that I had never before experienced. As mentioned above I interpreted that event in my then Judeo-Christian consciousness and channeled that energy into the church and Christian service.

I became an advocate for the transforming power of God and testified to that power weekly at church. I took on the role of a sort of lay minister, praying for people, for their healing and deliverance of whatever ailed them. I was the music director at the church and took on the responsibility of the music for the church services, leading music worship, writing and arranging music, and directing the choir and a vocal and instrumental ensemble. All of this was fulfilling and provided a source of purpose, personal validation, and creativity, which resulted in a lot of positive mirroring and ego-satisfaction for that shy, introverted boy of childhood. In many ways, my life in church music had become a big piece of the image that I presented to the world, a

---

54 Sanford, *Evil*, 49–51.

piece of my persona so to speak. This was an image with which my ego had become identified. I had, in fact, taken on the life of my father and grandfather who were both ministers in the church. For me it is interesting to note that my maternal grandfather had also experienced a "transformation" when he was thirty-three. He is reported to have been healed of what was then called a "mental breakdown" and at that time received a "call to preach." He then left his job as teacher and school principal to become a minister.

My own father reports that he "received a call from God at an early age to preach" and tells of standing on an old washtub as a child, pretending to be preaching. My brother heard the call of God at the age of twelve to be a missionary and followed that call into the ministry, serving as a missionary in Africa for thirty-five years. Another brother of mine became an ordained minister before following his interest in psychology and becoming a psychologist. The man who would become my father-in-law reported that he received a call from God at the age of five to become a missionary.

These deep unconscious patterns, these archetypes, emerge from our families of origin, culture, religion, and life itself. In fact, observation would suggest that certain families live out certain archetypal patterns. Simply put, an archetype is a typical and universal pattern or model of expression. There are families who are bankers, caregivers, politicians, priests, and ministers, artists, and craftsmen, to name just a few. The archetypes of priest/minister and teacher are predominant archetypes in my family going on three generations now, both of which I too was living out. It seems to me that archetypal patterns will both pull us and push us into circumstances, situations, and relationships that create the potentials for them to live out their energetic patterns.

My "transformation experience" in 1978 had ushered in an identification with the priest/minister archetype living within my family system. However, I was finding that I couldn't maintain that image or role. From this vantage point I can certainly see the value and importance of religion and the institutional church. I can also see the importance and value of those called to spend their lives serving such institutions. However, at the time, the struggle to maintain the life required to fit into that system, and what was emerging in my own spiritual journey, was too great. To maintain this image, I had to deny more and more of who I was discovering I was, and more and more of the truth that was living in my soul. I was coming to believe that the infallibility of biblical scripture was untenable for me, for what I said was apparently the opposite of what I meant.

Rather I was discovering that the Divine—this Other that I longed for—lived in the depths of my own soul and revealed himself or herself by direct encounter through my dreams. I was also coming to understand that same-sex desires and attractions, even same-sex love, was not something evil or sinful that I needed God's forgiveness and redemption for. Rather it was a relationship that needed to be embraced, loved, and understood. My transformation experience had not healed or taken away my same-sex attractions. Rather it had begun to open me up to the acceptance of and even the embracing of them as a vital and important part of who I was. As these opposing thoughts and energies gained strength, this shadow self began to break through in my dreams. Or perhaps it was because these shadow elements were appearing in my dreams that I became more and more aware of qualities and impulses that were in opposition to the life that I was living.

In the above dream the house is complete, suggesting that I had done sufficient inner work over the past two years by my reading, studying, tracking, and working with my dreams, that I was in a place where I could meet and embrace my shadow. Opening the door and letting this dark, shadowy figure in suggested that I was open to meeting and giving space to this Other in me—all those parts of myself that I had rejected, repressed, ignored, and refused to let live and, in some cases, didn't even know existed. They were now beginning to stir in me and demand recognition and relationship.

The dream said he "needed a place to stay." Also, the fact that the dream said this house was "not as royal" as other houses had been, but was "lovely" and exhibited a "generally good feeling" suggested that the grandiosity and inflation that had been present immediately following my transformation experience had lessened and that I was becoming more comfortable with myself. The presence of my wife in this house-dream and that we were standing together suggested the continuing evolution and commitment of our relationship, a shift in my relationship to her as well as an improved relationship with the inner masculine-feminine energies, and an improved relationship between the conscious and the unconscious.

The shadow tends to show up in dreams being the same sex as the dreamer and as stated, is often a shadowy, unknown, unappealing, despised, feared, and inferior figure. He may also take the form of same-sex encounters in dreams or spontaneous same-sex fantasies and attractions, even pulling us into sexual relationships with men in outer reality. We also project the shadow onto persons we know but can't stand or who behave in ways that we wouldn't or on persons we idealize and would like to be but can't allow ourselves to be. Such projections result in either negative feelings and conflicts or in an over-idealization of those persons. This denied, repressed, and rejected masculine energy would show up over and over again in me, in various guises, seeking acceptance and relationship, increasing the tension between my inner and outer worlds.

I dream that I am observing the following:

A wedding is taking place in Washington, D.C. A reporter goes to cover the event for the newspaper and takes Terry Zinn along as the photographer. The pictures he takes are ones not usually taken for wedding pictures—those pretty, well-posed photos that newspapers typically publish. The paper comes out and the guests are looking at it; it's full of Terry's pictures. Most of the photos are not as clear as they should be and some photos are actually fuzzy. The guests ask Terry about the photos and he says, "I just take pictures of what I see" meaning candid pictures. Then he walked away happy and laughing.

The wedding celebration now becomes a meeting with Dr. Evans and a committee. They are upset with the mayor and the way he is doing his job. Suddenly Dr. Evans says, "This is going to shock the community but let's impeach the mayor," which they do. (Journal, 3-3-80)

Terry Zinn was a high school student in the school where I taught. He was considered a stud athlete, a troublemaker and into drugs—a certain masculinity opposite of and foreign to me. Thus, he represented a shadow figure.

The dream took place in Washington D.C., the place where the nation's laws are made, and so represented my psyche's self-regulating system. A wedding symbolizes the union of opposites. The photographer wasn't interested in taking pictures that maintained the "well-posed photos" that are usually presented to the public (newspaper). This suggested that the unconscious was saying "Things aren't as clear and as perfect as you think they are. They are even fuzzy."

The photographer, however, didn't seem to care, saying "I just take what I see." His "not caring, laughing, happy, walk-away attitude" implied the presence of the shadow and a potential shift in my own attitude and in the image that I presented to the public (candid, fuzzy, and not as clear or as perfect). This part of the dream showed me that "things are not as clear and as well-defined as you think they are." These "fuzzy" images also suggested a shift in my way of seeing, from a masculine, solar way of seeing things, to a more diffuse, fuzzy, feminine, moonlit, or lunar way. The former is marked by the ability to think clearly, to discern and judge, to calculate, analyze, and follow a line of logic or the rule of law. The latter mode is characterized by the ability to investigate reality through the senses, and to know through emotions, dreams, the imagination, and to receive insights intuitively—all ways of seeing or relating to the world that were not valued in the parsonage family in which I was raised.

The dream then shifted and the wedding became a meeting. Dr. Evans, the man at the end of my dream, was the superintendent of the school system where I taught. Thus, he and his committee represented the power or authority in my psychic life to make decisions over the complex that fed my current life. Simply put, a complex is a collection of images and ideas, perceptions and memories formed around a central theme derived from one or more archetypes or universal patterns of experience. These patterns have a common emotional tone that when activated contributes to certain behaviors and affects whether a person is conscious of them or not. Common complexes are a mother complex, father complex, ego complex, or inferiority complex.

In any event, in my dream, the committee decided to impeach the mayor. The mayor oversees the workings of a city and like a ruling king represents the ruling consciousness. This part of the dream showed that my psyche's self-regulating system—another "inner committee"—was overthrowing my current ego-consciousness, which was ruling my life.

That same night I dream another dream about the photographer in the above dream. In this dream

> *Terry Zinn is riding in an airplane. He falls out. I observe. When I see him on the ground, his eyes and ears are bandaged but he is alive, for which I am both surprised and relieved. He is put into an ambulance. My daughter and I follow him, airborne behind the ambulance. My daughter wants to see if it is really Terry Zinn. We go up real close and zero in. Sure enough, it is him. Suddenly the ambulance starts backing up fast and pulls off to the right and stops on the side of the road.*
>
> *Terry gets out. His eyes are no longer bandaged. I now enter the dream and go over to him and put my hands on him and say, "It is going to be all right." He takes my hand and feebly says, "I want to make my peace with God." I put my arms around him and draw him close and pray a simple prayer of reconciliation. I hear him feebly praying after me. Then I continue praying and ask God to heal him.* (Journal, 3-3-80)

The airplane symbolized my ego's inflated and elevated status, which I was enjoying in the church from my newly found power. I was "flying high" so to speak since my January transformation experience. However, hidden in this ego-consciousness was the shadow, the opposite of the Bible-reading, churchgoing, praying, meditating, power-of-God-testifying guy who, no longer able to sustain this elevated and inflated attitude and position, fell to earth, bringing me back to the reality of my unconscious situation.

I am not as I appear.

What I say is opposite of what I mean.

I fell back to earth and set in motion the reconciliation and healing of ego and shadow—this other man in me—as the end of the dream suggested. Even today as I recall this dream tears roll down my checks. I am overcome with strong emotion as I remember the feeling of that moment as I embraced this other man in me, pulling him to myself, reconciling him to me and God. As Thich Nhat Hanh says, "The first person you must reconcile with is yourself, . . . The rest is just a matter of time."[55]

I call this dream "the Fall" as it ushered in a series of dreams over the next several months that ultimately resulted in my resigning my position as Director of Music in the church. and eventually leaving the church. Many saw this as "my fall from grace" saying such things as "Sheldon is living his dark side." But the dreams set me on a path of self-discovery, on a path to discovering the Divine within and on the hero's path of my soul's journey. This path would involve "leaving my parents' home" and the "parsonage consciousness" and entailed a "radical transformation of conventional attitudes." This journey would become the working out and manifestation of the admonition of the voice I'd heard that January morning in 1978, "Listen to your dreams for I will speak to you through them."

Although I had always enjoyed a good rapport with the people I attended church with and had always had a good response to my music and musical leadership there, this dream ushered in a change. I began to experience growing tension, a growing dislike for the job, and a growing dissatisfaction with my life. I began to dread Sundays, and I lost my desire and energy for writing and arranging music. I began to notice a disconnect between me and the music, between me and

55 Nhat Hanh, quoted in "The Buddha Flower Opens," 23.

the people to whom I ministered, between the beliefs that I held and what was emerging inside me. This was a disconnect that my current consciousness couldn't seem to solve no matter how hard I tried. The rapport between me and the people suddenly changed. Suddenly it was like a wall had appeared and the flow of the music stopped. No matter how I tried to force it, I became more anxious and irritable. I lost desire and energy for what had once brought me joy.

The dreams, however, continued nightly, like a damn had broken and a river had come gushing forth. I began to realize that my dreams were trying to tell me something. It was like a plan of some kind was being revealed through them—a plan that didn't seem to much care about the life that I was living.

During this time I had a series of dreams that spoke directly to my growing tension with my identification with music and my role as music director. On December 4, 1980, I dreamed

> *An airfreight van drives up and stops in our driveway. I go out. The van is delivering a piano from Africa. The piano is all folded up and in a box. I am surprised that it arrived so soon. I had expected it to arrive after Mark and Sarah. My brother is the airfreight man and I help him unload the boxed piano.*
>
> *As we are carrying the boxed piano into the house, a car drives up. In it are Mark and his wife, Sarah, my mom, and my dad. Mark gets out. When I see him I notice that he has matured, and I know it is because of the difficulty and responsibilities of doing the job all by himself in Africa that had "mellowed" him. He had also gained weight. When I saw him, I felt a strong emotion, a strange closeness and compassion for him—so much so that I wanted to hug him but I*

> *couldn't because I was carrying the boxed piano. Finally, the desire became so great that I sat the piano down and ran and hugged him. This surprised everybody because it was not my normal behavior toward Mark.* (Journal, 12-04-80)

The dream centered on a piano. The piano symbolized my music. My life had been dedicated to music and especially music in the church. In many ways, music was a large part of my identity—the major way I expressed my feelings and creativity. In the dream the piano was all folded up and in a box.

The piano came by airfreight. Since air is a symbol of Spirit, this suggested to me that Spirit had sent me a message that the life I had dedicated to music—that particular identity and way of expressing myself—was coming to an end, being "boxed up." In the dream I was carrying the piano. Although the musician and my life in music had been folded up and put in a box, I was still carrying it around. The spirit in me revealed that that was the reason for the feeling I was having pertaining to the music job. The spirit had folded up the piano, but I was still trying to carry it around in the church music job. That was the source of my frustration and dislike for the job. I was going against the spirit in me—against the unconscious—against the soul's longing. I was attempting to carry around a life that was no longer in God's will or in the plan of the greater purpose of the unconscious other.

While I was carrying the piano, a car drove up containing Mark and his wife, and my mom and dad. A car is a way of getting from one place to another and therefore can symbolize ego- consciousness. Another consciousness containing four people had arrived. Since the number four symbolizes wholeness, this suggested to me that my wholeness might be contained in this other consciousness.

When I saw Mark, I was moved emotionally and felt a strange closeness to him and compassion for him. At the time Mark was a missionary in Africa ministering to the indigenous people in various tribal systems. So, Mark could represent or symbolize the missionary-minister part of me.

What does Africa symbolize? Africa was often referred to as the "dark continent" because up until the 20th century little was known about this mysterious land. My association of "dark continent" to Africa suggested that it symbolized the unconscious realm. Putting these two ideas together, Mark represented that part of me that was a missionary-minister to the unconscious.

The feeling for Mark and, therefore, the feeling for this aspect of me became so great that I set the piano down and went to embrace him. I set the piano down! I must therefore set music down in order to embrace this other masculine aspect.

Understood symbolically, the dream seemed to say that my life that had been identified with music and its role in the church was all folded up and put away in a box. I was to set it down and embrace another part of me—the missionary-minister to the unconscious part of me—because of a deep and strange closeness I felt for it.

Did this mean I was to dedicate my life to working with the unconscious or did Mark simply represent some unconscious aspect of my personality that hadn't yet been revealed—some masculine energy that had this connection to the indigenous world? I didn't know for sure. I would have to wait and see. However, one thing *was* for sure. According to the dream, this move would surprise everybody because it wouldn't display my normal behavior—it wasn't *my* way of being. My normal behavior and what would be expected of me by most people I knew would be for me to continue in music, in service to the church.

It wouldn't be normal for me to stop working in music, but the dream seemed to be leading in that direction.

The second dream in this series came the following night, on December 5, 1980. I dream

> *The committee, like a church board, is meeting to evaluate the church music position. They hire someone else. I am not even considered. I am surprised at that. They tell me they no longer need that masculine image up in front.* (Journal, 12-05-80)

In reality, the evaluation of the church music director's position was coming up within the month. So, was this an objective dream—a dream that related to the literal facts of an outer event? Was the church board actually going to do this? Or was this a subjective dream dealing with my own inner and spiritual life? Although I had no way of knowing if, at the unconscious level, the church board felt the way the dream said they felt, there was no indication that this was an objective dream—a dream that refers to a literal external reality. Therefore, I took the dream as my own inner spiritual advisory board that was evaluating the music director part of me. This spiritual board hired somebody else for the job. In fact, my own spiritual guidance system—that part of me that was interested in my spiritual life—didn't even consider me for the job because they no longer needed "that masculine image up in front." The dream was saying that my inner guidance system didn't want the music image—this particular "masculine image"—up in front, and dominant or primary anymore.

This dream seemed to confirm the insights gained from the first dream and even speak more specifically to the issue. The parts of me in charge of my spiritual life needed a different "*masculine image up in front.*" This spoke directly to a change in the masculine image. They wanted a different identity. The masculinity identified with the music director was no longer beneficial to my spiritual health.

These two dreams had pretty well convinced me that to continue as the director of music would not be in the will of God, that is, it would not be in agreement with the direction and movement of the unconscious and my soul. However, a third dream came to further substantiate the messages of these first two dreams. The third dream came on December 11, 1980, one week after the first dream. I dreamed

> *I am up in front of the church of my childhood. I am leading songs or singing or getting ready to. My back is turned to the congregation. I face the congregation, and somebody says, "Don't you see who is here?" I look around and suddenly I see Mark and Sarah in the congregation. I am overjoyed and quickly go to greet them. I clasp Mark's hand in my hands and put my arm around his neck. My wife and I stay in the pew with Mark and Sarah. The people on the other end of the pew move down so we can sit together. I sit by Mark and we all sit on the right end of the pew.* (Journal, 12-11-80)

This dream showed the final move from the masculine image as music director to the new image symbolized by Mark. The words "up in front" connected to the previous dream where the church board said they needed "a different masculine image up in front." Again, I went to Mark, who I had determined was a symbol for the "missionary-minister to the unconscious aspect of me" and with great feeling and joy clasped his hand in mine and put my arms around his neck. I did this in public—like a public confession of my acceptance of this part of me. This time I stayed with this aspect, sitting on the right end of the pew. Since the direction *right* often stands for consciousness, this act indicated that I was moving toward making a conscious decision to leave the music director's position and identity.

The tension between these two worlds became so great that finally I couldn't maintain the outer structure any longer and gave in to the demands of the dreams. I accepted the dream's call for a "new masculine image up in front." One month from the time of the second dream of this series I resigned from my position as the church music director and my life in church music, and embraced the dream's call to become a "minister to the unconscious" and to discover how "God may speak through dreams."

This decision threw me into a time of confusion, questioning, and doubt. Had I made the right decision? Was I going against God's will? Was I being deceived as some believed? Who was I now? What was I to do with my life? What *was* God's will? It was like I was adrift, having left the shore of what was safe and comfortable, of what I knew and had been taught to be true and right, and was now drifting into open sea, unable to return to the home shore, and yet having no view of another land in sight. My same-sex desires returned. I remember getting into my car late one night and driving for miles, crying, blinded by tears to the point that I had difficulty seeing the road. Feeling the loss of all that I had been and somehow all that I had longed to be and all that others had longed for me to be, I cried out to God, "Did I dare trust my dreams?"

A few weeks later I went to bed with these questions on my mind. That night I had the following dream. It was January 1981, three years after I was told to listen to my dreams and just a few weeks after resigning the church music job in response to listening to my dreams. I dream that

> *I call a radio talk show on a Christian radio station, to ask one of the guests, an authority on the Bible and God's will, "How do I know that my dreams are God confirming in me and showing me His will or just the unconscious mirroring back to me what I am doing?" He says, "The simple fact that dreams are a universal part of man's experience says that God must have a reason for them and intends to use them. But he has given us minds and abilities to discern how God may speak through them. To find the answer to that question is our job."* (Journal, 1-08-81)

The message was clear! "God has a reason for dreams and intends to use them. It is my job to discover just how God may speak through dreams." In this dream the unconscious chose a Christian radio station in my local area to get this message to me. This Christian radio station was a modern-day method of and symbol for spreading God's word in my community. The talk show was another symbol for revealing how God worked in the lives of people today. Both were accepted by my own church and traditional training as valid ministries. Therefore, taken inwardly, this meant that my own personal spiritual guidance system was confirming the value of dreams and leading me further into their study and use. This dream felt comforting and gave me courage to continue on despite personal doubts and criticisms from my extended family and friends.

Thus began my journey to find the answer to that question—to discover how God might speak through dreams. Shortly thereafter the Ministerial Association in the county where I lived invited a minister and a Jungian analyst to present a course on dreams. I attended this course, which ironically was held at the church I attended and where I had served as music director. After the presentation I introduced myself to the analyst and within months began analysis, a decision that would change the direction of my life.

Looking back, I now understand that this event was a synchronicity, an event where my inner and outer worlds intersected in a meaningful way. It would prove to be just one of many synchronicities that would show up and keep me on my path.

Notes and Exercises

The shadow refers to the dark, feared, unwanted, unknown and rejected parts of ourselves, parts that don't fit into the ideal image we have for ourselves or the image that others have for us. These parts don't cease to exist. Rather they continue to live in the unconscious where they form a kind of secondary personality, an alter-ego so to speak, which causes us to behave in ways that don't fit into our ideal view of our self.

A man's shadow contains rejected, unacknowledged and repressed masculine qualities. Although we tend to think of the shadow in negative terms, it actually contains many positive, even vital qualities of "unlived life" that, if related to in appropriate ways, enhances a man's life.

The shadow will show up in dreams as a same-sex figure, often as a murky, unappealing, despised, feared or inferior figure. We first meet our shadow in others. We meet our negative shadows in people we can't stand, people we can't tolerate, people that trigger an exaggerated reaction of anger and judgment. We meet our positive shadow in people that we idealize, people we think are better than us, people we long to be like.

List three people or types of people you can't stand—people you have difficulty tolerating and tend to resist. Now make a list the things you can't stand about them. Using the words on your list, write a paragraph describing your shadow. Begin "My negative shadow is . . ."

List three people or types of people you idealize—people you wish you could be like. List the qualities about them that you idealize. Now write a paragraph describing your positive shadow beginning "My positive shadow is . . ."

Can you imagine yourself doing these things? In order to begin to own your shadow material, rewrite your paragraphs in first person beginning "I am . . ." Next speak them out loud to yourself in the mirror. How does that make you feel?

CHAPTER FIVE

Honoring the Witch

Eight months after "The Fall" dream I dream

> *I meet a beautiful young woman at work. Either I have a new job, or she gets a job in the same place where I work. I go to my mother and ask her about her mink coat. She perceives that I want it and says, "Why yes, son. You may have my mink coat." She thinks that I want it for myself, but I know I really want it for this young woman as a gift. My mother kisses me on my face, either on my forehead, nose, or mouth as she gives me the mink coat. I go back to my office and hang the long mink coat over my chair.*
>
> *While my back is turned, the beautiful young woman comes in and sees the coat and admires it. I turn and notice her. I go over and put the coat on and model it for her with various crazy fun actions. She thinks it is my coat. I let her think it while I continue to "show it off." She says, "I thought I'd be the first to receive a coat like that."*
>
> *I say, "This coat is for you. It is yours."* (Journal, 11-25-80)

This dream is typical of a dream that features the "anima" in Jungian psychology. Not only is there an unconscious masculine image living in the soul of a man, also living in his soul is an unconscious feminine image that expresses archetypal feminine qualities and traits.[56] This feminine image may appear positive one moment and negative the next.[57] In dreams she may show up as a young girl, a beautiful woman, a dancer, a nymph, a goddess, a good fairy, a saint, a witch, a whore, or a seductress.[58]

According to Jungian theory, developing a relationship with this "inner woman" or the "anima" opens a man up to emotionality and to a broader spirituality by creating a new conscious attitude that includes intuitive processes, creativity, imagination, and psychic sensitivity. According to Jung, she is the archetype of life itself[59] and an image of his soul.[60] As such this inner female image draws a man into life in search of that which is unconscious in him through the process of projection. In fact, through this process of projection, she often becomes a mediator between a man and his unconscious[61] as the behind-the-scenes element in a man's moods, reactions, impulses, and whatever else is spontaneous in psychic life.[62]

This is energy that lives of itself and makes us live a life behind consciousness that cannot be completely integrated but from which consciousness arises.[63] It is believed that the anima as an archetype influences a man's interactions with women and his attitudes toward

---

56 Jung, *Collected Works 7,* par. 297.

57 Jung, *Collected Works 9, Part 1,* par. 356.

58 Ibid.

59 Jung, *Collected Works 9, Part 1,* par. 66.

60 Jung, *Collected Works 6,* par. 808 and *Collected Works 9,* par. 55.

61 Jung, *Collected Works 10,* par. 715/378.

62 Jung, *Collected Works 9,* Part 1, par. 57

63 Ibid.

them. It is my experience that this inner feminine energy not only influences a man's interactions with women but can also draw a man into same-sex relationships in her attempt to connect him to the unconscious masculine living in his soul. I hypothesize that this inner woman can fall in love with a man right through a man's ego and pull him into a relationship with that man. This idea will be explored in a later chapter.

A beautiful young woman, the personification of my unconscious feminine qualities, made her appearance in this dream. Immediately I went to my mother and asked for her mink coat because I wanted to give it to this beautiful woman. This suggested that while I was shifting my loyalty from my mother to my inner feminine and another soul figure, I was projecting my mother-image or mother complex onto her. In other words, my anima, my own inner woman, came under the spell of the mother, wrapped so to speak in her image, symbolized by my giving the woman my mother's mink coat.

It is believed that in a man's psychology, invariably the anima first appears mingled with the mother-image. This now became my psychological task and another part of my soul's journey: to differentiate the anima (as an image of my own soul) from the mother and come into a relationship with her. This would be done so that I could be true to my own inner feminine and her life in me, in order for me to be true to my own soul's life.

Over the next several years, this feminine energy would appear in my dreams and fantasies, in my moods and inspirations in various forms, inviting me into a relationship with her, a relationship that continues today. As I continued my study of and my work with my own dreams, I began to differentiate this inner feminine energy from the mother complex and from her contamination with the unconscious masculine. This process began to remove the mink coat (the mother material), from the anima and the anima began to speak her truth, the truth of my own soul.

However, I found it difficult to trust her, to trust my feelings and my intuition. I felt ambivalent about trusting the dreams, questioning whether I could trust this growing relationship with the unconscious, scared to trust this voice in me. This is mirrored in the following "witch" dreams.

I dream

> *A young girl is being chased from place to place, being accused by people that there is something strange about her, not right. They chase her up against a door and she cries out "Okay, I'm a witch. I'm a witch" and sobs. I have an idea she's not really a witch, but that the people keep accusing her, and she just gives in or says she is to stop the chasing and conflict.* (Journal, 1-13-81)

I dialog with this young girl.

> *Sheldon: Who are you?*
>
> *Young girl: I am your soul reborn that is trying to guide you into truth, your truth, but you keep doubting, fearing that perhaps, Jung, Dean Franz, these classes you are taking, the dreams themselves are anti-Christ, of the devil, even accusing this place we are holding the meetings—the Unity Church—of being evil because of their theology. You keep accusing me, wondering if I am Satan. I am still weak and cannot withstand the conflict, so I am just giving in to stop the conflict. I'll be a witch if that is what you want me to be and if that will stop you from harassing me.*

Sheldon: How can I be sure that you are not a witch?

Young girl: You can't. You can only trust me that I'm not.

Sheldon: How can I trust you?

Young girl: You can start by honoring me, by listening to me. You have prayed for reconstruction of your masculine-feminine relationship. That is happening. Trust the events in your life. Your soul contains much repressed and unlived life. Anything that opposes your current identity will be seen as wrong to you—even of the devil. Don't be afraid. Believe and she will be healed. (Journal, 1-13-81)

The girl informed me that it was my attitude that was the problem. The girl's shift from first person to third person suggested that this problem was not just personal but had a nonpersonal element—or perhaps archetypal elements—to it. The task was to meet the archetypal feminine image with sufficient openness to benefit from her inspirational energy and yet resist falling wholly under the sway of the primitive unconscious.[64] This dream suggested that my attitude toward the feminine ran the risk of making her a witch or keeping her a witch, that is, in the primitive unconscious. Here she would "bewitch" me from time to time with spells of moodiness, irritability, and sexual acting out, causing me to seek a man who would free me from her controlling, castrating, and seductive spell. I had come to notice through the years that when I felt under the spell of a mood, such as irritable, rejected, lonely, guilty, misunderstood, and disappointed, my same-sex fantasies and attractions would become activated, increasing in their intensity.

One week later I dream

64 Watsky, "Anima."

> *We, my family of origin, are moving. A man is helping us. He sets some things down. One falls over and breaks. He doesn't seem concerned about it and kind of laughs it off. Then a disheveled girl appears. She is a complete mess, especially her hair. They are holding her down and cutting her hair by force. She doesn't want it cut.* (Journal, 1-20-81)

This dream continued to mirror my ongoing difficulty and struggle with my parental complex and the church. The man helping with the move was a pillar of masculine authority in the church I attended. While I had left the church music position, thus making some movement, I was still questioning this journey into the unconscious and the value or "rightness" of listening to my dreams. This dream showed that "they" were holding the girl down and cutting her hair against her will. A reference to "they" in dreams can often represent some unknown collective or societal attitude, some social or organizational rule that expects one to comply with the rules and laws of that ruling consciousness.

Although this might refer to the law of the church and my family of origin, it most certainly showed that I was still contained in some collective, societal, or ruling attitude that was forcing its belief and attitude on my anima, forcing her to come under its rules, under its power, and cutting off her wisdom, which was symbolized by the cutting of her hair.

Hair often symbolizes the life-force, wisdom, and spiritual inspiration, strength, and power.[65] To cut the hair is a symbol of submission.[66] While the dream suggested that I was attempting to come into a relationship with my feminine side, it showed that I was doing this

---

65 Cooper, *Illustrated Encyclopaedia*, 77.

66 Tresidder, *Symbols and Their Meanings*, 18.

by trying to force her to come under a ruling collective attitude rather than relating to her for who she was. The dream seemed to be saying "Sheldon, you are cutting off the wisdom and life-force of your soul by the attitude you are holding toward the feminine."

In the midst of my struggle with fear, doubt, and ambivalence mirrored by these "witch dreams" I dream

> *I meet a man who travels all over the world to different countries to help people. He goes to one country that is several hundred years behind. In fact, he has never seen a culture so primitive. He says the only way he was able to relate to the members of this culture was because of his study at the Jung Institute. I tell him that he just gave me confirmation about my studying Jung's psychology.* (Journal, 1-17-81)

As I worked on this dream I came to understand that the country referred to in the dream was the country of the unconscious, and it referred not only to my own unconscious life but to the unconscious life of the world in which I lived. We like to imagine that our primitive traits have long since disappeared but we only have to look at the terrible things that have happened throughout modern history, even today, to recognize that they live on in us as we unconsciously them act out. This dream continued to confirm that my study of Jungian psychology would help me understand the primitive country of my own unconscious. Two weeks later I dream

> *I am walking through a hall in a public building, like a train station. I meet Hilda. We have been involved in each other's healing and search for wholeness. I have just left an "animal house," a place where all kinds of animals are kept*

> *penned up. It is my duty to care for them. These animals are wild animals but have been made very tame. In fact, their instincts are missing. I know that if they can find and eat a particular food, their instincts will return, but then they will be wild animals again. I leave their cage doors open. I do this on purpose and without anybody knowing it so that the animals will find this food, this "magic potent," and become wild again. I do this knowing it is breaking the rules of this "animal house" or clinic/zoo. Hilda used to work at this "animal house" and she wants to know about the animals. In fact, she left them in my care. I know that I have set the animals free.*
>
> *Hilda becomes aware of this, and it triggers in her years and years of pent up feelings and emotions. It triggers memories and dreams from childhood, and she becomes hysterical and uncontrollable. She becomes violet as all these pent up feelings surge through her. I know that she doesn't want to hurt me, but she begins directing all this hysterical violence toward me and shoots me in the stomach. As she begins to shoot me, I realize this is a moment I have lived before in a dream that I had in my early teens or preteen years in which I was shot in the stomach. However, this time I felt no pain and I didn't die.* (Journal, 2-3-81)

Hilda was a colleague of mine, fifteen years my senior, a very bright, intuitive, independent woman who taught English and literature. She introduced me to many Jungian writers and was a strong supporter of my journey. As the daughter of a minister, she too had been raised in a parsonage and had faced conflicts similar to mine in her own journey to selfhood. Hilda had been a consistent figure in my dreams through the years, representing aspects of my anima and inner wisdom. Overall, she was a trusted inner figure and guide.

This dream suggested a shift in my attitude toward the feminine. Instead of trying to subdue her by force as represented in the previous dream (holding her down and cutting her hair against her will), this dream showed me opening up to her and her pent up feelings. This dream was the beginning of the healing of my relationship with the feminine in me, my emotions, feelings, intuitions, creativity, imagination, and psychic sensitivity, my own inner wisdom—all that I had repressed or not allowed into my experience in order to become the man I had become. This feminine as a symbol of life itself would also include those rejected and denied masculine parts of me as well as my soul, that all-encompassing center of wholeness.

The feminine is one of the doorways to the shadow and to the Self as an experience of wholeness. This idea was reflected by that aspect of the dream that stated: "Hilda and I have been involved in each other's healing and search for wholeness." The dream showed that I was beginning to get in touch with my instincts as suggested by the fact that I left the door open so the animals could get out and get the food that would "make them wild again"—that would put them back in touch with their natural instinctual natures, which the dream said "are missing."

As the dream itself suggested, animals represent instincts when they appear in dreams.[67] Animals represent the instinctive forces in man, *forces that know the way when man feels completely lost.*[68] One only has to think of the helpful animals in myths and fairy tales wherein an animal saves the hero by showing him something nearby that he had not seen. Sometimes the animals do more than that; they solve the

67 Hannah, The Cat, Dog and Horse Lectures, 55.

68 Jung, *Visions*, Vol. 1, 139, in Hannah, 58.

entire problem.[69] English psychologist and Jung biographer Barbara Hannah in the book, The Cat, Dog and Horse Lectures, which features a seminar she gave in Zürich in 1954 on the images of the cat, dog, and horse in psychic life of humankind, addressing dreams, mythology, and culture points out that "[i]n all natural situations, . . . the instincts are far better protection than all the intellectual wisdom in the world . . ."[70] Hannah also tells us how much nearer animals live to God's will—to their true nature—than we do, noting that "if you follow the way of nature you will quite naturally come to your own law"[71] and "if we follow the laws of our own nature, they quite naturally will lead us to the right end,"[72] that is, "to a state of completeness [the Self], to what we really are."[73] But it isn't just the case of simply following the instinct; it is seeing the *meaning* in the instinct.[74] Animals as representatives of instincts in our dreams connect us to laws of our own nature if we can but understand their meaning!

The fact that the "wild" animals had been "tamed" to such an extent that their instincts were "missing" suggested that I was not in a good relationship with my instincts, that I was cut off from them, having relegated them to some place in my unconscious, some "animal house." To *tame* means "to domesticate and make tractable"; "to deprive of courage, ardor, or zest"; "to deprive of interest, excitement, or attractiveness"; "to make dull"; "to soften and tone down" as well as "to harness or control and render useful, as a source of power." Taming the instincts may have a positive and necessary benefit at various stages in psycho-social-sexual development, such as the domestication,

---

69 Hannah, The Cat, Dog and Horse Lectures, 57.

70 Ibid.

71 Ibid.

72 Jung, *Visions*, Vol. 1, 139, in Hannah, 58.

73 Hannah, *Archetypal Symbolism of Animals*, 8.

74 Ibid.

harnessing, and control of aggression or sexuality in order to fit into the rules of a society or an organization. However, there comes a time when the rules of that societal or organizational structure may begin to stifle one's growing need to embrace another life that is calling, a life more in tune with the laws of one's own nature, that state of completeness of what we really are.

This dream indicated that I was opening the doorway to the laws of my own nature, who I really was, by allowing the animals, the instincts, to find the "magical potent," the food that would return them to their wild and natural state. In that process I would have to deal with the anger and rage of the feminine as she remembered years and years of pent up (repressed) feelings and emotions, recalling dreams and memories from childhood that released a hysterical and uncontrollable violence directed toward me.

This is what I call the revenge of the repressed and unlived life! This repressed and unlived life will do all manner of things to get *into* life—pull us into an extramarital affair, get us addicted to drugs or pornography, call us to a men's room on a summer afternoon to have sex with an unknown man, cause us to quit a job and move across the country, put us into a depression, make us anxious, wake us with the terror of a nightmare, or employ a thousand other means of getting our attention.

The feminine figure in the dream started shooting me in the stomach. The dream ended by reminding me of another dream in which I was shot in the stomach. Although the dream said that I had this dream in my teens, the dream that I remembered was one I had some time in my twenties. However, this dream did reference the teenage boy dream.

In my twenties I dream that I remember a dream where

> *I am a teenage boy in a thatched-roof hut. Suddenly a man appears at the door of the hut with a gun. He shoots me in the stomach. I awaken from the dream believing that I had been shot and feeling the pain in my stomach.* (Journal, date unknown).

This dream of being shot in the stomach had three references: me as a teenager, me as a man in his twenties, and the current dream, me as a man at age thirty-seven. All three references occurred at critical stages in a man's development. The task of the adolescent male was to more fully embrace his developing masculinity, his phallic energy, and move out and away from mother and his family into the world and to begin to fit into the larger cultural and societal demands. It was both an expansion and a curtailing—an expansion into his developing masculinity and growing independence into his male peer group and a resurgence of oedipal energy, but this time with a surrogate mother figure, the girl friend, unencumbered by the incest taboo.[75]

It was also curtailing of the regressive tendency to remain more closely with the family and with the mother, or in my case, the life of the parsonage. At this point I was ambivalent as to whether this gunshot to the stomach of the adolescent male and then again to the stomach of the twenty-something young man was an expansion. By expansion, I mean a killing of the boy's inclinations to remain with the mother and the milieu of the parsonage, thus pushing him into the rigors of his masculine, phallic development. Or was it a curtailing of these masculine energies, a killing of his phallic energy and masculine development, thus keeping him stuck in the mother symbol and in

75 Monick, *Castration and Male Rage*, 29.

the external searching for a more expanded masculine in same-sex encounters?

I'm inclined to think that the dream of the teenage boy was a killing of the masculine energy that wanted and longed for expression. I am reminded of another dream that I had during my adolescence. In this dream *I am standing naked in the locker room following gym class. I look down and see that I have both a penis and a vagina. I take my penis and roll it up and stick it up into my vagina.* The dream speaks for itself. It's significant that the dream of being shot in the stomach surfaced again in my twenties, around the time that I was stopping my same-sex relationships and increasing my commitment to my wife, my family, and a life that was then more congruent with my family and religious beliefs. This included an increased commitment to the church, suggesting that the dream referred to another curtailing and expansion—the death of the adolescent attitude and transformation of my pubescent erotic drive into a striving for social standing and collective approval, with the church even becoming a surrogate mother of sorts.

However, I think the reference to this dream at age thirty-seven has quite a different meaning. I think it was an expansion of Phallos that was now able to let the feminine in without the fear of castration. It was an expansion designed to embrace my instincts and was also a further departure from the comforts of the collective dream, the cultural family, the religious family, and the mother church. It signified my coming into a relationship with the laws of my own nature. I would come to understand that this drive to come into a relationship with the laws of my own nature was behind my same-sex attractions.

The gun imagery certainly has its masculine and phallic symbolism. The bullets are symbolic of the penetration by aggressive and potentially destructive aspects of the masculine energy, reminiscent of the bull energy that was chasing me in the dream three years earlier.

The difference between this dream of being shot in the stomach at age thirty-seven and the previous dreams is that I did not feel the pain and I did not die. This would suggest that I was now able to withstand, to take in, and to survive the return of this repressed energy—this Other that longed to live.

In the chakra system the stomach area is the location of the third chakra. Basically, chakras are spinning energy centers that receive and transmit the subtle energies that are believed to be necessary for physical and emotional health. Each chakra is thought to be associated with a certain level of consciousness, certain organs of the body, certain emotions and developmental stages. The third chakra represents the development of one's personality, self-esteem, and ego. It is the place of personal power, courage, and one's expression in the world. The spiritual and emotional challenges that are associated with the third chakra are trust, fear and intimidation, self-confidence, self-respect, competence and skills in the outer world, care of oneself and others, sensitivity to criticism, aggression, defensiveness, decision-making ability, and competitiveness.[76] So the dream showed that I was being "hit" in these areas of development. I would have to face my fears, to face where my self-confidence and self-respect and competence came from. I would have to address my sensitivity to criticism, my repressed aggression, and my defensiveness in order to embrace the laws of my own nature and become truly myself.

This dream came to me at the age of thirty-seven, a time for another developmental task but a different one—the transformation of individuation. A man must make two sacrifices before individuation can occur: (1) the childish longing for the past, especially the longing for the mother and the comfort and security she represents, which may get

---

76 Myss, *Why People Don't Heal*, 59.

projected onto belief systems, cultural and societal institutions and (2) adult pride in his accomplishments. If these two sacrifices are made, then individuation can occur.

This has to do with the integration of the feminine without danger to Phallos.[77] Integration of the feminine is the capacity to value a man's growing consciousness of himself as an interior being with an interior life that is in keeping with the laws of his own nature.[78] This now became my journey—to find this man inside me as Phallos and not in some men's restroom as phallus. Could it be that this was the transformation—the transformation of individuation—that was started and even intended that January morning in 1978 when I had been told to listen to my dreams?

Following the dream where I released the animals, I had a series of dreams of the "witch-girl" of the earlier dream. At first, she was dressed in torn and dirty clothes. Her hair was long and disheveled. These dreams showed the condition of my inner feminine and my relationship to her. I had neglected this part of my soul. I had not tended to her needs or her life and therefore I had not tended to *my* life. I had not given her the value she deserved. Therefore, I had not given the life of my soul the value it longed for. I had kept her in service to the parsonage—in service to the age of the parson—both the personal parson's life that I was raised in as well as the archetypal. It was the end of this age, an end to the age of the parson.

In these dreams of the "witch-girl" I was washing, combing, and styling her hair. Each dream showed the hair becoming less disheveled and more and more attractive. Her clothes became clean and less tattered. These dreams mirrored my improved relationship with the feminine and also my inner life. I began to honor and listen to this soul

---

77 Monick, *Castration and Male Rage*, 65.

78 Ibid.

figure—the wisdom and life of my own soul. To actually integrate her life into my life, however, would require a new masculine image "up in front" as the "church board dream" had indicated, a masculine image that was not contained in the parsonage consciousness but one that could follow the wisdom and promptings of my own soul.

Notes and Exercises

A man has an inner woman. This inner woman is shaped by a man's experience with his mother and other important women in his life while growing up. Various expressions of a man's mother complex include over-idealization of women, fear of women, anger at women, distrust of women, guilt when asserting self, detachment from feelings, over-valuing sexual experience and undervaluing emotional responses.[79] A man's anima or inner woman is often under the spell of the mother. This creates problems in his relationships when he projects his inner woman or feminine feelings onto his partner. For example, anger, moodiness, and irritability are often signs of an anima under the spell of the mother complex. One of the tasks of a man is to separate his inner feminine from his mother's feelings so that he can be true to himself and his own feelings. *(Refer to Appendix My Parents, for a description of my mother's emotional style.)*

> *Describe your mother's emotional style. What emotions did your mother express (e.g. anger, disgust, sadness, shame, fear, joy, happiness, surprise, etc.) and how did she express them (crying spells, rages, withdrawal, blame, creative acts, etc.)? Which ones describe you? How do you express your*

79 Ellis, G.H. MD. Re-Membering Frankenstein, Chapter 1, par. 77

emotions? Can you express your emotions without guilt or discomfort? What emotions do you find difficult to express? How is your emotional style like your mother's emotional style? How is it different?

From your answers, describe your anima or inner woman.

CHAPTER SIX

The Emerging Self

"Trust that which gives you meaning and accept it as your guide."

—Carl Jung

Dreams are nature's way of attempting to bring to consciousness the unconscious material that is often at the root of our emotional, psychological, mental, physical, and spiritual conflicts. They are also nature's way of revealing to us the parts of ourselves that have never been realized—potential ways of being that we may need to acknowledge, listen to, and integrate into our lives if we are to grow toward wholeness and healing and become the persons we were born to be. Dreams help us get in touch with these unknown and unacknowledged parts. The dreams hold up a mirror to show us what is going on at the deeper, unconscious level. It is as if the dreams show us the inside story. Therefore, to be in contact with the dreams is to have the hope of altering one's conscious standpoint in the light of a larger reality and more complete point of view. In my case, my journey was none other than my individuation and my struggle for an authentic expression of the Self.

Over the next several years, my dreams commented on every area of my life—my relationships, my sexuality, my profession, my spiritual life, my marriage, my health, and even my past and my future. By paying attention to my dreams I had to face and come to terms with parts of me that I had repressed, parts of me that I didn't like, parts I didn't want to be and couldn't accept, pain that I didn't want to face, as well as parts of me that had never been conscious, parts of me that longed for life, longed to be loved, lived, and expressed. As mentioned earlier, I discovered that deep within me lived an unknown land—a land with its own characters, its own laws, and its own functions. In this land there was a story being written and played out, the goals and purposes of which were independent of external factors or my conscious ego desires. Each night I was allowed to see a page in the story. And slowly I began to live that story.

Four days after my initial meeting with Jungian analyst Dean Frantz, I dream

> *I am in an older department store. There is a new manager who has rearranged the layout of the store and added some new departments. I work at this store and am upset and irritated with this new manager because he has changed the area where I work and the special place where I hang my hairbrush. He has moved it. I question the new manager about this act and where my hairbrush is. I feel like he has no right to move my working area and my personal hairbrush without at least telling me. I have worked in this store for a long time. He shows no concern for my feelings and is unimpressed with my tenure and seniority. He points to a pile of hairbrushes lying on a shelf under a table. I begin to look for my hairbrush. I pick up a couple, but I don't find mine. These hairbrushes have hair bristles. Mine has vinyl or plastic teeth. I am now at my working station and think that*

I'll just hang my hairbrush up in its new place. Something inside me seems to indicate I get a new one.

Now I see a sign that is hanging from the ceiling near my station that says "counseling." The new manager has added new departments in order to compete with other stores and remain in business. He has added personal service departments, one of which is counseling. People are coming out of the counseling area saying how beautifully it is decorated.

I decide to go in and see the area. There is a small waiting area. I push open a partially opened door and look inside. It is a restroom with a shower in it and part of an older building with tall ceilings. The walls are plastered. The room is painted a deep royal blue. The shower is running. I notice that where the water hits the wall, the dark blue is washing away and white or at least a lighter blue is showing through. I wonder why the shower is running with no one in it and that they must have turned the water on before the paint got completely dry or else the continuing hitting of the water is wearing the blue paint off. (Journal, 2-27-81)

This dream indicated that my psychic structure was being rearranged; not only rearranged but new departments were being added in order for me to stay in business, that is, in order for me to remain alive and viable, to have some usefulness and purpose. A new manager had changed the area where I worked and had gotten rid of my hairbrush. A hairbrush has to do with maintaining my hair and, by extension, my appearance or image. My hair and how it looks has always been important to me. I remember one time my father took me to get my hair cut and had the barber give me what was then called a "pineapple" hair cut—very short except right at the front, which was left longer, like the leaves of a pineapple. I was six or seven years old at the time, and I remember being excited about my new cut. But when I returned home, my mother was very upset and even cried because I had gotten my hair cut so short. I felt so bad that I ran and hid behind the sofa.

This early reaction reveals how sensitive my emerging masculine energy was to the power of the emotions of the feminine and how important my hair and its appearance would become to me and even to my sense of Self. Thus, like the witch dream where the hair was being forcibly cut, another dream showing that someone messing with the way I maintained my hair was significant; it focused on something very important to me. Besides my personal associations to hair, throughout time and across cultures, hair and hairstyling carried heavy cultural meaning for men. In many cultures the grooming of hair was a rite of passage, sometimes tied to religious rituals and could confer power or status. As I have noted earlier, hair symbolizes the life-force. Hair on the head is linked with individual spirit or the life-force of a person[80] and the power of thought, virility, higher powers and inspiration,[81] spiritualized energy, and the spiritual assets of a person.[82] Hair then is a symbol of my life-force and spiritual energy.

This new manager had tossed my way of managing my thinking and spiritual self into a box with all the other employees without even consulting me. An experience of the Self, the center and unifying principle of the psyche and source of life that contains our wholeness, is a defeat for the ego because it requires the ego to expand it one-sided point of view.[83] And although one might argue or question my calling this "new manager" the Self, it's apparent from Jungian psychology

80 Tresidder, *Symbols and Their Meaning*, 18.

81 Cooper, *Illustrated Encyclopaedia*, 77.

82 Cirlot, *Dictionary of Symbols*, 153.

83 Jung, *Collected Works 14*, par. 778.

that behind all psychological phenomena, including dreams, is a larger entity that guides the journey. This entity is called the Self[84] or, as I have discussed elsewhere, the Soul.

In the rearranging of my psychic structure, a "counseling section" had been added. When I enter into this counseling section, I found a shower with the water running. Water is a symbol of the unconscious, the source of all potential existence, and is associated with the Great Mother and the feminine principle,[85] an emblem of fluidity, dissolution, birth, and regeneration.[86] This dream is an invitation to step into the shower and subject myself to the unconscious. Immersion in water symbolizes the death of the old and the rebirth into the new as the rite of baptism represents. Water dreams suggest the emergence of the alchemical stage of the *solutio.* For the alchemist, the *solutio* was a stage in the process of returning the differentiated matter to its original undifferentiated state—like a return to the womb for rebirth.[87] This is what takes place in the psychotherapy process. The fixed aspects of the personality do not allow for change. They are established and sure of their rightness. For change or transformation to occur, these fixed aspects must first be dissolved. This is done by the analytic process, which examines the products of the unconscious and puts the established ego attitudes in question.[88]

This theme of water and the invitation to enter psychoanalysis, my journey through the unconscious, continued in another dream I had about two weeks later.

---

84 Wilkerson, *Jung, the Self and Dreamwork.*

85 Ibid., 188.

86 Ibid., 112.

87 Edinger, *Anatomy of the Psyche*, 47.

88 Ibid., 47–48.

I am on a trip to Florida with a man, a woman, and a dog. We stop to eat. While eating I tell the man that because of recent rains, the roads are under water, inferring that we won't be able to get to Florida. He says probably not the northern roads, which are the ones we are taking. He says the roads near the ocean usually get covered first. We see a map and realize the roads that we are taking are also covered with water. I suggest we stay a couple of days for the water to go down, but instead we contact a man who is a specialist at getting people through to Florida when the roads are covered with water.

We get ready to leave. We carry out three folding tables, but the car is not there. We store the tables in the church foyer. Finally, we are ready to leave. I go in to get the lady, but she is sleeping and isn't ready yet.

The special driver arrives. He says that he is not the greatest guide, but that he has helped many people get through the water-covered roads. He invites us to get into his vehicle. (Journal, 3-15-81)

The dream showed that I was traveling to another state, suggesting another state of consciousness. My personal associations of Florida are sunshine, oranges, health, restoration, and the fountain of youth. Florida means "flowering Easter" and was named by Ponce de Leon for Spain's Easter Celebration of Flowers.[89] The word *Florida* is from the Spanish word *florida,* which means "florid, flowery, and full of flowers." Flowers symbolize beauty, spring, youth, and gentleness, but also innocence, peace, spiritual perfection, the brevity of life, and the joy

89 Florida Quick Facts: Ben's Guide to U.S. Government.

of paradise.[90] Because of a flower's shape, the flower is the image of the center and thus an archetypal image of the soul.[91] Florida's connection to Easter reinforces the idea of resurrection and new life, connecting it to the resurrection of Christ. Christ, according to Jung, is an apt symbol of the Self.[92]

The dream was clear. I was on a journey to another state of consciousness, but it also showed that I was somewhat hesitant or resistant to this process. I pointed out that the roads were covered with water and that we needed to wait until it went down. This would suggest that I wanted to wait for a more "favorable time" until the current crisis or unconscious pressure passed.

But the dream didn't much care and offered a specialist that could get us through the water to Florida. When we were finally ready to go and carry the tables out, the car was not there, that is, the way, the means, wasn't there.

Cars often represent ego-consciousness since it is the ego that moves us through life. The fact that the car wasn't there appeared to be another obstacle to the dream's goal—to get to Florida. The car not being there suggested that I was not yet ready to take this journey, which mirrored the ego's continuing ambivalence and conflict about it. This resistance was also indicated by the "sleeping lady." But she pointed out why she was sleeping. From my journal:

> *Sheldon: Why aren't you ready to go, sleeping lady?*
>
> *Sleeping lady: I'm tired. I've been doing all the work. Besides, the specialist hasn't arrived yet.*

---

90 Tresidder, p. 90

91 Cirlot, p. 110

92 Jung, *Collected Works* 9, 23–35.

Sheldon: I think you're lazy. I don't think you want me to get to Florida.

Sleeping lady: I'm not lazy. I'm waiting for the specialist. He hasn't come yet, has he?

Sheldon: No.

Sleeping lady: When are you going to contact him? I have brought you this far. Now you must make a conscious choice to continue. But you need a specialist to help you on to Florida, the state of renewal and wholeness.

Sheldon: I've already contacted the specialist.

Sleeping lady: Yes, in the dream, but when are you going to contact him in outer life?

Sheldon: I will do it soon.

Sleeping lady: When?

Sheldon: In the next couple of days.

Sleeping lady: Okay.

Specialist: Hello. I'm here. Get in. This vehicle is a special kind for getting through the water. (Journal, 3-15-81)

The dream also showed me carrying three rectangular tables that I was to take with me. Geometric shapes are universal symbols that often appear in dreams; as such they may provide another layer of meaning. Throughout history, numbers and shapes have been ascribed long and often detailed, complicated meanings. Simply put, the number 3 indicates creative power and growth, moving toward overcoming duality, and connects with the triangle that symbolizes aspiration toward a higher unity.[93] The rectangular shape indicates the number 4, referring to its four sides. The number 4 produces the first solid figure and is symbolic of a certain wholeness, totality, and completion.[94] Combining

93 Cirlot, 351

94 Cooper, 115

the number 3 with the number 4 we have the number 7. The number 7 has a long symbolic history, but basically 7 is a symbol of completeness and the totality of the created universe (3 the sky + 4 the earth). It is the first number which contains both the spiritual and the temporal[95] and expresses the creation within that man evolves.

Carrying around these three tables indicated that I was carrying around energy that was moving toward a new wholeness. Momentarily, while waiting for the car, I put the tables in the foyer of the church. This suggested that I was still contained somewhat in the mother church and the life of the parsonage. From my journal:

> *Sheldon: Tables, why do I store you in the church?*
>
> *Tables: Because you are still contained in the church. But notice you stored us in the foyer, close to the door, close to the outer extremity of the collective church opinion. But you know you only stored them until the vehicle comes. You are not quite ready for this journey . . .* (Journal, 3-15-81)

Tables also symbolize connection and communication. We sit around tables to eat and talk with family and friends. We sit around tables in meetings to discuss ideas. The presence of tables suggested that this journey would include communication—communication with the unconscious—but also communication between me and the specialist. This dream further indicated movement and confirmation of my journey into analysis. The specialist is the analyst. The vehicle is the analysis. One final observation is that when I first left to load the tables, the car, the energy for transformation, was not there. We needed a special vehicle. This suggested that I couldn't make this journey in

95 Ibid., 117

my usual way of travel, in my usual ego-consciousness or manner of doing things. It would require a new point of view.

This journey to Florida continued as evidenced in another dream, a dream which added meaning to the journey and began to provide more insights into my same-sex desires and attractions.

> *I am watching a movie on TV with my father and mother. In the movie there is a train with an erect penis in each car. There are three cars. They are large penises, probably eight or nine inches, not abnormally large, but larger than average. The train is going on a track on a mountain.*
>
> *The movie takes place in Florida. At the end of the movie, I see a house. I come out of the house and see eggs all around the house in the shrubs and flower beds.*
>
> *My father is upset about the movie. But I say every church should see this movie. The penis is a symbol for the Self, the God-stamped image within each person. Florida is the same meaning and the eggs are the symbol of new life and of the tomb, that when broken, new life comes out of, like Christ coming out of the tomb. I tell him that when one meets Christ, that is just the beginning of finding God. We have been wrong in teaching that when we accept Christ, we have found God, or wholeness. The Bible says that Christ is the doorway to God. So when we come to Christ and accept Him, we have put ourselves in the position to find God and thus Wholeness. That is a lifetime process. My father thinks this explanation is tremendous.*
>
> *There is now a young man who is trying to decide whether to take a music director position for a Christian TV show. He has seen this movie and says, "I have always*

> *wanted to go to Florida. Now I know how to get there." He turns down the music position because he wants to go to Florida.* (Journal, 4-26-81)

The central image in this dream is the erect penis. As detailed earlier, the penis is itself a phallic symbol.[96] I repeat the symbolic meaning of the penis here because the penis as symbol became extremely critical in understanding what compelled me to seek it, in understanding what power it held for and over me, and what I was longing for in seeking it in same-sex encounters. As a phallic symbol, it is a symbol of power and fertility as well as male sexuality.[97] The phallus is also the source of life and libido, the creator and worker of miracles,[98] and often stands for the creative divinity.[99] A man's phallus expresses his creative power, is his way of entering the body, of experiencing another person, the instrument of his passion and the provider of ecstasy, giving an experience of transcendence.[100] "These three elements—creation, joining with another, and ecstasy—are common ground binding together the opposites of sensuality and spirituality, making Phallos the uniting symbol it is."[101] Historically the erected phallus was worshiped throughout antiquity and was associated with the bull-gods as previously discussed. Thus the phallus can be a symbol of the inner God-image and of the Jungian Self,[102] the archetype of wholeness—that unifying center that brings together and integrates the many layers of psyche, and yet is

---

96 Stevens, "The Penis itself is a Phallic Symbols?"

97 Ibid.

98 Jung, *Collected Works 5,* par. 146.

99 Ibid., par. 183.

100 Monick, *Castration and Male Rage,* 17.

101 Ibid.

102 Wilkerson, *Jung, the Self and Dreamwork.*

considered to be beyond the psyche, serving a transcendent function.[103] As such, the Self is the ability to unite opposites in a new form, and to unite them in ways that we as individuals cannot consciously do ourselves.[104] So while the erect penis in this dream can certainly refer to my own masculinity and sexuality, as well as the focus of my same-sex desires, fantasies and attractions, it also transcends sexuality and represents the Self—the longing for wholeness and the union of opposites and the individual life of my soul, the emerging Self.

The second part of this dream stated directly that the penis was an image of the Self, identifying it as an inner God-stamped image within men. Furthermore, the dream associated the Self with the state of Florida as suggested in the previous dream. It posited that the eggs are the symbol of new life and of the tomb, and when they are broken, new life emerges, like Christ coming out of the tomb.

The fact that my father liked and accepted my interpretation and explanation of this dream suggested that my ruling consciousness, symbolized by my father, was undergoing a transformation, a change. The end of this dream again mirrored my ongoing conflict: whether to return to my former life, referenced by the man's questioning whether to take a music position for a Christian TV station, or embrace a new life and go to Florida. The latter option represented the resurrection and transformation of the masculine. The dream ended with the man choosing Florida. The unconscious continued to push and pull me toward analysis and a new state of consciousness.

The next two years would continue to challenge me to face this unconscious Other in me and embrace a more conscious and accepting relationship of him and his relationship to me as the man I had

---

103 Ibid.

104 Ibid.

become and to the feminine in both my inner and outer lives. The dreams continued to reflect this journey and be my guide. I dream

> *I am at the doctor. My wife tells me that I must have another circumcision to remove more of the extra skin. My wife and another female have made the arrangements. My wife tells the doctor that I enjoy stuffing it, referring to sexual intercourse. I know the doctor is surprised that I enjoy "stuffing it." He doesn't see me that way. The doctor tells my wife that this will enhance my pleasure in really stuffing. I do not want to go to the hospital. It seems that I just got out of the hospital for something else. I object but it is still necessary. I don't see the need for this other circumcision. I go to the admission desk to fill out the forms.* (Journal, 1-29-82)

The theme of this dream was circumcision, which is the world's oldest planned surgical procedure, predating recorded history. Some suggest that it began as a less severe form of emasculating a captured enemy. In some cultures circumcision was associated with purity and spiritual and intellectual development. In others it was endowed with great honor and importance as a rite of passage into adulthood. In Jewish tradition, circumcision was a physical sign of the Jews' covenant with God. In various indigenous cultures some males are not circumcised until they reached the age of twelve or thirteen. These males are required to take the pain without showing emotion to prove their manhood. In contemporary pagan practices, circumcision seems to have associated this rite either with puberty or with approaching marriage. For some, circumcision was done for purification; for others it was a mark of subjugation; for others it was a blood sacrifice. For still others it was a test of bravery and self-control as part of a rite of passage into manhood. In any case, circumcision was an important ritual associated with certain initiations and rites of passage.

I have already discussed the penis as a phallic symbol representing the sacred masculine in man as the manifestation of his inner self and the source of life, libido, creativity, and the object of his own soul. Thus, the removal of the foreskin was a cutting away of the outer covering to reveal more of the sacred masculine and my own soul. The feminine was leading me into a cutting away of the outer coverings to allow for more of my authentic masculinity to be revealed, a cutting away of the outer learned and external support systems.

Coming into a faithful relationship with my authentic inner feminine self is what assisted me in breaking free from the mother. The fact that the dreams showed my wife articulating that I needed another circumcision suggested that it was also my commitment to and my relationship with her that was contributing to this new masculine. This required a masculine development that served the anima as my inner feminine soul figure instead of the mother—whether the literal mother or the symbolic one.

The dream said that I needed to have "another circumcision to remove more of the extra skin." This additional "cutting away" suggested more analysis and more work to allow for more of my individual masculine consciousness to be revealed, as well as my capacity to withstand the pain of initiation into my adult individual self. My own association was that the foreskin around the penis could symbolize the feminine, the mother, the church, the parsonage—all the "coverings" that had contained my masculinity. This was being cut away, which according to the dream, would enhance sexual intercourse. That is, it would enhance my creative relationship with the feminine. This idea of "cutting away from the feminine container" was reinforced in another dream about three weeks later.

I dream

> *My father is dead. I am the husband of my mother, a close relationship in every way except sexual. Another man comes into my mother's life and starts to take her away from me. I hate him. I am hurt and do terrible things to him and run and hide. My brothers come and find me. My mother and this man come to get me. I'm sure they, especially this man, will be very angry with me and punish me severely. However, he doesn't. He tells me they are going away for a few days on their honeymoon. My mother says that she left me food and the man who is now my mother's husband tells me that when they return, he will take me fishing.* (Journal, 2-17-82)

Besides mirroring the fact that this old masculine, symbolized by my father, was dead, this dream also mirrored my life as a child. I had been my mother's companion as a child and teen. I did many of the things for her and with her. I was the one who helped her around the house, went shopping with her, and participated in her sewing, knitting and arts and craft interests. I became her companion to the point of sacrificing my wants and needs to satisfy hers. I struggled as a child between what I wanted to do and what I knew my mother wanted me to do, and usually gave into her because I couldn't stand the hurt and disappointment that she expressed when I didn't. My father, being under the same "spell," was unable to provide the masculine stance to help me hold my ground against the mother. I carried this same relationship over in service to the church, which in many ways became my surrogate and symbolic mother.

This dream also showed my attachment to my inner feminine to the extent that she was contaminated with and under the spell of the personal and archetypal mother. In my personal work I had been making the break—"cutting myself away" from my identification with the feminine to allow more of my masculine self to be revealed as the above circumcision dream had mandated. This dream confirmed this by showing that my mother was getting a new husband, thus setting me free to be the child.

This new husband, the new masculine figure would, after his honeymoon—which symbolized the consummation of this new inner relationship—return to develop a father-son relationship with me. The dream said that together we would go fishing. This meant that I now had access to a new masculine energy in me that would assist me in searching the waters of the unconscious for the psychic elements (the fish) that would develop a new consciousness. This was both a confirming dream and a dream showing there was still more work to be done. Another dream indicated the development of this masculine voice in me. I dream

> *My wife is on the phone talking to the landlord of the house we live in. She is pushing the landlord about the house and I am feeling uncomfortable with her conversation, feeling like we shouldn't be pushing her. I tell my wife to back off but she keeps talking and I then realize she is trying to find out what the landlord's plan is for the house: if they are planning to rent it again or do they want us to move.*
>
> *The landlord tells us that her husband says, "It is always best to follow one's spirit rather than directions when doing something. Even in my work where there are specific ways of doing things, if my senses and intuition say to do it another way, I always follow that." She says that he also says that this will always take longer to get the thing accomplished but is*

> *it the best way. "When faced with two ways of doing things, always follow the spirit's voice in you, the inner knowing."* (Journal, 2-28-82)

This dream continued to show my discomfort with the feminine voice in me that pushed me to confront the ruling authority regarding possible change. But it is in her persistence that I discovered this masculine Other in me that said it was best to follow one's inner knowing rather than conventional directions. This was further support for following the dreams and the inner experience. However, to do that meant that I had to bear the feelings of being wrong, even looking wrong, and having to bear the feelings of disappointing people by not falling into what they expected me to be and to do—not following their directions—not following the collective voice of the church and parsonage when the spirit in me said "no."

I dream that

> *I am in an upstairs classroom at church. I leave and walk out of the church and go to a place where my wife and I are enjoying a meal. I look at my watch and see that it is almost twenty minutes after the hour. I say we must leave because the boat leaves at twenty after. My wife and I are going on a trip across the ocean. It is on a large ocean liner and cruise boat. We are going to Spain. Another man with us is also going to Spain, but he is flying.*
>
> *We go to board the ship. My wife gets on the ship. I go to the hotel to pick up our luggage. I enter the room and pick up the suitcase. There is a Spanish young man there, a hotel clerk. I say to him, "el tiempo ha llegado."*

He says, "la hora" correcting my use of "tiempo" in this situation.

I say, "thank you." The feeling was one of gratitude for correcting my use of Spanish for in that way I will learn to speak correct Spanish. There is an older lady with us. We look out the window and see my wife standing on the deck of the boat. She is dressed in her black and white pants suite, one of my favorite outfits.

The lady says, "My, doesn't she look beautiful?" I agree. The lady asks if I get seasick. I tell her that I didn't the last time I was out on the ocean. The Spanish man tells me if I do get seasick to sit up straight and breathe like this, showing me short, deep breaths. But I think I should buy some Lomotil. I leave the hotel with the suitcase and try to find a drugstore to buy Lomotil. The boat is about to leave. I know there is a drugstore on the boat and if I need Lomotil they will have some. (Journal, 3-25-82)

This dream showed that the time had arrived for the journey to begin. The dream's correction of my use of "*tiempo,*" which refers to a "period of time," to "*la hora,*" which refers to a "specific time or hour," emphasized a definite start time for this journey. The dream showed that my wife and I were on this journey together. The ship or the container for this journey was analysis and the dream said even though the process might cause some discomfort the process itself would provide whatever I needed. The goal was a new country, suggestive again of a new consciousness. To honor and integrate the meaning of this dream and to move it forward I wrote the following poem:

Sitting,
Eating lunch with friends

I look
It's time.
The ship leaves soon.
We must go.
I've come to get my luggage.
El tiempo ha llegado.
He turns.
"La hora," he replies.
I look at him
"La hora?"
And then I knew
Yes. La hora.
Thank you.
Through the window I see her
Beautiful she is
Dressed in black and white
Standing,
Waiting
On the ship.
Motion sickness?
No, not I.
Have you anything?
No, nothing.
Perhaps I should.
Lomotil will be good.
The drugstores
They don't have it.
And it's time to board the ship.
The ship, ah yes, the ship.
There is a drugstore there

And they will have Lomotil
Should I have need of it.
On board at last
On board the ship.
And now it's time to leave
Where are we going? She and I?
I do not know
Spain perhaps . . .
As least across the sea.

The last stanza of this poem had moved the dream from an invitation to start this journey to being on board and ready to leave.

The above dream began with me walking out of the church. My ongoing conflict with the church and what was emerging in my dreams and inner life was mirrored in the following dream. I dream

> *A female parishioner and I are talking to the minister's wife who is very concerned about the church and all the problems in the church. She indicates that she believes that a lot of the fault lies with her husband, the minister, and she doesn't understand why he can't see that, why he can't change. The parishioner begins to tell the minister's wife about unconscious root judgments. I then tell her that because of her husband's childhood background, there are a lot of unconscious things working in him. I go on to say that much of what is happening in the church is the result of his (the minister's) unconscious projections, judgments, and strivings.*
>
> *I say, "For example, perhaps his father asked him to do something once and while he went ahead and did it, he made an unconscious judgment of hate toward his father that he*

> *is now reaping in his life. It is that judgment that keeps him bound from breaking from this pattern."*
>
> *The minister's wife gets very smart-alecky, almost making fun of me. She says, "Oh, is that so? And how do you propose to know that? And what do you suggest we do about it?" She then says, "Do you still believe that the unconscious makes judgments that the conscious mind doesn't know anything about?" I tell her "yes and that was the error in your message last Sunday when you said if you commit all to God, He cleanses the unconscious so that those roots are all made clean and no longer work negatively in your life, the idea that it is a 'zap' and all the unconscious is purified."* (Journal, 4-25-82)

While the dream reflected the inner conflict I was having with the church and circumstances of my current life, this dream could also be understood as a further confrontation with my inner parsonage family, my own father-minister and mother-minister-wife, my own parental complex, the "parsonage" in me that was being projected onto the church-minister situation. This dream also showed my increased awareness in the power of the unconscious to influence the environment through projection. It also showed that I was confronting the minimizing, disbelieving, ridiculing voice in me that questioned the power of the unconscious.

A few weeks later I awakened early and lay thinking about my last therapy session and my decision to go into analysis. From my journal:

> *Do I really need to go into analysis? Do I want to do all the work that I know it will require? How can I afford it? I remember the "circumcision dream" where I had expressed*

the same attitude of not wanting to undergo another circumcision but the inner feminine had already arranged it, and I did go to the admitting desk for admittance. Yes! It is a must. But the next six years are very important for my children as they go through middle school and high school. I want to be available to go through it with them, not off studying and writing, thus not sharing their very important moments.

Perhaps I can do both. I lay listening to the birds singing. What a beautiful chorus. They sing from their own inborn instinctive nature, doing exactly what God destined them to do. They probably don't care whether anybody listens or not. They are just doing their God-given job. I should take a lesson from them. Funny, some are just chirps and others are a melody. I wonder if the chirpers feel inferior or wrong because of their song. I think not. It probably wouldn't enter whatever awareness they may have to think of themselves as inferior or wrong because of their song. The morning is beautiful, and my destiny continues to grow. I too must sing my song. (Journal, 5-13-82)

I fall back to sleep and have the first of several dreams that would mirror watershed moments in my spiritual journey to find and come into relationship with this other man living in my soul. I dream

It is announced on a Christian radio station that today is the day that Christ is coming back. My wife and I go outside and see thousands and thousands of people from all over the world walking to a hill for His coming. We stand back from them and observe. It seems like we are standing at a stone square, like some kind of altar. We see my grandfather and his second wife walking up from the left. They are coming to join the throngs of people.

My wife suggests that we have them come and pray with us. I tell her no. Then several beautiful rainbows in arches appear over the hill. I don't believe Christ is going to come like these people think He is. Then suddenly out of the eastern skies, four beautiful blue clouds begin to form and then roll out toward us. It is a beautiful display. I then recognize that this is the way the Bible says that Christ will come, and I know that He is coming. The clouds form a design in the sky like a four-leaf clover. I know they are ready for the Christ to break through.

I then fear that He will say I wasn't a believer because I didn't join all the people but stayed back as if I did not believe in Him. Then I think I will just be very honest with Him and let Him see me as I really am. I do not have any fear of His knowing that I didn't think He was actually going to come this way. I hear someone say something about this "being my own Armageddon." I then experience a kind of paralysis, which seems to me like a psychic change, a power beyond me, doing something to me. I think that I must experience this for Christ to come and it is okay. (Journal, 5-13-82)

This was a powerful dream with a numinous quality. In this dream I was facing the ultimate teaching and goal of the Christian story, the coming of Christ. In the world in which I was raised, Christ was the supreme character in history, a chief force in modern life for much of the Western world. He is considered one of the greatest teachers of the ages, the founder of Christianity. He is the object of faith and worship as the Son of God and savior of sinners. His power is the chief regenerating force of mankind and the mainspring of all our progress in the uplifting of the human race. He is the hope of man. In Him God and man meet, the great miracle, the incarnation of God in human form. Christ is considered the highest type of man, the representative man, the real Son of Man, the Logos, the image of God, the expression of God in humanity, the reconciler of men to God and men to each other and to themselves.

According to my "parsonage consciousness," Christ as the Son of God was now sitting at the right hand of the Father in heaven guiding the eternal conflict between the power of righteousness and that of evil, with certain victory for Christ as set forth in the biblical account in Revelation.

The dream also indicated that this was my personal Armageddon. The term *Armageddo*n refers to the final battle at the end of the world between the forces of good and evil[105] and pertains to any great and crucial conflict. Symbolically this dream suggested the end of an era, the end of my world as I had known it, and the birth of a new consciousness to be ushered in by the coming of the symbolic Christ.

This was a critical dream in my individuation process. The departure from the collective mind for my own individual path was symbolized by my staying back and not joining all the people and by my not believing that Christ was actually going to come in the way they believed. This was my meeting of the Self, the divine within my own soul, this Other in me that longed for life. It is when I decided to be honest with Him, this inner divine image, and to let Him see me as I really was in order that I might lose my fear of Him, knowing that I didn't believe that He would come like everyone else thought He would. And it was in that moment that I experienced the paralysis, the psychic

105 Revelation 16:1(NIV)

shift, the power beyond my own that I was willing to experience for the inner Christ to come, that is, for the Divine to be born in me.

The rainbows also confirmed this agreement between me and this other transcendent Self—the inner Christ—and suggested both an end of something and the hope of a new beginning and wholeness. Rainbows appear after the rain, after the storm, as the sun's rays reflect on the droplets of water. The rainbow contained the seven colors, symbolizing complete unity. Genesis says "When I gather the clouds over the earth and the bow appears in the clouds, I will recall the Covenant between myself and you and every living creature of every kind. . . . And God said to Noah, this is the sign of the covenant I have established between myself and every living thing."[106]

This dream was a confirmation of a covenant between me and the divine. Rainbows unified the observer by allowing him to find his real self so he might create wholeness. I am reminded of the "circumcision dream" that was also a sign of a commitment between man and his God or between me and this Other *in* me. This was a watershed dream in that it ushered in a psychic shift that would help me make difficult decisions in my spiritual journey. This was the coming of Christ but the coming of the Christ as an inner psychic experience. We must leave the outer Christ and allow the spirit of truth, the inner counselor, the Holy Spirit, lead us and create in us His will.

After I stopped participating in the music program at church, my family and I slowly stopped supporting and attending some of the church services and activities, especially the Sunday night and midweek services. Having been such a visible presence in the church and so active in the integral workings of it in multiple capacities, this change in behavior was quite noticeable.

---

106 Genesis 9:14–17 (New Jerusalem Bible, Standard Edition)

On May 17, 1982, the minister called me and asked me to meet him to talk about my affiliation with the church. This caused me anxiety. The night before I was to meet with the minister, I dream

> *I see an area with several snakes. They are different sizes. One very large snake sees me and starts after me. He chases me, trying to bite me. I try to find a butcher knife to kill it, to cut it in two, but I can't find one. The snake keeps chasing me trying to bite me. As the dream ends, I am standing face to face with the snake. Its tongue is trying to bite the front of my legs.* (Journal, 5-18-82)

Clearly the dream showed my anxiety in facing the minister to discuss my affiliation with the church. The central figure in this dream was the snake. The snake has a complicated and ambivalent symbolic history and it is beyond our purview to detail all of that here. Suffice it to say that the snake carries both evil and destructive characteristics as well as healing and transformative ones. In the Bible the snake takes on both roles. In the Garden of Eden, the serpent tempts the feminine to disobey God's law to not eat from the tree of good and evil. This disobedience resulted in Adam and Eve being thrown out of the garden.

Later, when God instructed Moses to make a bronze serpent and put it on a pole so the people could be healed from snakebites, the snake became the symbol of that which saves and heals.[107] Later, in John 3:14 (NIV), John indicates that this bronze serpent was a foreshadowing of Christ being raised on the cross. By looking to the cross of Christ people would be saved from their sins just as the Israelites had been saved

107 Numbers 21:5–7.

from snake bites by looking to the upraised snake in the wilderness. So, the snake, as Jung has observed, symbolizes the cure affected by what caused the ailment. The snake becomes the source of the healing of the wound caused by the snake itself. This is the situation where like cures like. This suggests the healing aspects of same-sex imagery. *A wound caused by the masculine is healed by the masculine.* The projection of the wounded masculine onto another man in same-sex imagery can be understood as symbolic of the longing for that healing. The snake as a symbol holding these two opposing meanings becomes a primary symbol for renewal and rebirth, emphasized again in the shedding of its skin, the releasing or a crawling out of an old consciousness or skin into a new one.

For me this conversation with the minister would symbolize my facing the masculine Father-God image of the parsonage. It would be a watershed moment, a defining moment where the decision must be made whether to follow the spirit in the matter of my own soul—this other man in me, as the man in the earlier dream had instructed—or obey the directions as defined by the institutional church and the symbolic father.

The snake was set to attack my legs. Legs are what hold us up. Legs are our relationship to the earth, to the ground that we stand on. Jung has suggested that the snake often appears in dreams when the conscious mind is deviating from its instinctual basis.[108] Would I be able to face and trust my instincts in this conversation with the minister? From my journal:

> *The options seem to come down to coming under the structure, rules, and expectations of this particular church*

108 Jung, *Collected Works 9*, i, par. 282.

body—following the directions—or to sever my relationship with this body. My dreams, my own intuition, my instincts, and my study and reading during my prayer and meditation times all indicate that it is time to leave home, a time to leave the parsonage. This is the beginning of my individuation, that inner vow to risk everything to embrace and follow God's voice in me, the Christ within, the Self, this Other in me that has its own wisdom, its own guidance, God speaking in the dreams. Perhaps this is the real meaning of the church's teaching on sanctification—to bring my own conscious ego into relation to the God within—a total commitment to this Divine Center.

The founder of the tradition in which I was raised, John Wesley, says, "Holiness is a single-mindedness toward a Divine Center." He goes on to say that holiness is none other than the whole mind [wholeness] which was in Christ Jesus.[109] *For Western man Christ is the symbol of man's transcendent, transpersonal Self, the divine living in man, the totality of his being. Wynkook, in her book,* Theology of Love, *says that "Man is a dynamic being reacting and responding to life, searching, reaching out, needing fulfillment. He is a hemisphere looking for his other half."*[110]*This is often what I feel in my homosexual desires, attractions, and sexual encounters, a longing for my other half—the man he is. Perhaps it is the longing for the love of a man, how to get him inside me, how to be the man he is.*

Self-love is as necessary to wholeness as love for others, but love for others, even for God, requires a measure of

---

109 Wesley, *Works, VI*, 70–72.

110 Wynkoop, *Theology of Love*, 141.

self-acceptance and self-esteem that holds the "ego" in self-conscious identity and respect. Holiness is love locked into the True Center. In being "true", all of the self and progressively all of life come into harmony and wholeness. The essence of humility and true personal moral grandeur is to set one's heart on God.[111]

Wynkoop's discussion on the meaning of moral grandeur speaks deeply to me as it relates to my decision pertaining to the church and the next step in my spiritual journey. My own personal moral integrity is at stake. Christ as the symbol of my divine center demands decision. It is not only desirable and possible but mandatory. Holiness or sanctification is single-mindedness to a divine center. It doesn't matter if this divine center is seen as right or wrong according to a particular society or religious system. The decision to break from the church is a moral decision that puts my integrity at stake.

The decision to maintain my break with the Sunday night and Wednesday night services and other points on theology and polity of the church is a necessary step in my own developing moral sense of integrity, a necessary step in the development of my own masculinity. It is a very symbolic move and decision that must be made. From this point my whole sense of integrity and moral structure will move. Not to make this decision will be spiritual suicide. If I do not follow what the spirit indicates is my obedience to this divine center within me, I will fall back into darkness and will not be worth anything—not to my wife, not to my children, not to my community.

---

111 Ibid., 141, 158.

If I don't move in accordance with my intuitive understanding of God's will for my life as I discern it and as the Holy Spirit reveals it to me, I will become like those who are "tossed to and fro." I will never again be able to trust myself and my judgments. That is, my center will become outer, worldly, and other than. I will know this and hate myself for it. I will know that I didn't have what it took to follow my own truth, to do what I knew was right. This will be spiritual death because it will be disobedience to the will of the inner Christ for my life—to this Other living in me. This journey in theological language is my own personal holiness and sanctification.

Sunday night and Wednesday services are no longer meaningful spiritual activities for me and my family. So, we sever our support for them by not attending. This does not mean these activities are not meaningful spiritual activities for others. This does not mean that we will never again attend these activities. It does mean they are no longer a part of our regular weekly spiritual practice.

While I have resigned my official position as director of music, I am glad to continue serving the church and God by leading the music on Sunday morning. However, if this causes division and negative attitudes in the church because of my lack of support of other church program and polity, I willingly and lovingly step aside and for the present will sit in the congregation and worship.

If I do not follow what I feel and know, this deep inner knowing that "this is the way, walk ye in it," I will not respect myself or ever again be able to trust myself and my thinking, my discernment, the spirit and "God-will sense" that

> *is growing and developing in me. I will become a "house divided against itself," a house that cannot stand.* (Journal, 5-18-82)

The meeting with the minister would further clarify that this relationship with the church was becoming irreconcilable. A decision had to be made. Slowly we just stopped attending. I do not remember a definite end date. We visited other churches in the community and attended one for a time. It was a time of drifting, trying to find a place to fit in. Recently my son, reflecting on these years, wrote in his blog:

> *The old saying "Nothing ever stays the same" is definitely true with my family's life in conjunction with the church. Circumstances of life, decisions, and personal growth led to my family leaving the church and after going to a few other churches for several years, the church years in a traditional sense were done. I don't think that went over well with my grandparents, but my dad was moving on . . . When I was seventeen, I was never made to go to church again. I'm sure when people talked among themselves, they were very critical and maybe even judgmental of my parents' decision during those years. Looking back, it was the start of something bigger and maybe even freeing.*

During the next few years my relationship with my wife and my relationship with my children and making sure the needs of their lives were being met were my priorities. My need to hold them together somehow held *me* together. There were ball games, tennis matches, band contests, cheerleading camps, girlfriends, boyfriends, the drama of teenage girls, teenage boys experimenting with alcohol and sex, and my son's interest in modeling and trips to Indianapolis to the John Robert Power School of Modeling. My job as high school Spanish teacher also held me together. Besides the daily teaching tasks, there were Spanish club meetings, student trips to Mexico, and other teaching duties. My dreams consistently mirrored the commitment that my wife and I had made to each other for this journey and the role, both inner and outer, that she would play in that journey. This all provided an outer container while I did my inner work. During this time my dreams became my constant companions and source of spiritual sustenance. They were the voices connecting me to the emerging self—this other man that was living in my soul.

Notes and Exercises

The Self is the center and unifying principle of the psyche and source of life that contains our wholeness. Creating a relationship with the Self is experienced as a defeat for the ego because it requires the ego expand its one-sided point of view.

The Self often appears in our dreams as images of a circle or sphere or a square. It may also appear as animals such as, for instance, snakes, owls, swans, dolphins, bees, elephants, lions, tigers, bears, eagles, hawks; as spiritual and religious figures such as Christ, Buddha, Atman, and as plants and flowers such as a tree, rose, lotus, lily.

> *Recall a dream about a circle or a square (e.g., table, window or some other circular or square object), an animal, a religious or spiritual figure, a tree or a flower. As you focus on that image, notice what comes to you. What do you feel? What thoughts or memories come to mind? Ask the image if it has a message for you? What is that message? How does*

that image want to connect you to something else in you? How might it want to expand your point of view and help you see things from a different perspective? Since dreams are expressions of the Self (Soul), this can be a way to begin a relationship with the Self, the Other in you.

CHAPTER SEVEN

The Call of the Swan Maiden

Five years had passed since the dream where I turned to face the bull that had chased me up a tree to prevent me from returning to the town where I lived. Facing and beginning to integrate the bull energy, that powerful masculine energy from some ancient time that was also somehow connected to the lunar energies of the ancient goddess, had resulted in a slow evolution of consciousness and changes in my relationships in the outer world.

As stated, I ended my same-sex relationships, and my wife and I sold our home in order to free ourselves from the financial burden of the bookstore that we owned and operated. Working with this energy as it revealed itself in my dreams also initiated the journey out of the institutional church and the parsonage consciousness in which I had been raised. The dreams continued to directly and clearly address the importance of the past as to the origins of my life patterns, including my same-sex attractions. They even made a statement about the origin of my homosexuality. The dreams indicated a path forward into a new life, the life of this Other living in my soul.

I dream that

> *I go to the church in which I was raised to hear the minister preach. He is telling the congregation about his ancestry and heritage. He tells them that he came from the jungles of Africa and that his rejection of the highly emotional African heritage has made him the way he is. I know that he has discovered this because he has been reading a book on how people make unconscious judgments. He has discovered that generations of our heritage still live in and through us unconsciously. His sermon is a confession of that reality to the congregation, a kind of setting things right. I know it is the rejection of his African heritage that resulted in him believing in the theology he believes in. I wonder if I should stop him and pray for the breaking of these unconscious judgments. Instead I leave without speaking to him. I have come to hear this final sermon before he moves, a kind of farewell.* (Journal, 5-16-83)

This dream referenced the ancestry of the minister as being from Africa. One of theories on the origin of the human race states that all humans came out of Africa.[112] Did this dream reference such an origin in general or did it simply refer to the origin of this particular man or my own ancestral origin? I do not know the ancestral history of the minister in this dream. But the dream stated that it was the rejection of his "highly emotional African heritage" that caused the minister to believe in a certain theology, in this case a Christian and biblical theology. Theology is the systematic study of the existence and nature of the Divine and its relationship to and influence upon other beings. Was this dream suggesting that this masculine minister part of me

---

112 Reuters. *Did We Come Out of Africa? Studies Collide.*

believed what he did because he was cut off from the emotional truth of his pre-Christian, more earth- and nature-based African history?

This dream also continued the theme of the previous dream wherein I told the minister's wife that we make unconscious root judgments that affect our lives. The minister in this dream was my former pastor. He represented my traditional Christian training and theology and the evangelical minister in me, the "parson" from the parsonage in which I was raised. This dream showed that this part of me was beginning to alter its point of view about the roles that the unconscious and our past play in our development and beliefs—not just our personal past but the ancestral past as well.

This dream also hinted at the split, the departure so to speak, from our pre-Christian and earth-related connections symbolized by the reference to the "African jungle." This theme of the influence of our ancestors on our lives was reflected in another dream.

> *I tell my dad that the beliefs and fantasies that our grandparents and great-grandparents lived throughout their lives in their work, their religion, and daily living are important in discovering why a person is the way he or she is, why a person has a particular problem, a particular disease, or a particular lifestyle. I tell him there will be a new psychology called "biological archetypal psychology."* (Journal, 7-9-83)

Twenty years later with my journey into shamanism and energy medicine I would discover the truth of this dream—that the stories of our ancestors continue to vibrate in our energy bodies, influencing our lives unconsciously.

Bobby McFerrin, a genius of improvisation and a genre-bending vocal magician who "sings the territory between music, mystery, and spirit" tells the story of a woman who came backstage after one of his shows to tell him that she had just spent a year studying African languages that were extinct or near extinct and she wanted to know how he knew these languages. Bobby told her that he didn't know what she was talking about, that he just opened his mouth and sang whatever came out, because to him that *was* a language. The woman told Bobby that she'd heard moments of precise phrasing of extinct African languages in his vocalizations.

Bobby said that incident caused him to start thinking that we are embodied memories of our ancestors. He had his father in him. He in turn was a memory of *his* father and so on and so on. Bobby wondered if he was accessing some ancestral memory when he sang and, if so, how far back did it go? Maybe a very long way indeed.[113]

This reflection by Bobby McFerrin agrees with what the Inca shamans teach. We each carry all of our past including our ancestral past in our luminous energy field. Do these memories emerge in our dreams? Do they influence our desires, our interests, and our longings? Shamanism asserts that we can access this information through "imaginal sight." Imaginal sight will be explored in Chapter 16.

Sometimes when I am doing energy work, I notice a strong urge to vocalize sounds or utterances—what some churches might call "speaking in tongues." Somewhere deep inside me, out of some space come these utterances, which I then speak. Clients have told me that they have found this "language"—these utterances—very powerful, comforting, and healing. Perhaps they are the memory of an ancient medicine man or woman or healer or perhaps they are the language of the energy itself, the energy in vocal form, which is accessed and expressed.

113 NPR. On Being.

This awareness and understanding came years after I'd had the dream I mention above. At the time the dream simply caused me to reflect on the stories of my ancestors and to begin to see how the archetypal patterns of my ancestors had influenced my own life's path. Both my maternal grandparents and great-grandparents were farmers, thus closely associated with the earth, nature, and the rhythms of planting and harvesting and symbolically with Mother Earth and the feminine—the Great Goddess of the ancient world. My maternal grandfather left the farm and went the way of higher education, becoming a teacher and school principal, symbolizing the rise of the masculine and the mind or spirit over earth and matter. As previously mentioned, in his thirties my maternal grandfather experienced a spontaneous healing and born-again experience. The story goes that while he was recovering from an illness at the family farm God instantly healed him from the illness and "saved him."

After this healing and born-again experience, he began attending church and eventually was called to preach. He became a minister and rose through the ranks to become the district superintendent of the Northeast Indiana Conference. Symbolically this was the rise of the masculine in both his professional pursuits, the masculine as it found its expression in the archetypes of the teacher and the minister-savior.

His son followed in the path of the farmer while his daughter, my mother, married a minister and carried on the path of the minister-savior archetype. This minister-savior archetype became dominant, cut off from the archetype of the farmer and its connection to the earth and nature. Financial power came through the maternal great-grandmother's family who were wealthy farmers.

My maternal grandmother's family also farmed. It is interesting to me that my grandmother also left the farm to become a teacher. She married my grandfather who had also left the farm to become an educator and eventually a minister. This mirrors the story that my mother lived out in her life, marrying a minister. While my mother says she always wanted to be a teacher or a librarian, she did not pursue either of those paths, but lived her life out as a minister's wife. The story of the teacher was passed on to me and one of my brothers while my other two brothers followed the path of the minister-savior archetype.

I don't know much about my father's ancestors. My father's parents died before my father turned twenty-five and before I was born. I only know that my paternal grandfather was a factory worker and my paternal grandmother a housewife. My father was one of nine siblings. He accepted Christ as his savior at an early age and felt "called to preach" at age sixteen. He became the minister in the parsonage in which I was raised. Given the archetypal stories of these two family lines, full of teachers, ministers, and before that, farmers and earth keepers, it's no wonder that I would fall under their spell.

The challenge is to become conscious of the archetypal patterns in one's life and to build an awakened relationship with them so as to not live them out unconsciously as fate. The dream's reference to a "biological-archetypal psychology" suggested the influences of both biology—the influence of inherited family patterns—and the influence of archetypes—transcendent and universal patterns swimming in the collective unconscious—on a person's life's path. This is none other than Jung's concept of the two-million-year-old man that lives in every one of us, connecting us to the archetypal foundations of all human experiences, back to the hominid, mammalian, and reptilian ancestors who live on in the structures of our minds and brains.[114] Not only do we harbor within us this two million-year-old man, we also harbor the universe itself, and beyond that, the divine, which connects

---

114 Stevens, *Two-Million Year Old Man*, 5.

us to the "primordial other," the "indigenous one" of the psyche and its wisdom. This two-million-year-old man "supports our finite existence and animates our dreams."[115]

The presence of the "farmer archetype" and its association with the earth and with looking after the land would show up frequently in my dreams. One such dream showed the psychic connection to the earth and to an ancient past, a past that longed to be remembered. It offered a window of insight into the longing that was fueling my same-sex attractions. I dream

> *I am in the country with some people. We are in a barn. There are two rooms. They are empty and all cleaned out. The rooms have been swept clean and have a tidy look. The scene changes and now we are outside in a field, as if the building has become a field. The grass is the floor and the partitions are the trees and bushes. We walk upon this scene and come around a partition that corresponds to the wall between the two rooms of the barn and yet it is outside as trees and bushes.*
>
> *As we come around this section, I see a round table with four chrome legs sitting in the corner. I wonder why someone would put a round table there. There is a tablecloth over the table, covering the top. I lift the tablecloth off and there is a beautiful antique, intricately carved wood table. I recognize its antique value by the carvings. I realize that someone has hidden it there to save it, to protect it, and to guard it. The thought was that no one would find it hidden in this corner. I notice the four chrome-like legs. I know the table*

---

115 Ibid.

was covered to conceal its antique value, and one would not know by looking at its legs that it was of any value because the legs are chrome. I also see a small child's antique chair against the wall.

The scene changes and we are back in the barn. There is an old woman with me. She seems disguised in some way. Either she removed layers of skin or masks or else her face slowly changes images several times. Finally, she looks into a mirror and says she looks like herself. She is an old woman with white hair. Her hair is carried up on the back of her head.

I climb upon the chair and lookout through the window. I see a battle going on between a white man and some Indians. The white man is on the left and the land from which he fights is flat and barren. The Indians are on the right. The right side has forests and trees. The battle rages. The white man uses guns and the Indians use bows and arrows. The Indians are covered with mud and/or paint, like warriors. Finally, the battle ends and the ground is covered with white men's bodies. The white man has been destroyed.

The Indians go back into the trees and forest. Now the ground and scene become cold and hard. I see the bodies change into clumps of grass and rocks with kind of a barren desert or prairie look. Now, no one would know that a battle had just taken place.

As I watch, an Indian comes out of the trees. He is covered with dark mud and paint, carrying a spear. He looks like some kind of a disguised spirit. He comes to where I am. He does not speak, only looks at me. I am drawn to him. I kiss him. I see the table. He motions for me to sit at the table.

He sits on one side and I sit on the other. He reaches out his hands and I reach out mine. We grasp hands. I feel very close to him. Suddenly it is like he becomes a bird and flies up above me and yet he is still there, or it is like a bird leaves from his chest and flies up above us. As the three of us are there, the atmosphere becomes very charged with energy or electricity of an almost numinous feeling.

I become sexually aroused and begin to masturbate, all the time looking directly into his eyes as if we are connected somehow. As I masturbate, the Indian holds my left hand with both his hands. He does not say anything, but it is like he knows exactly what is happening. That is, he knows the significance of the act, although he remains connected to me on what is like a spiritual level. I stand up and ejaculate large amounts of semen all over the table. As I finish, he leans up and kisses me and lets go of my hand and disappears back into the forest.

I am left with a numinous feeling of having been visited by a god or someone very close and special, a part of me.

Now the table is my table. As the Indian disappears into the woods he turns and looks at me with warm, understanding, loving, and knowing eyes. Then slowly the dark savage look returns, and he disappears into the trees. The bird comes to the table and eats the semen. The energy vibrating through me is indescribable. (Journal, 7-29-83)

This dream left me with a numinous feeling as if something powerful had taken place in my psyche. Somehow I felt that I had come to possess the table. It was mine and it was extremely important! Its circular shape suggested a mandala, a symbol of wholeness and the

Self. What had happened *in* me between the Indian *and* me was an extremely important psychic and spiritual experience. Perhaps it was an initiation into the spirit or another realm of the spirit. Perhaps it was the activation of an ancient memory living in my psychic past. Perhaps it was symbolic of a "blood pact" between me and this other ancient man living in me.

Critical to the meaning of this dream as it related to same-sex attractions and behaviors were the motifs of masturbation and semen-eating, both of which are the focus of same-sex fantasies and behaviors. When we are able to remove the erotic element from sexual fantasies and dreams, we get at the underlying symbolic meaning. The symbolic meaning and mythological history and ritual of masturbation and semen-eating will be detailed in the chapter entitled "Manifestations of the Self in Male Same-Sex Behaviors." However, I will briefly discuss the symbolism of masturbation here. In general, it represents man's first contact with the "sacred other" and is a symbol of self-creation. In Egyptian mythology "Atum proceeded to create the first creatures, Shu and Tefnut, male and female. Pyramid Utterance 527 says: 'Atum was creative in that he proceeded to masturbate with himself . . .; he put his penis in his hand that he might obtain the pleasure of emission thereby and there were born brother and sister—that is Shu and Tefnut.'"[116] The act emphasized the bisexual character of Atum and the self-sufficiency of the High God, that is, the psyche.[117] This is to say that masturbation emphasizes the bisexual character of the Self and the self-sufficiency of the psyche to create from and out of itself. Masturbation remained a popular Creation motif in various ancient cultures. According to Greek mythology, Hermes was said to have invented the ritual of masturbation as an act of self-contemplation,

---

116 Clark, *Myth and Symbol in Ancient Egypt*, 42.

117 Ibid.

leading to the comprehension of the God, just as intercourse led to the comprehension of the Goddess.[118]

The dream's reference of the Indian becoming a bird or a bird leaving from his heart and hovering above us is symbolic of the indigenous spirit and soul. A bird is a universal symbol of Spirit, spiritualization, and the soul.[119] The dream showed this soul image eating the semen, a symbol of the fertilizing life-force itself. Ingesting semen was an ancient practice. (The practice and its symbolic meaning will be discussed more fully later.) Suffice it to say here that ingesting semen is the symbolic act of taking in the life-force and wisdom of the masculine Other and in some traditions of God himself as the sacred Other.[120] I am speaking here of psychic processes that are often unconscious sources of such dreams and fantasies and not their literal manifestations.

The idea that in this dream I had contacted and brought to life some ancient memory in me is suggested by another dream I had a couple of weeks later. I dream

> *I am with some people. We are opening a coffin. We are opening the coffin to release the dead person. He stands up. In opening the coffin, I say we must open it in a proper manner so as not to offend the spirit of the dead. The feeling is that we must respect this person's ancestral or ancient heritage or ritual and not violate his customs. He walks and moves just like he is alive, yet I know he is different, like he isn't really flesh and blood, somehow different, indestructible. I think now that we Americans have discovered we can release the dead from their graves, we will go to cemeteries and release*

---

118 hobbithills.blogspot.com/.../caduceushermesaphroditeserpentandrogyn.html.

119 Cooper, *Illustrated Encyclopaedia*, 20–21; Cirlot, *Dictionary of Symbols*, 26–28.

120 Mandal, *Semen and Culture*.

lots of dead people. I am concerned about this because I think they could start ruling over us and even if we fought against them, we could not kill them because they are indestructible. (Journal, 8-15-83)

This dream came after I had participated in a Communion service at the church I attended. During the taking of the Eucharist I entered into a meditative dialog with the bread and grape juice, asking the elements as symbols of the Christ and the Self to come alive in me. In applying the death and resurrection of Christ to psychic life, one could say that if one's chosen life is cut off from his or her true self, cut off from the life of the inner Christ or one's authentic divine nature, he or she crucifies that Self, hangs it on a cross so to speak and buries it, forcing it into the tomb of the unconscious. Later, when he or she comes into a relationship with the inner Christ or the Self, it is resurrected and makes itself known to consciousness. The person must then allow the inner Christ or the Self to work in and through the ego, establishing what Jung calls the "ego-Self axis." The opening of the coffin and releasing the dead person symbolized aspects of me that I was bringing back to life or parts of me that were coming to life in me, coming into consciousness.

In thinking about this in the context of the Christian story it can be understood as symbolic of the Pentecost experience where Christ sent his agent the Holy Spirit to empower man. For he who died in Christ was raised with a new body, an indestructible body, symbolic of the resurrection of the "Ego-Self relationship." My reference in the dream to my fear that this indestructible part would rule over us mirrored the ego's fear of losing its control as the center of life, and also the importance of releasing and relating to repressed and archetypal material in an appropriate manner. To reach wholeness, this "Other" had to be confronted as an independent fact, as another personality to which I was tied, an inner "I-Thou." Its laws could not be derived from my subjective rationality but operated on autonomous terms of its own, irrespective of and at times contrary to and in opposition to consciousness or the ego's desires—even able to overrule and even submerge the ego at times.

This seemed to connect with my feeling in the dream of opening the coffin in a proper manner, with a proper attitude, so as not to offend the rules and ritual of the spirit as being rejected and split-off. One must hold a proper attitude toward this process so as not to be possessed by or fall under the spell of the unconscious and repressed material or of the archetype itself.

> *I dream that my son and I are going to Switzerland. Prior to leaving I go to a store and ask a female clerk if she has* Playboy *magazine. She opens a drawer and takes out a magazine. It isn't* Playboy *but another, more sexually explicit magazine. She turns the pages. I see pictures of people defecating and other pictures of nudity and people engaged in explicit sex acts. I see a full page picture of naked buttocks with a turd sticking straight out of the anus. I know that this magazine has both men and women in sex acts whereas* Playboy *only has women. I keep looking to see if I can see a nude man and his penis. The clerk says that she usually has* Playboy *on the magazine rack. I tell her that I want to see the want ads in it because I want to buy a Playboy bunny earring for my son. I don't find the* Playboy *magazine.*
>
> *The scene changes and now we are in Switzerland, going up a mountain. There is a feeling of anticipation.* (Journal, 9-1-83)

The goal of this dream was to get to Switzerland. I associated Switzerland with Carl Jung, the Jung Institute in Zurich, and my desire to study there. I also associated it with my own analysis, and my desire to buy a Playboy bunny earring for my son, which I associated with adolescent sexuality and the emerging masculine self—especially the heterosexual self and the masculine self that seeks its other half as feminine.

The first goal of this dream was met. The dream ended with us in Switzerland. However, I did not find a Playboy bunny earring. Before getting to Switzerland the dream showed a regression into adolescent sexuality symbolized by the reference to *Playboy* and other "girlie" or pornographic magazines. It also featured the continuing challenge of sorting out my feminine and masculine energies, symbolized by my desire to see a nude man and his penis (the masculine) and my desire to buy a Playboy bunny (the feminine) for my teenage son. Neither desire was successful in this dream suggesting that the unconscious or the soul would not allow such a regression.

One of the central images in this dream was the full-page picture of nude buttocks with a turd sticking out of the anus. Defecation and references to the anus have to do with ego development and especially overcoming the mother, both literally and symbolically. Anality represents self-assertion, the assertion of existence, power, possession, and control over the mother, objects, and people, as well as over oneself. In its strictest sense, it is egotism. But in our development it is necessary to strive for an ego, including aggression.

In its extreme form it is sadism. In mythology it is the dragon-killing power deed where the hero overcomes the dragon, which is symbolic of the ego separating from the maternal unconscious. It is the very attitude of will and power expression par excellence.[121] This same motif is represented in the dream by my wanting to see a man and woman having sex so that I could see a nude man and his penis. I have already established the symbolic meaning of the penis.

In this dream I was still looking for this male image, the creative fertilizing energy of the mana character, the Self that confers health and salvation and establishes my authentic masculine image. However, its absence suggested that the unconscious was saying that I couldn't find what I was looking for in a porn magazine.

After the unsuccessful attempts to find the masculine, the dream shifted and the unconscious showed me and my son, my adolescent attitude, traveling up a mountain in Switzerland. I have learned that the end of a dream is important as it shows the direction the unconscious is moving. Thus, the mountain became an important point of consideration. From the top of a mountain a man could get a greater perspective on things. He may often see where the desert ends and the prairie begins and where the ocean stops and the land begins. Throughout history, mountains have symbolized constancy, eternity, firmness, and stillness. Mountaintops are associated with sun, rain, and thunder gods and, in early traditions, were associated with the feminine godhead. The mountain was the earth and female. The sky, clouds, thunder, and lightning were the fecundating male.[122] The shape of the mountain itself suggests a female breast. On the spiritual level mountaintops represent the state of full consciousness.[123] Pilgrimages up sacred mountains symbolize aspiration and renunciation of worldly desires.[124]

---

121 Whitmont, *Symbolic Quest*, 241.

122 Cooper, J.C., 110

123 Ibid.

124 Ibid.

Perhaps the deepest symbolism of the mountain is one that imparts a sacred character by uniting the concept of mass, as an expression of being, with the idea of verticality. Thus, the mountain becomes a symbol for a union of opposites. Just like the cross or the Cosmic Tree, wherever its location, the mountain becomes the center of the world whose peak is the point of contact between heaven and earth, the center through which the world-axis passes.[125] Thus traveling up a mountain was once again symbolic of my individuation journey, my search for the union of these opposing forces in me and the discovery of my individual self.

The association of this journey up the mountain in Switzerland to Jung and the union or marriage of opposites was reinforced by another dream I had a couple of months later. I dream that

> *My wife and I are invited to be in Jung's wedding. This marriage has been arranged by Jung's children and he is going along with it. We get there after the wedding is over but in time for the reception. As we enter the reception area there are six usher-greeters standing, three on each side of the railing of the steps. The first, a lady, bends over the railing and reaches to welcome us. It seems this lets us know we are properly received. I notice the three usher-greeters on the left are also bending and hanging out over the railing to welcome us. Members of both Jung's family and my family are there. There are two tables that contain food for the reception. However, there is something about having run out of water or not having any water. I say that is the reason my mother always carries her own thermos of water.* (Journal, 11-1-83)

125 Cirlot, 219-221

All aspects of a dream represent parts of us. In this one there was a wedding, a union, a joining together going on inside of me. It seemed to me that this wedding was the marriage of Jungian psychology or psyche and soul and my Christian theology or God and Spirit, symbolized by the fact that both Jung's family and my family were present for it. The fact that my wife and I arrived in time for the reception suggested that both the masculine and feminine parts were accepting of this marriage as well as being accepted *by* this marriage. Jung going along with this wedding suggested that Jung's spirit in me was also in agreement with this union.

The wedding reception featured food but no water. Food suggested knowledge or understanding. We have expressions like "food for thought" and "food for the soul." Water, on the other hand, stands for Spirit and the life-force. In the Bible, John 8:38 (NIV) states, "Whoever believes in me, as the Scriptures has said, streams of living water will flow from within him.' By this he meant the Spirit, whom those who believed in him were later to receive. . ." (NIV)

The dream suggested that Jungian psychology would offer a kind of nourishment or food for me—knowledge—but it wouldn't offer the life of the Spirit (water). The dream said that this was why "my mother always carries her own thermos of water." While this dream image could refer to my personal mother and her creative life, it could also refer to the archetypal mother, the Great Mother, who is also my mother.

The Great Mother was further hinted at by the dream's reference to the "thermos of water." The "thermos of water" connects with symbol of the vase. The vase, water-pot, or pitcher is a universal symbol for the Great Mother. It contains the cosmic waters as the feminine receptive principle, the life source. It stands for acceptance, fertility, and the heart. As the maternal symbol, the vase implied nourishment and flowing waters and was a symbol for the ultimate Divine source. Mother is also a symbol of the unconscious, the source of all life. The dream was pointing to the fact that although Jungian psychology will provide me with food, it won't provide me a connection to the source of life, a connection with Spirit. That, the dream says, comes from the feminine.

Looking back at this dream thirty-five years later in light of how my journey had taken me into shamanism—which in many ways is a return to earth, nature, and spirit in nature, the Great Goddess, Divine Feminine, and the Great Mother herself, I can see how the seed of that journey was planted even in this early dream. But that awareness and development would come many years later and after a long journey into my own unconscious. At this point I understood the reference to "my mother carries her own water" as symbolic of my relationship to my own unconscious that would bring forth the living water of the spirit living in my own soul. Symbolism is an instrument of knowledge that reveals aspects of reality that escape other modes of expression.[126] In fact, most human thought and behavior is symbolic rather than literal.[127] Jung asserted that "empirical truth never frees a man from his bondage to the senses." Rather, it is the symbolic truth which, for example, "*puts water in the place of mother* and spirit or fire in the place of father" that frees the libido and allows it to move to a spiritual level of development. [italics mine][128]

The year is 1984. It is the year I would turn forty. In retrospect it was the beginning of the emergence of a new life. Perhaps the notion that "life begins at forty" has some basis in psychological development. While the idea that "life begins at forty" is a twentieth-century notion

---

126 Cooper, *Illustrated Encyclopaedia*, 7.

127 Barnhouse, *Homosexuality: Symbolic Confusion*, 14.

128 Jung, *Symbols of Transformation*, 226.

credited to American psychologist Walter Pitkin and made popular by his self-help book of the same name, he wasn't the first to express it. The origin of the phrase goes back to the great nineteenth-century German philosopher Arthur Schopenhauer who said: "The first forty years of life give us the text: the next thirty supply the commentary."[129] Certainly the text of my first forty years provided the context out of which the next thirty-plus years would emerge, as the dreams began to comment on my life. Slowly there would be a shift from an awareness of "Spirit over matter" as had been the theme of the parsonage to one of "Spirit as one with matter," Spirit as an intelligence in nature and matter, even a wisdom and intelligence in the nature and matter in my own soul. The dreams and my response to them would come together to form a path forward.

I dream

> *There is a war in our country against homosexuals. There is much shooting. I am hiding between some wooden benches in a church. Someone sees me and shoots me. I think of all the pain caused to the families of homosexuals. It reminds me of the days of slavery and the bitter battle to free the slaves and all the terrible things people did to the slaves and those who had slaves. I think how it will feel for my family to have me taken away because I am homosexual. I wonder what it will feel like to be killed. I see myself being taken away and allowing myself to be taken away by not denying that I am homosexual. I accept the consequences of being homosexual.* (Journal, 1-16-84)

---

129 Life Begins at Forty, The Phrase Finder. www.phrases.org.uk

This dream mirrored both the inner and outer conflicts regarding homosexuality in the culture in which I was raised and, to a great extent, in the culture of the eighties. The dream also showed the movement in my unconscious toward the acceptance of my homosexuality, which I have come to understand is a symbol for this other masculine image living in my soul—a masculinity that was different from the masculinity of the parsonage. The dream also showed my willingness to accept the consequences of being this self. However, this acceptance would usher in a more direct confrontation with the opposing forces living in my soul.

> *I am in the basement. A sandy-haired young man climbs into the basement through a window. His face looks like it has a lady's stocking over it. It doesn't but he looks like that to disguise his identity. He says, "I am your adversary." We wrestle each other. The dream ends before anybody wins, while we are still wrestling.* (Journal, 1-22-84)

I had been analyzing my dreams for six years when this dream came to me. In this work I had taken great pains to understand my same-sex attractions and to come into a relationship and integrate this other man living in me. Although my relationship with the church and my role in it had changed, I had not yet left the institutional church, given that I was visiting other churches in the community. And yet, friends within the church and my extended family continued to feel that I had somehow lost my way. While I had ended all same-sex relationships, homosexual images and attractions had once again entered my dreams and fantasies.

The "adversary dream" is not without an archetypal source. As great literature, myths, and fairy tales show, the adversary is a key figure in such stories and therefore archetypal. As an archetype the adversary is one who strives against another with a design to oppose or resist him. The purpose of the adversary is to prevent the protagonist or hero or heroine of the story from achieving his or her goal. This creates a conflict or obstacles that must be resolved or overcome.

In my dream, was this adversarial other opposing my emerging consciousness, thus tempting me to regress back into my former life? Or was it that which was emerging—the future me—that opposed my urge to remain in the past? I am reminded of the biblical story of Jacob wrestling with a man until daybreak (Genesis 32: 24, NIV). Jungian analyst, John Sanford, commenting on this biblical story, says that everyone wrestling with his or her spiritual or psychological experiences, refusing to let them go until their meaning is discovered, is having a Jacob experience.[130] Sanford goes on to say "[w]hat began as a struggle in his [Jacob's] mind with his shadow, led to a struggle with the Unknown, and so the whole of the unconscious seized Jacob's ego and wrestled with it. Behind Jacob's wrestling match is the archetype of totality, what Jung calls the Self or God-image in the soul."[131] This encounter with the "Other" results in reconciliation, which was the request of the masculine image falling out of the plane in "the Fall" dream. As Jacob's story unfolds, the estranged brothers—Jacob and Esau—are reconciled. Jacob is reconciled to himself and to his God. The reconciliation of the estranged brothers suggests the psychological reconciliation of ego and shadow or for me the reconciliation between my ego and the same-sex other living in my soul.

In the dream, my story was not yet complete. I awoke while I was still wrestling with this adversary, symbolizing that some opposing force was at work in me. The instinctual masculine energy that entered

130 Sanford, *Man Who Wrestled with God*, 40.

131 Ibid., 40–41.

my dream six years earlier as a bull chasing me was now wrestling with me in the human form, albeit still disguised. This wrestling was multi-faceted. On one hand I was continuing to wrestle with my same-sex attractions. On the other hand I was still wrestling with leaving the church, the parsonage that in that earlier dream I had been instructed to leave in order to heal. On still on another front I was starting to wrestle with the meaning of my life. Why was I here? What was mine to do? I was also beginning to notice a growing dissatisfaction with teaching and a desire to become a Jungian analyst. My task now became to make meaning of this struggle with this Other in me in order to derive its gift.

In this I was reminded of Christ's saying "Settle matters quickly with your adversary who is taking you to court. Do it while you are still with him on the way, or he may hand you over to the judge, and the judge may hand you over to the officer, and you may be thrown into prison. I tell you the truth; you will not get out until you have paid the last penny."[132] This suggested the psychological truth of the importance of coming to terms with the shadow or other unconscious aspects when they present themselves. Otherwise they may retreat to the unconscious where they may continue to act out unconsciously and wreak havoc on your life. "When an inner situation is not made conscious, it happens outside as fate. That is to say, when the individual remains undivided and does not become conscious of his inner opposite, the world must perforce act out the conflict and be torn into opposing halves."[133] There is a price to pay for unconsciousness.

Because of the powerful effect of this dream, I came to understand that this adversary represented some numinous antagonist, some spiritual power that held some viewpoint that was struggling to come into

---

132 Matthew 5:25, NIV.

133 Carl Jung, Aion, Christ: A Symbol of the Self, Pages 70-71.

consciousness. The wrestling was for acceptance, for in acceptance, the ego and consciousness is changed. It is in our struggles that we have the opportunity to become aware of opposing forces in us.

The appearance of the stocking on the man's face prevented the face from being clear or recognizable. I was not yet able to clearly see the face of this Other in me. Thus, the adversary came disguised, lest my ego could not endure the actual person. God often comes disguised. The Self and the longing of the soul often lie hidden behind the shadow.[134] The facial features looked like a stocking was over them and thus had the appearance of not being developed, resembling a fetus or an undeveloped face. This adversary symbolized the unconscious aspect that opposed my current ego-conscious attitude but had not yet fully developed. It was an image or face that was yet to be.

This movement toward acceptance of myself was followed one month later by a dream that pointed to further union with this opposite Other. I dream

> *I leave something in the care of a man. I call later to ask for it. He says, "closed," meaning he is not available at this time. I walk out of the building I am in to see if I can find out why he isn't available. I see him making out with a woman and realize that was why he wasn't available. He didn't want to be disturbed. The man seems sinister. I see two teenage girls dressed for a costume party walking. One is dressed as a witch. I ask her to scare this man or put a spell on him so that he will return what he is holding of mine. Suddenly the man throws me a sock. In the sock is a gold ring, like a wedding band. I know that it is valuable*

134 Sanford, *Man Who Wrestled with God*, 40-41.

> *and important. I look down and see my glasses. I pick them up.* (Journal, 2-17-84)

I have this dream after a time of prayer and meditation in which I give God my contradictions and ask God for wholeness and wisdom and especially to bring about the marriage of my unconscious and conscious so that my ego will be in relation with the unconscious. The dream showed that some dark, sinister masculine shadow part of me was holding something of mine that I wanted. However, it wasn't available to me because this unconscious masculine part was involved with some feminine part, held under her spell.

This was a successful dream in that the goal of the dream was met. I was able to retrieve what I had left in the care of this unconscious masculine part. It turns out that it was a ring, a wedding band. The ring as a circle was a symbol for wholeness. The ring as a wedding band suggested it was a symbol of unending love, unity, the union of the opposites, and the inner marriage. The ring was delivered to me in a sock. Socks are clothing for the feet. This reminded me of an earlier dream where I was preparing for my marriage and I found a pair of socks in my suitcase to *complete the wedding clothes*. Footwear is a symbol of liberty; its symbolic meaning is linked with that of the foot. According to psychoanalytic thought, the foot is a phallic symbol. To others the foot is symbolic of the soul. It is also symbolic of the relationship and the point of contact between the body and the earth.[135]

For me the foot held an erotic attraction, and part of that fantasy or acting out ritual would be the removing of the sock that held the foot that was the point of sexual contact with the man. For the dream to present the ring—a symbol of love, unity, wholeness, and inner

---

135 Cirlot, p. 111

marriage—with my same-sex behaviors, was significant. So while the foot, as psychoanalytic thought suggests, was a point of contact with the masculine for me, it also contained association to the soul and contact with the earth. This suggested that my wholeness and inner marriage and unity was to be found in my relationship to the feminine and the earth. I get this from the shadow, from this other man living in me—the masculine that had been rejected in the life of the parsonage. This dream showed that this relationship and unity was coming. After receiving the ring, I looked down and found my glasses. That is, I found my way of seeing.

Two weeks later I dream

> *I am lying in bed. I sense that I am dying. Suddenly I take off and fly through the air, way up into the sky. Really it is more like I am carried through the sky by some force. It is night. I remain in the same position I was in bed, just soaring through the air, high up into the sky. I keep soaring until I see a ring of fire in the sky. When I see this ring of fire or come to this ring of fire, I am transformed by it.* (Journal, 3-5-84)

This dream would usher in a four-year struggle with my same-sex desires and attractions and with the purpose and meaning of my life—"the treasure hard to find." This would usher in a new consciousness—one that began to trust the spirit in the matter of my soul—a spirit that opposed my current life—a spirit that would not only bring me face to face with the meaning of my same-sex attractions but would continue to confirm my leaving the institutional church. It would also lead me out of teaching and initiate a move to Indianapolis to become a clinical social worker. This same spirit would eventually lead me to study mind-body therapies, call me and instruct me on how to use art to heal, and call me to study shamanism and energy medicine. Finally, in the end I would discover the archetype of the Green Man and the presence of another masculine spirit, another Divine Masculine, the "Earth Masculine" living in my soul as shaman-healer. But that realization was still years away.

Some weeks later I dream

> *A spiritual healer is speaking and says that homosexuality is when the animi descends down on the animus and attaches itself to the animus . . . I pray and ask God to break the anima from the animus and to return the animus to its rightful position in the masculine . . .* (Dream Journal, 3-10-84)

Archetypes are preexistent, or latent, internally determined patterns of being and behaving and of perceiving and responding that *preform* our experiences in a certain typical way.[136]

As such they govern emotions and behavior and are powerful forces that demand their due, recognized or not. Each archetype has characteristic drives, emotions, and needs that shape personality and if consciously recognized and honored help a man really be himself, motivating him to lead a deeply meaningful life because what he does is connected to the archetypal layer of his psyche.[137] Archetypes contain information that program the individual to behave in certain specific ways while permitting such behavior to be adapted appropriately to environmental circumstances.[138] While certain specific external stimuli may release the program, some internal apparatus decides which

136 Jung, *Collected Works* 9, i, 66; and Bolen, *Gods in Everyman*, 6.

137 Bolen, *Gods in Everyman*, 5–6.

138 Stevens, *Archetypes*, 52.

of the program options is to be put into effect.[139] The archetype is the common origin of both the behavioral and psychic events.[140]

Two of the dominant archetypes that Jung identified as operating in the human psyche are the anima and animus. The anima is the archetype of the feminine operating within the unconscious of a man,[141] and the animus is the archetype of the masculine operating within the unconscious of a woman.[142] James Hillman points out that the archetypes cannot be confined to human gender and shows how anima and animus work equally in both sexes.[143] Thus the archetype of the masculine (animus) is a major dominant force in the psyche of a man. In my own work, I had a dream that simply said, "the animus lives in a man too."

According to Jungian psychology, it is the anima in men and the animus in women that, in projection, attract them to the other sex in relationships. Since anima and animus operate in both men and women, they may be responsible for same-sex attraction as well. I have already shown how the phallus as Phallos is a symbol for the archetypal masculine (God) as a companion and co-creator with the feminine (Goddess) in antiquity, supporting the idea that the masculine archetype is *coequal* with the feminine principle as an originating force in the psyche.[144]

My dream suggested that the configuration of the masculine and feminine archetypes and their relationship to each other results in the masculine Phallos being more fascinating and attractive to some men than others. Why are some men attracted to women while others are

---

139 Stevens, Ibid., 53–54.

140 Ibid., 62.

141 Jung, *Collected Works 5,* 266.

142 Ibid., 267.

143 Hillman, *Anima,* 51–65.

144 Monick, *Phallos,* 73.

attracted to men and still others are attracted to both? While modern research suggests that brain chemistry is strongly involved with our lust, attractions, and attachments,[145] I propose that the attraction also holds some unconscious purpose that if understood facilitates its integration, helping the person to become more fully him or herself and to fulfill that purpose.

The dream revealed that how the masculine archetype manifests in any one man is a factor of the masculine/feminine (anima/animus) balance in his psyche and the configuration or relationship of the archetypes in his deep unconscious. The dream supported and confirmed that it is the configuration and mutual influence of the archetypes and their relationships in the psyche that determines a man's character and his fate.[146]

The archetypes want to be known. They make their presence known in our dreams in order that we pay attention to what we are neglecting. It's our task to find the archetype's blessing and to read—in the archetype's expression in our dreams and its manifestation in our lives—some divine message that unravels its meaning.[147] This dream also suggested that the ego had some influence on the configuration and relationship of the archetypal system and how it would manifest. I had to work with the archetype or archetypal configuration that was at the root of my sexuality, realizing that the process of individuation included the archetype or archetypes that are basic to my individual psychic structure.[148] This dream was pretty clear as to the archetypal configuration that was at the core of my homosexuality and same-sex attraction and suggested a way forward in my development.

---

145 Fisher, *Brains Do It.*

146 Guggenbuhl-Craig, *Eros on Crutches*, 28.

147 Wink, *Unmasking the Powers*, 117–125.

148 Guggenbuhl-Craig, *Eros on Crutches*, 24.

The "animi" configuration refers to undifferentiated masculine/feminine (animus/anima) energy. Its attachment to animus, my own masculinity, resulted in an inner relationship that manifested as homosexuality. This "animi" is understood as the archetypal form of my inner feminine under the influence of an unconscious masculine characteristic or some unconscious man in me. An unconscious man, trying to get into consciousness, had taken hold of my anima. The anima is an agent of the Self that typically seduces one into sexual relationships to express an unexpressed need of the Self.

This struggle is common to every man. Heterosexual men are shamed for their sexuality and often driven to pornography and other sexual compulsions, which can be understood as abuse by their animas. This is parallel to the homosexual man who feels derided for his same-sex attraction. We each have an anima that is actively using the libido of sexuality to project a part of the Self onto a lover. Therefore, when my anima, my impulse for life, goes off with this other unconscious man, she takes the male ego along and involves me in homosexual relationships. In this instance, the anima is under an aspect of some unconscious masculine energy in me that is then projected onto and searched for in the other man.

Just as the anima archetype in men and the animus archetype in women are responsible for other-sex relationships, the dream said that the animi archetype of undifferentiated masculine-feminine energy was the psychic condition that initiated and mediated the homosexual aspect of my bisexuality, attracting me to men. I would also say that the anima may fall in love with a man right through the ego and in so doing, drag me into relationship with that man. One could say that the relationship is really between the anima and the other man. The ego provides the vehicle for this to happen.

The dream stated that I "pray and ask God to break the anima from the animus and to return the animus to its proper position in the masculine." Although this part of the dream might be understood as my inability to accept my homosexuality and my unconscious wish for some "miracle" solution or remedy (intervention by God), it is, from an archetypal point of view, the task of freeing the maiden (anima) from the dragon (unconscious) that is the subject of many myths and fairy tales. I understand this as the spiritual task of differentiating my feminine element (anima) from its identification with my unconscious masculine element (animus) and giving the masculine its proper place in the masculine. Whether this differentiation and return of the masculine to the masculine (the homosexual desire) was to be expressed in symbol as an inner symbolic experience or in behavior as a return to an outer homosexual relationship or both was not clear at this time.

Another dream would appear a few months later to indicate the personal decision I was to make concerning my homosexuality. This dream resulted in a lengthy journey into the psychological interpretation of the ballet *Swan Lake* and how the archetypal dimensions of the *Swan Lake* story spoke to my own homosexuality and psycho-spiritual development. This analytical work became the turning point in my individuation process and set me on a path to discover the meaning of my same-sex desires. I dream

> I *am at school. It is the sixth period. A male student comes in and walks up to the desk. He tells me that this is the last day he will be in class. The reason is that he has to work starting at the time of the class. The work has something to do with writing. It seems that he got a scholarship from one of the local factories in town, which is payment for him to work for them in writing. He goes to school until the sixth*

period and then he works for them. He tells me that he got too much money to turn it down. He pats his back pocket where his wallet is when he says this.

While I am talking with him, a woman comes in and sits down in the back of the class. I think it is the new Spanish teacher who has come to observe my teaching. I become a little anxious about talking to this student and not teaching the class, fearing that she will judge me not as a good teacher since I am spending time talking to this student and letting the rest of the class go. I look at the clock. It is 2:40. I think that isn't so bad, meaning not so much time wasted.

The lady comes to the desk. She is the mother of the male student. I notice that she lays a book down on my desk, a black and white book. I glance at it and think the title is The Sheldon-Sam Story. *I think it must be a book about my same-sex relationship with this man, but I didn't know one existed. Meanwhile I tell the student that he will fail these nine weeks because of missing the rest of the classes. His mother says that they had planned for that.*

I average out his grades for the first nine weeks; he gets an A. *Since the grade for the last nine weeks will be an* F, *his average will be a* C. *I tell the student that whatever he gets on the semester test will average into that. I tell him that he can play around with different grades to see what he can make on the semester average. It is like he can see what his semester average will be by what grade he decides he wants to get on the semester test. His mother asks if he can come in the mornings to get help and make up the class. She suggests twenty minutes. I don't think that is much time. I tell her that I am at school by twenty minutes to eight.*

The student doesn't want to do that. They leave. As they leave, I say, "When one has a conflict of priorities one must follow the heart."

The mother says, "Especially when it involves so much," pointing to her back pocket. I know that she is referring to the large amount of money this scholarship and job gave her son. After they leave, I look at the book she put down on the desk. It isn't The Sheldon-Sam Story but The Swan Lake Story. *I open it up. It is written in Spanish and above every or almost every line is an English translation in handwriting. I notice that some chapters are in English and the handwritten translations are in Spanish. As I open the book, other books unfold out of it. One is a book of poetry and others are literary classics. Hilda is now there and says, "That is an excellent book" referring to the book on poetry. It seems like four or five books unfold.* (Journal, 8-84)

On the day before this dream my wife and I sat on the porch of our home on a hot August afternoon talking about my homosexual needs. I told her that I wished I could return to a previous homosexual relationship—a relationship that had ended six years before. As the dream suggested, I think the book that the lady in the dream laid on my desk was a specific reference to that former relationship. Because of the intensity and the importance of that discussion with my wife and the dream's specific reference to that relationship, I conclude that the dream was speaking to my desire to return to a homosexual relationship as the solution to my homosexual needs. However, the unconscious suggested to me that the intention of my homosexual desires was not about returning to an actual homosexual relationship but rather lay somehow in the story of *Swan Lake* since that was the actual name of the book in the dream.

The dream also stated that "when there is a conflict of priorities, one must follow the heart." "Following one's heart" is often interpreted to mean following some "subjective feeling or desire." However, the heart, as James Hillman, Henry Corbin, and others have suggested, is the place of "imaginal sight," the place of seeing things as they really or essentially are. To see with the heart is to see images as they arise in the imagination as "real" figures, not something that we have made up but as beings actually presented to us as genuinely created, authentic creatures. We misunderstand the mode of being of these figures in our dreams or the persons of our imaginings and fantasies. We believe these figures are subjectively real when they are instead *imaginally* real. Or, we believe these figures are externally real when they are *essentially* real.

In other words, we confuse imaginal with subjective and internal, and we mistake essential for external and objective.[149] To "follow the heart" means to follow "imaginal sight." To follow "imaginal sight" means to follow the essential meaning of the image living in the soul. To follow the essential meaning means to recognize that much of what we call projection is an attempt by the psyche to experience things beyond ourselves as imaginal presences, an attempt to restore both heart and image to the matter—the "stuff"—in our lives.[150] We must begin to allow the images to express their imaginal reality. This will be discussed more fully in the chapters "The Soul's Next Manifestation" and "The Matter of the Heart and the Heart of Matter." For now, let me return to the dream.

---

149 Hillman, *Thought of the Heart*, 6.

150 Ibid., 29–30.

The reference to "a conflict of priorities" in the dream might mirror the conflict of priorities in my life between staying within the belief structure of my family of origin and the parsonage or the more liberal one that was emerging in me. This latter priority meant remaining in a heterosexual relationship versus returning to a homosexual relationship—or even what would emerge some four years later, a conflict between remaining a teacher or becoming a therapist, or a conflict between staying in the town where we lived or moving to Indianapolis to pursue another life. But for the time being this dream had called my attention to explore what the ballet *Swan Lake* might have to say about this dream and the context of me wanting to return to a same-sex relationship.

For modern man, myth is born when the outer images and events are recognized as carriers and therefore symbols of the patterns of energy at work within the individual or collective psyche. The ballet *Swan Lake* became a template to show how the characters in the ballet could be understood as characters of my own soul on which I was projecting the spiritual intent of my attractions as my desire for union—the reconciliation of the outer and inner man—and the sacrifice that is often necessary in order to be true to the purpose of one's soul. I provide a brief summary of the story and its message for me in the context of the dream and the soul conflict at that time.

> Swan Lake *involves a beautiful princess, a passionate prince, and a really major obstacle to their happiness. That obstacle is the wicked sorcerer von Rothbart who captures the Princess Odette and turns her into a swan by day. Only if a young man pledges his love and marries her can the evil spell be broken. But should he betray her, she will remain a swan forever.*

A childhood friend of Prince Siegfried leads the court and villagers in a celebration of the prince's coming-of-age. The Queen Mother offers the prince his present, a crossbow. She reminds him that as he is to become king, he must choose a bride at the following evening's ball. Realizing the days of his carefree youth are over, Siegfried leaves the festivities to seek the solace of the woods.

Later that night, in a moonlit clearing by the lake, the prince meets the mysterious Odette, who explains her fate. The prince is smitten and vows that he will save her. Von Rothbart suddenly appears and the prince draws his bow. But Odette shields the sorcerer's body with hers, realizing that should he die before the spell is broken, her destiny would be sealed. Von Rothbart disappears and Odette withdraws, as the awestruck prince looks on.

At the ball, eligible royal princesses arrive from foreign lands, all eager to be chosen as the prince's bride and future queen. They present their native dances, but the prince's thoughts are only of Odette. Suddenly, von Rothbart arrives with his daughter Odile who is disguised as a black swan and appears identical to Odette. The prince is enraptured and they exit together as von Rothbart holds the court in thrall, dancing with each of the princesses. Siegfried and Odile return, she beguiles him, and the prince announces he will marry her. Von Rothbart demands he swear fidelity, and just as he does, the prince realizes he is the victim of a heinous plot. In a startling moment of clarity, he envisions the woman he truly loves and rushes to join her at the lakeside.

A great storm rages as the prince arrives and asks Odette for forgiveness. She says she has no choice but to kill herself.

The prince declares he will die with her. Von Rothbart appears and the lovers throw themselves into the lake. Von Rothbart is vanquished, his power destroyed— but not before he witnesses the lovers' ultimate triumph as their spirits rise heavenward, united at last in life after death.

I am fully aware that I projected my unconscious onto my interpretation of *Swan Lake*. Thus, my interpretation speaks to my psychic configuration and associations and may or may not have larger meaning. The ballet *Swan Lake* shows the psychological problem that exists when the man's anima—his inner feminine—has fallen under the influence of some unconscious content. It reveals what happens when the ego attempts to free the anima from the conditions established by the mother, and what path is necessary for resolving the conflict. I am suggesting that certain homosexual desires or drives occur when such a tendency in the unconscious cannot get into consciousness and therefore takes hold of the anima. As I have stated earlier, in the case of male homosexuality, it is some unconscious masculine aspect that for some reason cannot get into consciousness that seizes the anima seeking life and its realization. "She [the impulse for life] is unfaithful and goes off with this other man—an unconscious characteristic of his own—without his noticing it"[151] and leads him into homosexual relationships in an attempt to bring into consciousness and experience the missing characteristic. The ego must free the anima from the unconscious point of view so that she will be his lover alone, united with him in a conscious relationship. If the ego cannot do this, then for the sake of love, the sake of following the center, he must follow her in death. This not only frees her from the unconscious content but

151 Von Franz, *Redemption Motifs*. 40.

results in the sacrifice of his own ego position, which was what was needed in the first place.

Furthermore, the anima of the male homosexual is under the influence of an unconscious aspect of the Self. This is the God image, which corresponds to an unconscious characteristic of his own male image that has been experienced too little or not at all. The anima goes off with this unconscious man and leads the ego into sexual relationships with other men onto whom the man projects this unconscious masculine characteristic through the anima in an attempt to make it conscious and a part of human experience. If the male homosexual can make the anima conscious and sacrifice his ego position to follow her inwardly, she will lead him to this other self that will manifest itself as the union of his ego-consciousness with the unconscious aspect. This union results in the strengthening of the masculine image and his male identity and in my case connected me to an earthy, pre-Christian male spirit.

Now I return to the importance of the swan as a symbol of the masculine sun-god of death and rebirth, the feminine goddess as anima and soul-image, and the union of these opposites as the Self in its male-female aspect. The swan as death and rebirth symbolizes the death of Siegfried's ego-consciousness that was contained in the mother, and the rebirth of his ego in its new form, one united with the anima, Odette. As a symbol of the anima, the swan represents the feminine spirit (wisdom) that aided Siegfried in his journey to this new relationship with the feminine. The swan as symbol of the Self is represented by the union of Siegfried and Odette as an inner union of opposites: the Self in its male-female aspect.

At the root of this movement is the swan as a symbol of desire itself. The swan "always points to the complete satisfaction of a desire, the swan song being a particular allusion to desire, which brings about its own death."[152] The swan, anticipating the good things of another world, that is, another consciousness, sings in the day of its death. Siegfried, now serving the same God as the swan maiden, willingly follows her in this death. This is why Socrates says, "And I too believing myself to be the consecrated servant of the same God and the fellow servant of the swans . . . would not go out of life less merrily than the swans . . . ."[153]

The ego now serves the same God as the anima, the God being the Self as it manifests in the individual man. It is the desire and purpose of the anima to lead the ego to the experience of the Self that the male experiences in an essentially masculine way.[154] This is of prime importance for the male homosexual. For the ego, in its desire for the masculine, goes inward in search of itself, that is, its self-realization, fulfillment, and completion, and brings about its own death through a union with the missing characteristic, resulting in a new world, a new consciousness. Thus homosexuality, understood symbolically, may indeed be a swan song, resulting in the birth of a new ego-consciousness, an ego-consciousness grounded in the Self. In my case the dream, in calling my attention to *Swan Lake*, indicated that my path was not to return to an external homosexual relationship but rather to follow the inner life. This new Self emerged as a masculine image of a man whose spirit was one with the earth and nature, the Earth Masculine.

In the thirty years since I had these dreams and did this analytical work on *Swan Lake* much has happened in the field of sexuality, and especially in the gay, lesbian, bisexual, and transgendered world as science continues to seek to understand the origins and development of sexual orientation. Homosexuality is much more visible and more accepted in our culture than it was in the early eighties. Many states

---

152 Cirlot, *Dictionary of Symbols,* 232.

153 Plato, *Symposium,* 62.

154 Ulanov, *The Feminine in Jungian Psychology,* 212.

now recognize same-sex marriage. We have openly gay persons in every area of life. The symbolic conclusions drawn from my work with my own same-sex desires should in no way be interpreted to mean that homosexuality is not a viable and valid expression of human feeling and behavior any more than understanding the symbolic meaning of heterosexuality invalidates or minimizes heterosexual expression and behavior. How a person decides to live and express his or her sexual desires and needs is a choice that must be left to the individual. The symbolic meaning does not render the literal and physical expression invalid. Rather, understanding the symbolic or inner meaning may allow further integration of the personality in ways that actually enhance relationships and their myriad sexual expressions.

Let's now look at the inner meanings of same-sex fantasies, attractions, and behaviors.

Notes and Exercises

The parts of the soul want to be known. They make themselves known in our dreams to get us to pay attention to what we are neglecting. It is our task to find their blessings--to discern some divine message that reveals their meanings. These soul parts can be understood as archetypal configurations that if not understood live out their lives in us as fate.

Archetypes are universal patterns of being and behavior, of perceiving and responding, that form our experiences in certain typical ways. There are as many archetypes as there are ways of being. Examples of archetypes are mother, father, savior, healer, devil, villain, seducer, teacher, banker, minister, homosexual, heterosexual, patriarchy, and bisexual. Generations of families that continue to follow a particular profession or job might be said to fall under the spell of that archetype and live it out, sometimes unconsciously, continuing to live out a family story (e.g., banker, minister, accountant, teacher, doctor, etc.). There is nothing wrong with living out a family story as long as it is also *your* story, providing meaning, fulfillment and purpose.

What are the archetypes (patterns) that live in your family? Have you identified with one or more of those archetypes? Which ones? Have you ever felt conflicted by your family's archetypal story? Which one(s) are living out through you and your life?

We tend to be born with certain archetypal configurations—those that are natural to us and our soul. However, sometimes we fall under the spell other archetypes that are not natural to us. To discover your primary archetypes or for a more in-depth study of archetypes, check out listings for archetypes in the resources section at the end of the book.

Once you have an idea of your personal archetype(s), how do they call to you? In what ways are you already living your personal archetype? What changes do you need to make to honor your personal archetypes?

CHAPTER EIGHT

Manifestations of the Self in Male Same-Sex Behaviors

I dream that

> *I perform oral sex on a man who is an officer in the military. When I finish I turn to go. The man orders me to go out into the field and perform oral sex on all the soldiers. Because I had performed oral sex on him, I have been initiated into this group and am now under the command of this officer. This is a military unit and I am to perform oral sex on all the soldiers.* (Journal, 1-3-85).
>
> *Later that night I dream that I am in the military. I am lined up with other soldiers on a field. We are doing drills in the nude. We are told to bend over. As I do, the man behind me performs anal intercourse on me.* (Journal, 1-3-85)

Sex divested of its biological function serves the purposes of the soul.[155] Anal intercourse, oral sex, and masturbation are central themes in same-sex dreams, fantasies, and behaviors. Operating on the idea

155 Harding, *Psychic Energy.*

that spiritual meaning is born when images and behaviors are recognized as carriers and therefore symbols of patterns of energy at work within the individual, we can begin to explore the symbolic meaning and spiritual intent or unconscious purpose of such desires, fantasies, and attractions. Symbolism reveals aspects of reality that escape other modes of expression.[156]

As pointed out earlier, most human thought and behavior is symbolic rather than literal.[157] The symbol carries the unconscious projection,[158] and it is the symbol that moves the energy from one realm to another.[159] To understand the meanings of the symbols that carry this energy as it plays within the man who has same-sex attractions is to gain some insight into what it is that he actually seeks through these acts and fantasies. To give symbolic meaning is not intended to diminish the sexual aspect, nor is it to negate or deny the biological and environmental determiners of homosexuality and same-sex attraction. Rather, it is an attempt to bring meaning and understanding to these same-sex fantasies and behaviors, a meaning that might contribute to the actual realization and fulfillment of their unconscious purpose and spiritual intent. When the unconscious purpose of a behavior has been fulfilled, the energy moves to another level of development.[160]

In the dreams and fantasies of men, unconscious masculine energy may express itself in the image of a homosexual.[161] As a phallic expression of the unconscious, he simultaneously represents the chthonic aspect of the masculine and ultimately the initiating spirit.[162] In certain

---

156 Cooper, *Illustrated Encyclopaedia*, 7.

157 Barnhouse, *Homosexuality: Symbolic Confusion*, 34.

158 Jung, *Collected Works 14*, 476.

159 Jacobi, *Complex/Archetype/Symbol*, 100.

160 Jung, *Collected Works 7*, 107.

161 Te Paske, *Rape and Ritual*, 113.

162 Ibid.

expressions of homosexuality it seems that some part of the man is under the influence of this chthonic aspect of the masculine. This part seeks a sexual relationship with a man onto whom this unconscious masculinity is projected. Thus, same-sex attraction can be understood as the longing for the concrete manifestation of that potential that is contained in the Soul and corresponds to the quest for the soul's realization. In homosexual love, the partner often becomes the carrier of the soul image and through the power of the relationship may unconsciously assist his lover, as the initiating spirit, in bringing that potential to birth in himself.[163]

The anima as the feminine image and urge for life in a man's soul initiates the development of the personality[164] and brings about not only feminine elements but also a dominant masculinity.[165] In the previous chapter I suggested that this soul image may initiate a same-sex relationship at times by falling in love with a man right through the ego in an attempt to establish a relationship between the man and this unconscious other living in his soul. The soul longs for the inner unity and wholeness of the personality and becomes the agent for this union.[166]As symbol, the same-sex partner becomes the carrier of the unconscious image that longs for consciousness.

I am operating on the assertions of quantum physics that everything is energy, both the physical plane of matter and the more abstract plane of the mind. I'm also operating on the idea that all behavior and thought are symbolic. Therefore, sexual fantasies and behaviors are symbolic expressions of energy at work in an individual but whose purposes are for the most part unconscious.

---

163 Sanford, *Invisible Partners,* 94–98.

164 Ulanov, *The Feminine in Jungian Psychology,* 241.

165 Ibid., 212.

166 Von Franz, *Aurora Consurgens,* 214.

In discussing so-called perversions, the late noted Jungian psychoanalyst and homeopathic physician Edward Whitmont in his book *Return of the Goddess* says that same-sex oral and anal sexuality can be understood as meaningful patterns of energy as it plays at creation and development, expressing basic, unconscious, and unacknowledged urges for the purpose of balancing a one-sided position. As such, they are archetypal in that they express the call of a basic power that is essentially of a religious and numinous or spiritual character.[167]

The focal point of the energy in anal intercourse, fellatio, and masturbation is the penis. This yearning for contact with the male organ represents symbolically a deep need for connection with the soul, represented by the phallus, which I have shown elsewhere is a symbol for the Divine Masculine and the creative masculine spirit.[168] The symbol and the libido or psychic energy associated with it are unknown quantities, hard to recognize, never quite definable,[169] something little known or completely unknown.[170] Psychic energy is the common denominator of all symbols. Their common meaning lies in the fact that they are all analogies of the same thing.[171]

For example, phallic symbols are supposed to stand for the penis and nothing more. However, psychologically speaking, the penis is indeed itself but also a symbol of something more, the meaning of which is not necessarily easy to determine. Primitive people, like the ancients, would never confuse the phallus as a ritualistic symbol with the penis. For the primitive, "the phallus always means the creative mana, the power of healing and fertility, the 'extraordinarily potent,' .

167 Whitmont, *Return of the Goddess,* 250.

168 Sanford, *Invisible Partners,* 96.

169 Jung, *Collected Works 16,* par. 340.

170 Jung, *Collected Works 5,* 222.

171 Ibid.

. . whose equivalents in mythology and in dreams are the *bull* [italics mine], the ass, the pomegranate, the yoni, and the he-goat, the lightening, the horse's hoof, the dance, the magical cohabitation in the furrow, and the menstrual fluid, to mention only a few of the thousand other analogies. That which underlies all the analogies, and sexuality itself, is the archetypal image whose character is hard to define, but whose nearest psychological equivalent in perhaps the primitive mana-symbol."[172]

As detailed in chapter 1, the phallus is the source of life and libido, the creator and worker of miracles, the inseminator of the earth. It stands for the creative divinity working in darkness to create a living thing.[173] No matter how clearly a phallus symbol appears as such, it does not denote the sexual organ. It is *always* a symbol for the libido. A symbol points to something real or to a structure in the world. The phallus, the erect penis, is the symbol of archetypal masculine and points to archetypal masculinity as an originating psychic force.

Given that sexuality is "a fundamental expression of psychic energy"[174] and "in its symbolic dimension has a spiritual function,"[175] same-sex anal intercourse can be understood as the sexual manifestation of the spiritual desire of an aspect of the individual to surrender to the masculine spirit of the soul, which contains his unconscious masculine image that longs for relatedness and connection but gets projected onto the other man. The desire inherent in anal intercourse is to surrender to the soul's longing for some unconscious and unrealized aspect represented by the phallus. In my own experience of anal intercourse, whether in fantasy or acting it out with another man, I

---

172 Jung, *Collected Works 16*, par. 340.

173 Jung, *Collected Works* 5, 124, 97, 436.

174 Whitmont, *Return of the Goddess*, 250.

175 Ulanov, *The Feminine in Jungian Psychology*, 14.

had the experience of complete abandonment of myself, a giving of myself over to this other man without reservation, saying "do with me as you want. I am yours." I longed to be ravished by him, carried off and raped by him, impregnated by his spirit, and indoctrinated into his mysteries so that I could give birth to the other man in me—the man I imaged him to be.

In my own journey I found it helpful to understand some of the archetypal and symbolic expressions of this behavior. In certain primitive societies there is widespread belief that anal intercourse between men promotes psychic growth. In these societies, semen as male bodily fluid is believed to carry the masculinity of the ancestral spirits and is interjected anally by the initiating men.[176] Such may be the meaning behind dream and fantasy material of homosexual intercourse and the unconscious purpose of actual anal intercourse between men. This behavior, whether fantasy or acted out, suggests the need for integration of the unconscious masculine. This type of erotic relationship stands as the foundation of the initiation rituals in which innumerable "hoaxes" are practiced on the novices. In one such instance, they are placed in a hut as the older men rattle sticks and threaten the youths with anal penetration by the ancestral spirits, which they personify. While such a practice may seem ludicrous to modern man, to the natives it assists in forming character of the highest value by initiating the men with the ancestral spirits. It is a case of the "lowest" turned into the "highest." What is meant by "ancestral spirits" is what we call "conscience," that inner voice that tells a man what is socially right and *what he ought to do*.[177]

---

176 TePaske. *Rape and Ritual*, 112, quoting John Layard. "Homoeroticism in Primitive Society as a Function of the Self," Journal of Analytical Psychology, 4.2, 251.

177 112–113.

The natives say that the ancestral spirits cannot come into a young initiate through the mouth because that is where the mother penetrates with her breast during the boy's infancy. Rather, the male influences must come in through the anus where a man can penetrate.[178]

In ancient times the feeling of being "penetrated" by, or of "receiving" a god—a basic archetypal power—was represented by the sexual act.[179] The penis is a symbol of the creative phallic power of the Self, and the anus as the place of penetration becomes a symbol of the prime place of origin.[180] This association and union of the penis with the anus in anal intercourse connect anal intercourse to the theory of anal propagation and the symbolic meaning of defection. Jung suggested that when an object such as the phallus, which has been revered and worshipped throughout history, is related by the unconscious to the anal region, we have to conclude that this is a way of expressing respect and attention for these areas, much like a child feels for these forbidden areas.[181] Naturally, traces of this infantile interest linger in the adult, but such fascination isn't only related to the psychology of the child. An oriental fairy tale tells of Crusaders who would anoint themselves with the excrement of the Pope in order to make themselves more formidable, suggesting that the anal region is closely connected with great respect.[182]

One of Jung's patients who had a special admiration for her father fantasized him sitting on a toilet in a dignified manner while people filed past, greeting him profusely.[183] Another of Jung's patients once dreamt that "she saw the Crucifix formed of excrement on the bottom

---

178 Ibid., 113.

179 Jung, *Collected Works 10*, 337–337n.

180 Jung, *Collected Works 5*, 161.

181 Ibid., 189.

182 Ibid.

183 Ibid.

of a blue-flowered chamber-pot."[184] Jung tells of a young girl who contracted the habit of sitting for hours on the toilet. On one occasion her father went to the toilet and asked her whatever was she doing. Whereupon the girl replied that she was "doing a little cart and two ponies." So the child was making a little cart and two ponies, things that she particularly wanted at the moment. In this way one can make whatever one wishes.[185]

Jung points out that children often value things very differently from us. For example, young children connect defecation with propagation. Children think that this is how things are produced or made.[186]

These two ideas—the initiatory significance of homosexual penetration believed by the natives and the anal birth theory believed by children—come together in the modern-day fantasy I discuss below. This fantasy began spontaneously in late adolescence and continued into early midlife when, in analysis, its symbolic meaning and psychospiritual intent became known. At that moment the fantasy lost its power and ended as suddenly as it had begun.

> *It is Friday night. I go to a house. I enter a room where I see many men. I contact one of the men and we go into a room where he performs anal intercourse on me. I know that he has made me pregnant. I then eat a large meal. The idea is to make me have to defecate. I stay the entire weekend, which symbolizes the growing child in me made by the sexual act with the man.*
>
> *Finally, I have to defecate and know it is time for the delivery. I go to a room where there is a table. The man who*

184 Ibid.

185 Ibid., 189–190.

186 Ibid.

> *performed the anal intercourse on me is there to "deliver the bowel movement." He makes me undress and lay on the table. He straps my feet and legs up in a delivery position. At last I defecate. The man, serving as doctor, catches the feces as it comes out. I have delivered. I leave. The weekend is finished.* (Journal, 1981)

This fantasy, as perverse as it may seem, can be understood as the psychospiritual need to be initiated by the masculine, and impregnated by his spirit (anal intercourse) in order to give birth (defecation) to the unconscious masculine that is embodied in and comes forth from the Self (phallus). The fantasy ended with the masturbatory act, ejaculating at the moment of defecating. The association of the ejaculation of semen with the act of defecation supports the infantile theory that "that is how things are produced" in that it connects the act of defecation with the symbolic act of self-creation (masturbation) It is the creation or birth by the infantile route.[187] In this case, the desired object is the unconscious man as carrier of the archetypal masculine. Mythology teaches us that the first men were made from earth and clay. "The Latin *lutum*, which really means 'mud,' also had the metaphorical meaning of 'filth.'"[188]

The alchemists believed that the lowest value allies itself to the highest and made this intimate connection between excrement and gold. They sought their *prima materia* in excrement, one of the arcane substances from which it was hoped that the mystic figure of the *filius philosophorum* (the Self) would emerge.[189] Anal intercourse may therefore be understood as the sexual manifestation of the spiritual desire—the unconscious and natural instinct—of some aspect of the man's

---

187 Ibid., 191.

188 Ibid.

189 Ibid., 189.

unconscious with which the ego may have overly identified to surrender to the experience of being penetrated by the "Divine Masculine." This Divine Masculine, residing in the soul, embodies the unconscious and unrelated masculinity that longs for realization and consciousness—a way to get into life. The question is: What *is* it that longs to get into life? The answer to that question for my own life will evolve in the coming chapters.

While anal intercourse symbolizes the psyche's longing for the realization of the soul and specifically the spiritual need of an impregnation from the chthonic masculine to beget a new and more differentiated masculinity, the homosexual act of fellatio expresses the spiritual need of the masculine to validate and affirm the unconscious masculinity and male identity embodied in the soul.

I dream

> *I am having highly active sex with an unknown male. The feeling in the dream is a very forceful feeling like the unity of two pieces of machinery that work together in a unified pattern or symmetrical pattern forming a whole operation. The sex is oral sex with each male sucking the other man's penis with deep forceful movements. It is like they are forming a whole, even a circle in this act.* (Journal, 2-2-85)

Whitmont suggests that "oral sexuality expresses a dependency need and often represents the unacknowledged worship of the phallic power."[190] Thus to have one's phallus orally "worshipped" is to have it validated in oneself. To offer fellatio to the other is to make him feel that power within and through his body.[191]

---

190 Whitmont, *Return of the Goddess*, 251.

191 Ibid.

The word *valid* comes from the Latin word *validus* meaning "strong and powerful," and from *valere* meaning "to be strong and to have power." To validate something is to make it strong and to give it power and authority. Therefore fellatio can be understood as the psyche's unconscious and natural desire (instinct) to give power and authority to the phallic spirit and to the unconscious masculine characteristics that are embodied in the soul and, in the final analysis, express the individual's desire to give value to his own unique masculinity. It is not without reason that the mouth—the organ of prime importance in fellatio—becomes the validating and empowering agent.

First and foremost, the mouth has a nutritive significance and connects fellatio to the symbolism of eating. This meaning is illustrated in the ancient habit of sacred kings who ate a penis upon their accession to the throne. The genitals of the defeated king were eaten by the victor as a way to pass the phallic spirit from the old king of "god" to the next. A King's "manliness" or "sacred power" dwelt in his genitals because that was his point of contact with the Goddess.[192] Barbara Walker, who points out this belief and practices of ancient man in *The Woman's Encyclopedia of Myths and Secrets*, continues, "God-eating was a universal custom descended from the earliest beginnings of civilization, when it was usually a genuine cannibal feast."[193] In these instances, the king was not only killed, but the people ate his body and drank his blood, believing that the king's life would then pass into them and unite them. The goal was to take on the nature of the king or god by eating him.

Lest we think that this kind of thinking is too far removed from modern-day practice to have any validity, we need only remember the Christian ritual of Holy Communion that states that by eating

---

192 Walker, *Woman's Encyclopedia of Myths and Secrets*, 143.

193 Ibid., 136.

the bread, the symbol of Christ's body, and by drinking the wine, the symbol of His blood, the believer actually partakes of the nature and spirit of Christ.[194] Therefore, fellatio may be understood to express in symbolic form the primitive and mythical belief that by eating the part of the body that carries the projection of the unconscious characteristic or energy that longs to be experienced the individual actually "takes into" himself some of the nature of that energy and becomes a partaker—one who himself has a portion of the energy projected onto and carried by the body part. This means that for the male, fellatio may be understood as a ritual whereby "eating of the penis," the symbol of the soul and carrier of the unconscious and unrelated masculinity, and drinking of the semen, the symbol of the generative and empowering male agent, he actually participates in the masculine energy of his partner and takes into himself the life of the other that somehow assists him in bringing to life in himself his own masculinity. In my personal experience with oral sex, I, as experienced in anal intercourse, experienced a sense of abandoned of myself, a completely giving myself over to the other man. It was like he was going to eat me completely up, like he couldn't get enough of me. The complete abandonment, of my giving myself over to the other, was part of what made this act so erotic and highly charged—the abandonment of myself to this Other in me that I projected onto the other man. But who was this Other in me?

Whitmont's idea that fellatio expresses the need to validate the masculine, that is, to give value to the unconscious and unrelated masculinity, suggests that oral sex is an expression of the feeling function and indicates an inadequately development masculine feeling-value level. Robert Johnson defines feeling, one of Jung's four psychic functions, as "the act of valuing."[195] One values what one feels, and one begins to feel

194 Matthew 26: 26–29 NIV.

195 Johnson, *He*, 35.

what one values. "Orally worshipping" the penis in the act of fellatio is an attempt to feel the masculine by giving it value, validity, power, and authority. This is an attempt to develop a masculine feeling-value or to value a masculine feeling as opposed to a feminine feeling. Or perhaps it is the need to value a different masculine feeling-value from the one a man may be identified with. For example, I was raised in a home with a rather passive masculine image except in its role as a voice for the patriarchal God that tended to subject Nature, the feminine, the body, sensuality and sexual expression that didn't fit the Biblical interpretation to its control. The part of my own soul that didn't fit into that model became repressed, split off and in its longing to get into consciousness became projected onto the penis in the act of fellatio. I would come to understand over time that this other masculine-feeling value was the one that was missing in the church parsonage. It was the masculine as a divine spirit in nature, in my *own* nature!

The mouth as the valuing agent contains taste buds—sensors that taste what is. The word *taste* means "to test by touch, to experience, to receive the sensation of" and derives from words meaning "test" and "trial," a hint that fellatio may even be an attempt at or a substitution for the missing masculine initiation that indoctrinates the young male into a masculine feeling-value level of experience—what it feels (tastes) like to be a man.

Seen in this light, fellatio, the desire to transfer the masculine feeling or masculine value from one man to another, seems to parallel the lack of and need for identification with the father or perhaps a different father image. In certain aspects of homosexuality, the male consciousness and masculine feeling-value-identity symbolized by the father (the old king), is believed to not have been constellated or passed on in the father-son relationship. In this instance, the goal of fellatio is the transfer of this phallic spirit and unconscious masculinity, including a masculine feeling-value, from the Self (the king) to the ego (the son). In other cases of same-sex attraction it would appear that the father image with which the boy has identified is not congruent with the one living in his own soul. It is the longing of that masculine image that gets projected onto the other man in its attempt to be validated through the act of oral sex.

However, the libido does not stop at the nutritive meaning of the mouth but actually returns to the unconscious through the mouth, through being devoured and swallowed.[196] For the mouth is also a symbol for the devouring aspect of the Great Mother and is symbolic of the entrance to the underworld or the unconscious. In such a regression the energy leaves the personal psychology of the individual and returns to the prenatal condition where it then erupts into the collective psyche. Here the libido returns to an undeveloped state or a not fully formed condition where it may remain stuck. However, it can also break free from the unconscious condition and return to consciousness with new possibilities.[197]

The energy may remain stuck at the nutritive significance of the mouth, literally stuck in the mouth in compulsive fellatio, for example, perpetuating, in this example, the mother-son bond. This bond has traditionally been one of the views to explain homosexuality, for this energy may enter the collective unconscious where it contacts the deeper, creative, archetypal, and non-personal masculine that can truly empower, bring to life, validate, give authority and value to the unconscious masculine and male identity that longs to be experienced and felt. This can be the longing for a masculinity different from the one in which a person was raised. Think back on my own example of being

196 Jung, *Collected Works 5*, 419.

197 Ibid.

raised in an evangelical minister's home with a certain masculine point of view or a masculinity different from the one living in my soul.

This level of experience touched on the symbolical truth that the male partner who has carried the projection of the missing masculinity (i.e., the missing father, the missing Green Man, Earth Masculine, etc.) is replaced by the inner libido-fire of the archetypal masculine that offers the energy another level of expression—that of an inner experience and a new consciousness. This was what the unconscious wanted in the first place. Again, the mouth becomes the symbol that carries the projection of the point of contact and source of this fire.

Jung pointed out that for an infant, the mouth has an exclusively nutritive significance. However, it soon takes on another significance as the organ of speech. The mouth becomes the expression of emotional forces, of libido itself. As such it becomes a prime place of origin. The most important discovery ever made by primitive man, the discovery of fire, came out of the mouth.[198] For example, certain texts state that "[f]rom his [Atman] mouth, the fire-hole (yoni), and from his hands, he brought forth fire."[199] And "[f]rom the mouth came speech, and from speech fire."[200]

Fire as a manifestation of psychic energy that came forth from the mouth places the mouth, symbolically, as the point of contact for receiving the fire—the "transforming, purifying, life-giving and generative power of the sun"[201] as the inner libido-fire of the creative phallic spirit that validates and empowers the unconscious and the unrelated masculinity that is projected onto and carried by the penis in the act of fellatio.

---

198 Ibid., 161.

199 Ibid., 160.

200 Ibid., 161.

201 Cooper. *Illustrated Encyclopaedia*, 66.

What actually happens, according to Jung, in incest and womb fantasies (which fellatio must surely be) is "... that the libido immerses itself in the unconscious, thereby provoking infantile reactions, affects, opinions and attitudes from the personal sphere [shadow] but at the same time activating collective images (archetypes) which have a compensatory and curative meaning ...."[202]

Understood symbolically as a spiritual and inner experience, the partners in the act of fellatio actually form a union—a circle of energy that attempts to fulfill and complete the other's need for the masculine as the above dream suggests. The partner performing the act validates and empowers the male factor of his partner in his "act of oral worship" and then takes this energy into himself. This is the very same energy that, through the act, his partner releases to return to the unconscious where it activates and makes contact with the archetypal masculine. In so doing, it brings it to life, constellating it in the other so that it can in fact empower the unconscious characteristics of his own male image.

The union in this exchange of energies is an attempt to heal the split between the ego's masculinity and the deeper masculine nature of the soul—the reconciliation of the outer man and the inner man—and serves the spiritual concern of personal destiny and Self-realization. It advances the "real, authentic self" as an expression of the transpersonal function of the Divine Masculine that stands outside ego yet longs to be experienced and lived. In my personal story it turns out that this was the longing of the Green Man, the Divine Masculine in nature, the spirit in matter and ultimately the inner shaman-healer that wanted to be recognized, experienced, and given place in my life and more broadly in the culture. The evolution of this discovery will emerge in the remaining chapters.

---

202 Jung., *Collected Works 5*, 420.

American Jungian analyst (the first significant Jungian psychoanalyst in the United States), Esther Harding, says that sexuality divested of its biological function serves the purposes of psyche.[203] I have suggested ways that the sexual experience of anal intercourse and fellatio might serve those purposes in male homosexuality and same-sex relationships. Another sexual act that has many and varied reasons and purposes is masturbation. James Hillman in his essay, "The Masturbation Inhibition," says "it is the [psychological] constellation that determines the masturbation experience."[204] That is, it is the fantasy and mythical material surrounding the experience that gives masturbation its purpose and its meaning.

That masturbation has many and varied reasons and purposes making its meaning difficult to grasp is stated most succinctly in a one-line dream that I had while struggling with the meaning of my own masturbatory needs. The voice of the dream simply said, "Masturbation is a mystery." The word *mystery* comes from the Greek words "*mysterion* meaning the secret worship of a deity [i.e., archetype], a secret thing, from *mystes* meaning one initiated into the mysteries, from *myein* meaning to initiate into the mysteries, and from *myein* meaning to shut the eyes." In strictest use, *mystery* "implies the thing's incapacity for comprehension by human reason, but in loose use only its extremely mystifying quality," something unexplained, unknown, or kept secret, a problem, a demand for a solution difficult to find which, if not found, will put one into a predicament. Mystery is a profound secret that has to do with rites, practices, or doctrines revealed only to initiates.[205] Mircea Eliade, in discussing the revelation of mystery in *The Sacred and the Profane*, says that "myth relates a sacred history,

---

203 Harding, *Psychic Energy*.

204 Hillman, *Loose Ends*, 120.

205 Ibid.

that is, a primordial event that took place at the beginning of time, . . .[and] tells how something was accomplished, began to be. . . . [T]o relate a sacred history is equivalent to revealing a mystery."[206]

One of the earliest accounts of the masturbation motif is found in Egyptian mythology.

R. T. Rundle Clark in his study *Myth and Symbol in Ancient Egypt* reports that the god Atum created the first creatures, Shu and Tefnut, male and female through masturbation. "Pyramid Utterance 527 says: 'Atum was creative in that he proceeded to masturbate with himself . . . ; he put his penis in his hand that he might obtain the pleasure of emission thereby and there were born brother and sister—that is Shu and Tefnut.'"[207] Masturbation remained a popular creation motif through Egyptian history. It emphasized the bisexual character of Atum and the self-sufficiency of the High God, that is, the psyche.[208] That is to say that masturbation emphasizes the bisexual character of the Self and the self-sufficiency of the psyche to create from and out of itself. Clark continues. "As time went on the gods grew more personal. Atum became more of a man and less of an abstract principle. He became exclusively male and his hand, which had performed the creative act, became his consort. . . . This hand-goddess was called Iusas—'she comes and is mighty'. . . ."[209] Although Jung says the hand "actually has a phallic meaning, . . ."[210] here in Egyptian mythology the hand becomes the Goddess and takes on the character of the anima.

Associated with the masturbation account for Shu and Tefnut is another myth that has them "spat forth from the Creator's mouth."[211]

---

206 Eliade, *Sacred and the Profane*, 95.

207 Clark, *Myth and Symbol in Ancient Egypt*, 42.

208 Ibid.

209 Ibid., 43.

210 Jung, *Collected Works 5*, 185.

211 Clark, *Myth and Symbol in Ancient Egypt*, 43.

Utterance 600 of the Pyramid Texts says: "You spat forth as Shu, you expectorated as Tefnut, you put your arms around them in an act of Ka-giving, so that you *ka* divine spirit might be in them."[212] According to Clark,

> The masturbation tale belongs to a primitive naturalistic view of the world which can only account for creation in terms of physical generation, whereas the spitting motif expresses creation through the Divine Word or entry of the breath of life. . . . The masturbation motif stresses the reproductive aspect of life but behind it lies the mystery of life itself, the breath of the Divine Soul [the creative spirit]. Hence the generation of Shu and Tefnut has to be described in terms of both the masturbation and the spitting myths—they are, in fact, complementary, not alternative. . . . The Coffin text . . . is quite definite on this point.[213]

Shu speaking to Atum-Re says, "This was the manner of your engendering: You conceived with your mouth and you gave birth from your hand in the pleasure of emission. . ."[214]

The mythology and archetypal sources of masturbation suggest that masturbation is, as stated earlier, a creation motif of the psyche's desire and ability to create itself out of itself. It is the desire of undifferentiated energy, original oneness. As such, for example, the son only knows himself as oneness with his mother, to create itself out of itself, to separate itself from itself as in the son's desire to separate himself from the mother. While this mother can certainly be the personal mother,

212 Ibid.

213 Ibid., 44.

214 Coffin Texts, III, 334j quoted in Clark, *Myth and Symbol in Ancient Egypt*, 44.

this mother can also refer to the unconscious in which the man's ego may be identified in some way. Masturbation can be understood as the psyche's unconscious and natural desire (instinct) to separate itself from itself, create itself out of itself. Masturbation expresses the psyche's desire to become conscious of itself as differentiated masculine and feminine energies or ego and other energies.

The serpent exclaims in the Coffin Texts: ". . . He the Indwelling Soul it was who made the universe in that he copulated with his fist and took pleasure of emission. . . ."[215] The desire to create, to give birth to that which exists in the mind or in the Divine spirit—the unconscious—that is, the soul, lies behind the masturbation experience.

In this way, masturbation can then be understood as the desire of undifferentiated energy, the original Oneness (i.e., the ego's oneness with mother—personal, archetypal or otherwise— that is, the unconscious) to create itself out of that containment. Compare this with "Atum was creative in that he proceeded to masturbate with himself . . . and thereby were born brother and sister—Shu and Tefnut."[216] That is, by the act of masturbation he brought forth the opposites—the duality, the beginning of consciousness. Thus, masturbation might symbolize the ego's unconscious desire to come into a creative relationship with the soul as a response to its desire to separate him from that which he is identified with. That is, the soul attracts his energy toward the penis in an attempt to integrate his unconscious masculine energy, to come into a relationship with Phallos, the Divine Masculine.

According to Greek mythology, Hermes was said to have invented the ritual of masturbation. According to Greek thought, masturbation was considered a ritual of self-love. Hermes' caduceus was called a masturbatory symbol massaged by the serpent that embraced it. As an

215 Ibid., 51.

216 Ibid, 42

act of self-contemplation, the hermit's masturbation would lead to the comprehension of the God just as intercourse led to the comprehension of the Goddess.[217]

The ancient gods and goddesses of mythology can be understood as archetypal images, that is, concrete forms in which the primitive mind conceived certain qualities, states, and affections to exist and operate.[218] They are symbolic of the various expressions of psychic energy. Hermes, as "one of the Aegean Great Mother's primal serpent-consorts, . . . [and] the original 'hermaphrodite' united in one body with Aphrodite,"[219] is a symbol of undifferentiated psyche energy—energy that expresses itself as both masculine and feminine. One of the main reasons for this, according to Jung, is that the female lies hidden in the male just as the male lies hidden in the female.[220] Thus Hermes' bisexuality. Hermes' masturbation is a striving for differentiation leading to the comprehension of the masculine (god) as a separate being from the feminine (goddess). The word *comprehend* comes from the Latin words *comprehendere,* to "seize, lay hold of, comprehend"; and, *com-*, "with" and *prehendere*, or *prendere*, "to catch hold of, seize, and means to grasp, to give meaning to, to understand fully, to contain, include, enclose, and embody." Therefore, as Hillman also suggested, masturbation is the archetypal act of introversion and self-contemplation where the ego turns inward in its need to comprehend, that is, grasp (literally the penis), include, and embody the unconscious and unrelated masculinity embodied in the Self/soul, represented by the phallus.[221]

---

217 Walker, *Woman's Encyclopedia of Myths and Secrets*, 397.

218 Onians, *Origens of European Thought*, 359.

219 Walker, *Women's Encyclopedia of Myths and Secrets*, 395.

220 Jung, *Collected Works 5,* 221.

221 Hillman, Loose Ends, 118–121.

If the ancient belief that a man's "manliness" and "holiness" (the "real-self") dwelt in his genitals because that was the point of contact with the Goddess-queen expresses an archetypal and psychic reality, then masturbation is an attempt to contact the Goddess (i.e., mother, unconscious) in an effort to find (grasp) and affirm the unconscious masculine qualities that remain in her grip—a manifestation of the Hermes myth. Masturbation is a sacred act in that it repeats the primordial event—the creation of the masculine out of the feminine, the original act of differentiation and separation of the masculine and the feminine, the establishment of the masculine as a separate entity. For the male masturbation can be understood as an initiatory act into the experience of self-hood, an initiation into the experience of the other (inner) man that carries the unconscious and unrelated masculinity that gets projected onto the penis as Phallos.

Traditionally, psychology has attempted to explain the cause of homosexuality as resulting from an overprotective mother and an absent father. Modern brain research has started to show that sexual orientation and what we are attracted to sexually is a far more complicated matter. While certain aspects of homosexuality may be a man's attempt to separate from over- identification with the personal mother or his own feminine nature, it may also be the rising up of archetypal masculine in its desire for a new male form, *a new masculine consciousness*. For example, I would argue that when a man or a society has become too one-sided and out of balance in its identification with a solar, patriarchal masculine consciousness, the chthonic, Earth Masculine will rise up to bring balance. The task will be to make this new masculine image conscious and not just live it out in sexual relationships. Rather, we must understand that this is a masculine that lives in unity with the earth, in unity with the Goddess, with the feminine forces as her consort and companion, living *with* her, not *over* her.

In masturbation, the penis becomes the symbol for the split-off masculinity embodied in the Self that longs to be "grasped" and attached to and embodied in the ego in its service to the masculine individual "real-self." This is precisely why masturbation has been viewed so unfavorably by society in general and especially by certain social institutions, (e.g., the church, marriage). Masturbation is an act against the collective values of the social order, discipline of, and service to the group, marriage, and procreation of the species that these institutions symbolize. It is an act in support of the individual whose purposes may appear to be in opposition to the purposes of the group.[222] Thus, masturbation is anti-collective consciousness and pro-individual consciousness. The individual contains both poles within himself/herself so that the conflict is an inner conflict between the needs and purposes of individual and collective values. For example, seeking sexual relief or sexual pleasure through masturbation may be at the expense or rejection of the feminine or collective procreative needs of the individual. Excessive masturbation might lead to a habit so pervasive that it could prevent the individual from being able to reconcile his own masculine-feminine relationship thereby making it impossible to commit to the feminine in a way that is beneficial to her. John Moore in his book, *Sexuality and Spirituality,* asserts that exploitation of the feminine by the masculine through self-indulgent pleasure-seeking at the expense of oneself and of another and the rejection of the feminine by the masculine through fear of emasculation, castration or impotence are related to the drive to kill and destroy.[223]

I suggest that the negative and destructive aspects of masturbation result only if the "real-self," acquired through the integration of the unconscious, and unrelated masculinity as symbolized by

222 Moore, *Sexuality and Spirituality*, 47.

223 Ibid., 61.

the masturbation experience, is not integrated into the relationship with the feminine in some creative form or expression meaningful to her. Therefore, on the personal level the need for and the purpose of masturbation can only be understood in light of the mythical material that is hidden in the fantasy that is constellated in the masturbatory experience.

Hillman says the secret feelings and fantasies present in masturbation present patterns of our individuation and suggests that the inhibition inherent in the masturbatory act actually contributes to this process by fostering intrapsychic tension that prolongs the circulation or rotation of the psychic energy.[224] This constellates the unconscious material in the forms of images (the gods and goddesses) and allows the ego to come into contact with these inner figures through the fantasy—a kind of active imagination. Masturbation, says Hillman, is "an attempt at active imagination at its most fundamental level."[225]

These inner figures are symbols of the split-off parts of the individual that remain in the unconscious as unlived psychic life that longs to be related to the ego and integrated into consciousness and experienced. They symbolize the energy at work in the psychic development of the individual and suggest the direction that individuation must take. All of this must happen if the individual is to continue toward wholeness and if the psyche is to reach its goal of self-realization.

To understand the symbolic meanings of these images is to reveal the myth (the mystery) that is attempting to live through the masturbatory act. This, in turn, indicates what is actually happening in the unconscious, that is, the myth hidden in the fantasy tells what the unconscious purpose is in the masturbation experience. To begin to

224 Hillman *Loose Ends*, 120–121.

225 Ibid., 223

reveal the mystery of masturbation is to recognize that the outer act is symbolic of patterns of energy at work within the individual.

For example, a heterosexual fantasy might indicate the need for further development in the area of the relationship with the feminine through integration of unconscious and unrelated qualities of a feminine nature such as a particular attitude toward the feminine (inner or outer) that is part of the soul's longing. In the case of the male homosexual and his homosexual fantasy where the energy of the fantasy has as its goal a man, the male body, or the male organ, masturbation is the psyche's unconscious and natural desire (instinct) to constellate, affirm, and grasp ("take hold of") the split-off and therefore unconscious and unrelated masculinity embodied in the Self, represented by the penis, and to attach it to the ego by way of the hand. Here masturbation has a healing and integrative purpose as illustrated in the following dream of mine.

> *I have a disease of the penis. It is athlete's foot or something similar. I am in what seems like a military unit. I am to receive a shot every day into my penis, which will cure the disease. I have to go every day to the doctor and have him give me the shot. I think he will really get used to seeing my penis and make some joke about him saying things like, "Well, get him out," or "Drop your pants and let's see him today." I know that I will get used to this and used to the shots and that they won't hurt. A teenage boy suggests that I wrap a strip of cloth around my penis with the syringe against the penis and the needle stuck into the penis and then every day give myself the shot. The idea is that through the movement of the penis I'd inject myself with the shot that would cure the disease.* (Journal, 8-25-83*)*

At the time of this dream I was in midlife. Throughout my life my need to masturbate had been met with periods of exemplary efforts at self-discipline in order to deal with the guilt and negative feelings toward masturbation that had resulted from religious training concerning sex and the conflict that it caused in my marriage. Both of these mental constructs were in conflict with my deeper intuitive feeling that masturbation was not only "okay" but a healthy, meaningful, and necessary expression of my sexuality. Again, my homosexual needs and fantasies suggested the soul's need to establish a different masculinity, one more congruent with my own soul as an individual separate from my identification with the feminine, the mother, and the masculine image and the collective institution and values, i.e., the parsonage, in which I was raised. The disease on the penis represented my uneasiness with my own authentic masculinity—my own soul's truth—a truth that was in conflict with my ego-consciousness at the time. To masturbate resulted in guilt, hurt, and pain in my relationship with my wife. However, submitting to her demands that I not masturbate only forced me further into identifying with the group or collective values from which the unconscious was trying to free me.

I had not yet developed sufficient masculine ego strength to risk embracing freely my own masculinity—the masculine spirit in nature, in my own nature—symbolized by my masturbation. The dream suggested that regular and ritual masturbation was the "shot" referenced in the dream. It was the integration that was needed to remedy this uneasiness, this dis-ease that I felt toward my own developing masculinity in my struggle to establish and accept my own spiritual masculine soul-self. An adolescent male telling me how to give myself the shot suggested a return to some unresolved or uncompleted masculine development from my adolescent years.

The dream relayed that I would "get used to the shots and that they won't hurt." This suggested that eventually I would become comfortable with my individual masculinity and my relationship with my soul. This followed the hypothesis that in certain cases and aspects of homosexuality the feminine (anima)—that urge for creation and life—"goes off with the unconscious man" and seeks a homosexual relationship onto which the man projects his unconscious and unrelated masculinity in an attempt to bring it into consciousness. However, I suggest it is also the anima who drives the man to masturbation in her desire to connect his ego to the deeper and unrelated masculinity of the soul from which he is cut off in her desire to develop a dominant masculinity. This dominant masculinity can then relate and support her needs instead of the mother's needs, or the old masculine needs, or the collective's needs and demands. However, if we understand that the bull and the Green Man as they appeared in my dreams and paintings represent the masculine spirit that is in nature, that fertilizing agent that, like the feminine, works toward life and creation, then it may well be that it is this unconscious masculine itself, this other that drives the man to masturbate in its desire to be embraced an integrated into a man's living experience.

The task is to become aware of just what this masculine energy is in the life of the man. Then we find the unconscious and spiritual purpose of the masturbatory act. What is it that longs to become conscious in this symbolic act of creation? For to only act this urge out in compulsory masturbation interferes with the task at hand, the task of bringing into consciousness that which lies buried in the soul. In my own life I would notice that whenever I felt exhausted, overwhelmed, fragmented and "out of touch" with myself, or unable to respond to life from my own truth out of fear or doubt, or whenever I found myself caught in feelings of guilt, shame, or feeling inadequate and wrong, I would often have same-sex dreams or find myself caught in same-sex fantasies. This would also happen if I had too much exposure to the feminine—whether inner or outer. Other ways that I responded to these states would entail my going in search of a man in some men's restroom to have sex with in order reconnect to some archetypal masculine image living in my soul.

Phallos, the erect penis, is the symbol of archetypal masculinity.[226] When Phallos enters a situation, an apprehension of masculine divinity takes place that could not take place without it, for Phallos carries the masculine inner god-image.[227] Phallos or archetypal masculinity is that transcendent function of the masculine that stands outside consciousness, yet longs to be experienced in its raw archetypal power. Phallos points to a mysterious and unknown reality that cannot be apprehended in any other way, indicating that phallos functions archetypally, with its own energy.[228] Thus, as the late Jungian analyst and author Eugene Monick asserts, Phallos "is thus an appropriate metaphor for the unconscious itself, and specifically, *the masculine mode of the unconscious* [italics mine]."[229]

So, whether it's anal intercourse, oral sex, or masturbation, I see that behind these acts are the soul's longing to express itself, the soul's longing to live its life—whatever that may be for the man. I am the receptacle, the vessel as well as the egg, that the vessel holds. I am the place where this union of the masculine and feminine energies occurs. I am the place where the psychic fertilization happens. It happens in me. These external acts are just manifestations of the internal process. It is the urge to fertilize, validate, and bring into creation that unconscious

---

226 Monick, *Phallos*, 32.

227 Ibid., 13–20.

228 Ibid., 20.

229 Ibid., 17.

man, the soul of me that longs to live. It is the urge to create that which lives in the soul as my authentic and true self.

The task is to become conscious of this Other in me. Certainly one can enjoy these acts in sexual relations with another man but to miss the unconscious or spiritual meaning is to miss the intent of these energies and to avoid the task of discovery that these sexual desires and attractions demand. I suggest the task is the birth of a new consciousness. Just like on the biological level, where the function of sexual relationship is a child, an offspring, a continuation of the human race, the task of sex at the soul's level, removed from its biological function, is the birth of a new self, a new awareness, and the continuation of the evolution of human consciousness.

These energies are the masculine and feminine energies at play. While some may assert that behind homosexuality is an over identification with the mother or the feminine and the need to separate from such an identification, I also assert that behind these homosexual urges is the drive to separate from an over-identification with the father or the masculine that isn't congruent with the imprint or truth of a man's own soul. It is an attempt to unite the split between his current consciousness and one that longs to live.

Whether a man's fantasies and attractions are toward a woman, a man, or both, behind them all is the creative response of the masculine and feminine, spirit and soul, in their longings to create a new and evolving consciousness. If we are willing to wrestle with the conflicts that these attractions cause in our lives, if we are willing to seek the meaning of these desires, slowly the birth of a new consciousness emerges. In so doing, we come to a greater understanding of all the opposing forces operating in our inner and outer worlds. Physical phallus is simultaneously and paradoxically spiritual Phallos. Sexuality that incorporates lower physical phallus becomes a manifestation of the sacred and the divine. Higher, solar, spiritual Phallos and lower, chthonic, physical phallus are manifestation of a single reality—spirit in nature.[230]

The part of the soul that is potentially accessible to an individual's consciousness as "the absolute individual meaning of one's individual life"[231] is that part of the Self in its raw archetypal solar/chthonic masculine form. This is an originating force in the psyche that seeks its place in consciousness as the "ground" of the soul. As such, it is unique to each particular man. When we recognize that images are the mediating world between the physical and the spiritual, between the mind and the body, between spirit and matter, between the inner and the outer, we discover a pathway to the individual meaning of our individual lives. For me, what emerged was the archetype of Green Man and the "shaman-healer."

The birth of that discovery will reveal itself in the remaining chapters.

Notes and Exercises

Sex removed from its biological function serves the purposes of the soul. Images and behaviors are carriers of patterns of energy at work in the individual and reveal the symbolic meaning and spiritual intent of such desires, fantasies and attractions. To understand the meaning of the symbols that carry the energy in our sexual attractions and fantasies gives us insight into what we actually seek through our sexual behaviors and fantasies.

---

230 Ibid., 65.

231 Von Franz, *Way of the Dream*, 283.

Write out one of your primary erotic fantasies. Circle the characters in your fantasy. Are they male or female, human or animal? What is the main action? Vaginal intercourse? Anal intercourse? Oral sex? Whipping and spanking? Tender and loving? Aggressive and dominating? What role do you play? What role do the others play in your fantasy? Are they subduing or being subdued? What is the most erotic part of this fantasy? Is it a body part? Which body part? What about that body part turns you on? Is it the action that turns you on? What turns you on the most?

All the characters in your fantasy are parts of you, energy in you that have taken these forms to get a message to you. What parts do they represent? What wants to be validated? What wants to be worshipped? What part wants to worship you? What part wants to be penetrated? What wants to be created? What wants to be owned, embodied, lived? The partners, whether in actual sex or in fantasies, becomes the carrier of the soul images that longs for expression.

Using your associations to the images in your fantasy and the answers to the above questions, write out the inner symbolic or spiritual meaning of your fantasy.

CHAPTER NINE

Looking in the Mirror

My dreams continued to indicate that my same-sex desires and attractions were not only about having sex with a man. Rather they were about what wanted to come into consciousness in me through the creative union of these energies in my soul that I projected onto and sought for in a man. I dream that

> *I tell someone that the Atman is the true self. It is necessary for some men to project this aspect, the Atman, onto and search for him in another man.* (Journal, 2-15-86)

Atman refers to the innermost essence of each individual, the supreme universal self. It is Sanskrit for breath and soul. According to Hindu philosophy, *Atman* refers to the non-material self that never changes, one's real self or essence. This again is "the treasure hard to find" that the earlier dream suggested stood behind my homosexuality and same-sex attractions. But what *was* my real self or essence? How *did* it wish to manifest? Who *was* this Atman? A symbol points to something unknown and mysterious and is often the precursor to a transformation.[232] Therefore the man that attracted me was a symbol

232 Jung, *Psychological Types*, 473–5.

that carried this projection. But what was the meaning? What was this essence that was projected onto this other man? What was it that wanted to come into consciousness?

As I meditated on this question, the word *coyote* suddenly came into my awareness. Why the word *coyote*? Coyote comes from *coyolle* and *coyotl*, which mean a "prairie wolf," and is related to the wolf. I recall the active imagination I did with the boy in the dream that I released from the parsonage that a later dream identified as my homosexual self. In that dream the boy also took the image of a green snake and a wolf all in one. (See the introduction.) In that work the green snake-wolf-boy identified himself as *instincts, drives, needs, my younger brother, my other self, my primitive self, the part of me that desires the masculine.*

The animal is also the symbolic carrier of the Self, one's true self and essence.[233] As such the animal becomes a symbol for the Atman. Coyote is a trickster figure, appearing at times as the Creator himself. At other times he is the messenger, the culture hero, and the fool with the ability of the transformer. In some stories he is a handsome young man. In others he is an animal. Yet others present him as just a power, a sacred one.[234] As a transformer, the coyote is a demiurge, a skilled workman and creator, a lunar animal, and the spirit of the night. As such he has a dual nature. On one hand he is a culture hero and imparts knowledge of arts and crafts and secures fire and sun. On the other he is a bullying, licentious, greedy, erotic, and fumbling dupe. The wolf is the companion of the coyote and his beloved brother. Could it be that the wolf in me sought his companion and brother, the coyote, in my same-sex attractions and desires? But what was this coyote-spirit that I sought?

---

233 Jung, *Collected Works 14*, par. 283.

234 Kazakova, *Encyclopedia Mythica*.

The trickster is the first rudimentary stage in the development of the hero myth in which the hero is instinctual, uninhibited, and often childish. The fundamental goal of initiation lies in taming the original trickster-like wildness of the juvenile nature. There are three kinds of initiation. First, there is the arousal and violence of a Dionysian Thunder Act such as a violent uprising of the unconscious. This one might be experienced with a serious illness. A second initiation is a submission to a religion, and a third initiation involves not integrating oneself with any religious doctrine or secular group consciousness, but rather liberating oneself from any state that is too rigid, too fixed, or too final. This third way is marked by a transcendence of any confining existing patterns, and a segue to a more expanded and mature stage of development, resulting in a union of conscious with the unconscious and the realization of the transcendent function by which man achieves his fullest potential and the Self.[235] It appears that the third way is the way of my initiation—to choose one's destiny or purpose. The symbols of transcendence, of which the phallus is one, are the symbols that represent man's striving to attain this goal. These provide the way for the unconscious to enter consciousness.

The symbols are manifold but at the most archaic levels of this symbolism is the trickster figure. But now he is no longer the lawless would-be hero, but the shaman, the medicine man, a primitive master of initiation.[236] The coyote is the shamanic spirit whose magical practices and flight of initiation symbolized by his antics stamp him as a primate master of initiation. Here I also connect the swan maiden of my work on *Swan Lake*. A swan maiden is also known as the shaman's spirit wife—intuition working through a medium—an individual who is capable of obtaining knowledge of distant events of either the future

---

235 Jung and Von Franz, eds., *Man and His Symbols*, 146.
236 Ibid., 147.

or the past. This confirms my initial hunch that the coyote was the shaman. He was my shamanic spirit, the shaman in me.

The trickster is not only sexual but also the messenger, a god of the crossroads, and finally, the leader of souls to and from the Underworld. His phallus therefore penetrates from the known into the unknown, seeking spiritual messages of deliverance and healing. The shaman's spirit first entered my consciousness in the form of the coyote as I reflected on the meaning of the Atman—my true self and essence—that I project onto a man in my sexual desire for him. Could it be that my homosexuality on the spiritual level was my desire to seek this spirit in me, to penetrate the unknown, the unconscious, seeking messages of deliverance and healing? But how could I bring this unconscious Other into consciousness? How could I embody this other man rather than seek him in the body of another?

Three nights later I dream that

> *I am at my analytical session. The analyst asks me how I would change a seed. I think this is a trick question and that the analyst really knows you can't change a seed, so I say in a kind of smartass way, "How do I know you can change a seed?"*
>
> *He says, "If you could, how would you do it?"*
>
> *I still think that he is just trying to get me to attempt something that he knows is impossible, just to prove some point, and make me realize that you can't change a seed. So I say, "You can't change a seed."*
>
> *He says, "Let me give you one other bit of information." He says, "You can change a seed."*
>
> *My attitude changes. I am very grateful and humbled, and I thank him for giving me this bit of information. I say*

> *with the information that it can actually be done, I will tell you how I would do it. I say, "First, I would cross a seed with another seed. The result of these two seeds would be a seed slightly different from the other two. I would then cross this seed with another completely different seed and continue this process. Eventually the seed that I have would be completely different from the original seed."*
>
> *He says, "That is exactly right." I now realize that he was asking me difficult questions in order to break into me. He felt that I had come far enough in my analysis that he could confront my shadow and/or my ego-held views and expose some unconscious part of me. He was confronting a part of me that he knew I was but that I didn't yet know because he knew that it was time that I realized this part. He felt that I was strong enough to face it.* (Journal, 2-18-86)

This dream is about the potential for change and the psyche's capacity to change. A seed is a potential, something not yet manifest. To cross-fertilize one seed with another suggests a process of integrating the fertilizing agent from one seed into the other. By integrating (cross-fertilizing) various seeds or contents from the unconscious, we create a new seed, a new way of being, and a new consciousness.

I dream

> *I am with a woman. We are standing on some rocks overlooking the sea. Out from a cave under the rocks that we are standing on comes a canoe with a man in it. He is rather strange looking in that his nose, mouth, and chin area is elongated like a prehistoric or primitive man. The woman and he try to communicate.* (Journal, 2-28-86)

I decide to dialog with this man.

Sheldon: Hello, sir. Where do you come from?

Man: I come from the deep center of your being, far in the center of the earth.

Sheldon: Who are you?

Man: I am your primitive man. I am the unconscious man. Do not be afraid of me. I will not hurt you. In many ways I am more civilized that you or your culture. For I respect all life and nature. It would never occur to me to do some of the things your people do. I am gentle with life. I respect all life and I am a friend to all animals. I am one with nature. I can even walk in great storms and not be hurt, for the storms respect me. I am one with them. I am the friend to the great wild animals. They would not hurt me because I respect them and love them. We are one family. I know your ways. I will not hurt the lady. I will care for her. Do not be afraid of me. I want to be your friend. I know the ways of the great sea, and of the forests, the caves, and the mountains. I am Neanderthal man or like the ape-man but more human, not an ape. I am your primitive or instinctive man, your primitive masculinity, your primitive wisdom. I know things you don't know. I am your primitive and natural masculinity.

Sheldon: And I too want to be your friend.

Man: I want the lady.

I *then see him carrying the lady off. The feeling is one of great tenderness, protection, and inquisitiveness. I get the feeling that I am to be the observer of this relationship. It definitely isn't me that he wants. It is the lady. It is like he has come for the purpose of finding her.*

> *They go off in the boat. I remember the last seen of* Swan Lake *where Siegfried and Odette go off in the canoe made from a tree. As I watch the man and the lady disembark and walk off into the woods. I know that he has found a most precious thing, what he has been searching for all his life. He is very loving, very gentle, and protective of her. He is her protector. She is new to him. He doesn't know her ways, but he has a sense of reverence for her, of great strength. He will care for her, protect her, provide food for her, and she will instruct him in her ways—ways he knows nothing about. She will teach him all that she knows, and he will protect her from all the dangers of the jungle because he knows the ways of the jungle and of the sea. I know that he has found a part of himself that he lost a long time ago.* (Journal, 2-28-86)

I have discovered the primitive man in me, this Other masculine in me. However, it isn't me he wants, but the feminine. They each have a wisdom the other knows nothing of. However, they will teach each other. I am to be an observer of this. Each dream is a seed. By integrating these seeds from the unconscious, I am making a new seed as the earlier dream suggested. At this point in my journey the inner relationship with my same-sex images begins to change.

I dream

> *I am with Roger. We embrace and kiss. We become sexually aroused. I want us to climax in our pants like I used to do with Sam. But Roger doesn't want to because it will be too messy. He would rather take our penises out and masturbate them but first he goes home to get a towel to wrap his penis in to catch the semen.*

> *While he is gone to get this towel, I have a complete change of heart. I decide I don't want to climax because I know Roger doesn't really want to. I go find Roger and tell him. Roger and I work together and have a good relationship, an intimate working relationship because of intimate knowledge we know about each other from the experience of embracing, kissing, and him knowing that I wanted to climax in our pants.* (Journal, 4-27-86)

At the time of this dream, Roger was the music director at the church where I attended. He had been asked to leave that position because he wasn't doing the job the church wanted, and I had been asked by the church to take his job. Roger was in fact a very talented and creative musician and therefore could represent my own inner creative masculine energy as well as my former life as the church music director. The dream showed the current situation—the invitation to take the job as church music director symbolized by my embracing Roger—as a same-sex encounter.

Sexual desire can symbolize the arousal and movement of libido as creative psychic energy. To climax represents the desire to release that energy, to express it somehow, the urge to fulfill or complete the desire by discharging it. It symbolizes the movement toward the completion of a desire or goal. In this dream I did not fulfill this desire. I did not release this energy by climaxing because the Roger in me really didn't want to, although he was willing if he could wrap his penis in something so it wouldn't be so messy. The dream showed that by honoring the Roger in me, by containing the energy and not climaxing, we were able to work together and have a good relationship. An intimate relationship developed between these two parts of me, and according to the dream, this intimate relationship developed because of consciousness, that is, what we knew about each other.

While I could certainly apply this dream to the decision not to take the church music position (symbolized by the fact that Roger—my old and former life of church music director—and I didn't climax together in the dream), this dream also shed light on my homosexuality and same-sex desires in general and the direction they were to take. Although, according to my knowledge, Roger was a heterosexual male, the dream also suggested that I was making a choice not to return to the former life of same-sex encounters or a same-sex relationship. This was represented by my reference that associated this sexual encounter with Roger with my former same-sex relationship with Sam. It would just be too messy. And while the dreams showed that part of me was trying to find a way to have such a relationship that wouldn't be messy, I knew that part didn't really want such a relationship. In honoring that part, I choose not to have such a sexual encounter.

I have shown elsewhere that the penis is a symbol of Phallos, that sacred Other in man, which exists as a divine, powerful, creative life-force in the depths of his soul. This life-force longs to be embraced, experienced, and lived. Heinz Westman in his book *Structure of Biblical Myths: The Ontogenesis of the Psyche* suggests that the penis is a symbol for continual birth and renewal.[237] This desire is aroused in another dream that I had some two months earlier. I dream

> *I am with a man. We are around his apartment house. We go onto the porch and are standing at the door. It is dark and shadowy. I kiss him. We embrace and kiss passionately. I become very sexually aroused and erected. I am about to*

237 Westman, *Structure of Biblical Myths*, 321.

climax when I remember that I told my wife that when my sexual desires returned that she would be the first to know. I think if I climax, then I will have given it somewhere else first and that will hurt her. I walk home. Upon arriving home there is another couple there that we have invited for dinner. (Journal, 2-14-86)

In both of these dreams I become sexually aroused by embracing and kissing the other man. In both dreams I want to climax, and fulfill and complete the goal of self-gratification, but I don't. In this dream it is because I had promised my wife that she would be the first to know if my sexual desire for a man returned. In the previous dream it was because I knew that Roger, while willing to climax in his pants if he could not make a mess, really didn't want to. It was in honoring these others in me that shifted my intent. These dreams mirrored a change happening at the unconscious level, a change in my inner masculine and feminine relationship. From my journal:

On the day of the "Roger dream" I attended a lecture on homosexuality. The presenter, a social scientist who worked with the Kinsey Institute, stated that from their research (1) family has nothing to do with making a homosexual, that there are no differences in the family life of the heterosexual or the homosexual, (2) peer pressure has nothing to do with making a homosexual, (3) recruitment or the homosexual subculture does not make homosexuals, and (4) there is no homosexual phase, but that the evidence is conclusive that homosexuality is the result of a biological-hormonal situation.

If homosexuality is completely biological, the result of prenatal hormonal influences that affect the emotional patterns of the individual then the dream where my analyst tells me that I am not getting at the truth of my dreams—that I am emotionally a homosexual would mean that I am biologically a homosexual or at least biologically programmed a homosexual. Does this also mean that all sexual attraction including bisexuality is the result of a biological-hormonal situation? So what can I do? Can I never experience the emotional completeness without the male lover? Is there anything in my dreams to indicate that the unconscious is demanding that I be who and what I am—a homosexual and live as one? What about the dream that refers to homosexuality as the "treasure hard to find?" But what is "the treasure hard to find?" The esoteric traditions say the God within. Analytical psychology would say the Self, that individually determined authentic self that is uniquely me.

I don't want to divorce my wife. I don't want to break up our family and cause whatever trauma that might do to our children. Yet, I want to feel again what it feels like to be with a man.

In the second dream above I don't complete the homosexual act because of my promise to my wife. Instead I return home where there are now four people—two men and two women. Since the number four often symbolizes wholeness, does this suggest that my wholeness is with the feminine rather than going off with the masculine? In the other dream the male image, although willing if he can avoid the mess in his pants, doesn't really want to have this same-sex encounter. This dream suggests that to let my energies go in the direction of a same-sex relationship would make a mess. Since the mess is in my pants, I am the one that will be "messed." This also suggests that the climax, the release of this energy, while feeling good and accomplishing some form of self-gratification is really wasted, not directed in some meaningful and fulfilling way but simply creates a mess.

What can I do symbolically that would be the same as a homosexual affair, a same-sex lover relationship? Since the homosexuality urge can be symbolic of searching for the lost parts of oneself and bringing to consciousness the inner man or the yet unknown self, doing something would offer the opportunity for personal growth and the development and fulfillment of other parts of me that long to be realized. I'm afraid that the unconscious is demanding that I become who I really am and embrace that. Is that the only way to realize the Self? Must it be constellated in the Other and experienced in a sexual relationship?

Anthony Stevens in his book Archetypes *says relationship and sex are the two requirements for individuation.*[238] *Since I have the homosexual need, does that mean I can't individuate and experience the Self that a male lover would constellate and bring to life? Stevens goes on to say that in "homosexual love, the partner, as carrier of the Self, . . . through the highly charged medium of the relationship, unconsciously assists his lover to bring similar potential to birth in himself. This is the very essence of the individuation relationship. For individuation to occur, marriage and*

238 Sevens, *Archetypes*, 198–199.

> *reproduction are not essential, but relationship and sexuality are."*[239]
>
> *Continuing, Stevens says that people have a choice between "inner" and "outer" individuation, that psychic functions are more important. According to Stevens, ultimately it matters little whether conscious expression is also acted out in behavior. Consciousness is the key.*[240] (Journal, 4-27-86)

These two dreams, as well as others, continued to suggest that my individuation was an "inner" one. My homosexual and same-sex energies were not to go into outer same-sex relationships but were to be contained and directed otherwise. Stevens says that psychic functions are most important. The psyche functions in symbols. So whatever becomes a symbol for the part of the Self that is projected onto a man in the homosexual relationship can bring about the birth of this Other just as effectively as the actual man in the same-sex relationship. Following the voice of the dreams, this Other in me becomes the path to the Self, to this Other in me—the Atman and the continuing birth and rebirth of this phallic energy.

Two months later I dream

> *Rob Lowe is speaking at a spiritual conference. He tells about his life. He tells that he first married a woman. Then he divorced this woman and married a man. At first I don't think he is referring to a homosexual relationship but then he says something that lets me know this marriage was a sexual relationship. He then says that he divorced this man*

239 Ibid.

240 Ibid., 199.

> *and married another woman. He says that also during this time he was into drugs and alcohol. But through some kind of a spiritual rebirth all this changed, and he is now sharing his story.* (Journal, 6-28-86)

The same night that I had this dream my wife dreams that

> *We are married but decide to get divorced. This is because I want to find out if I can find fulfillment in another life-style—in homosexuality and with a man. My wife decides that she can let me to this. So we divorce and go our separate ways. During this time, I realize that my fulfillment wasn't in another man and my wife realizes that she doesn't need me to be fulfilled. So we come back together and tell each other this. We decide to get remarried. After this our relationship is different, no jealously.* (Journal, 6-28-86)

Both dreams indicated a shift between the masculine and feminine energies in me and suggested that the individuation process and psychological and spiritual development occurred in the further differentiation of the masculine and feminine energies. Both dreams mirrored the original union of the masculine and feminine. Both dreams went on to mirror the separation of the masculine and feminine where both go off to find the Other. The masculine went off to strengthen itself with a male relationship and the feminine went off to allow this.

In this process both found out that they were complete within themselves. The masculine didn't need the homosexual relationship for fulfillment and the feminine was complete without the masculine that she had been married to. The two energies then came back and remarried with this new awareness, and the relationship between them, between the masculine and the feminine energies, was changed. It was no longer a jealous relationship.

Jealousy is an unhappy or angry feeling caused by the belief that someone you love likes or is liked by someone else. These dreams indicated that happiness and fulfillment were not found in some external Other but reside within us—not only within each of us individually but that the answer to the relationship lies inside our relationship! From my journal:

> *The man with same-sex desires and attractions must have an affair with himself through his relationship with the images arising from the unconscious. In the process he will find and bring to consciousness this other self that is all too often seen only in projected form. Projection is a natural and therefore instinctive response of the unconscious to constellate the unconscious material with the purpose of mirroring back to the ego the unconscious side of his personality. Homosexuality is a spiritual phenomenon whose goal is the Self, the Atman, the creative genius or creative spirit of a yet unknown consciousness, this other man is in me.*
>
> *He is me. He possesses qualities, states and ways of being and feeling that are in me. It is my desire to touch him, embrace him, kiss him, love him, hold him, cherish him, and ultimately know him and enter into relationship with him, which manifests itself as the desire behind my homosexual urge. His eyes are kind and gentle, full of love and understanding, and yet somehow almost amusingly wicked for he knows the vilest in me and yet he loves me still.*
>
> *In my active imagination I hold a conversation with my other self by looking at my own image in the mirror. It was the most synthesizing experience I have ever had. I now see the two of me, both images of myself that are uniting. It is no*

longer the other man out there who has carried the image of this other self, but he is me that looks back at me in the mirror. I now feel myself carrying this self with me. The two of us are walking together—two separate aspects, yet both are me. I feel a new sense of unity in myself. He is my homosexual lover, my homosexual brother, and he is me. (Journal, 1985)

It would be years later, during my training in shamanic healing, before I would understand the significance of this mirror exercise or who it was that was looking back at me in the mirror, who it was that I was embracing, and who was embracing me.

Moving ahead twenty-six years, I dream that

Hundreds of people showed up at my office seeking energy healing. A voice in the dream tells me that I am not to work with them until I have completed the "mirror exercise" because I am not sufficiently protected. (Journal, 2011)

In 2013 I continued my training in shamanic healing by taking the course "Walking with Protection." On the third day of this training the leaders announced that we were going to do a "mirror exercise." I immediately remembered my dream and felt an energetic response in my body. As the process goes, a candle is placed in front of a smoked mirror. We were to stare at our image in the mirror and just notice what occurred. There were four mirrors.

In the first mirror we were to simply acknowledge the realm of spirit, the unconscious, and the archetype of the smoking mirrors. In the second and third mirrors we were to look in and notice what we saw. At the fourth mirror we were to thank the spirit and the archetype of the smoking mirrors.

The first two times I did this, nothing much happened. On the third time we were to ask a question as we peered into the mirror at our reflection. Since I had had this dream about the "mirror exercise" I asked the question "What is it that I need to see or know that is related to the dream?" Suddenly it was like a portal opened and I saw into a realm that went on forever, like there was no end. I saw behind me throngs of people, long lines of them; they looked like medicine men and women. They said, "We have your back."

I went to the next mirror and looked in. I saw myself and then slowly, the image began to change, going through several shapes until finally stopping at the image of an old and ancient man. The only way I can describe him is by the terms *Earth Man* or *Earth Masculine.* He simply smiled a "knowing" smile and slightly nodded in an affirming, validating way.

That night I dream

> *I walk into a building with three or four floors. The building is full of people. I realize that they are souls needing to be set free. As I walk through each floor they begin to file out of the building, being set free. I am now outside the building and the last of them has come out. It is like they simply go off into space. I now notice a woman standing beside me. She starts to walk back into the building and I ask, "Where are you going?" She says, "To tend to the children that they left behind."* (Journal, 5-15-13)

The connection of the mirror exercise that I did in 1985 with this experience in 2013 is another sign along the way that behind my homosexual urges was the desire of this other man, this other consciousness, this ancient earth-man from the past that first revealed himself as a bull chasing me in 1978 and then as a coyote in my work on the Atman dream in 1986. I am still coming to understand what it means to embody this other man.

Notes and Exercises

Relationship and sexuality are essential for individuation—becoming our authentic, individual self. People have a choice between inner and outer individuation. It matters little whether conscious expression is also acted out in behavior. Psychic functions are most important. Consciousness if the key.

> *Reflect on your sexual desires. Are you sexually attracted to women, to men or to both? How do you express your erotic longings? Do you express them within a committed relationship that is satisfying to both you and your partner Do you and your partner have conflicts over sex? What are the conflicts? Do you act out your erotic desires in destructive or addictive ways, such as compulsive masturbation, excessive use of pornography or in frequent and multiple affairs? Do you go on-line in search of cyber-sex to satisfy some longing?*

As adults we can express our sexuality however we want and with whomever we want. But when our sexuality becomes destructive, creating conflicts and pain, either externally with our partners or internally with other parts of ourselves, we need to explore what those conflicts are about. The more compulsive, impulsive, and addictive our sexual behaviors are, the more some unconscious Other is trying to get into consciousness.

The objects or persons onto whom we project our erotic longings can be understood as parts of ourselves that we long to embrace and give life to. They are our mirrors, mirroring back to us the unconscious and split off parts of ourselves that long to live, that long to be accepted and loved. To embrace these parts, we must have an affair with ourselves through the images arising in our dreams and fantasies as a way to bring into consciousness this other self that is all too often seen only in projected form.

> *Think of a sexual dream or fantasy. Notice the object of your desire. If this person is someone you know, ask the image to change to represent some part of you. Now imagine that you are looking at the part of you in a mirror. What do you see? What do you feel? What qualities does that image possess? Just let your imagination go. Feel your desire to touch him/her, to embrace him/her, to kiss him/her, to cherish him/her, to know him/her, to enter into a relationship with him/her. Notice his/her eyes. What do you notice? Are they kind and gentle, full of love and understanding? Or are they seductive, impish or amusingly wicked? Hold a conversation with this other. See if you can feel love for this Other. Can it feel love for you? Imagine that you can embrace this part of you and hold this part of you in acceptance and love. Imagine that this man/woman is no longer the Other that has carried this image of this Other, but is you looking back at you. Feel yourself carrying this self in you, walking together as one.*

CHAPTER TEN

Same-Sex Attractions and the Interplay of the Masculine and Feminine

I dream that

> *My wife and I are reading a book. We each have our own copy of the same book. A man tells us the Jung himself was confused on whether to call homosexuals, homosexuals, saying "One time Jung would refer to them as homosexuals and then after the next session with them he would refer to them as heterosexuals when he wrote in their records."*
>
> *This man takes a pencil and draws a circle around the paragraph in the books that we are reading where it states that Jung himself says that in his own writings. He circles it first in my wife's book and then in mine.* (Journal, 1-20-87)

For me, Jung symbolized the wise old man, a representative of wisdom and meaning that symbolized the preexisting knowledge living in the soul. This dream brought attention to my confusion about my own sexuality—sometimes I was a heterosexual and other times I was a homosexual. The fact that the man drew a circle around this passage in both my book and my wife's book emphasized the importance of this observation.

From the point of view of the unconscious there are two energy systems at work in me. At one time the heterosexual energy system was at work, and at another time the homosexual energy system was at work. Sometimes I was drawn to the feminine (the heterosexual) and at other times I was drawn to the masculine (the homosexual). I would call these archetypal (typical and universal) systems that operate within the psyche as expressions of how the masculine and feminine energies may interact. Dreams show things as they are at the unconscious, thus my confusion: Was I gay? Was I straight? Or was I both—bisexual? Or was I neither?

This is just one of the myriad ways the psyche functions. The soul expresses itself in images of the masculine and the feminine. In my own journey, the interplay of these two archetypal energies became critical in understanding the energy that expressed itself in my same-sex attractions. It was this inner relationship between the masculine and feminine energies that began to reveal to me the meaning and purpose of the longing behind this other man living in my soul.

Critical to this discussion is what I mean by masculine and feminine energies. While this next section may become laborious for some, I ask you to bear with me as I take you through my own journey of defining masculine and feminine. I will say at the onset of this discussion that by *masculine* and *feminine* I am not referring simply to men and women or to male and female but rather to a complex of energies that express themselves in certain patterns of thought, emotion, and behavior that appear in both men and women. I will then give examples of how these two archetypal energies played out in my own life and how my same-sex attractions played into this masculine-feminine relationship.

John Moore in his book *Sexuality and Spirituality* correlates the masculine and feminine with the right and left brain hemispheres respectively. Moore defines the feminine as the active, group, procreative purpose of the psyche that serves the survival of the group or species. It corresponds to the left-brain hemisphere and is directed toward procreation and physical survival. From this arises dispositions toward a legion of inclinations, preoccupations, and behavioral traits, for example, habit, tradition, conservatism, protection, defense, productivity, expansion, and longevity.[241]

According to Moore, "the feminine is centrifugal (moves from the center outwards) proliferates, expands, multiplies, works in terms of continuous movement in linear, passing, or historical time (being concerned with the past and future). The feminine is group—or family—identified . . . ."[242] According to Moore's definition, my loyalty and service to collective values, to my family and family values, to religion and religious values, or any institutional system and its values, would be an expression of and an identification with and service to the feminine.

On the other hand, Moore defines the masculine as individuality in both men and women and says that it corresponds to the right brain hemisphere. According to Moore, the masculine "tends toward the abstract, the ideal, the inner meaning, the metaphysical, the immanent and the visualized perfection."[243] According to Moore the masculine "is centripetal (withdrawing towar ds a center), penetrating and withdrawing pulsation . . . being only concerned with the immediate, the moment now. It is individual self-concerned and self-sacrificial.[244]

---

241 Moore, *Spirituality and Sexuality*, 15.

242 Ibid.

243 Ibid., 29–30.

244 Ibid., 30.

According to this definition, any interest or desire in me that would go against collective values and beliefs, go against family, religious, or institutional values for my own individual voice and personal needs, would be masculine.

The feminine, as defined by Moore, serves the sexual-socio-economic-procreative-collective purpose of life and is *centrifugal, moving from the center outward.* The masculine serves the spiritual concern of personal destiny and self-realization—the advancement of what Moore calls the "real-self;" it is *centripetal, withdrawing toward a center.*[245] Using Moore's definitions, the interplay between the masculine and feminine can be understood as the interplay between my personal and individual needs of my "real-self" and the demands and expectations of family and collective values.

I dream

> *I am walking on a sandy beach although I am not aware of an ocean. I am walking with Hilda, a man, and a small boy. We come to a high sand wall. I know that we have to get into some place by climbing this wall of sand. I attempt it but slide back down. It seems we all attempt it. Hilda is giving the instructions.*
>
> *Finally I get to the top and clear away sand, which reveals the tunnel area that we are trying to get to. I think that all I have to do is pull the wall down and we'll be in. However, instead, the wall caves in and forms a path on which we can walk. There is a lady inside showing us the way.* (Journal, 7-8-87)

245 Ibid.

At the time of this dream I was working on understanding the meanings of my attractions to same-sex anal sex, oral sex, and masturbation. According to Moore's definition, this activity itself is a masculine endeavor. On one hand these behaviors and my attraction and interest in them went against the primary collective values of the 1970s and certainly went against the family and religious values in which I was raised (Moore's feminine), on the other hand they served as an individual journey in search of their inner personal meaning (Moore's masculine).

On the day prior to this dream I had spent time at the library researching Jung's collected works on masturbation. As I was leaving the library and heading to my car, it dawned on me that I hadn't looked up any references to the hand—the auxiliary organ in masturbation. So I went back to the library. However, when I went to the shelf where Jung's works were stored, the shelf had been cleared.

As I was looking around in the nearby areas for the books, I "came upon" Anthony Stevens's book *Archetypes*. I was happy about this because I needed it to footnote my reference to Stevens's idea on initiation and homosexuality. As I browsed the book, I immediately came upon a quote that I had used in my writing at the time but whose source I hadn't been able to locate. I felt this to be a synchronicity. Given the circumstances under which I rediscovered this book, I decided to reread Stevens's book. As I did, I came across his definitions of the masculine and feminine. I noticed that in his definitions the movements of the masculine and feminine energies were the exact opposite of Moore's definitions.

Stevens says the masculine is essentially *centrifugal, outgoing, and extraverted.* According to him, the masculine is energetic, dynamic, and assertive and its realms are heaven and spirit. In its phallic, penetrating aspect it arouses, produces, and creates. In its aggressive form it combats and destroys. It is positive and impulsive, but also disciplined and ascetic.[246]

On the other hand, Stevens says it is the feminine that is *centripetal, in-turning, and introverted*, concerned with the realms of earth, nature, the womb, home, and family—giving form to the energy of the masculine and bringing life out of darkness.[247]

The discrepancy between how these two scholars described the movement of the masculine and feminine energies caused me to call into question my use of Moore's definitions in my own work on the masculine and feminine as it related to my own homosexual/heterosexual conflict. In fact, these opposing viewpoints felt like an obstacle to my moving forward, just as the dream had shown a large sand wall in the way of my journey. However, the dream also showed that in my climbing the wall, in my facing this seeming contradiction of the masculine and feminine expressions—and by extension the seeming contradiction between my homosexual and heterosexual selves—I not only discovered the destination for which I was searching, but the wall itself became the path on which I could walk.

In other words, that which seemed like an obstacle became a path forward. According to the dream, the feminine was showing me the way.

I considered this dream, the rediscovery of Anthony Stevens's book, and the context under which it all occurred, to be a synchronicity and a significant one. It was none other than the voice of the Self where the inner and the outer worlds came together in a meaningful way to further clarify and direct my work on the masculine and feminine and their interplay in my heterosexual-homosexual dance.

---

246 Stevens, *Archetypes*, 176.

247 Ibid., 208–209.

As already discussed, Jung calls the masculine and feminine "animus" and "anima" respectively.[248] The terms *anima* and *animus* as used in Jungian psychology are complex and represent what are often contradictory and paradoxical figures. I don't claim to understand all their proposed technical roles in psychoanalytic theory. Rather I will use the terms in a very general sense as the feminine and masculine energies in me and how their interplay seemed to play out in my same-sex attractions and my heterosexual and homosexual conflict.

Animus as an archetype represents an *instinctive drive* related to the masculine as a basic force of life. As the masculine it is related to active initiative, aggression, assertiveness, the search for meaning, creativity, and one's capacity for discrimination, separation, and judgment.[249] According to Jungian theory, ". . . the animus consists of a woman's unconscious capacity to focus on, evaluate, discern her reactions, her unconscious rationality, her power aspirations, her opinions, her argumentativeness, her aggression, her capacities to differentiate, her expectation of how one "ought to be" and "what one ought to do," as well as her potential for relationship to creative meaning, clarity, self-expression, and the spiritual contents of her life."[250]

This description of the animus would broadly encompass both Moore's and Stevens's definition of the masculine as tending toward the energetic, dynamic, assertive, aggressive, penetrating, creative, abstract, ideal, and metaphysical, self, concerned with spirituality, personal destiny, and self-realization. The difference is that Moore says this masculine energy is in-turning and introverted while Stevens says this energy is out-going and extraverted.

---

248 Whitmont, *Symbolic Quest*, 215.

249 Jung, *Aion*, 14–15.

250 Ulanov, *The Feminine in Jungian Psychology*, 41.

As the contra sexual element in a woman, the animus expresses qualities traditionally associated with a man and behaves in women as he would in a man.[251] These include the capacity "to penetrate, separate, take charge, initiate, create, stand firmly and over against, to articulate and express meaning."[252] According to Jungian theory, "the nuclear core of the animus archetype is represented by male images such as the laborer, judge, teacher, monk, Prince Charming, prophet, magician or rapist."[253] In mythology the animus is represented in tales having to do with the masculine such as the "conquering hero, the great king, or wise man, and is symbolized by male deities such as Zeus, Dionysus, Apollo, Pan or the Devil and the animals associated with male deities such as the bull, goat, dog or eagle."[254]

In my work I have met the judge, the teacher, the monk, the prophet, the magician, and the wise man, as well as the rapist in my own dreams. I have also met the animals associated with the animus—such as the bull, the goat/ram, and dog, suggesting that this masculine archetypal energy is not only a component of the woman but also of the man.

The anima archetype on the other hand represents the *instinctive drive* related to the feminine, as "drive elements which are related to life as life, as an unpremeditated, spontaneous, natural phenomenon, to the life of the instincts, the life of the flesh, the life of concreteness, of earth, or emotionality, directed toward people and things. It is a drive toward involvement, the instinctual connectedness to other people and the containing community or group."[255]

---

251 Monick, *Phallos*, 125.

252 Ulanov, *The Feminine in Jungian Psychology*, 42.

253 Ibid., 41.

254 Ibid.

255 Whitmont, *The Symbolic Quest*, 189.

Again, this description of the anima would broadly embrace both Moore's and Stevens's definition of the feminine as serving the natural and instinctual sexual-socio-economic-procreative purposes of collective survival. This difference is again in the direction this energy flows. Moore says the feminine energy is extraverted and moves out from the center while Stevens says the feminine energy is in-turning and introverted. The very fact that a series of synchronistic events brought this seeming conflict to my attention suggests that it must have some meaning for my own psychic life.

Was there and is there both an introverted-masculine/extraverted-feminine and an extraverted-masculine/introverted-feminine dynamic living in me? And if so, was that the source of my sexual conflict? Was it also possible to have other combinations operating in the unconscious? And if so, how did they influence one's sexual inclinations and attractions? Were these archetypal patterns that seek expression? Such a discussion is beyond the scope of this book except to say that how the masculine and feminine energies are formed and how they relate to each other in the unconscious may influence a man's relationship to these energies in the outer world. But let me return to the task at hand, to describe my own inner masculine and feminine story.

As an archetype, anima "consists of the man's unconscious urges, his moods, emotional aspirations, anxieties, fears, inflations and depressions, as well as his potential for emotion and relationship."[256] According to Jungian theory she personifies the contrasexual elements in a man, expressing the qualities of tenderness, sensitivity, deviousness, seduction, indefiniteness, feeling, receptivity, elusiveness, jealousy, and creative containing and yielding.[257] The nuclear core of the anima is represented by images from harlot, witch, martyr, sister, peasant,

---

256 Ibid.

257 Ulanov, *The Feminine in Jungian Psychology*, 38.

gypsy, beloved, muse, to saint, goddess, and spiritual guide. She is represented in mythology having to do with the feminine in all its forms, such as Mother Earth, love, or wisdom, and is symbolized by animals like the cow, dove, owl, and cat.[258]

Since archetypes are the foundation stones of the psychic structure[259] they cannot be confined to human gender—such as anima only in men and animus only in women. Rather, the pairing of anima and animus, these masculine and feminine archetypes, takes place inside each of us.[260] I once had a dream that simply said, "a man has an animus too." Not only does the relationship to father and brother shape the woman's connection to the realm of the masculine, but the relationship to father and other primary males also shapes a man's connection to the masculine.

While "actualization of the masculine occurs predominately through the father figure,"[261] behind the personal father stands the world of archetypal masculine. The objective, nonpersonal aspect of the animus complex is archetypal masculinity represented most succinctly as Phallos.[262] The personal aspect of the animus complex is the associational shell that is built around the archetypal core. This shell consists of those characteristics of the masculine activated by a man's experiences with the primary masculine figures during his developmental years. These figures include his father, grandfather, brothers, uncles, teachers, and coaches, among others. This associational shell becomes the image of how a man experiences the masculine and perceives himself to be and thus how he reacts in the world as a man.

---

258 Ibid., 37.

259 Jung, *Collected Works,* 9ii, par. 40.

260 Hillman, *Anima,* 175.

261 Ibid., 210.

262 Monick, *Phallos,* 124.

In my own experience I also came to recognize that it wasn't only the men in my life that influenced my masculine image, it was also the animus or masculine characteristics of my mother and grandmother and other primary women that influenced the development of the associational shell of my masculine image. These become part of the point of view standing behind the anima in the anima-animus relationship as they play out their stories.

The characteristics of archetypal masculine, Phallos, which do not become activated in a man's experience, accumulate in the unconscious, forming what Jung calls the shadow. These shadow elements may also become associated or attached to this anima-animus syzygy or inner masculine-feminine relationship. The masculine-feminine atmosphere in the parsonage, as reflected by my father and mother, influenced the associational shells of my own anima-animus relationship. (See the appendix for a description of my father and mother's personalities.)

Based on the personality of my father and the role he played in my life, the shell of my animus or the original orientation of my inner masculine image can be described as dogmatic; rigid; bound by rules of right and wrong; passive; having difficulty tolerating tension; avoids confrontation; is overly spiritualized; afraid of the anger and tears of women; slow to anger with difficulty expressing any negative emotions; sentimental; infantile; afraid of aggression; deprived sexually and sensually; overly sensitive to criticism; guilt ridden; doubtful; controlled by the opinions of others; afraid; uncertain; unable to express its needs without feeling guilty unless they are approved by God, the church, or mother, with a need to be right.

On the other hand, it is also supportive of the arts; gentle; caring; helpful; emotional; sentimental; self-sacrificing; a people pleaser; and takes loyalty, responsibility, and commitment seriously. Because of my father's obsession with spiritual things—church; God's will; spiritual laws; right and wrong according to God's views as expressed in the Bible; the archetypal core of my animus is the image of the spiritual guide/healer/wise man/teacher/prophet, all of which—according to the personally acquired shell—must renounce; sacrifice; and deny the sensual and the sexual, as well as the physical and earthy side, of my individual needs.

When an image in the nuclear core of the animus (Phallos) different from the image with which a man has identified through his associational shell, begins to rise from the depths of the unconscious and seek consciousness, an internal conflict and struggle ensues between the masculine image with which the ego has identified—the associational shell of the animus—and the image emerging from his soul. When one archetypal image of the masculine begins to lose its power and fall away, another one will rise to take its place. In my own journey I would discover that another expression of Phallos, who first entered my dreams as a bull, was rising into my consciousness to compensate for the one-sided masculine image of the parsonage.

Likewise, based on the personality of my mother and her influence, the original orientation of my inner feminine—or the shell of my anima—can be described as creative; artistic; musical; sensitive and moody; easily given to melancholy; insecure; has difficulty expressing feelings; is manipulative; easily overwhelmed; shy and introverted; self-righteous and judgmental; insecure; fearful and indecisive; perfectionistic; rigid and controlling; reliable; dependable and task-oriented, with a tendency to hide feelings and to serve and please others for the purpose of maintaining a certain image.

As with the animus, when other aspects in the core of the anima archetype begin to seek consciousness that are different from the inner feminine image that a man has internalized or with which he has identified, she will seek ways to connect him to that life through dreams, intuitions, compulsions, and desires—including sexual ones. For she, being the archetype of life itself, seeks to bring this new life into consciousness. For me these repressed or unknown aspects of the anima's life manifested as intuitions, hunches, moods, personal interests, and attractions, including sexual ones, appearing early on in my dreams as a witch-like disheveled young girl. Resolving this relationship between the bull and the witch became crucial in bringing to consciousness this other man living in my soul.

From my experience of the interplay of the masculine-feminine energies in the parsonage, my masculine energy—the animus—was overly identified with the feminine, falling under her spell, controlled by the fear of upsetting her, of disappointing her, or making her cry. Thus, my animus became rather passive, accommodating, and oriented toward serving the feminine—whether that was my own inner feminine, the personal mother, or one of her many collective manifestations such as the church. My anima, on the other hand, retreated into her creative side of art and music for validation and value.

In response, my masculine image sought validation for the masculine from some other man who could connect him to and give him the confidence and authority to stand up to the inner masculine-feminine dynamic. As the unconscious and yet unacknowledged and therefore undeveloped sides of my masculine-feminine energies began to assert themselves more and more in my dreams, my relationships with both the masculine and the feminine began to change, and my relationships to the outer masculine and feminine also began to change—both in their human and symbolic expressions.

As I began to distinguish between my anima energy and my mother energy, I came to understand that my anima energy was centripetal, in-turning, and introverted. This was how Stevens had defined the feminine: In-turning, going into the womb of the unconscious, and giving form to the energy of the unconscious masculine that was attached to her, bringing that life out of its darkness and unconscious state[263] into consciousness and connecting me to the aspects of the Self that were mine to inhabit.

As mentioned above, while a man's masculine image is shaped by the father, typical masculine attributes and drives that have not been actualized in the personal relationship with the father or other pertinent male figures nevertheless press for realization as potentials that want to take form.[264] For example, when male aggressiveness is not adequately actualized in the father-son relationship, there is not sufficient energy for the son to maintain his own ego stand, especially against the mother—personal or symbolic—but also against other men—actual or symbolic. Nor can he maintain his stance against his own inner feminine, often falling under her spell.

For example, when the negative side of the anima is strongly activated, she softens the man and can make him touchy, irritable, moody, jealous, vain, and unadjusted.[265] In my own case, when I felt overwhelmed by the feminine, too much cared for by the feminine, too smothered by the feminine, or overly controlled by her—to the point where I couldn't find and express my own masculine voice—I would then have the urge to connect with the masculine through a need to masturbate or seek out a man with which to have sexual contact. I would project my unconscious and split-off aggression onto a man and submit myself to him in an aggressive act of anal intercourse hoping to get something of him inside me. Ironically, while I was being passive in this interaction it also felt somehow aggressive, given that I was taking action by entering a men's restroom and searching out this masculine

---

263 Stevens, *Archetype Revisited*, 209.

264 Whitmont, *The Symbolic Quest*, 212.

265 Jung, *Collected Works 9*, i, par. 144.

energy (Stevens's masculine). In such cases, the not-yet-actualized animus aspect, in this case the masculine assertiveness, needed to be investigated and aroused. Given that the anima as a man's capacity for sexual relatedness has an erotic and emotional character,[266] this not-yet-realized animus becomes the point of view behind the anima that she then translates into homosexual feelings as a way to get into life.

In my own life I came to understand that my father complex, with all its shadow components, took the form of this search for the masculine in same-sex relationships. While the anima itself is feminine and influenced by the mother, she can become contaminated by the animus and fall under the spell of the father complex. In these situations the anima or the man's inner feminine aspect is more acutely under the point of view of the masculine. For such a man, life may be sought in the masculine and not in the feminine. This is the case of undifferentiated masculine and feminine energies.

I dream

> *My wife, a child, and I are standing in a wooded area. There is a path in the center of this wooded area, and I know there is a bull in this area. We are standing at one end of this path and can dimly see the bull standing at the other end. The bull charges toward us and begins to chase us. We turn and run into a barn or shed. I close the door and put a piece of wood down over it to hold the door shut. But the bull charges right through the door. I think I should have known a piece of wood wouldn't hold a bull.*
>
> *We then run out the door of the barn. The door is now a regular door with a knob. I close the door behind us. I*

266 Jung, *Collected Works 17*, par. 338.

know the bull can't get out of this door or that he won't come through this door. I then go back and look in through a window. I see a corral. In one corner is a calf. I also see a dog. I think, Well, the bull won't hurt the other animals and he won't hurt the dog. *I look over and see a teenage boy standing in the building. It is like he is looking for a way to get out. I didn't realize that he was inside or that we had left him there.* (Journal, 4-17-87)

As I mediated on this dream, suddenly the dog in the dream came face-to-face with my face. I saw that this wasn't a dog at all, but a young woman who was wearing a dog's mask. I could see behind and under the mask and see this young woman. I engaged her in conversation:

Sheldon: "Hello, young woman. Hi. I thought you were a dog."

Young woman: "No, I am not a dog. I only wear this mask that makes me appear as a dog so that the bull won't hurt me. Neither am I a bitch. You try to make me into a bitch. You make me wear a mask because you won't accept me as part of you. You won't humanize me. You make me remain a dog. But under this mask I am a beautiful young woman. I am your anima. I am your feminine intuition, your feminine instincts, your companion, your friend. I am your protector, the guardian of your treasure. I am the feminine feelings that are still in the unconscious, that is, in the animal state. Don't mask your feelings. Don't mask your feminine nature." (Journal, 4-17-87)

Jungian analyst Marie von Franz says that when a man dreams that a woman he loves has turned into a dog, it suggests that the anima, which should have a human field of experience, a human expression, has been overwhelmed by a drive, has regressed into a prehuman form of expression through the influence of inner complexes. Such a dream image means that another completely unconscious complex has contaminated the anima with its content, exercising a destructive and damaging influence on her. The inner life, which had reached a human level of experience or the potential for a human experience, continues to be under or has once again fallen under the spell of the unconscious. In such cases, the cursed anima needs the help of the hero to get out its state, for she cannot free herself.

I have already written in some detail on the meaning of the bull in chapter 1 where I discuss the dream in which a bull chased me up a tree. Once again the bull—as a symbol of the raw, chthonic masculine, pre-Christian phallic god that was also connected to the feminine moon-goddess and ancient nature religions as my androgynous and undifferentiated bisexual nature—was chasing me. However, this time the dream showed that I was able to contain this energy. In being able to contain this energy I was able to "see" into myself as represented by my looking through a window into the barn. There I discovered a calf, a dog, and a teenage boy who had been left, trapped in the place of the instincts, caught between the bull and the feminine voice in me, but was now looking for a way out.

The fact that the dreams showed my feminine energies disguised as a dog—an animus or masculine image—because she was afraid of the bull, suggested that I was still afraid of this bull energy in me. I was still afraid of my own voice, my own masculinity, and/or my own androgynous nature. This dream also suggested that I was not relating to my inner feminine directly, but only through the unconscious masculine energy symbolized by the dog.

The anima has been called the emissary of the Self. The Self is the image of wholeness that contains all the potentialities living in the soul. As its emissary, the anima longs to connect a man to all the potentials living in his soul that are his unique and individual Self, his soul's longing and purpose. Again, I would argue that certain archetypes or archetypal configurations take hold of the anima in their longing to get into life. In many ways we are just the playgrounds for the gods and goddesses, those archetypal forces that stand behind all manifestation, to live out their archetypal stories. While I suspect that we are born with particular imprints that are ours to manifest, the environment activates the archetype, which mediates the experience and the behavior. Archetypes are the organizing schemata by which the innate becomes personal. If we are able to wake up, at least to some extent, we are then able to become co-creators in their dance, participants with a voice that can interact with their images, developing a relationship with these forces—even influencing them—so they don't live out *their* lives as *our* fate.

Although I continued to wrestle with same-sex attractions and the urge to live them out in relationships with men, my nine-year journey into my dreams had resulted in a shift in my understanding of this other man living in my soul and his relationship to the feminine. My relationship with these energies began to influence the decisions I made in my life. Looking back, I see more clearly how the decisions I made and would make were in response to these voices.

At the time of this dream I was facing another conflict between the outer-ego life and what was emerging inside of me. I had come into conflict with my life as a high school teacher. In my journey thus far, I had slowly been untangling from the life of the parsonage, given that the early dream had suggested this was critical for my healing. I had left my identification with music and especially my role as church music director and performer. I had for the most part left the institutional church of my childhood. Such decisions had required another point of view—a point of view that was more congruent with the man I was discovering myself to be. These decisions also required the development of another masculine consciousness that could support this changing point of view in how I saw myself and the world—and myself *in* the world.

Now I was facing another conflict. I noticed that I had become weary of teaching school. It no longer satisfied my soul. I dreaded going to work. Perhaps, just as I had fallen under the spell of the obedient mother-son relationship in my obedient service to mother church, I had also fallen under the spell of the teacher archetype—both of which were patterns in my family system. While both lives had served me well and supported my ego's life, both eventually came into conflict with what was emerging in my soul. My soul was longing for something else. Five nights after my work on the above dream, I dream

> *My friend Sam and his wife have returned. They brought with them friends from California. They are putting on a play. My wife is in the play. She has a table with a projection screen, and she is to roll out the table with the projection screen. There is also a second cart with the projection screen that another lady has.*
>
> *Sam is in the singing group, with a group of kids. His friend is leading the group. They sing a song, "She's a strong man-woman. He's a strong woman-man."*
>
> *I say, "Well, praise God! Androgyny has finally come to the church." I say this so that the preacher's wife sitting*

> *behind a partition can hear me. I know that by the time these kids are adults, the idea of androgyny will be common knowledge and accepted facts in their lives and that the whole of theological doctrine will have to change. The idea is that the biblical understanding—Christian-theological doctrine—will have to change to incorporate this fact and the reality of androgyny.* (Journal, 4-22-87)

Sam, as stated previously, is a heterosexual male with whom I had had sexual encounters. This masculine energy, along with its feminine side (represented by his wife), had returned and brought with it another unknown couple, representing other unconscious masculine and feminine energies. After this former masculine energy returned, it began to sing about a woman being a *strong man-woman* and a man being a *strong woman-man,* emphasizing the reality of androgyny and the animus-anima pairing.

The dream's reference to church symbolized my former life in the parsonage that had been so identified with the life of church and collective religious values of my family (Moore's definition of the feminine). This dream showed the emergence of my androgynous nature, suggesting that it would influence my entire belief system.

In discussing this dream, my analyst told me that the further one goes in analysis the more androgynous one becomes.

However, the previous dream, where my inner feminine was wearing the mask of the dog, showed me that I was still under the spell of an inner complex and still not relating to my masculine and feminine energies in a healthy, human, and conscious way; these energies were not in a good relationship. This also meant that I was not in a good relationship with my androgynous nature. Ultimately it meant that I was not in a good relationship with myself, my own soul.

As stated earlier, in our dreams we get a kind of photograph of how the unconscious looks at a conscious situation.[267] The scenario of the dream revealed the inner, unconscious conditions under which I lived—these were the inner conditions under which the teenage boy was trapped. Certainly this teenage boy could represent parts of me that remained trapped in the teenage years of the parsonage; parts of me that I was unable to develop and embrace; parts of me that I had sought to claim in my same-sex relationships. But this teenage boy also represented my future, the future me that was yet to be, my current undeveloped or developing masculinity. This masculine energy was caught in this inner masculine-and-feminine dilemma.

The dream showed that my anima, my feminine, was contaminated, and under the influence of unconscious masculine energy. My task was now to free the anima, my feminine energy, from her contamination by this unconscious material, from the mask she wore. This process would require a shift in my relationship to the feminine that would free her and the teenage boy—this other developing masculine energy—from their unconscious states. We could say that my anima, my feminine nature, was under the spell of the masculine, thus her attraction—and mine—to men who represented a different kind of masculine image.

As I continued to hold my same-sex attractions in the vessel of an inner experience, I slowly became aware of the "two-spirit archetype"—the berdache—living in my soul. It would not only become the healing of the split in me but would become an avenue for me to serve the collective. In indigenous cultures, this two-spirit archetype finds expression in the tribal medicine man, medicine woman, or shaman. This person, being both masculine and feminine, is able to mediate between the worlds, not just between men and women, but also between

---

267 Von Franz, *Dreams: A Study of the Dreams.*

the physical and the spiritual. (That piece of my journey will be detailed in a future chapter.)

I came to understand that the anima as an agent of the unconscious connected me to the greater potentials living in my soul. I also discovered that it would take the development of a different masculine consciousness for me to be true to her. Six weeks later I dream

> *Dr. Jones, my high school principal, tells me that he dreamed he changed jobs and that a lady has entered his life. There is some feeling that he is having an affair with this lady. Dr. Jones tells me that he thinks this dream is crazy. I tell Dr. Jones that the dream is indicating that he will be changing jobs and that the lady in his dream is the anima. I tell him that Jung says that anima is the archetype of life itself and entangles a man in life and disentangles him from it. I explain that in the dream she symbolizes this new job, for it is she that will draw him into a new job.*
>
> *I now notice there is another man there. He is my age or slightly younger, dark-complected and thin. I know that we are very good friends, close, and intimate, like brothers. We are nude, lying down beside each other. He is very warm, open, uninhibited toward me, and touches me. I put my hand on his chest. He is very receptive to this. There is a feeling of closeness, like a bond between us. I then move my hand down to his groin area.*
>
> *He is surprised and shocked by this and asks, "What are you doing?" indicating that this relationship is not a sexual one and that homosexuality is not the motivation for our closeness and that he is not homosexual and is not*

interested in such a relationship nor has any such desire. (Journal, 6-12-87)

This dream relayed that my masculine principle was undergoing a job change. A job is symbolic of an exchange of energy. We put energy into some effort and then we receive payment in return. The dream indicated that my masculine principle was going to have a change in its energy system, in how it functioned energetically. The dream said that it was the anima, my inner feminine, that was instigating this change and would actually draw me into this new relationship (job). The end of the dream suggested that the new job or position for the masculine was relationship with the masculine, but not a sexual one. This new relationship was one of the heart, of the soul, one of love—but was not to include the sexual. I remember the *Swan Lake* dream where the feminine told me when there was a conflict of priorities, one must follow the heart. This is the change that the dream said the anima was drawing me into.

This dream is another example that continued to confirm my growing awareness that my same-sex desires were often about something other than sex. The setting for this dream was the school where I was then teaching. Dr. Jones was the principal of the school. He represented my ruling masculine consciousness that was then operating under the complex of energies related to the collective values of an educational institution (Moore's feminine) and under the archetypal expression of the archetype of the teacher, one of the core images of the animus. The dream said this energy was going to get a new job.

At the time of this dream I was becoming more and more dissatisfied in my job as a high school teacher. I was having increasing difficulty maintaining that ego structure. Once again I found myself in a conflict of the soul.

Although the dream confirmed that I was tempted to project this conflict onto a man and seek its solution in a same-sex encounter, the unconscious had another point of view, indicated by the other man in me not allowing me to engage in the sexual relationship. This was a heart issue, a soul issue, indicated by the man allowing me to place my hand on his chest and heart areas—but not the groin. The dream was clear. This conflict was not a sexual issue, nor was the solution a sexual one!

When we have difficulties, whether they are with a partner, a profession, or something else, and ignore the situation from the outside and look at it from within with a kind of relative exclusion of the outer situation, this forces the situation into the vessel for the purpose of introversion, where it may be understood as a drama playing out inside us.

This wasn't about my job as teacher, or my relationship with my wife, or my homosexuality. It was about the interplay of energies inside of me. It is anthropomorphic to say that the unconscious is always benevolent, for it is up to consciousness to make decisions. Consciousness must decide. It was up to me to decide what this dream meant.

Whitmont says that the next stage of one's development is comprised of that which attracts one and yet also causes fear. Certainly, this desire to leave teaching, to change the ego's position and its current level of external comfort and go off into the unknown to explore my interests in dreams and Jungian psychology and perhaps become a therapist or analyst, met both those criteria. It attracted me greatly, like a passion drawing me toward some as of yet unknown destiny. While I would come to understand that this longing was about my own individuation and coming to understand the urge behind my own homosexuality, at the time I only knew that something inside me was calling me. It was surrounded by both fear and excitement and would become a necessary step in my own development, but that decision was still over a year away.

In the meantime the dreams continued to demonstrate the interplay between the masculine and the feminine and the growing relationship to the anima and this other man living in my soul.

Phallos, as archetypal masculine, stands behind the animus—whether in a man or a woman. Attributes of Phallos that are not constellated in a boy's development remain in the unconscious and may attach to the anima. To the extent that the masculine and feminine are undifferentiated, the unconscious characteristics take hold of the anima in their attempt to get into life. This often sets up a conflict within the inner masculine-feminine relationship and its relationship to the greater purposes of the Self or soul.

For example, whenever my spontaneous aggressive masculine rose up, it was reprimanded and punished as selfishness by my father, or my mother would become upset and break into tears for which I would then feel guilty. So I would adjust my behavior accordingly. I began to understand intuitively what the rules of the parsonage were and responded in turn, driving the parts of me that didn't fit into that image underground and into the unconscious.

These reactions and perspectives of my parents were not only their personal views but were also projected to be the view of God as they understood Him, thus further splitting me off from my own divine nature. My father lived his aggressive and assertive animus out in the pulpit, in dogmatic, loud preaching, putting forth the "sperma" or "word of God." Whenever his own voice came into conflict with the church's teachings, he admitted to feeling guilty. Therefore, he would adjust his thinking, submitting to the demands and expectations of the collective and coming into service to her—whether that be my mother or God's church.

In the parsonage, self-concern and self-will had to be repressed, for they were perceived to be evil. Somehow, natural masculine assertiveness and aggressiveness were interpreted as self-concern and self-will and therefore selfishness and an act against God. Not only were physical aggression and assertiveness deemed inappropriate, but the assertion of beliefs or thoughts that didn't fit into the "parsonage system" (Moore's masculine) were also judged to be self-centered and wrong, rising against God himself. Raw phallic masculinity remained unactualized. Yet this energy continued to exist and it continually strove for realization in my same-sex attractions and fantasies.

This masculine energy, pressing for realization and embodiment, can be understood as my father's unexpressed masculinity—the raw, sexual, earthy, chthonic phallic power—even the power to think differently. These aspects of archetypal masculine remained unconscious in the father-son relationship and attached themselves to my anima. They then sought themselves in my submitting myself to the raw sexual energy of a man.

Looking back over my life from this vantage point and where my own journey led me, I can say that I became the carrier of my father's unlived life and unconscious longing. However, that realization would come only after a long journey into my own inner world. In the beginning, my own male image took on the point of view of the masculine-feminine relationship in the parsonage—sacrificing itself for the feminine, whether that be Mother, or the collective thinking of the church, or any other collective institution whose values were accepted by the religious system of the parsonage (Moore's feminine).

I lived the first thirty-four years of my life in this manner: serving Mother and the feminine as my father had. This was my acquired anima-animus relationship. And while that life seemed to work for my father, slowly it stopped working for me. Even though I could access the creative musician and teacher sides of my anima and use them effectively in service to the church and education for many years, she began to express her dissatisfaction with both these expressions. I would fall into fits of irritability, moodiness, and self-criticism. If I attempted to disagree with, reject, or question the laws and rules of the church and therefore the parsonage, I would be criticized and made to feel guilty and wrong and I would be told that I was disobeying God. This would trigger my desire for a same-sex encounter in my attempt to reestablish a connection to my own masculine self.

As I continued to work with my own masculine and feminine energies, I came to identify both their extraverted and introverted expressions in me. In working with my brother, James Shalley, Psy.D., we came to refer to them as dynamic and static. For example, the static masculine can be defined as the energy that creates systems of order, makes and keeps rules, maintains hierarchical systems, preserves social norms, preserves proper conduct, enforces the shoulds, demands obedience, seeks peace, tends toward perfectionism and inflexibility, sets limits, is oriented toward the group, is disciplined and fits into group expectations, has reasoned behaviors, is rational, and would be characterized as the ruling king or queen. This masculine energy has a stabilizing effect and could be called "the Stabilizer." This masculine would pair up with and be in service to Moore's feminine as the sexual-socio-economic-procreative-collective purpose of life that is occupied with habit; tradition; conservatism; and defense and protection.[268]

The dynamic side of the masculine energy is "the Initiator." This energy is aggressive and assertive; goal-oriented; initiates and conquers; strives for accomplishments; pursues individual interests; goes its own way; strives, challenges and confronts; masters goals; is outward

---

268 Moore, *Sexuality and Spirituality*, 15.

directed; does battle; is fascinated with force, movement, speed and strength; and is objective and analytical. This masculine energy is associated with the hero and the warrior and would actually include both Moore's and Stevens's description of the masculine as well as Jung's definition of the animus.

The static side of the feminine energy might be called "the Responder." This energy is oriented toward others; nurtures, accepts, holds and contains; shelters, protects, affirms; takes care of; expresses confidence, security and optimism; trusts in the basic values of life, and takes on the role of the nurturing parent. This would correspond to both Moore's and Stevens's description of the feminine.

The dynamic side of the feminine energy is spontaneous; open to experience; urges change; enjoys the playful and unexpected; liberates and inspires; is open to new insights, values personal experience; creates new possibilities; is charming, playful and seductive; and gives birth to what is emerging from within. This energy manifests as the visionary; the dreamer; the artist; the child at play; the muse; and Dionysus. This energy could be called "the Transformer" and corresponds more or less with Jung's description of the anima.

Of course, the expression of these aspects in actual life experience isn't so clear-cut. Rather, the energies become mixed with each other, contaminating each other. Sometimes attributes of each are operating at the same time. The task is to recognize each energy, learn how to live in relationship with it, and balance it with all the other expressions—and to be able to discern when to honor one or the other for whatever is needed in any given situation.

Moving forward I had to recognize the experience of the dynamic feminine in her spontaneous, liberating, and inspiring creative way of bringing to birth in me that which wanted to come into consciousness. I must use the responding, nurturing, mothering feminine to hold and nurture what was wanting birth, to value it, and to trust its development. Then I must activate the initiating side of the masculine to move forward into life in a way that brought into existence that which the anima and the dynamic and transforming side of the feminine wanted to bring into consciousness. I would then need to use the static masculine—the stabilizing aspect of the masculine energy—to create a new order for me, a new consciousness, a new way of being in the world, one that was more congruent with my own psychic structure.

While I didn't see or understand this process at this point in my journey, looking back I can see its evolution in my life and how the symbolic meaning of my same-sex attractions played into that process. Ultimately it was my same-sex attractions that pulled me into a new consciousness and world view.

I discovered that the transformer energy in me, my anima, held a different point of view from its original orientation in the parsonage. This point of view came into conflict with the static masculine that supported the Judeo-Christian patriarchal system of the parsonage in which I was raised and lived. Since the dynamic masculine, the initiating masculine energy, was insufficiently constellated in my father-son relationship, this operated at the unconscious level and sought its life in my same-sex encounters as an unconscious attempt to both validate and honor the unintegrated and split-off masculinity through oral sex and masturbation and to get that energy into me via anal intercourse. The task was to honor the emerging point of view of my anima in her desire to connect me to the masculine-feminine relationship that was mine to inhabit, and then initiate conscious action to bring that into conscious experience. That would mean honoring my own inner knowing and "real-self" (Moore's masculine) and taking action in the world (Stevens's masculine). Ultimately it would mean leaving home and taking on the hero's journey.

As I continued to distinguish and separate out the voice of my anima, my own inner feminine truth, from the voices of the parental complexes, I began to discover my own thoughts and to find my own feelings, my own values, and my own voice. I discovered what was important and authentic in me and to me. To be true to the anima as a voice separate from the images of the masculine and feminine that ruled the parsonage required that I also develop a new masculine consciousness, one that could be true to her voice in me, one that was able to stand up *for* her.

I discovered that this was what she wanted all along, for me to be true to my own masculine-feminine relationship—the one living in me as my own individual archetypal truth. However, my masculine image, my animus, was under the spell of my father complex. I needed another kind of male image, another masculine consciousness, another masculine feeling. I needed the pre-Christian, sensual, earthy chthonic masculine, the bull nature of antiquity—that masculine energy that lived as Spirit in nature and *in* the very nature of my own being—that male image that was co-creator with the Goddess. This was her lover. This was her companion.

When I couldn't hold that relationship with her by failing to acknowledge and live this deeper truth of this Other, she would seek him elsewhere. She, as the emissary of the Self, would, through same-sex encounters, project this soul aspect onto a man in the external world who would both ravage her and rapture her into these masculine mysteries. By doing so she introduced me into the mystery of the masculine lying dormant in my soul.

To this endeavor she was committed.

Notes and Exercises

The soul expresses itself in images of the masculine and feminine. The interplay of these two archetypal energies are critical in understanding not only same-sex attractions but all forms of sexual attraction. Masculine and feminine refer to a complex of energies that express themselves in certain patterns of thought, emotion and behavior that appear in both men and women.

The feminine refers to the group, procreative purpose of the psyche that is oriented toward the survival of the group or species, serving the collective values of home and family, religious values and institutional system, tending toward maintaining tradition, protection and conservatism. In its creative aspect, the feminine is associated with the earth, nature and the womb, giving form to the energy of the masculine and bringing life out of darkness.

The masculine tends toward the abstract, the ideal, and the inner meaning. It is self-concerned, serving the spiritual concern of personal destiny and self-realization and the advancement of the "real-self." Its realms are heaven and spirit. It is dynamic, assertive, and in its phallic, penetrating aspect arouses, fertilizes, and creates.

In general, the feminine services group and collective values while the masculine serves personal and individual values. How these masculine and feminine energies relate to each other in the unconscious influences a man's relationship to these energies in the outer world including his sexual relationships. Our parents' relationship to each other as well as their relationships to us influence the formation of our masculine and feminine energies.

Describe your father's personality and the role he played in your life. Describe your mother's personality and the role that she played in your life. (See Appendix: My Parents for an example.) Which parent reinforced the feminine qualities as defined above? Which parent reinforced the masculine qualities? What qualities are missing in your father? What qualities are missing in your mother? What characteristics of your father do you exhibit? What characteristics of your mother do you exhibit? How do these masculine and feminine energies play out in you? How do these masculine and feminine energies play out in your sexual relationships? What masculine and feminine qualities do you seek in your sexual fantasies or in your sexual relationships? Write out a description of the relationship between your inner masculine and feminine energies.

CHAPTER ELEVEN

Caught in an Archetypal Tale

My analyst tells me that he had a dream about me. He dreams that

> *I call him and tell him that I'm being held at Calvary Church. I say "They really have me. Therefore, I can't make it to my session." My analyst says that he understands and when I can talk about it, to call him and we will reschedule.* (Journal, 7-29-87)

In response to this dream, my analyst asks me if I feel caught in some kind of a closed, rigid system. At the time of this dream I was caught in the struggles between my heterosexual and homosexual selves, between staying married or divorcing, between continuing to teach high school Spanish or to leave teaching and purse my interest in becoming a Jungian analyst. I was also experiencing a growing conflict about whether or not to continue or stop my therapy and analysis.

Our discussion that particular day centered on the conflict between my heterosexual self and my desire to remain married and my homosexual self with its desire to be free of the marriage so it could spontaneously pursue same-sex relationships. Living within the bounds of marriage and my commitment to my wife felt like a system that I was caught in from the perspective of my homosexual self. But my analyst's dream didn't say I was being held by my marriage or by my relationship to my wife, but by Calvary Church. What if my association to my literal marriage was a projection of the inner marriage?

The "inner marriage" is the often stated goal of a Jungian analysis—the union of the opposites, the union of the masculine and feminine, the conscious and the unconscious—which brings about the birth of the Self and one's unique individual destiny. His dream said that I was "being held at Calvary Church." "Being held" suggests "beyond my control." Something *had* me. Some power was holding me against my will, against my ego's will, or my conscious will. The dream said this power was Calvary Church, suggesting this system was the "church system." The dream also said, "They really got me." Why did the dream say "they?" Why didn't the dream say "it," since "it" would be the natural and appropriate pronoun to refer back to the word *church* as a singular noun?

Could it be that my analyst's unconscious had picked up on these conflicts and viewed them as an archetypal story, like the one played out in the Christian Church? Certainly my psychic system had been indoctrinated into and contained in the Christian story by the mere fact that I was born into and lived in a fundamentalist Christian minister's home. Was I still caught in the personal story of the parsonage from which the earlier dream had told me I must free myself in order to heal the homosexual self? Or did my analyst's dream point to something else—an archetypal story playing out in me that transcended the literal church and my own personal story?

During this time my wife and I had many intense and serious conversations about our relationship and my same-sex attractions and whether to divorce or remain married. She was becoming clearer that she was no longer able to carry my homosexual energies. At times she felt that she was just a substitute for my same-sex attractions, and even felt that sometimes the sex we had was nothing more than masturbatory fantasies on my part. We also had many discussions about my desire to leave teaching and move to Indianapolis in order for me to go back to school and become a therapist. Either one of these decisions—to divorce after twenty-one years of marriage or to leave teaching after twenty years—would disrupt our lives.

As mentioned above, if we ignore a conflicting situation from the outside and look at it from within with a kind of relative exclusion of the outer situation, this forces the situation into an inner vessel where it can be understood as a drama playing out inside us. The question, of course, is what was the drama? If my analyst's dream suggested that I was being held in some archetypal story, what was the story?

The church is a mother symbol. We speak of mother church. To the extent that the church serves the collective purposes, it corresponds with Moore's definition of the feminine as the active, group, procreative purpose of the psyche that serves the survival of the group or species.[269] Calvary refers to the place of the Crucifixion of Christ on the cross. The cross or tree is another mother symbol. This is the archetypal story of the death of son-ego and his return to the mother for rebirth and transformation. Numerous myths tell how the hero was enclosed in the maternal tree trunk.[270] The various meanings of the tree as sun, Tree of Paradise, mother, and even as phallus are explained by the fact that it is a symbol of libido. The basic underlying reality is the libido. However, it is not the real mother who is symbolized here but the libido of the son whose object was once the mother.

Every sun myth illustrates the idea of entering into the mother in order to be reborn through her. But here the incest prohibition

---

269 Moore, *Spirituality and Sexuality*, 15.

270 Jung, *Collected Works 5*, 219.

intervenes. As Jung points out, the incest prohibition acts as an obstacle and stimulates the creative imagination to find avenues for the self-realization of the libido. Consequently, every rebirth myth devises every conceivable kind of mother analogy for the purpose of canalizing the libido into new forms and effectively preventing it from regressing to actual incest.[271] In this way the libido becomes spiritualized.

This is also a way of understanding the Christian story—a rebirth and transformation of the soul-image (Christ) through death and resurrection. My analyst's dream said that I was caught in such a system. If I considered that the tree was basically a mother symbol, then the meaning of this mode of burial became clear. The dead were delivered back to the mother for rebirth. This seemed to be an adequate explanation if we hold that the tree or cross is only a mother symbol. However, the tree is a much more diverse and complicated symbol, representing not only the mother or the feminine, it is also a phallic and masculine symbol. The tree became another symbol for my bisexuality.

The cross itself is a symbol of primordial androgyny and nature's dualism, again suggesting the bisexuality that is inherent in nature. Beyond that, the cross is a symbol of the union of the opposites, the union of the masculine and feminine, with the vertical line representing the connection with the spiritual, the heavens, the masculine, and the horizontal representing nature, the earth, and the feminine.[272] As such, being held on the cross represents the integration of man's soul into the union of opposing forces: the masculine and feminine, the spiritual and the earthy or, in my case, the heterosexual and the homosexual awaiting the birth of the new man. Being held at Calvary

---

271 Ibid., 222.

272 Cooper, *Illustrated Encyclopaedia*, 45.

Church suggested containment. Containment signifies the latent state that precedes regeneration.[273]

According to my analyst's dream I was caught in the archetypal process of transformation and self-realization of libido, the sacrifice of the ego-self for the realization of this other man living in my soul. Jung has suggested that "No man can change himself into anything from sheer reason: he can only change into what he potentially is. When such a change becomes necessary, the previous mode of adaptation, already in a state of decay, is unconsciously compensated by the archetype of another mode."[274]

Seen in this light, it is really the transformation, rebirth, and realization of the masculine God-image that began chasing me as a bull in my dream nine years ago. It seemed that this was a process that would not let me go—thus held in Calvary Church, held in the crucible of the conscious and unconscious energies—awaiting the resurrection of the Self. As Helen Luke so aptly puts it, ". . . the true peace does not come until one has been through all the struggles of the ego, and until one has accepted boundaries and conflict—to the bitter end. That's what the whole Christian story is about. That's what the cross is."

Many men with same-sex attractions find themselves suffering silently in the church. These are often sensitive, loyal, and responsible men who feel a great sense of commitment to their upbringing, their families, and to God. Unfortunately, these loyalties often force an abduction of the Self—an abduction of that true, unique, authentic, individual sacred Self living in the soul. This unconscious Other often becomes projected onto the church, and we fall under the spell of the archetypal Mother/Father complex and God-image.

---

273 Jung, 236.

274 Ibid.

Yet the longing of this other man breaks through in same-sex fantasies and attractions, compulsive masturbation, and secret homosexual encounters and affairs. Suffering under a conflict of priorities—how to be loyal to both the church, our families, and ourselves—we face the great challenge of withdrawing this projected Self from the church and giving ourselves permission to embrace our own sacred masculine and to live our own lives as determined by our relationship with the Divine living in our own souls. This will most certainly be a Herculean task, but for many it is a necessity task. This process often feels like being nailed to the cross as we hold the tensions of these opposing forces, waiting for the resurrection of the new God-image—one that can embrace our homosexual and bisexual natures.

Holding this tension was frequently extremely difficult for me to maintain. At times there was a strong desire to choose one side over the other—a man over my wife. But something inside me would not permit it. I refused to say that I was one or the other. Somewhere deep inside I knew that I was both, and that I could hold both within. I could relate to the feminine and masculine energies within me and allow them to work in creative ways, bringing to birth the other man living in my soul. How I lived these energies out in my sexual life was another issue that the unconscious continued to speak to.

I dream

> *Sam and his wife have returned for a visit. Sam wants to continue our sexual relationship where it left off when he moved away. I tell him that I have matured and grown beyond that and don't want to and can't continue that relationship. This sense of maturing has something to do with my relationship with my wife. I can't do that to her anymore.*

> *The dream shifts and I am telling my analyst about this dream. My analyst says, "Being a scientist, it (meaning the scientific discovery that I had made as a scientist) has become a part of you."* (Journal, 8-10-87)

As the tensions regarding my unhappiness and dissatisfaction with teaching school and my inner struggle to leave that profession and follow the growing desire to go back to school and become a therapist increased, my same-sex desires and attractions also increased significantly. I found myself again wanting to seek out men with whom to have sex. Such a decision would completely disrupt and destroy my life as I knew it. My wife and I had agreed that if I made choices again to have extramarital affairs or decided that I needed to live a homosexual life, we would end our marriage. But to leave teaching would also disrupt our lives. Such a decision would require a move and result in a significant loss of income. It would require me to withdraw retirement monies in order to make this change happen. Such a decision seemed risky, impractical, and even irrational from the ego's point of view. Why would I do such a thing?

Yet there was a voice in me—more than a voice. Some might call it a "calling." Something inside me told me that if I wasn't able to follow what I knew to be right for me I could never trust myself again. What was the right decision? Divorce? Leave teaching? I had been here before in my decision to stop my same-sex relationships and in my decision to leave the church music position and ultimately the church. The anima had once again come under the influence of some aspect of the Self in her desire to connect me to my life. Could I remain loyal to her? Could I make that conscious? Could I trust my intuition, my inner knowing? Or would she drag me into sexual relationships with men in her attempt to get me to relate to this other man living in my soul?

This dream showed that the homosexual energies had returned with the return of Sam. But this dream continued to show the change happening at the unconscious level regarding my relationship to the masculine and feminine. Sam, as my former lover with whom I'd had a long- standing sexual relationship, carried the projection of my unconscious masculinity. I had ended that relationship in 1978. Here it was 1987 and this inner part of me had returned and wanted to "pick up where we left off." However, I could no longer engage in such a relationship due to my relationship with my wife, the feminine. I must now be loyal to her. The analyst said that the "scientist in me has become a part of me."

The word *science* comes from *sciens,* meaning "to know." Originally, it referred to a state or fact of knowing and knowledge, often as opposed to intuition and belief. Scientific knowledge is derived from observation, study, and experimentation carried out in order to determine the nature or principle of what is being studied.

This "scientific discovery" of my dream was the knowledge that I had acquired from my years of inner work, study, and writing on the meaning of my own homosexuality. It had become a part of my consciousness, a part of my "knowing." It is what I knew. Therefore, the relationship to my inner masculine had changed. I could no longer project it outside as a sexual relationship. The dream suggested that this had something to do with my relationship to my wife, and therefore, to the feminine.

This was the result of the hypothesis of my work on *Swan La*ke. My task was to free the anima from her contamination by unconscious masculine contents so that she no longer went off with the unconscious aspects of the Self, leading me into sexual relationships with other men in her attempt to relate me to this other man living in me. Rather by sorting out the voice of the anima from the voices of the parental complexes, from the voice of the shadow and the voices of other complexes, I was discovering how to remain faithful to her and to the deeper voice of the Self.

But why were my homosexual needs so much stronger then, after so many years? The closer we get to the Self—to the actual union of the opposites, to the union of the opposing forces—the greater becomes the temptation and the greater becomes the pull of energy into one-sidedness again, allowing the other side to fall back into the unconscious.

In the process of the journey there are always temptations to return to old ways of coping, old ways of managing fear and the unconscious stirrings of the soul. I could return to projecting this unconscious masculine energy onto a man and engage him in sex and for the moment feel relief, satisfaction, and a sense of completeness and wholeness. But my experience told me that the experience would be short-lived. Soon I'd be off again in search of another man, another sexual experience in my attempt to find and feel that sense of connection and completeness with this other man in me.

The alternative was to hold this masculine energy inside me and initiate movement to materialize this longing to leave teaching and step into this calling of the soul to become a therapist and analyst or whatever was longing to come into consciousness (Stevens's masculine). This dream was the call to act upon what I knew, what had become a part of me—to trust the dreams and the desires and promptings of the soul, even in the face of criticism, judgment, and misunderstanding by both the inner and outer voices.

I dream

> *A young girl, a dancer, tries out for a part in a musical play. The director, a strong matriarchal-type woman rejects her. The girl leaves and gets into another less prestigious show*

and becomes a success. Now the previous matriarchal-type woman director is after her, either to destroy her success or to get her to dance for her now that she has become such a success. Finally the other directors, a man and wife, and the previous matriarchal-type director and I sit down to discuss this situation. They all talk.

Finally, the matriarchal director asks me what I think. I say "When love comes, no matter in what form, e.g., person, talent, creative expression, etc., one must embrace it, and likewise when love goes one must let it go. Otherwise one does not live life to its fullest." (Journal, 8-15-87)

I woke up from this dream and reflected briefly on it. Once again the foursome—the two men and two women, a symbol of order and wholeness—had shown up to help me solve this dilemma. This time the mother symbol asked me what I thought. She asked me for my input, showing me some autonomy. I went back to sleep and dream the meaning of love. I dream

Love is simply energy directed toward a particular object or goal. Thus, the meaning of my statements "When love comes one must accept it and when it leaves one must let it go" means when energy is directed toward a particular object or goal, one must accept it, but when the energy is no longer directed toward that object or goal, one must let it go. (Journal, 8-15-87)

My energy that had once been directed toward teaching had gone. Therefore, I must let it go. My energy was moving in another direction. Therefore, I must accept it. Otherwise I would not live my life to the fullest. That ultimately is the goal of the Self, to live one's unique, individual life to the fullest. That is the longing of the soul and the task of life.

This dream also reflected a change in my relationship with the mother energy that had been in control of my creative feminine energy, the dancer, in me. This dream showed that I was able to relate to and state my position to this matriarchal or archetypal force that wanted to control or kill this energy. She was none other than the evil matriarch, the mythological equivalent of Medusa or the Snow Queen, who had sadistic punitive control over my masculine energy. This dream also showed my increased ability to think on my own and decide for myself about how best to think for myself and organize my life. This was tantamount to organizing my masculine energy in such a way as to free the anima, the symbol of my "life urge" from the life of the mother.

I dream

> *I am with another man. He is the son of the pilot of a plane. We are to go someplace. This other man is experienced in flying this plane. The plane is a very modern sleek-lined bird shape. To get into the plane we have to slide down a narrow passage. I am anxious about this. As I slide down I feel more uncertainty, more anxious about going on this flight. I slide into the plane. The sides of the plane are open but in a shape that is such that I know we can't fall out. I think there isn't enough room for my male friend to get in with me. But I move over to the right and he slides down in beside me. It is a very tight, close fit. Again I sense his experience in this, no anxiousness or fear in him. He is experienced in these things. This is all very familiar to him. He is at ease in the situation.* (Journal, 8-18-87)

This dream showed that this other masculine energy—this other man in me—and I had now joined together for the journey. The plane is a modern day symbol of the bird. The bird is often a symbol of the soul. This dream showed me getting into a close relationship with the masculine Other, a relationship that the dream showed me making room for. This suggested to me that I was able to hold this masculine energy, able to contain it within the vessel of my soul. It felt a little uncomfortable. While I was anxious about this relationship, this closeness with the Other, and about this journey, this other part of me knew the way and had experience with such things.

My entrance into the plane with the pilot could also be understood as a sexual image of vaginal or anal penetration by the masculine energy. In my opinion, intercourse is between the masculine and the feminine—whether that happens between a man and a woman, between two men, or between two women. My masculine projection, the pilot, was now in control but dependent on the plane, which is a feminine vessel. An airplane journey through the upper realms reinforced the idea that this was a spiritual journey for me. The sky and upper realms are often associated with spirit and the masculine. My masculine energies had penetrated the feminine vessel of the soul for a journey (Stevens's masculine).

That same night I dream

> *I am driving a car and come to an intersection. I want to turn right but it is a one-way street in the other direction so no right turn is allowed. However, there is a house on the corner that has built a contraption that is for some personal use, but they allow other cars who need to turn on that street to use it also. I drive up into the driveway wondering how one uses it.*

As I drive up, a garage door automatically opens. I drive in. I am now in an elevator that goes down, turns and goes down, turns and goes down, and moves my car through to the other side and out in the direction I needed to go but couldn't because of the one-way street. (Journal, 8-18-87)

While in the previous dream I was traveling through the sky, associated with the masculine and the spiritual, in this dream I was driving on earth and in order to go in the direction that I want to go, I have to go down into the earth, into the deep feminine. These two dreams showed the opposites. My journey was both one of the spirit and the masculine, and of the earth and the feminine. The fact that the two dreams came back-to-back suggested that my journey into Spirit must be grounded in the feminine in order to go in the direction that I wanted to go. The street was a one-way street for the general public, suggesting the "collective way." I employed something built for personal use so I could go in the opposite direction, suggesting further individuation, going against the natural collective opinion or flow.

These two dreams suggested that one part of my journey was through the vessel of the airplane—the "plane of air"—spirit, fantasy, and the imagination. In this part of my journey I was with the other masculine. From my journal:

Sheldon: Who are you?

Man: I am the part of you that wants to fly into the realm of ideas, fantasies, the realm of the masculine and spirit so that you can get to some other reality, some other point on earth. But that must become reality through internalization. That is what the second dream is about—going in and down—internalization that allows you to go in the direction

> *you want and need to go. The regular, normal streets of the collective rules represented by the one-way street won't take you in the direction you are to go. You have to make this turn but you can only make this turn—going against the collective voice—by going underground, by traveling through the dark, earthy, feminine side. It is a personal and individual journey indicated by the fact that the mechanism provided in the dream was for "personal use."* (Journal, 8-18-87)

These two dreams have moved the masculine and feminine from the personal to the archetypal, represented by the sky and the earth. This seems to confirm my analyst's dream that I was caught in an archetypal tale—the journey to find the "treasure hard to find" that the dream of so many years ago had told me was the goal of my homosexuality. Three nights later I dream

> *I see a father coming up one side of a glass divider. His young son is running up the other side of this divider. They meet at the top and the father picks up the son and embraces him.* (Journal, 8-21-87)

This dream conveyed the healing of the father-son relationship, the coming together of masculine energies, the reconciliation of the past and the future and the old and the new, that which was and that which was to come. If I consider the child in the dream as a symbol of the psyche's irresistible urge to fulfill itself, as Jung has suggested, and if I consider the father as not only the internalized father image, but also the old king or ruling consciousness, then this dream shows the father's acceptance of psyche's longing to fulfill itself. It is embraced, validated, and affirmed by the inner father. Perhaps with such approval and movement I could move forward on my journey. However, I felt increasingly caught in my life with no way out. From my journal:

> *I feel more and more unadapted to my life. It takes all of my energy just to maintain the structure of my life and carry out all the roles of my life—teacher, husband, father. I don't have any drive anymore. I just want to sit and sleep or watch TV. I feel no direction, no goals, nothing because it all seems too hopeless, no way out.*
>
> *The new school year has started. After the first day of teaching I already feel that I just can't keep this up. I have to find energy once I get into the classroom because I have to teach the class. So I do, but it is forced. I do just what I have to do to get through the day. It is all so uncreative to me, yet I don't have the energy or desire to work at making teaching creative and alive any more. Then I dislike myself because I am not teaching as well as I know I can. I am not doing the job that I am capable of or can do. So I just come home and sit and go through the motions of doing my father and husband duties as needed, like I'm on automatic pilot.*
>
> *It takes all of my energy to maintain this structure. It feels like there is a volcano rumbling around inside me that just wants to explode. In the extreme it materializes into a fantasy of just walking out of the school, quitting my job, filing for bankruptcy, and just leaving. If my wife will go, fine. If not, just leave her and the kids and go. But go where? I don't know, just some place where I can get into a new life. I don't even feel like going back to school and studying Jungian psychology although that is probably what I'd do. I'm feeling more and more like I don't have the ego strength or energy*

to do what is expected of me as far as making it in society, even to do what it takes to play the games of returning to school. I'm so tired. . . . (Journal, 8-31-87)

The increasing level of despair was accompanied by an increase in my same-sex attractions and fantasies. Once again, I wrestled with increased temptations to seek out some man with whom to have sex. However, my years in analysis had taught me that these urges weren't really about sex but some other need, something in me, some part of me that wanted to be accepted, embraced, listened to and validated, even loved. Something wanted to come into consciousness. But what was it?

One thing was certain: the dreams continued to indicate that I couldn't return to my former life. I dream

Sam has returned to the area. We have come together to do a concert for old times' sake or for a homecoming, or just to remember, but Sam is the only one doing anything. He is trying on different suits like we used to wear. I am giving him different suits from the rack of suits. Finally I give him his blue suit—the one he really looked good in and was his favorite. It is like this is the finale. He puts it on, but it doesn't fit him anymore. After trying on all the suits, Sam says he feels like he is trying to be seventeen years old again, trying to get into a suit that doesn't fit him anymore, and is no longer appropriate.

There is another man there, an older man. I don't know him. This man plays the piano. Sam says to this man, "I don't have anything. You have so much more than I do because you play the piano." Church is over. I say we should have sung

> *one last song together. It would have been exactly the old sound. At that point another man comes up and invites me to his church. I say that I will never come back to this church. As we pack up to leave I know that I can't have the same relationship with Sam that I once had. I get in my car, lay my head on the steering wheel, and cry.* (Journal, 12-10-87)

Here Sam, my previous lover, represented my old life—my old way of managing my life. This part of me was trying to fit back into the old life, symbolized by trying on all the suits—all the roles that he used to wear. Even his favorite one, the one he looked good in, no longer fit. Once again the unconscious was showing me that my relationship to my soul energy had changed. This part of me symbolized by Sam could no longer do things the way it used to. In dreams, clothes often symbolize the persona or images that we wear or present to the world or attitudes we hold. This part of me could no longer carry the projection of that former image. I just couldn't do it anymore. This was the death of the old life and I cried. We must grieve the death of the old life.

But the dream also made reference to another man who played the piano. While I do play the piano, I didn't know the man in the dream. A few days before the above dream I dreamed that

> *I see a rope hanging down from the sky with music attached to it. I know that it is my music. I climb up the rope and get the music. While climbing, there are times when I'm not sure if I will be able to climb all the way up. I'm not sure if my arms will hold me. But I do climb up and get the music.* (Journal, 11-30-87)

Is this the music that I was to play? I didn't yet know this piano-playing man in the other dream, so this part of me was still unconscious. I remembered that early morning back in 1981 at the very beginning of this journey. I lay in bed listening to the birds singing, thinking *Birds don't worry about their song; whether people like their songs or not. They just sing the songs given them.* In that early morning I had cried out from the depths of my soul, "I just want to sing my song." The dream showed that I had found my music. But I hadn't yet found how to play my music or even what my music *was*. But I had found it. And the previous dream had also been clear: I couldn't return to the old ways. I felt stuck with no way out. From my journal:

> *My wife tells me that she thinks if I stay in teaching that it will eventually kill me and that she supports me in whatever I decide to do. I do not enjoy teaching anymore, but I'm afraid to make a change. There is this conflict in me of just staying in teaching, resigning myself to this life, accepting that this is just the way it is, the way it must be, settling into the role of the teacher, trying to fit into the community, take my place in some meaningful way, and give up the other desires in me, my other needs, this other longing in me. This is the safest and most secure. This would be living under the spell of my father complex.*
>
> *This is the conflict between Moore's feminine as serving the collective and Moore's masculine as serving individual needs of the "real self." To remain teaching feels like death, resignation, putrification, stagnation, leaving me no options. It feels like all options and opportunities are closed and lost. On the other hand, to leave teaching feels like an opening up of possibilities of new options and new roads—opportunities*

> *and paths that simply are not available to me here. To remain as a high school teacher does feel like death. I'll just be going through the motions every day, playing the game.* (Journal, 11-29-87)

Two weeks later I dream:

> *There has been a huge snowstorm. I see a snowplow coming toward me to clear off the road. It is spraying the snow way out and piling it up deep and I fear that I will be buried under the snow and that it will be so high, deep, and heavy that I won't be able to get out and will die. However, when the snowplow passes, it sprays the snow out, covering me, but I am able to rather easily get free of it. I look back at the path that it left. The snow is piled very high on each side of the road.* (Journal, 12-15-87)

At the time of this dream as my journal entry had indicated I was still caught in the feeling that there was no way out of teaching, no way out of the demands of my life, no way to follow what my heart was pulling at me to do. At times I felt like just forgetting it all, giving up, resigning myself to the reality of the life that I was living, just accept it, and make the best of it. Perhaps this is what the dream was referring to. I felt frozen in my life, like a huge pile of frozen psychic life was going to overwhelm me, even bring about my death. James Hillman says that the psyche is a cold, cold region in its deepest levels. Snow is the consolidation of water, frozen water so to speak. Water is often a symbol of the unconscious, emotions, the feminine, and the life-force or spirit itself. These were frozen in me. But this dream showed that some masculine energy, represented by the snowplow, was plowing through this frozen life-force in me, opening up a path. I survived this process.

Whitmont in his book *The Symbolic Quest* says that archetypal patterns and the structuring of these "energy fields" that are constellated in one's life indicate the direction that psychological development is to take. These are to be followed if the development is to lead to a fulfillment of a person's true individuality. A given personality seems "called" to incarnate certain facets of the total range of human archetypes. Archetypes are the intermediators between genes and experience. They are the organizing schemata by which the innate becomes personal. A person will live these forms whether he knows about them or not. However, their more constructive aspects can be contacted if the person does know and can understand them.[275]

What were these archetypal forces that I was called to incarnate? How were these energy fields structured in me? What was the direction of my psychological development? What was the direction of my true individuality? Psychic predispositions are not isolated inner factors that can be separated from the outer world. Rather, world and archetype correspond to each other. That which our consciousness calls "world" and that which it calls "psyche" are not just two aspects of the total reality. Rather, world and psyche are two paths of development of the whole that belong together. [276]

A few nights later I dream

> *I find a very tiny kitten under the kitchen cupboard. I take a yardstick and, putting it behind the kitten, move it out and place a saucer of milk for the kitten to drink.* (Journal, 12-19-87)

---

275 Whitmont, *Symbolic Quest*, 112–113.

276 Ibid., 114.

Animals almost always represent instincts when we meet them in our dreams,[277] and as instincts animals often know the way when we feel completely lost.[278] Animals live their true natures and, in that, live closer to God's will than we do.[279] Dreaming of an animal is akin to returning to nature and of being reunited with something very healing.[280] Jung has suggested that if we can follow the way of nature, we will quite naturally come to our own law.[281]

Even though the dreams were showing some positive movement in the inner world, in the outer world things were going from bad to worse. Debt was piling up. Teaching was draining my energy. The conflict between my homosexual and heterosexual selves was increasing. Yet, in the midst of this growing despair, I discovered a kitten living within me.

Cats have appeared in my dreams on multiple occasions. Historically cats have been associated with the Goddess, the feminine, and the moon. Cats in my dreams have consistently represented my feelings, the instinctive feminine voice, even the anima herself. Here the dream showed me finding some young, tender, newly developing feeling growing in me, some feminine instinctive nature.

Psychologist Barbara Hannah tells us that our cat instinct can help us positively or, when uncontrolled, can endanger us on the negative side.[282] According to Hannah, our cat instinct can fight the darkness of the unconscious or cause us to lose our energy in wild untamed emotion. It can bring us destruction if used as black magic under the spell of the witch, or it can be healing energy if the magic is tamed and

277 Hannah, *The Cat, Dog and Horse Lectures*, 55.

278 Ibid., 57.

279 Ibid.

280 Ibid., 55.

281 Ibid., 57.

282 Ibid., 81.

used with a healing touch or purpose. Our cat instinct can relax us and heal our overworked egos or greatly overstrained attitude, or make us lazy and false. The cat can lead us away into the desert, away from our human relationships, into a purely autoerotic isolation, or it can give us access to the universal knowledge and make us truly self-reliant.[283]

For me, the kitten simply meant that in the midst of this rather desperate time of feeling there was no way out, the unconscious said "yes there is. There is a new growth in you, some aspect of your instinctive feminine nature that you must feed and care for." The dream showed me bringing this energy out into the open from under its hidden place under the kitchen cupboard. The kitchen itself is a place of transformation where we prepare and cook food for eating, symbolizing the integration of psychic material, corresponding to the alchemical process of the coagulation—embodying, incarnating, bringing something into manifestation. I was nurturing this energy, symbolized by the milk that I gave the kitten. Once again it was my relationship with the feminine that was both holding me together and indicating my way forward.

Once again the dreams continued to confirm and reinforce my growing awareness that my same-sex attractions weren't just about sexual desires for another man. Rather, behind these desires was the urge to embrace a life that was different from the one I was living. Certainly, I could choose a homosexual life as the life different from the one I was living. I could make it about sex and sexual attraction and seek some man with whom to possibly fall in love and live with in a homosexual relationship.

But was that the "treasure hard to find" that my earlier dream had told me was the goal of my homosexuality? I didn't think so. Even if I made that choice, I knew at this point in my journey that I would

---

283 Ibid.

still be looking for "that treasure" in the man I chose. In the end the "treasure hard to find" that I sought lived inside me, not out there in some Other. I discovered that the "treasure hard to find" was what I was looking for in my same-sex attractions.

I didn't know this at this time, but that would emerge in my journey.

I had become aware that I had been living the life of my parents, falling under the spell of the masculine-feminine dynamics and the God-image living in the parsonage. As my identification with the parental complexes began to fall apart and I began to withdraw my projections on to the church, the energy to live that life diminished to where I could no longer sustain it.

As previous chapters have detailed, I left church music and the church. Then I became aware that I was living the repressed and unconscious life of the parsonage through my same-sex fantasies, attractions, and sexual encounters with men—everything that was opposed to the parental complexes and the parsonage. But in both these situations I still wasn't living *my* life. I was simply living a life identified with the parsonage or one in opposition to it. Either way, I was still caught in the life of the parental complexes and that particular masculine-feminine story, caught in the archetypal tale. I had not yet found the "treasure hard to find."

I began to understand that my ego had identified with a certain cognitive, emotional, and behavioral pattern—a pattern that fit with and served the sexual-socio-economic-procreative-collective purpose of life (Moore's feminine). My homosexuality became a symbol for all that opposed that, not only in the parsonage but in the greater collective (Moore's masculine). For in the late '70s and early '80s homosexuality was far from being accepted. Even today the acceptance of gay, lesbian, bisexual, and transgendered community is far from complete. Thus homosexuality and my same-sex attractions became the symbol for my individuation, finding my own path separate from the collective values in which I was raised and in which I lived, both internally as well as externally.

As I identified my projections onto my same-sex fantasies and encounters as expressions of the masculine desire in me to leave the life with which my ego had identified, to break out of the collective spell into which I had fallen and give birth to a self that wanted to live (Moore's masculine as energy that "tends toward the "real-self), I was able to distinguish between the various voices in me. I was able to embrace the feminine in me, not mother as Moore's feminine that serves the sexual-socio-economic-procreative-collective purpose of life, but as that transforming feminine as defined by Stevens. This version of the feminine is the energy that introverts into the earth, nature, and the womb of the unconscious to give form to the energy that wants to come into life.

Consistently the feminine images in my dream were connecting me to my heart. As I became more comfortable listening to my heart and what my heart was telling me, I was able to engage Phallos as the initiating masculine directive (Stevens's masculine) to follow the heart. This newfound energy, which seemed more authentic to me, provided me with the energy and initiative to finally leave home and start on what was to become a journey of the heart. While that journey would begin in the external world in the next year with my decision to leave teaching, the realization of what was really vibrating in my soul was still years away. First I had to leave home.

Whether it is the heterosexual man who is attracted to having an affair with his secretary or his wife's best friend, or the man who sneaks upstairs in the middle of the night to masturbate to pornography, or the man who aggressively commits acts of violence or deceit against his teammates or, like me, a man who sought out men with whom to have sex—the urge behind these behaviors is something else, something that is wanting to get into consciousness, some unlived life that is longing to be lived, some part of us that longs for recognition, acceptance, integration, and yes, even love.

Some men just fly off on a motorcycle, have an affair, buy a new car, or quit their jobs during these struggling times. The challenge and the task are to withdraw these projections and hold them in the crucible of the inner vessel. When this inner experience does its work in us, it will bring forth that which is at the core of the longing and attraction. This will satisfy both the soul's longing and the ego's needs by bringing into consciousness that which is really longing to come to life. This is indeed a heroic task.

Notes and Exercises

Sometimes we fall under the spell of an archetypal story. An archetypal story is a typical, universal pattern that lives out in us, often without our awareness. Common archetypal stories are victim/rescuer, servant/master, mother/son, father/daughter, sinner/savior, innocent/villain, etc. We often project our unconscious parts into these stories. Once we get caught in the story, it plays out unconsciously and automatically as fate.

> *Where do you feel caught in your life? Where are you in conflict? How might you be projecting your mother complex—your service to mother or the feminine—onto some group or institution? How is that in conflict with or preventing you from honoring or living the masculine's desire for personal expression or to be yourself? How might the external conflict*

mirror an inner conflict between the masculine and feminine in you or other parts of you?

CHAPTER TWELVE

Same-Sex Attraction and the Hero's Journey

When an individual has succeeded in freeing himself from his traditional alliances in a responsible fashion, he will then be able to choose the direction of his life, which will ensure his own autonomy and the right to govern himself according to his own reason. I now turn to the next phase of my story, leaving the past behind to begin the process of governing myself according to the reasons of my own soul.

Mythology, fairy tales, religious traditions, world literature, and modern movies are strewn with stories of a man's journey to overcome some obstacle in his search for selfhood and his desire to fulfill a longing of the soul. Whether it is Perseus who rescued his future bride, Andromeda, from a monster; Prince Phillip who freed the maiden, lifeless Aurora, in *Sleeping Beauty* from the clutches of the witch; the biblical character Joseph who eventually reunited his family and saved a nation from starvation; King Arthur's quest to find the Holy Grail; or Luke in *Star Wars* who redeemed his father's darkness—they all ventured forth from the world as they knew it into unknown areas and uncharted paths where they encountered forces they had to overcome or endure in order to get the treasure they sought. Transformed by the process, they returned home to share their gift with their community or the world. In this process, a man must overcome multiple obstacles. If successful he frees this Other—the treasure hard to find—that lies hidden in his soul, and a new consciousness is born. I dream

> *I am living at home with my parents and my brothers. My father has established a lot of rules that don't allow us to do hardly anything. Everything I want to do, my father won't let me. According to him, these things are wrong, even evil. My brothers agree with him. Finally I confront my father and mother about these rules. I tell them it is their own fear of life that has made these rules. My mother just enforces the rules of my father.*
>
> *The scene changes and now I am with a group of people from a church. There are three spots, circles, on the bathroom wall. According to the people from the church, this is a sign that what I want to do is evil, a sign from the devil that confirms that what I want to do, even my confronting them, is evil. I tell them that those three spots are their own projections onto the wall, the projections of their own evil onto the wall and not the devil.*
>
> *The scene changes again and I meet Hilda. She tells me that I must leave home.* (Journal, 1-19-88)

This dream captured the masculine-feminine experience of the parsonage and the relationship of my own masculine-feminine energies. My father represented the fundamental Judeo-Christian patriarchal consciousness of the parsonage in which I was raised. My mother simply obeyed this masculine point of view. I was now confronting these voices in me. This dream also pointed out that we project what is unconscious in us outside—onto others and onto our environment.

In the end I meet once again the feminine figure Hilda and she tells me I must leave home.

As mentioned earlier earlier, Hilda has been a consistent figure in my dreams through the years, representing aspects of my anima and inner wisdom. Overall, she was a trusted inner figure and guide. This voice in me in this dream told me that I must leave home. I must leave the parental images and all their projections. I could no longer live under the rules of the masculine as represented by my father and as obeyed by my mother. Nine nights later I dream

> *I meet the minister of the church that I attend. He asks me about my plans to buy a new house. I tell him that I am "going for broke," meaning that I am going to put all my assets on the line to build this house. He responds in a way to show the seriousness of such a decision. I know that he is thinking that I can borrow the money from my parents, but I know that my parents don't have that kind of money. He tells me to investigate all possibilities.*
>
> *I talk to a man named Mr. Butler. He tells me that he got money he needed from his brother. I now see the minister walking down the street. He has lost a lot of weight and is very trim, appearing in good physical condition. I particularly notice that his shape has changed, especially how his legs and hips are attached causing a different shape from the buttocks and waist down, causing a different shaped butt. His butt is raised up higher and protruding.* (Journal, 1-28-88)

This dream indicated that I was putting everything that I had into building a new house, into building a new consciousness, a new psychic structure. The dream also said that I couldn't get the energy (money) that I needed for this new consciousness from the point of view of my parents. They didn't have what I needed. I must get it somewhere else, from Mr. Butler's brother. The end of this dream suggested the possible meaning of the dream's reference to Mr. Butler's brother. In this dream the minister's buttocks had changed shape. This dream showed the change in my own inner masculine minister-father image.

The body reveals the way a person is in the world, demonstrating a relationship between various parts of the body and a person's emotions and attitudes, even his consciousness.[284] Ron Kurtz in his book *The Body Reveals* points out that the pelvis assumes the position that expresses a person's set attitude toward living. For example, when the pelvis is tucked under, the tight buttocks allow for only a dribbling out of emotion and feeling. In this situation the person can't allow the pelvis to swing back and gather strength for the forward thrust associated with full emotional discharge. Emotions can, at best, only be squeezed out. In the opposite extreme where the pelvis is retracted, or held back, the individual is unable to release. In this situation a great charge has been gathered in the pelvic region but is unable to swing forward. Individuals with such a pelvic situation often have a fear of letting go.[285]

In general, a tight, contracted, and small pelvis is associated with immaturity and a lack of development of feelings of sexuality and instinctual drive or with a strong containment of these instinctual feelings.[286] The pelvis is the place where we carry our sexuality and phallic energy. The buttocks are also a symbol for the shadow, for what is "behind" us, unseen, out of view. We call a person an "ass-hole" or a

---

284 Kurtz, Ron, and Prestera, *Body Reveals*, ix.

285 Ibid., 60–61.

286 Ibid.

"butt-hole" when he acts in ways that are offensive or in ways that we would not. Thus the buttocks become the carrier for all that we reject and disdain, in my case, my rejected masculinity and sexuality. The buttocks are also connected to the symbolism of anality. Basically, anality represents self-assertion; assertion of existence, power, and control over mother, objects, and people as well as over oneself. It expresses the holding and wielding of might and power.[287] The dream showed that the minister-father masculine image in me had changed the way it held this energy. This suggested that the energy for this new psychic structure lay in how I held and carried my shadow energy and what I did with it. Currently held in its high, protracted position suggested that I was in the position of discharge and letting go.

I dream

> *I am reading a book on the sacredness of sexuality. I read a section on the sacredness of my homosexual needs and on the sacredness of watching pornography and masturbating. The book says these—homosexuality, watching pornography, and masturbating—are manifestations of the sacred experience of my anima.* (Journal, 1-27-88)

Why would I have such a dream? What was the unconscious trying to tell me? The word *sacred* means (1) dedicated or set apart for the service or worship of a deity, such as a tree sacred to the gods, (2) devoted exclusively to one service or one use as to a person or purpose, such as a fund sacred to charity, (3) worthy of religious veneration, holy, and (4) entitled to reverence and respect. Using these definitions, homosexuality, watching pornography, and masturbation are dedicated

---

287 Whitmont, *Symbolic Quest*, 241.

and set apart for the service of the anima, dedicated exclusively to her use in ways that are worthy of religious veneration or great respect and reverence, not to be profaned, violated, or made common. These expressions belong to the experience of the anima.

I have pointed out elsewhere that the anima is an archetype. As an archetype she is a powerful force in the unconscious, pulling us under her spell with a god-like fascination. Without knowing it we worship her. Mircea Eliade in his book *Image and Symbols* points out that sexuality has everywhere and always been a manifestation of the holy.[288] According to Eliade, the purpose of sexuality is to reveal to human beings that which is beyond ego, or in religious terms, that which is divine.[289]

Sexuality as symbol will broaden and deepen humanity's understanding of itself and of the enormous forces that live in the unconscious, which if not made conscious, will live out in harmful and destructive ways. If sexuality is to reveal that which is beyond ego, that which is transcendent or divine, then understanding its symbolic and sacred meaning becomes a means of self-knowledge about what our sexual compulsions are really about. Sexuality or to use the dream's references—homosexuality, watching pornography, and masturbating—*hold within their very manifestations revelations of the archetypal and sacred character of the unconscious.* To miss their meaning is to live them out unconsciously and remain stuck in the repetition of compulsive sex while missing what the soul is longing to bring into consciousness, its connection to the transcendent or the divine in us.

I dream

---

288 Eliade, *Images and Symbols,* 14.

289 Ibid.

> *I see a man reading a book. He tells me that he read something in the margin of a page that explains the problem that he and his wife are having. He shows this to me. It is a French word for woman, le femme. It is defined as "yes and no." The man smiles and laughs for now he understands his wife's dilemma, the reason she is acting like she is. (Journal, 2-01-88)*

At the time of this dream the man in the dream and his wife were friends of mine. They were having marital problems and both were in counseling. His wife had decided that she had been "too good" all of her life and now wanted to "be bad." She found herself attracted to another man, had become intrigued with another religion, and had decided to go back to school. She said that she had played a role all her life and now she wanted to live her life.

While this actually referred to what was happening in the life of these friends of mine, it also mirrored what was happening in my own life. Often the world around us will mirror to us our own conflicts if we are but willing to listen. My anima was tired of the role that I'd played all my life. She was attracted to another man, other masculine energy (my same-sex attractions), and another religion, and another sacred expression (the inner divine image), and wanted to go back to school and find another expression (my longing to leave teaching).

The dream mirrored my ambivalence not only about my sexuality but also about whether to leave home or not. This is my Hamlet's "To be or not to be," to choose life, my life, or not, which would be a kind of death—a suicide—much like Hamlet contemplated. The dream also emphasized the challenge of the anima; she was both "yes" and "no." She had no definite point of view and she had *all* points of view. That was the dilemma of the anima and thus the dilemma of the ego that had fallen under her spell. She was both "yes" and "no"—thus must consciousness decide.

But we can only decide if we have some hint as to what she is up to, for she will pull us into life and just as quickly destroy that life. Just as, over the past several years, I had struggled with the "yes and no" conflict about whether to leave church music or not, whether to leave the church or not, whether to leave my marriage or not, whether to embrace homosexuality or not, once again I was caught in this "yes and no" dilemma. This time it centered on whether to leave teaching or not, whether to stay put or move to another city and pursue my desire to become a psychotherapist.

My dreams continued to both show my dilemma and provide hints for the journey. I dream

> *I am sitting at a table with several others, both male and female. A woman named Regina is sitting at the table. She says that she had a dream. She sings the dream. She sings it in a beautiful, clear, very pleasing melodious, high soprano voice. It is simply beautiful. The last line of the dream that she sings is "And here I am at this place in my life again."*
>
> *When she finishes I turn to her and say "And that is exactly where you are in your life, at midlife where once again you must choose what you will do with your life just like you did at the beginning." I then say "No matter how this turns out (meaning the interpretation of her dream) with that beautiful voice, you must be singing someplace every week."* (Journal, 2-17-88)

This dream was clear about where I was in my life and what I must do. I was reminded of the previous references to "singing my song." This reference had marked my journey from its very beginning, starting when I lay in bed that morning listening to the singing of the birds and thinking *I just want to sing my song.* Later it manifested in the dream where I climbed the ladder to get "my music." The feminine in me had a dream to sing. As I reflected on this dream, the association that jumped out at me was that *Regina* means "queen." She is the feminine side of the king/queen syzygy that Jung speaks of in his book *Mysterium Coniunctionis.*

I opened this book to the last section on the king and queen, Rex and Regina, and my eyes fell on the last paragraph. It says

> *The Queen of Sheba, Wisdom, the royal art, and the "daughter of the philosophers" are all so interfused that the underlying psychologem (archetypal psychic structure) clearly emerges: the art is queen of the alchemist's heart, she is at once his mother, his daughter, and his beloved, and in his art and its allegories the drama of his own soul, his individuation process, is played out.*[290]

Its message is clear to me. My work with my dreams and my work to understand the meaning of my same-sex attractions—my archetypal psychic structure—was where the drama of my own soul and my individuation was being played out.

The day before I had this dream I'd entered my application for consideration in the three-year part-time evening MSW program at the IUPUI School of Social Work and decided that should I get accepted I would relocate to Indianapolis. I had also made contacts regarding possible teaching jobs in the Indianapolis area. The next night I dream

290 Jung, *Collected Works 14*, par. 543.

> *I am walking on the street where we used to live. I see the houses, including our former house. I notice the sky is turning deep, dark colors and realize a storm is coming. The storm hits and the houses are destroyed. I am now walking through the house where we used to live, viewing the rubble. I find three cats among the rubble.* (Journal, 2-18-88)

The house in this dream is the house where my wife and I had lived for thirteen of the first fourteen years of our marriage. During this time I had built an existence that fit into the collective view of the parsonage, taking my place in the life of a small town. I had built a professional career and become a community leader fully involved in the church. I had also become a father raising children and attending their academic and sports activities. I had opened and operated a Christian bookstore, building a life that served Moore's definition of the feminine—the sexual-socio-economic-procreative-collective purpose of existence.

In this house there had been moments of passion, moments of joy, even moments of ecstasy such as when our children were born, but there had also been much pain and tears. This was the house where I confessed my homosexuality to my wife. This was the house where I admitted to my same-sex affairs. This was the house where I shattered my wife's dream of what a marriage was supposed to be. This was the house that we had built together and that we had to sell to pay off the debt of the Christian bookstore. This house contained so much pain, so much loss, so much hurt, so much anger, so much betrayal. Yet somehow in the midst of it all, we had managed to make it through. We had managed to survive and eventually thrive. This house symbolized that old life.

The dream showed that a storm was destroying this house.

Basically, a storm symbolizes the creative intercourse between elements in the universe[291] and represents the creative power and vitality on which the cosmos depends.[292] Storms have dual creative-destructive symbolism.[293] Thus, psychic storms represent all those elements—both destructive and constructive—on which psychic life depends in its death, rebirth, and transformative processes. The psychic structure that once held me was being destroyed.

Storms are associated with the storm gods. Storm gods emphasize the father archetype that has to do with rain-provision and fertility. As such, storms are commonly identified with the bull and the earth religions. This beautiful description of the birth of the storm gods by Anthony Stevens in his book *Ariadne's Clue: A Guide to the Symbols of Humankind*, captures again the message of the archetypal tale described in the last chapter.

> All storm gods are symbolical products of a historical process set in motion by the discovery of agriculture and animal husbandry. The original supreme sky god gives way to them by a process of differentiation and specialization, his absolute sovereignty is diluted, and he declines into the more human role of the consort of the Great Mother. His union with her, as is the case of all such divine pairs . . . represents the hieros gamos (sacred marriage) necessary for renewal of the life-giving powers of the earth. With his demotion, the sky god may even yield precedence to the Great Mother goddess and her "son," who invariably turns out to be a vegetation god, who dies and rises again,

291 Cirlot, *Dictionary of Symbols*, 315.

292 Stevens, *Ariadne's Clue: A Guide to the Symbols of Humankind*, 182.

293 Tresidder, *Symbols and Their Meaning*, 111.

> guaranteeing the regenerative life of the crops as well as the eternal life of the soul.
>
> Dionysus (son of Zeus), Osiris (son of the Egyptian sky goddess), Aleion (son of the Phoenician Ba'al)—all were associated with suffering, death, resurrection, and initiation. The son of the sky god invariably shares the lot of humanity, and, through the provision of initiation rites into his sacred mysteries, assures redemption and eternal life.
>
> It was against the storm gods of fertility that the Semitic people produced their monotheistic, Messianic revolution. The triumph of Yahweh over Ba'al represented the reassertion of "heavenly" values over the "earthly" preoccupations with mere fecundity. Nevertheless, Jesus (son of God) conforms to the same historic tradition of those other sons of the sky god who underwent suffering, death, and resurrection to guarantee the eternal continuance of the cycles of life.[294]

Once again, the bull energy as the storm-god entered my dreams. The storm in this dream was none other than the Divine Masculine bringing the destructive, yet fertilizing, illuminating, and creative agent to my psyche. When we dream of storms, it is often representative of a sweeping change happening in the background of the psyche, a complete restructuring of the psyche resulting in a psychic shift and the birth of new growth, a new awareness, or a new consciousness. The dream suggested that my psychic life—once contained in that old structure—was being destroyed and dismantled, thus opening the potential for a rebuilding of my inner psychic house.

---

294 Stevens, *Ariadne's Clud*, 182-183.

In the midst of the rubble, I find three cats. I've already discussed the symbolic meaning of the cat. Primarily it is associated with the feminine as a basic instinctive drive in the psyche. My feminine instincts survived and the cats in my dream signified that I had found my connection to the feminine, my connection to the goddess energy, and by extension, my connection to the earth. Or perhaps it was in the rubble of this old consciousness that I was discovering my instinctive feminine nature. As the dreams through these past pages have illustrated, it was the feminine in all her seeming contradictions—her "yes" and her "no"—that was guiding this journey.

I dream

> *My wife, my children, and I are driving to Niagara Falls. We see a sign that says "Niagara Falls" with an arrow pointing the direction. I turn right to follow the sign. We are now traveling on a gravel road. I am surprised that it is a dirt road because the last time we went to Niagara Falls the road was a paved, dual-lane highway.*
>
> *As we drive on I see a paved freeway running parallel to this gravel road. I think that we should be on that road. We come to a small town and I ask a woman how to get to Niagara Falls. She tells us we have to go on the gravel road. I tell her that the last time we traveled on a paved freeway. She says, "Yes, but the lady who owns the land on which Niagara Falls sits has demanded that people not be allowed to use the highways. If they want to get to Niagara Falls, they must use the dirt road. We turn around and continue on. My teenage son is now driving. We come to a large drawbridge. It is closed. But as we drive right up to it, it opens up and*

the ends drops down and we drive right down, turn right, and go on to Niagara Falls. (Journal, 2-28-88)

This was a powerful and significant dream. It shows the direction of the soul. The waterfall mediated between above and below and was itself the incommensurable third.[295] When we are carrying open and unresolved conflicts, dreams and fantasies will occur which, like the waterfall, hold the tension of the opposites and thus prepare the synthesis.[296] If we can make the recognition of this Other in us as complete as possible, then conflict and disorientation occur—an equally strong "yes" and "no" that we can no longer keep separate by a rational decision. We can no longer hide the conflict behind a mask.

The conflict required a real solution, which required the emergence of the third—a solution in which the opposites could unite. Here the logical mind usually fails us because logically, there is no solution. The rational logical mind wanted me to choose—one or other—homosexuality or heterosexuality, my old masculine image or a new masculine image, my old life or a new life, the rejection of my spiritual past or a return to embrace the old spiritual church life. Logically and rationally, we can't see a third. The solution comes from the irrational or perhaps better said, from the nonrational, from nature, from the unconscious. As we hold the opposites, the unconscious acts symbolically, doing something that expresses both sides—thus the waterfall.

This dream again showed that my particular journey was an individual one. The feminine said that the way to Niagara Falls, the symbol for the union of these opposites, was not on the wide, paved, dual-lane highway that the collective traveled, but the single-lane gravel road. Even though the bridge—that which connects the opposites—was

295 Jung, *Collected Works 14*, par. 705.

296 Ibid.

closed, as we drove up to it, it opened and the way was revealed. At this point my teenage son was driving. My son represented a strong, aggressive, extraverted masculine. This developing masculinity was now driving me. This was both an encouraging dream and one that indicated the path I must take. Once again it was the feminine that was indicating the way. The land on which the waterfall stood—the union of the opposites and the goal—was owned by a woman and she had established the road to get there.

A few nights later I dream

> *I am at a military base. It is at the ocean. There is a huge submarine being stored in a building under the water. The military men release it. A huge very heavy- duty, powerful submarine shoots forth from under the water, going high into the air with great power. For a moment everyone, including me, is concerned and anxious as to whether it will land okay. The boat shoots way up, makes a complete turn, and lands on the ocean just fine. Everyone is relieved and happy. I know that the boat is on a mission somewhere.* (Journal, 3-3-88)

The night before this dream I had watched an adult gay-sex video and ejaculated spontaneously. Given this context, I could say that the dream showed how the unconscious experienced the watching of the same-sex video. Energy that had been stored in the unconscious (in the dark depths within the ocean) was being released with great force by aggressive masculine energy and finding its place where it could be seen in consciousness (on the ocean). On one hand this image was like an ejaculation—energy in the form of a large ship bursting forth from the unconscious depths that were holding it. The dream suggested that I had projected onto the same-sex video that masculine part of me—that masculine energy—that wanted to burst forth and live its life—its mission.

On the other hand it was like a birth, like a baby shooting forth from the womb (the ocean) at the time of birth. Ordained minister and depth psychologist Genia Pauli Haddon in her essay, "Delivering Yang-Femininity," calls this the thrusting power of the womb pushing toward birth. It is none other than the womb's birthing power, the initiator of all going forth, the outthrusting yang power that is at the heart of being.

The word *ejaculate* comes from "to throw out" whereas *womb-power* might better be described as "exertive." An old meaning of the word *exert* is "to thrust forth, to reveal." According to Haddon, yang femininity has for the most part remained unnamed, repressed, banished, and relegated to the shadow. Phallic energy generates goals and fuels purposeful activity toward them. Yang femininity pushes from within the actual life context. Forward movement orients toward the flowering forth of what has been gestating within the situation rather than toward an extrinsic goal. Womb power, in the service of bringing forth newness by the fullness of time, tends to push with what is being birthed, rather than insisting that things should be different in accordance with an extrinsic ideal.[297]

This dream could be understood as an example of how we project onto a pornography addiction or other sexual compulsive behavior or onto sex in general something unconscious, something that is longing to come into consciousness. In this case, the dream showed that my desire to watch a pornographic video and the resultant ejaculation was really about releasing a vessel, a container buried in the unconscious. The old container of my former life had dissolved, as shown by the

297 Haddon, "Delivering Yang-Femininity."

storm in the previous dream. I could no longer sustain it. This dream showed that behind my masturbatory act was the desire to bring a new vessel into consciousness—a ship that landed safely on the surface of the ocean—showing another way to journey the sea of life. The projection behind the masturbatory act was the act of psychic creation, a new life that was coming into consciousness—my particular mission.

Over the next several months my dreams continued to show this emerging consciousness and a path forward. I dream

> *My wife and I are walking in a wooded area. A lady passes us and comments on how beautiful this place is. We are walking in one direction and the lady is walking in the opposite direction. We then turn around and walk back in the other direction from which the lady had come. I see something standing by the path. It is an Old English Sheepdog. It is just standing there. It is a beautiful specimen of a dog, hair slightly tussled like blowing in the wind and as is their nature, hair hanging over the eyes.* (Journal, 3-22-88)

The night prior to this dream I had meditated and prayed for a dream that would help me know the direction that my deeper self, my soul-self wanted to go in. The Old English Sheepdog was a very important symbol with a long emotional history. Since I was a small boy I had always wanted this dog. When very young I had gone to a dog kennel with my father. I saw an Old English Sheepdog there. It was the kennel dog. Something inside me connected that day with that breed. Since that time I found these dogs to be fascinating, desirable, and exciting, attracting much energy. I used to stop by the magazine counters in stores and look for them in dog journals and read about them. I would seek them out in newspaper want ads. I have always said that one day I would have an Old English Sheepdog. In the dream the unconscious pulled from my long-standing desire for an Old English Sheepdog to serve as the symbol for the current longing in my soul.

The dog is a symbol of the object of instinctual desire. Whitmont points out that the dog is also a symbol for the "Wise Man" in his nature aspect. When not confronted consciously, he will enter unconsciously and automatically into any situation requiring initiative, action, and discrimination.[298] The dog is also a guiding protecting spirit, the guardian of the treasure.[299]

There was something playful about this dog of my dream. It was like he was just waiting for me to call to him. He was waiting to release boundless energy, yet he knew what he was doing. He was in a "stay" obedience command, standing in perfect form waiting for the command to be released so that he could come forth in boundless, emotional, loving energy. Like the previous dream where the submarine shot up into the air, released from its underground storage in response to my same-sex fantasy, the dog instinct as the guardian of the journey was awaiting my command.

My dissatisfaction and frustration with teaching continued to mount. I began to experience physical symptoms: chest pains, tension in my upper body and left arm. A physical exam showed no physical cause of my symptoms, but something was certainly affecting the area of my heart. My dreams continued to mirror my internal conflict, my ambivalence, my "yes" and "no" about leaving teaching, leaving the town in which we had raised our family, ultimately about leaving home. But they also showed movement happening in the unconscious—movement that pointed toward a solution and a path forward. I dream

298 Whitmont, *Symbolic Quest*, 207.

299 Ibid.

> *I am putting a sign on the steeple of a building. I cut the sign out of cardboard pieces and paint them green. I fasten them around the sides of a square steeple. On the green area I fasten the words "Dreams are for living" and "Life is made of dreams."* (Journal, 4-4-88)

This dream is clear. If I have dreams, they are for living, for dreams are the making of life. Yes, I had dreams, desires, and longings. My instincts were telling me to follow my dreams. But that required a different masculine energy. And while that masculine energy had been present in my dreams for this past year, initiating movement, I hadn't yet acted on it. Like the Old English Sheepdog standing on the path waiting, I just kept waiting. And then I dream

> *There is a large wooden pen. In it are two dogs. I know that I am to get something from one of the dogs. I stick my hand through a hole. I know the first dog is a mean dog and will bite me. That is not the dog I am to get something from. I go down into the ground, under the pen. There I find the other dog. I am not afraid of this dog. I stick my hand in and under to get to the dog's mouth so that I can get whatever I'm to get from the dog. The dog is an Old English Sheepdog.* (Journal, 4-10-88)

Here the dream shows me taking action. I take the something from the mouth of the dog, from the object of my desire, from the guardian of the treasure. Taking something from an animal is akin to taking on the energy of the animal, taking on its power. The next night I dream

> *I see a car. I don't know who is driving, but my brother and his wife are in the car. They are sitting in the front seat, my brother in the passenger's seat and his wife in the middle. The car stops and picks me up. I get in the back seat. Something is said about me not hugging my brother. This is because he has just returned from Africa and this is the first time I have seen him since his return. I say that I'll hug him later.* (Journal, 4-11-88)

This was a significant dream. In the time when I was trying to decide whether to leave the church music position and eventually the church, I had a series of "brother" dreams. At that time I established that my brother—a missionary to Africa—symbolized the part of me that was the minister to the unconscious, those dark and unknown aspects of myself. This was due to my general association with Africa as the "dark continent." During the middle of the nineteenth century, Africa was referred to it in this way because little was known about the mysterious land itself. While it is well-known that the African continent was mostly under European control until the late nineteenth century, the continent was still hardly mapped out and barely explored, even after the European powers divided the land among themselves. It was not until the twentieth century that those people occupying Africa were able to further explore the land and take full advantage of its abundant resources.

Today I would not refer to Africa as the "dark continent." But in the context of my consciousness at that time, Africa came to symbolize my dark, unknown unexplored shadow aspects. Just as my brother, the Christian missionary, was in Africa to bring the light of Christ to the people, I was trying to bring light and consciousness to the unknown, unexplored, and rejected aspects of myself.

Again, at that time, I was trying to decide whether to leave the teaching profession. So this part of me, the missionary to the unconscious, showed up. Interestingly there was no one driving the car. I got in but sat in the back seat and the dream reminded me that I did not hug my brother. I understood this dream as the unconscious mirroring to me my current consciousness as well as posing the question: Was I going to hug my brother, that part of me that served the unknown, unexplored parts of me? And remember that Mr. Butler told me that he had gotten money (energy) for his new house from his brother. Was I then going to take my position in the driver's seat and drive?

Eleven days after I had this dream I wrote my letter of resignation to the superintendent of schools. Shortly thereafter, I contacted potential employers in the Indianapolis area, and my wife and I began making plans to move there. Several months of struggle had finally come to an end. This is an example of how recording and interacting with your dreams can have a salutatory effect on consciousness, influencing the direction of one's life. Ten years earlier that voice had said to me "Listen to your dreams for I will speak to you through them." This voice had been speaking in the depths of my unconscious, pushing and pulling me, sometimes with great conflict, contradiction, and anxiety—as well as excitement—into and onto my path.

Now the decision had been made. I was leaving everything that was familiar, everything that I knew, not only physically—such as our home, my job, my friends, and a respected position in the community—but also ideologically. I was leaving a body of doctrine, myths, and beliefs. I was leaving home. Ironically, on July 4, the day of celebration commemorating our country's independence, my wife and I loaded all our belongings into a U-Haul truck, left the small town where we had lived for the past twenty-one years, and headed south into a life and an ideology yet to be discovered.

Notes and Exercises

Sexuality is a manifestation of the holy. In its symbolic and sacred meaning, sexual attraction becomes a means to self-knowledge revealing what our erotic longings are really about. To miss the symbolic meaning is to miss the other that the soul is longing to bring into consciousness.

Write down a sexual dream or sexual fantasy. Circle all the images in the dream or fantasy. List all your associations for each image. An association is any thought, feeling, memory, picture or literally anything that comes to mind when you reflect on the image. Ask yourself, what part of you does the image represents? Do this for each image in the dream, even objects, the dream's setting, environmental images, characters, and anything else you noticed in the dream. Once you have identified what parts of you the dream images represent, think of this as a story being played out in you, between your inner parts as energy in you. What is this story about? What part or parts of you are you engaging and interacting with in this dream or fantasy? What is the sex really about? How might this dream or fantasy reflect some spiritual meaning, some longing of the soul?

To think about our erotic longings and sexual desires in this way requires a shift in consciousness. We begin to see the hidden meanings in our behaviors. We realize that sometimes sex isn't just about sex. We become aware of the parts of us that we project onto and into sex as an attempt to get into life. To withdraw our projections and stop living them out in compulsive and destructive behaviors and carry them as parts of us that long for recognition, acceptance and love is to begin the hero's journey of living the life of the other. If this dream or fantasy wasn't about sex, but something else couched in sex to arouse you to something, what would this dream or fantasy be about? Who or what is it in you that wants to live? How do you begin that journey?

CHAPTER THIRTEEN

Archetypal Implications in Same-Sex Dreams, Fantasies, and Behaviors

I dream

> *There is a large bull running toward me, which I am to stop. I am somewhat anxious and not sure if I can stop it. I have two cardboard gates that I plan to put up in front of the bull to stop it. There are two sizes, a large one and a smaller one. There are men there to help me, but mostly it is my job. The bull is coming. I am holding up the smaller cardboard gate. A man at the other end sees the bull and indicates that I should use the larger, wider gate. He says, "wider, wider, wider." I put up the wider gate. The bull comes. I stop the bull with the cardboard gate and the bull falls down. I grab its horns and subdue it. The others come to assist.* (Journal, 12-31-89)

In many ways this dream could be a scene out of the Mithraic mysteries where the Roman god Mithras subdues and kills the sacred bull. In other esoteric teachings of Mithraism, Mithras himself was the bull that represented his lower nature, and by slaying the bull he was sacrificing himself for the redemption of humanity. Mithras, in the form of the slain bull, lay like Christ in a tomb for three days, before being resurrected to join with his Higher Self.

I have maintained throughout this book that the bull in my dreams represented the Earth Masculine. This is the masculine principle inhabiting nature, that generative male procreative humid force of the chthonic masculine that is also a symbol of the life-giving, death-dealing, regenerating forces of the chthonic feminine—the ancient Goddess herself. As such, it was the embodiment of my bisexuality and the shadow side of my patriarchal, fundamental Christian parsonage consciousness. In its first appearance in my dreams you may remember that the bull chased me up a tree. In its second appearance I was able to enclose and contain the bull in a barn. In this dream I physically subdued the bull. In this act of grabbing its horns, I was taking on the power of the bull, taking control of this energy. This was symbolic of embracing and integrating the bull energy.

In antiquity, ritual killing of bulls and washing in their blood was believed to be necessary for cleansing, eternal life, and salvation. This was followed by a meal of the bull's flesh. The adherents of Mithras believed that by eating the bull's flesh and drinking its blood they would be born again. Participation in this rite would give not only physical strength but lead to the immortality of the soul and to eternal life. This dream not only mirrored remnants of an ancient archetypal process, it showed a slight shift in the archetypal story—one from salvation through sacrifice, killing, and the drinking of blood. This, I will shortly show, is shadowed in the drinking of semen in the act of same-sex fellatio, to salvation through subduing, relating to, and the integration of the split-off, rejected shadow energy.

As we have established, archetypes are invisible fields of energy that determine human existence. They are the riverbeds along which psychic life flows. Like the invisible jet stream that determines the course of the weather, these hidden currents shape our lives. In many ways we fall under their spell and live out their lives unconsciously as fate. To wake up to the influence of an archetype is to begin to participate in its drama with some awareness.

Personal growth depends on our ability to transcend the limits of our personal stories. To do that we must recognize the multiple hidden meanings beneath our thoughts, desires, fantasies, and behaviors. Beneath our seemingly conscious lives is a whole other world. Understanding these hidden currents, these archetypal forces that lie beneath our drives, our obsessions, and our longings will radically change our view of ourselves and ultimately our personal stories and our lives.

A compulsion can be understood as a struggle against a part of the soul that continues to remain unconscious and is projected onto an object in the environment. We might think of it as an undifferentiated part of the Self that longs to be differentiated and brought into conscious life. In compulsive sex—whether it be masturbation, or oral or anal sex, for example—some part of the soul continues to be undifferentiated and placed onto or into the object of the desire in the outer world. To continue to repeat this behavior is to remain stuck in the personal story. To transcend the personal story is to get at the archetypal meaning or unconscious and nonpersonal meaning or purpose of the behavior.

Whenever we have a conflict or are caught in ambivalence about making a decision in a practical matter, the basis for such a dilemma is often our inability to distinguish between the concrete and the symbolic meanings of the pondered action. The concrete and the symbolic are two different levels of reality. These two levels need to be separated out and considered separately. When this is done, the objective decision is often easily reached. [300]

What is happening on the personal level, as troubling as that may be, is not as important as what is happening on the archetypal level. For example, a conflict between a son and his father on the personal level may be a manifestation of the archetypal story of the death of the old king—the death and destruction of a ruling consciousness. It may be that the ruling consciousness of the internalized father (in the son) is the source of the conflict—a consciousness that is in opposition to the one of the son or the one emerging in the son or the one wanting to emerge in the son. This conflict can certainly get projected out and onto the father-son relationship, resulting in fights, arguments, or outright rejection of the father if not understood from its archetypal source.

This aspect of the masculine longed to initiate me into its life. I could no longer kill or deny this energy as the Mithras ritual had done. Rather I had to allow it to initiate me into another masculine image. I dream

> *I am observing a male initiation rite of an indigenous tribe. In the ceremony the men are tied to a rope like a clothesline, naked with their erected penises hanging down. The tribal leader comes up and kisses the end of the erected penises. I am quite surprised by this action as I do not expect it. The scene changes and now I am one of the men in the tribe that is being initiated. I am tied to the rope in front of the tribe of men with my erected penis hanging down. A man comes up and kisses my penis on the head. I do*

300 Stevens, *Anatomy of the Psyche*, 138.

> *not ejaculate, which means that I pass the initiation into manhood.* (Journal, 7-2-91)

As my own personal consciousness evolved, I continued to have spontaneous same-sex fantasies and attractions, with periodic longings to act them out. However, my dreams also revealed to me that these desires were about something else. Over the next several months I had a series of dreams showing what was going on in my unconscious in the desire of this other masculine to find a consciousness that I didn't yet understand and a man I couldn't yet put a face on.

I dream

> *I am in the yard masturbating. I fear my mother is looking out the window and may see me. I move over to the left, to another part of the yard, so I am out of her sight. I ejaculate. I notice there is no feeling, no pleasure in the climax. The semen sprays out like a fan. I keep on masturbating. Finally I feel the pleasurable sensations begin. I keep on and ejaculate again with a normal pleasurable climax feeling. I masturbate fast to enjoy the feeling.* (Journal, 10-15-91)

I discussed at length the symbolic meaning of masturbation in chapter 8. Central to the meaning and purpose of masturbation is the dream or fantasy material that is the focus of the masturbation. I have discussed elsewhere that the penis as phallus becomes a symbol of the transcendent function that becomes the carrier of the aspect of the Self that transcends current ego-consciousness. I understood this dream as my attempt to get out from under the spell of Mother, not only the personal mother, but the collective institutions onto which I projected my mother complex.

This dream mirrored my ongoing attempt to come into a relationship with a masculinity that transcended my current consciousness and, by extension, the culture in which I was raised. This was none other than my ongoing desire for self-creation—the psyche's longing to bring into existence my own individual masculine consciousness. Masturbation can be understood as an act against the collective value.

At first the dream showed that I was having difficulty feeling this masculinity, difficulty enjoying or embracing this relationship with this masculine other. The dream suggested that eventually I did come to enjoy the feeling of this masculine other. To the extent that the penis as phallus is the symbol for the Self as Jung has suggested, the dream suggested that I might be hiding this relationship with the Self from the collective, still not able to embrace my own relationship to the Self, still under the fear of Mother.

A week later I dream

> *I am masturbating and have just ejaculated. I eat my semen. I expect it to taste like ordinary semen, a taste that I do not particularly like. However, the semen doesn't taste like regular semen, but in fact is very good—a taste that I like. I eat more.* (Journal, 10-23-91)

In this dream the masturbation led to my eating my semen. While this might seem disgusting and even pornographic, eating semen has a long ritual use in antiquity. These uses give some hint at the archetypal meaning and purpose of not only such actions in same-sex relationships, but in dreams and fantasies. Various traditions practiced the act of drinking semen. In Gnosticism, the elect bestowed "grace" on lesser initiates with a sacramental gift of their semen. In Tantrism, semen is imbued with magical powers and a "drink containing semen of a respected master is consumed by his disciples."[301]

A number of alchemical texts make reference to the act of ingesting one's seed and note that this ritual is still practiced by modern occultists who believe that semen "contains a real spiritual substance that is beneficial when consumed." They believe that "semen contains the "life-force" and gives one the extra energy needed to reach the higher mystical trances."[302] The Naasenes, a Christian Gnostic sect, practiced ritual masturbation in celebratory worship of the male power, ingesting the seminal emissions as the highest sort of sacrament.[303] Dutch missionaries in New Guinea observed that among many tribes "the male's semen was regarded as a sacred substance and was used in healing."[304]

Semen was ritually consumed in "Agape Feasts."[305] In these ancient rituals drinking semen was considered the drinking of life, itself.[306] Sacramental ingestion of semen was practiced in ancient Thrace and Greece as an act of transferring the virtues of the beloved to the lover. It was believed that this happened physically through the transmission of the semen, which contained a part of the soul.[307]

---

301 Danielou, quoted in "Suck like an Egyptian: Grail of the Christian 'Eucharist' is Founded on Ancient Semen-drinking Rites." Retrieved from zaidpub.com/.../spermo-gnosis-or-suck-like-an-egyptian-the-holy-grail-of-t...

302 Wilson. 1973. In "Suck Like an Egyptian." Retrieved from zaidpub.com/.../spermo-gnosis-or-suck-like-an-egyptian-the-holy-grail-of-t...

303 Conner, in zaidpub.com/.../spermo-gnosis-or-suck-like-an-egyptian-the-holy-grail-of-t...

304 Ingeborg Baldauf, *Boylove, Folksong and Literature*, 12–31.

305 Romer, *Testament*, 194.

306 Clair, *Sexual Mysticism in Christianity*. In Suck Like an Egyptian. Retrieved from zaidpub.com/.../spermo-gnosis-or-suck-like-an-egyptian-the-holy-grail-of-t...

307 Wellesley. *Sex and the Occult*, 34.

Lest we think that rituals such as drinking semen are no longer a part of current times, the Sambia of Papau New Guinea believe that both men and women are born with a *tingu*, the body part that allows for procreation. They believe that a woman's *tingu* is ready for reproduction when she first menstruates. However, a man's *tingu* is born shriveled and dried and the only way to fill it is to drink the "man milk," or semen, of other sexually mature men. The Sambia believe that by drinking the male essence of other men, the boys will become strong and virile. Done in the privacy of the forest, a boy will perform fellatio on young, usually unmarried men between the ages of thirteen and twenty-one. The boys are encouraged to "drink the male essence" as much as possible in order to become strong.[308]

These primitive and ancient processes linger in the psyche of modern man. A man fantasizes that he is sitting at a table with six or eight other men. They have gathered for a meal. Prior to the meal each man is to masturbate into his drink and pass it to the man on his left, who will drink it. The man masturbates into his drink and gives it to the next man to drink until all of the men have participated. He, being the man who started the ritual, then drinks the last man's semen. The ritual is complete. We continue with the meal. Another variation of this fantasy is that a glass of wine is passed around the table. Each man masturbates into the glass. Then the glass of wine is passed around a second time and each man drinks from the semen-wine solution. This can be understood as drinking in the male essence of the sacred archetypal masculine or the essence of Phallos, the phallic god himself. It doesn't take much imagination to make a connection between modern-day Communion in which wine is drunk as a symbol of the blood of Christ, and the ancient ritual of the young initiate drinking the semen

308 McKay. *8 Interesting (And Insane) Male Rites of Passages From Around the World.*

of the adult males as a way to take in the male essence, the transpersonal or transcendent masculine.

The fact that such acts have been practiced in various places in the world and by various traditions supports the idea of an archetypal process. I suggest that part and parcel of these ancient rituals was the desire to bring into consciousness a relationship with an unconscious Other, an Other that transcends the current consciousness. The task is to understand just what it is that longs to come into consciousness. This one must discern from the context of one's life and where the internal and external conflicts exist.

In the above dream I expect my semen, my masculine agency, to taste like ordinary semen. *Ordinary* suggests something common or normal with no distinctive features. Yet when I tasted it I liked its taste. This dream suggested increased acceptance of, even a liking for, my own individual masculine agency. For me, as the dreams would come to show, I was accepting and integrating my own individual masculine life-force—the Earth Masculine over the Judeo-Christian, patriarchal consciousness of the parsonage. I dream

> *I am walking through a sacred forest. I see a primitive tribe carrying out a ritual dance. The dancers, all male, are dancing around a fire dressed in their ritual costumes. I notice a particular male. I walk up to the edge and watch. The women are seated in a circle around the fire and the dance. I want to approach the dancer but I'm not sure it is appropriate to interrupt the ritual. He beckons to me to enter the sacred space and to dance with him.* (Journal, 12-15-91)

This was a powerful dream. This other masculine energy, the man connected to the sacred forest, to the fire, and to the dance of life, invited me to the dance. This dream ushered in a new relationship to the masculine, the one from which I had become split and estranged so many years ago, the one that was feared, the masculine of the body, the masculine of the sensual, the sexual, the masculine of the earth.

During the years that I was having these dreams the conflict between these two masculine images manifested in various ways. Even though I had left home—left my old life—I continued to feel torn apart, still not knowing just who I was. For example, while getting my MSW I found myself caught between the more traditional social work values of helping an individual *fit into* collective and social institutions in order to get his or her needs met and helping the individual become separate and individuated from the collective and social values in order to satisfy individual needs. I also found myself in conflict between working for a community agency in which I had to embrace the rules and laws of an institution and its collective values versus setting up a self-employed private psychotherapy practice. In addition, I experienced a conflict between the generally accepted therapeutic models of cognitive-behavioral therapy and short-term solution-focused therapy and my own individual interests in the unconscious and unconscious processes, Jungian-oriented dream work and the symbolic meaning of behaviors, psychoanalytic psychotherapy and alternative nontraditional mind-body therapies, and energy psychology. This longing was mirrored in the following dream.

I dream

> *I am discussing a case with two colleagues. The case is of a boy who masturbated into his excrement. I interpret it symbolically. The excrement is a symbol of the prima materia out of which the Self develops, and the act of masturbation is symbolic of the act of self-creation—the creative energies*

> *of Phallos. This action by the boy can be understood as the unconscious attempt—the unconscious longing to constellate the Self. When I finish and am walking back to my office, I notice how good it feels to have talked like this again—looking at the symbolic meaning.* (Journal, 3-93)

Again from my journal:

> *As I reflected on the dream and its feeling during the day, it comes to me that it hadn't been the ego that had spoken in my interpretation of the case, but the Self. I have this sudden awareness. The symbols live. Symbols are living energetic fields and the symbols heal. That is what I am about. That is my work. It is now a knowing. This is my journey!* (Journal, 3-93)

That night I dream

> *I have a new baby. It is in the shape of a phallus. The head of the baby is alive but its body is made of wood.* (Journal, 3-93)

Babies in dreams often reflect the birth of an idea, a new belief, a new project, or a new path. We often say "that is his baby" referring to a person's pet project or interest, creative endeavor, or responsibility. Given the powerful effect of the previous dream and my "sudden awareness" that "symbols are alive" and that "symbols heal," I see this dream telling me that this awareness is only an idea, a thought. Its body hasn't yet been realized or developed. It hasn't yet come fully alive. I haven't yet embodied this idea.

It is only now as I reflect on how my life led me into the study of and training in shamanic healing and energy medicine that I understand the full meaning and significance of these two dreams. It would take years before I would or could embody the sudden awareness of that day: that symbols are live energetic fields—even energetic or spiritual beings—that have the power to heal.

Because of the phallic shape of this baby and the fact that part of it was wood, I was reminded of Isis and Osiris. In this Egyptian creation myth Osiris is the king of Egypt. Isis, his sister, is his wife. One day out of jealousy, Set, Osiris' brother, kills Osiris so that he may be king instead. Set dismembers Osiris and scatters his body throughout the kingdom. Isis, who has great magical powers, decides to find her husband and bring him back to life long enough so that they might have a child. Isis roams the country, collecting the pieces of her husband's body.

There are many versions of this myth. In one of them Isis finds all the parts of Osiris's body except his penis. She reassembles them and then creates a phallus from wood and, through magic, is able to conceive the Divine Child.

While there are many meanings and implications of this myth for modern man, I will focus on its amplification for my own journey and particularly on these two dreams. My old consciousness, like the ruling king (Osiris), had been killed and dismembered in what was the death of my old masculine structure. Like Isis, my anima and inner feminine had been on a long journey of several years now gathering up the various parts of me and putting them (me) back together. Like the Egyptian myth where Isis couldn't find Osiris's penis because it had fallen into the river and been eaten by a fish, my phallic energy had fallen into the unconscious, which I then literally sought in men's restrooms—the unconscious longing to find a new consciousness, one congruent with the man living in my soul.

These two dreams showed the birth of a new emerging consciousness. This phallic shaped baby can also be understood as the emergence of the Self—my own unique individual Self—in that the phallus as symbol is often a carrier of the projection of the Self.

There is another amplification of this myth that I think deserves attention here. It is from a short but powerful article, "The Penis and Male Force—A Snippet from Isis and Osiris," posted on a WordPress blog, The Magic of the Ordinary: Encounter with Mystery, Politics and Sex, by Peregrin, March 6, 2015.

Peregrin writes:

> It is this loss of power that enables Osiris to later become a just and wise ruler and king. He needs to die to his inherited and assumed male role and become utterly impotent. Osiris's restoration is at the hands of and through the love and magic of Isis, the feminine. The once powerful king is rescued by a woman, who herself in some versions of the myth becomes disempowered and forgetful of her divine nature during her grief stricken wanderings.
>
> However, even when restored, Osiris is lacking his most vital and visible symbol of potency, his penis. The myth is clear—in order for Osiris to rule both the worlds, upper and lower, conscious and unconscious, he needs to give up his penis, his male power. He needs to accept the assistance of his wife and Goddess and have a new penis, one made from and connected to the earth. Only then is he fit to rule in truth and balance, linked to the greater earth.

On the spiritual level, this myth installs within us the eternal truth that the male force, including sexuality, is not the prerogative of the individual man, but is a gift from the Mother, from the earth. That is, sexual force in men and pubescent boys is not their own force but flows through their body via their connection to all life, and when transformed, respected and controlled, is a means by which they can connect more deeply to all life, to the earth.

This truth runs in direct contradiction to both conscious and unconscious attitudes to men and the male force within our culture. Common idioms and sexual slang position the penis as its own entity, its own force and it is not uncommon for pubescent boys to become so focused on and enamored of their penis they give it a name. The penis, so the boy learns from the world around him, has its own agenda, often in stark contradiction to the boy or man himself. This was graphically illustrated in the comedy show Seinfeld, where "Jerry the brain" played a chess game against "Jerry the penis" to decide if Jerry the man should continue dating and having sex with a woman he actually despised. Underlying the humour here is a dangerous meme of knowledge; the penis is separate from the man, yet it can control a man's actions. Men, we are told, think more with their dicks than their brain.

The Osiris myth opposes this enculturated view. His penis is from the earth, lovingly crafted by Isis. He rules by his acceptance of impotence and connection to both the earth and women. This truth is also shown forth (as well as many other things) in the Lovers tarot trump as painted

> by Pamela Colman Smith, where Adam looks to Eve, who looks to the angel.
>
> On a social level this truth indicates the need for men to give up male privilege. To accept we have assumed power, vitality, respect and force only through the fact that we are male, that we possess a penis. The power needs to be given back to whence it came, the larger world, women and the earth and we need to accept true, equal partnership with women—this is not a sexual partnership and applies equally to straight and gay men.
>
> The myth of Osiris and Isis gives us all this—and far, far more. Of course, we need not only to read it but to embody, chant, work and enact the myth. Then we will understand.[309]

It is my opinion that this shift in the powers of the masculine and feminine and their relationship to each other is one of the gifts that the LGBT community is offering to our society. It is none other than the rising up of another archetypal story of the relationship of the masculine and feminine energies and how these energies play out in our individual lives. I will develop this idea more fully in a later chapter.

This evolution is more than personal. It is also a transformation and evolution of our understanding and relationship to the Divine, to those transcendent realities that we call God and Goddess. This discussion of Osiris takes me all the way back to the first dream in my story, the dream where the bull was chasing me. The bull is a symbol for Osiris. It is the story of the creation of a new phallus, a new masculine consciousness, one created by and connected to the feminine and the

309 "The Penis and Male Force: A Snippet from Isis and Osiris."

earth. Like Osiris, whose new phallus was constructed by the feminine, it was the feminine, my own anima that, through the years, was connecting me to my new phallic energy, a new masculine image, the Earth Masculine, one connected more to the earth and the feminine as her consort and companion—the inner shaman-healer.

However, at this point in my journey I was still several years away from the full realization of just what that meant. I continued to have same-sex dreams as this energy continued to seek consciousness. I dream

> *I am with a man. He moves his feet so they touch my hands. I think that I will hold them like I used to do with a male lover. I fear he'll realize that I'm feeling sexually aroused and erotic toward him. However, he doesn't move his feet and I know that he is realizing that I haven't moved my hands. He starts gently rocking his feet back and forth. I don't object. I know he knows that we both want this. I become very aroused and get an erection. I want this but know that I can't because of my wife.*
>
> *The scene now changes. I now feel the man's mouth on my penis, not his actual mouth, but the presence, the heat, the breath and energy from his mouth. This so excites me that I ejaculate, releasing semen into his mouth.* (Journal, 3-27-94)

Certainly my wife in my dreams has, at times, referred to our relationship and how my commitment to that relationship prevented me from engaging in activities that she can't allow or go along with. A relationship with a man would fall into that category. However, an image in a dream is a symbol and as a symbol refers to something unconscious. So the question to ask is "What am I married to (besides my wife) that is preventing me from connecting with this other masculine energy?" At the time of this dream I was wrestling with the desire to become visible with my dream work by starting dream groups. I was caught in fear, self-doubt, and self-judgment, believing that I wasn't adequately trained, I didn't know enough. Additionally, the fact that I was going against traditional ways of thinking contributed to my struggle in making a decision, with following this desire. To give value to dreams and to the unconscious certainly went against my rational, logical, and traditional self to which I had been married for a long time. However, the dream showed that I did release semen, my creative life-force, into this other masculine. This dream would suggest that my energy was moving toward following that desire, the desire of this other masculine energy. A week or so later I dream

> *I am in bed with a man. We are touching and kissing. It is wonderful. My wife isn't as upset as in past similar situations.* (Journal, 4-08-94)

This dream came after I had started a dream group. Fear and self-doubt had been keeping me from following my desires to become more public with my dreamwork. This manifested as fear of my wife or the feminine to the extent that she symbolizes the feminine that is attached to collective values as opposed to individual desires. This dream showed a change in my relationship with that part of me that feared my relationship with the masculine. I was not as afraid to follow my individual desires that flew in the face of collective opinion and collective values and was beginning to accept my feelings and intuition about this desire.

At the time of these dreams I was struggling with my desires to work with dreams, my desire to become a Jungian analyst, my desire to work with adults doing inner spiritual work, to work with imagery and the imagination as a path for healing and transformation. This was the longing of my soul. I didn't want to work with children, with the schools and behavior problems that my current job was requiring of me. I felt constrained and again strapped in a collective system.

How could I satisfy that longing, that desire, and also take care of the practical side of life: paying my bills and providing a home for my wife and me. How could I follow my heart? This was the challenge that was presented to me. I found myself caught in fantasies and meditations of doing dreamwork and holding dream groups. Slowly my dreams began to suggest movement toward dreamwork and other expressions of working with the unconscious, such as sand play therapy, and art and painting and mind-body approaches to healing. I began to have an increasing awareness that reality lives inside of one and can be changed with imagery, visualization, and meditation. I would have dreams where I was back in the church, caught in conflict, struggling to get out, confronting voices from the past. The challenges to find my own masculine self and my own voice and to express it appropriately were represented in the following dreams and fantasies. I dream

> *I am to be in a play that is taking place in a church. I am playing the part of a woman. This is the first of four scenes. In this scene I am in bed with a man. We have just had sex. My opening line is "It feels so good to wake up like this." The line refers to being waked up by sex. I am called up in front to rehearse this scene. I don't have the lines learned yet, and I can't find the script. I say I need the first word of each scene as cues.* (Journal, 6-26-94)

During the time of this dream I was caught in several conflicts. Specifically, whether or not I should remain in private practice—which was not providing sufficient income to meet living expenses—or should I return to a job with an agency where income would be secure and health insurance would be a benefit? Did I stop working with children and follow my heart to work with adults in transformative processes of inner work and psychospiritual healing? Did I start analytical training at the Jung Institute or let go of that dream and longtime goal? I can see how this dream mirrored my then current situation. I was having difficulty finding my script, finding my lines, finding my voice. Given that I was a woman in this dream, I was having difficulty finding the voice of my feminine nature. But I did like being awakened by the creative process as mirrored by the sex in the dream. I dream

> *I am in an upstairs room. I am standing in front of a window, naked. I want to masturbate, but I think people can see me so I squat down. I wonder if people had seen me masturbating on other occasions. Just as I start to masturbate, a man with a child bursts through the door, which opened to a flight of stairs. I feel somewhat embarrassed that they came upon me naked and masturbating. I decide to go downstairs to the men's room and masturbate.* (Journal, 8-28-94)

To the extent that masturbation—among all the other things it may represent and speak to—is a remnant of an ancient archetypal creation myth, masturbation is about self-creation. During the months that I had these dreams, I continued to struggle to give birth to this new masculine Self, this other man living in my soul, to find the appropriate expression of this sacred masculine energy.

I dream

> *I am being initiated into a men's club. They strip me naked and lay me on a table. The men stand around me, masturbating. They ejaculate all over me.* (Journal, 8-28-94)

This series of dreams can be understood as reflections of ancient rituals of transcending an old ego structure. The men ejaculating all over me in this dream reminded me of the ancient ritual where Christian devotees were smeared with semen. It was believe that they absorbed this powerful liquid into their bodies and were thereby brought into living communion with God.[310] The sacramental use of semen, both eaten and rubbed on the body, also had a long tradition in Canaanite religion.[311] These dreams of masturbation, semen-eating, and being covered with semen could all be understood as remnants of ancient rituals, and suggested a dynamic and archetypal process occurring in the depths of my psyche—one that had to do with connecting me to a sacred and archetypal masculine. These powerful archetypal forces are often the energies behind the powerful, passionate and sometimes tumultuous relationships of both homosexual and heterosexual attraction as they play at creation and consciousness.

I slowly accepted the truth of my own being—my bisexuality and two-spirit nature, and the presence of a divine image living in me that was different from the one with which I was raised. As this process of acceptance began, I started making choices that were more congruent with my own interests, intuitions, and the growing awareness of my connection to the earth, nature, the energetic world, and the shaman-healer. In so doing, the same-sex dreams began to diminish and finally

---

310 Allegro, *Sacred Mushroom and the Cross*, 57-61

311 Ibid.

ended—except on rare occasions. I also came to understand that when such a dream or spontaneous fantasy did occur, it was a message from Spirit to step more fully into my individual path and to integrate more of the other man living in my soul and to let him sing his song.

As time went on, my dreams continued to point the way. They were my constant companions through this process, keeping me both grounded and connected to something that allowed me to slowly integrate work, family, sexuality, and purpose into a new life congruent with the man living in my soul.

Notes and Exercises

Personal growth depends on our ability to transcend the limits of our personal stories. Understanding the archetypal forces that lie beneath our drives, obsessions and longings will radically change our view of ourselves and ultimately our lives. Masturbation, oral and anal sex have archetypal implications.

Masturbation is related to the archetypal story of creation. Archetypally, oral sex is related to eating the penis of the conquered king as a way to take on his power and drinking the semen as a way take in fertilizing life force of the masculine. Anal intercourse understood archetypally is the way to get the spirit of the masculine in the initiate or youth.[312]

> *When caught in the compulsive need to masturbate, ask yourself what is wanting to be created in your life? What are you wanting to create? What is unfulfilled in you? What do you long to bring into life? Are your beliefs working for you?*

312 TePaske. *Rape and Ritual*, 113.

Is your job fulfilling? Is there something that you are wanting to do? Masturbation can be understood as an act of creation of the Self. Who do you want to be? What do you want to do? Where is your old story not working?

When caught in urge to seek out oral sex, do you want to give oral sex or do you want to receive it? Which role do you like most? Which role do you most fantasize about? Giving oral sex suggests the need to receive, to take in the masculine energy and to worship some aspect of the masculine that is missing in you. What is missing? Are you feeling overwhelmed by the feminine in any form—wife, mother, an institution, feelings, for instance? Do you force the Other to submit to you? Is this about split off or unacknowledged aggression that is trying to get expressed? If you are not able to exercise power in your life to act on something, you might find yourself seeking out oral sex as a way to take in the masculine energy that you can't mobilize. If you long to be the recipient of oral sex, this can be understood as the archetypal need to be validated and worshipped, with the other bowing at your own phallic power. Where do you need to feel validated? Worshipped? Made to feel important?

When caught in the compulsive need for anal sex, this can be remnants of the primitive man's way of getting the spirits of the masculine into the novice or initiate. Ultimately, it may be the desire to be impregnated by the masculine. This can also be an expression of split off and unacknowledged aggression, as anal intercourse can be quite aggressive in that it's a taking of the Other, even a rape. Again, what role do you most like to play—the one penetrating or the one receiving? Do you need to have or take somebody? That is an act of aggression, an act of power over another. What are you projecting onto this Other that you need to own within yourself? Even in consenting partners, these archetypal stories such as dominance/submission, victim/persecutor, innocent/villain play out. Ask yourself how are these archetypal stories are playing out in your life?

CHAPTER FOURTEEN

The Music Begins

"All life sings. It is your birthright to express your soul through song, adding to the universal song of life."

—Sandra Ingerman, *Walking in the Light*

I dream

I am in an office with two Jungian analysts. One of the analysts is working on one of my dreams. I say, "You have what ego-consciousness does and you have what the unconscious does. It is these two working together that influences a life."

The other analyst then draws a model of three circles. He says the other analyst doesn't accept this piece—God—pointing to the third circle. This analyst says "There are three things that influence a life—the unconscious, which is revealed through dreams, ego-consciousness, which is the I you know yourself to be, and God, which is a force that transcends both and acts on its own. It is all three that determine one's life." (Journal, 8-14-94)

I have maintained throughout this book that there is some divine spirit or transcendent purpose in my same-sex attractions and fantasies. This divine spirit is that numinous and highly charged transpersonal vital life-giving energy that responded to my cries in 1981 to sing my song by coming to me in a dream as powerful swirling rings of energy described in a previous chapter. I have maintained that this divine spirit and transcendent reality carries the highest creative function and ultimate reality of the psyche and invokes the sacrifice of the ego on behalf of its purposes.

Three years after our move to Indianapolis, I completed my Master of Social Work degree and began a second career as a clinical social worker and therapist for a community mental health center. The MSW degree and job as a therapist provided the container for me to continue to pursue my interest in dreams and psychotherapy and provided me a new lease on life—one that was more congruent with the images that I had discovered living in my soul.

My original plan had been that once I obtained my MSW degree and gained some clinical experience I would pursue my interest in Jungian psychology and begin analytical training to become a Jungian analyst. However, once I completed the MSW and began my work as a therapist, I found that my motivation and need to continue such training had decreased. Also, the logistics of paying off a school loan that had been necessary to get the MSW—an additional minimum of five years of study and the projected $50,000-plus it would cost to pursue analytical training at that time—seemed beyond my grasp.

Although my dreams continued to bring up the topic of studying at a Jungian institute and becoming a Jungian analyst, I began to understand those dreams as symbolic of a process happening inside me. They referred to my continuing individuation process rather than my potential striving to achieve the more tangible goal of becoming an actual Jungian analyst. I still hold some sadness around the loss of that dream. However, I came to understand through years of working with my dreams that there is indeed a process in the psyche that seeks its goals independently of external factors or the ego's desires—a process that provides a path to self-discovery, healing, personal growth, and even one's destiny.

As stated earlier, when the unconscious purpose of a behavior has been fulfilled, the energy then moves on to a next gradient or level of development. [313] As I came to understand that the internal spiritual and symbolic meanings of my same-sex dreams, fantasies, and attractions were my soul's desire to bring alive another man living in me, I began to make choices to give that man life. This energy had become the impetus to the many changes I had already made, including leaving my former life as musician, church leader, and high school teacher, to become a psychotherapist. In many ways becoming a psychotherapist was yet another projection of my own soul's longing for healing and expression.

As I settled into my life as a therapist, my dreams began to point me in another direction—one I had not anticipated or ever contemplated—shamanism and energy medicine.

I dream

> *A woman is sick. I am called to come heal her. I go to the house where the woman lives. Her husband comes out to meet me as I walk up to the house. He stops me and says he doesn't know me and won't let me in the house to see his wife. A lady, his wife's mother, comes to the door and says, "He's okay. I called him to come." He then lets me enter.*

---

313 Jung, *Collected Works 7*, 107.

I go to the sick lady's room. She is in bed. I sit on a chair beside the bed and just sit quietly with her. Suddenly I see myself with bird feathers—like a headdress you might see a Native American wearing in a Native American dance. I'm just sitting there with this feather headdress on. I then realize that I take the lady's ill energy into me and it is transformed, that is, it is healed and made healthy as it passes through my energy and returns to her, much like blood is cleansed by passing it through one of those machines that removes contamination from diseased blood.

I wake up with a peaceful, healed feeling and a sense of "okay-ness" and purpose. (Journal, 4-21-96)

Although this dream may be understood as the continued healing of my own feminine, it might also be understood as a call from the feminine to become an energy healer. This theme of the call of the feminine and energy healing continued in another dream. I dream

I am with a chiropractor and energy healer. She is training a group of us to heal pain in the body through energy. She demonstrates by touching the area where the pain is located and then touching the herb that is needed for the healing. She then touches the body in various places to balance the energy. It is the balancing of the energy that eliminates the pain. I ask her how she knows what herb to use. She says that she sees it. She sees the herb the body needs. The body tells her. (Journal, 8-25-96)

I dream

My daughter and I are walking in the town where we used to live. We are walking on familiar streets. We come to

> *another street and turn left. Suddenly we are walking in a different place. Everything is different. We turn again, trying to figure out where we are when we meet a man, a woman, and a little girl living in a house up on stilts. We don't know them, but they look vaguely familiar. We tell them we were in Bluffton, and we made a turn and suddenly we aren't in the small mid-western town anymore.* (Journal, 09-10-00)

Either I woke up and went over this dream in my mind, or I woke up in the dream and went over the dream. I then dream

> *What has happened is that we had walked into another dimension. Upon this realization, my body is filled with chills. I realize that this is what happens to people who can see into the spirit realm. They go into another dimension. I then practice going into this other dimension, moving back and forth between the two realities. I go into the other dimension and then struggle and struggle to come back. My body is very heavy. I can't move. I have difficulty swallowing. I know there is this other realm or reality happening simultaneously. I had walked into that realm. I am discovering that I can do it at will, move in and out of these two dimensions at will or consciously. It is for the purpose of seeing into this other realm, to see the sources of people's problems and to help them heal. It is a strange and powerful, yet somewhat frightening experience because it is almost like I can't get back.* (Journal, 9-10-00)

It would be several years before I would understand the implications and importance of this dream. As I began my study of and training in shamanism, I discovered that central to shamanic healing practices is what is called "shamanic journeying." When journeying, the shaman enters into an altered state of consciousness and travels outside of time into the hidden realms, which are called non-ordinary reality or the spirit realm. In these hidden realms one is able to see the root cause of problems. In these realms are helping spirits, compassionate spirits, who offer their guidance and also their healing and help on behalf of all life on earth.[314]

I dream

> *I am with a man and a woman. A lady comes for healing. We use hypnosis. We all have a part in putting her into trance. She is driving a car around a large circle. Suddenly the outside of the car bursts into flames. The lady is propelled around the track under the power of this energy. I recognize this is divine healing energy and know that she is being healed. She goes around the track several times. Finally she is again driving the car and drives up and stops. We know she is healed, an expression of divine power and energy.* (Journal, 9-27-00)

Again, this dream can be understood on multiple levels. First, it spoke to the continuing healing of the feminine in me and the work that I was doing at the time on my relationship to the feminine. Second, since the woman came for healing, it might also refer to the movement in my life toward mind-body medicine and energy healing. As a result of these dreams and the study on mind-body medicine and energy healing that these dreams increasingly brought alive in me, a spiritual

---

314 Ingerman, "Shamanism: Healing of Individuals and the Planet."

element began to emerge in my therapy practice. By "spiritual element" I'm referring to the invisible realm of energy at the root of emotional and physical problems. In general we are unaware of this spiritual or invisible energetic dimension of our problems.

Behind the form of any problem is formless energy. The basic stuff of the unconscious is at its core pure energy—formless energy that is malleable to human intention. We can both access and interact with this energy. Our expectation itself causes our energy to flow out into the world and affect other energy systems. As we get in touch with the unconscious through our dreams, and other avenues such as writing, art, dance, and other forms of Active Imagination, we have the capacity to shape that energy into forms.

There is a magic within each of us that we continually deny because it lies in the realm of the imagination—in the imaginal realm. It is the imaginal realm that gives power to the symbols and activates their power to heal. The previous dream had told me that symbols are alive. They are living patterns of energy, vibrating with information. Jung has pointed out that "an image or word or act is symbolic when it intends more than it says, when it implies more than its immediate meaning."[315] I have maintained throughout this book that I saw the images in my same-sex dreams, fantasies, and behaviors as symbolic of something else, some other man living in my soul that wanted expression. As I increasingly integrated this man into consciousness, I awakened to another reality—the reality of the energetic world. This would slowly result in a change in my consciousness and my world view.

When a person is unable to express what he or she thinks or feels, that person may create a symptom to express it for him. In this way the symptom becomes a symbol or takes on a symbolic meaning.

---

315 Whitmont, *Symbolic Quest*, 9.

Seeing something as a symbol allows one to get in touch with something indefinable, intuitive, or imaginative, or to get a feeling-sense of something than cannot be known in any other way.[316] Symptoms are manifestations of the unconscious and are therefore symbols of the unconscious. Since the core of the unconscious is pure energy that may be manipulated by human intention, we have the capacity, even the power, to interact with that energy in ways that transform it, as the above dreams suggest.

American psychologist Jeanne Achterberg distinguishes two types of imagery that play a role in healing. She states that "in preverbal imagery, the imagination acts upon one's own physical being to alter cellular, biochemical, and physiological activity."[317] On the other hand, "transpersonal imagery embodies the assumption that information can be transmitted from the consciousness of one person to the physical substrate of others."[318]

According to Achterberg, transpersonal imagery can exist or act across persons, functioning as a bridge to connect the conscious, imaginal content of one person with the conscious or unconscious, physiological or psychological activities or experience of another.[319] To see fantasies and dreams and even behaviors as functions of the imaginal realm connects the conscious mind and the energy in the unconscious. The pure energy that is vibrating at the core of the unconscious is then brought under the will of consciousness in a way that consciousness can go on to shape the energy into viable and healing forms through imagery that is held with intention. These images of the unconscious

---

316 Ibid., 16.

317 Achterberg, *Healing Images*, 450.

318 Ibid., 5.

319 Achterberg, *Healing Images*, 450.

contain the seeds of a new and better adaptation. This adaptation can be facilitated by interaction with the energy at the core of the symbol.

I have meditated since I was in my early twenties. Over the years my meditations often became times wherein I had visionary experiences. The increase of these visionary experiences coincided with my dreams of seeing energy, healing energy, and of seeing other realms. Following one particular meditation I went back to bed and had the following visionary-dream experience:

> *A feeling comes over me that something is happening to my body, like something is taking me over or possessing me. I can't move. I feel paralyzed. I feel frightened, like I'm losing all control. I look (although my eyes are not open) and see a spirit-like being, a mass of vapor like an entity of some kind. Within this vapor is a demon-like face, evil, extremely scary. I am frightened. I struggle to speak, still having some capacity to call out and I call out in the name of Jesus and demand that it leave. It does. As it does I become fully conscious and I see a message dimly written in the vapors but I can't make the words out.* (Journal, 1-6-01)

I struggled to understand this experience. Was this simply a dream or visionary experience? Or were there actual spirit beings that could enter and take over the body? Was this a manifestation of my own fears or some unknown, unacceptable part of me that I projected outside—some repressed psychic content? I know from my study and work with dreams that during sleep the body alternates between REM (rapid eye movement) and NREM (non-rapid eye movement) sleep. During NREM sleep, the body relaxes and restores itself. At the end of NREM, sleep shifts back to REM.

In the REM state, eyes move quickly and dreams occur, but the rest of the body remains very relaxed. Its muscles are "turned off" during REM sleep. This is to prevent any acting out of one's dreams. However, if you happen to become aware or wake up before the REM cycle has finished, you may notice that you cannot move or speak. It is like a part of the brain wakes up before the part of brain that allows movement awakens. So my paralysis in this case could have been that I had awakened from this dream before the REM cycle completed itself.

There are also phenomena called hypnagogia and hypnopompia. Hypnagogia is the transitional state from wakefulness to sleep. Hypnopompia denotes the onset of wakefulness. Mental phenomena that occur during these stages of "threshold consciousness" include lucid dreaming, hallucinations, and sleep paralysis. During these transitions from a sleep state to a waking state the dream images get projected out and are seen as living outside the dream. These are rather common experiences and can certainly explain my experience.

I began to wonder what might have happened if I had not been so frightened and had just relaxed into the experience? Had my fear made the image of my dream appear demonic? Had my fear made it appear fearful? Was it some evil in me? Would it have become friendly and benevolent if I'd accepted it or offered it love instead of demanding that it leave?

During the time of this experience I was studying the work of Dr. Brian Weiss, a Yale trained psychiatrist and chairman emeritus of psychiatry at the Mount Sinai Medical Center in Miami. As a traditional psychotherapist, Dr. Weiss was astonished and skeptical when one of his patients began recalling past-life traumas that seemed to hold the key to her recurring nightmares and anxiety attacks. His skepticism was eroded, however, when she began to channel messages from "the space between lives," which contained remarkable revelations about Dr. Weiss's family and his dead son.[320]

Prior to my reading of Dr. Weiss's books telling of his experiences and his regression and past-life therapies, I would have seen this experience as a dream or vision and interpreted it as a manifestation of my unconscious. I would have deemed it to be some piece of my (Jungian) shadow, some rejected part of myself, that because of my failure to accept it or value it, had become so repressed that it took on a demonic, evil quality. I decided to meditate and explore the meaning of this experience. As I meditate,

> *I have the sensation of floating and am aware that I am flying. I see the entire world at times. I remember many scenes from my life—this current life and what seem like other lifetimes. My eyes suddenly hurt as if they are suddenly filled with sand. I realize that I am in a sandstorm. Suddenly everything goes black. I am buried under sand. Then I am floating again above this scene. I see a large family sitting at a long table. I see the backs of women. A little boy is at the end. I am the little boy.*
>
> *I then ask the meaning of the dream-visionary experience. I am told "It is the spirit form of the distressed soul, Jaime, who committed suicide. He is caught, unable to move on due to his tragic and premature death. He needs forgiveness and help to move on." Not knowing what to do in such a situation, I simply say to him, "I forgive you. Continue your soul's journey."* (Journal, 12-01-01)

---

320 Weiss, *Many Lives, Many Masters*, Back Cover.

The week prior to this experience, Jaime, the father of a child client of mine, had in fact committed suicide. Was this experience simply my attempt to deal with this suicide? Or are their spirit-souls floating around us as Dr. Weiss believes—some waiting to reincarnate and others trapped in this earthly realm, needing assistance to complete their transition to the spirit realm?

Years later in my training in shamanic healing I would learn the technique of shamanic journeying (mentioned earlier), wherein we are able to journey to non-ordinary realms. I would learn to assist souls—who hadn't been able to make a complete transition after death—to complete their transition. I would discover that entities come to us from the other side for assistance and healing. As I look back over my life's journey and where I ended up I see more clearly how my dreams and meditative experiences were already preparing me, even introducing and instructing me—initiating me in many ways into the shamanic-healer path.

I have a dream that really started me on my current journey. I dream

> *My wife, her employer, and I are invited to the home of an oriental family for a meal. After the meal the man suggests that we paint. He gets some paints and paper. We paint. I put globs of paint on what is a very large canvas and begin smearing them around, mixing them.*
>
> *As I smear the paint around I notice that shapes and images appear and a picture emerges. I stop and look at it. I see a large house, a bull that has gored or knocked a man off a horse. There is background scenery. I look at Betty's employer's painting. He has painted a stone tablet. I think he has painted Christ, but as I look closer, I see it is Moses.*

> *I comment on how he made Moses look like he was coming right out of the stone.* (Journal, 1-12-02)

This dream with its painting of the bull and the horse carried me back to the first dream that had started me on this path. It was the dream where I was blind and riding a horse. I kept falling off and decided to return to the small town where I lived. But at that moment a bull came out of nowhere and chased me up a tree, preventing me from returning to the past.

This dream with the painting of the bull and horse images seemed more than a random occurrence. At the time, I was in a dream group. I shared this dream with the group and they were of the opinion that I must paint. I had never painted anything except for the painting of the rings that I had done after seeing them in a dream back in 1981 (as presented in chapter 2). The dream group suggested that I simply follow the process in the dream and see what happened. Following the dream's suggestion, I painted colors into a background. I then stared into the background and painted what I saw. It might be part of an animal such as a bird's beak or an animal's eye, a person's nose, eye, or hand. I then developed that image and let the painting emerge.

At first I brought little detail to the images. As I continued to paint, however, more detail emerged, defining the images more clearly. I credit the artist, the late Rae Witvoet, who saw my initial work and encouraged me to "just paint" and "not to worry about what it looked like." She emphasized painting as self-expression. Rae's advice set me free to paint and to trust myself to paint whatever images I saw or whatever images wanted to appear.

This painting dream became another critical voice from the unconscious without which I would have missed much of my life. Besides the dream's invitation to paint, which became a path for my continued healing and psycho-spiritual evolution—the soul's attempt to heal the mind-body, spirit-matter split in me—my wife's employer's presence in the dream and his painting of Moses needs comment.

The employer in the dream was an attorney in real life and thus symbolized a part of me that had to do with interpreting and maintaining the law of my psyche. In the Bible, Moses led the Israelites out of captivity and received the Ten Commandments from God. He is also associated with the idea of "taken out" and "drawn forth," referring to the fact that Moses was "taken out of the water" by Pharaoh's daughter. This latter reference connects with my comment in the dream that the painting of Moses looked like he was "coming right out of the stone." This meaning, which would materialize in my paintings, became an avenue not only for me to bring out images living in my soul, freeing them from their captivity in the unconscious, but also became a way to interact with the archetypal world of Spirit.

Following the process outlined in the dream, I paint a horse coming out of water.

Figure 2. *Steed Rising from the Sea*

As I finished painting this horse coming out of the water, my eye caught the word *Mercurius* on a page of Jung's *Mysterium Coniunctionis* lying open on the floor. I felt impressed to begin reading as if there were some connection between the painting and the book or the word *Mercurius.* I read several pages but—nothing. Some sixty pages later I came across a reference to the Atharva-veda and the sun-god Rohita. The passage reads "In Hymn XIII, I of the *Atharva-veda* he is praised together with his wife Rohini. Of her it says: 'Rise up, O steed, that art within the waters,' and 'The steed that is within the waters is risen up.'"[321]

Jung speaks of this within the context of the union of spirit with material reality. Of the hymn, Jung says Rohini, the wife of sun-god

321 Jung, *Collected Works* Vol. XIV, par. 735.

Rohita, represents the anima.[322] The water represents Mercurius. Both represent the unconscious. Therefore, in the painting, the water represents Mercurius or the unconscious and the horse refers to Rohita, the queen or anima. This suggests that the picture of the horse rising from the water represents the union of the spirit and matter. I consider this painting and the discovery of this passage in Jung's writing to be a synchronicity. It reinforced the movement in me toward the union of spirit and matter, and my belief that spirit resides in and is one with matter or nature. It also represented a return to an ancient belief that "Nature, including human nature, contains within itself a directing intelligence which is the source of all knowledge concerning the nature of a person's being and becoming."[323]

I recall a dream that I had over a year earlier:

> *I am with a group of people. We are on a trip for two weeks into the deep jungle. I am traveling in a jeep. The guide/director has been here before. We travel this road deep into the jungle. There are native men all along the path, in the trees, serving as lookouts. They have guns.*
>
> *As we get deeper into the jungle the road becomes narrower and narrower. The driver has to drive the jeep through the narrowing space—like maneuver the jeep so as not to hit the sides of this bridge like construction. The natives are laughing, friendly. They know the guide. He has been here before with groups. It is like the task he has to do. It all seems in fun—like a test, although one gets the sense that even if he hits the side, it wouldn't be any big deal. They'd*

322 Ibid., par. 736.

323 Stein, *Betrayal of Soul in Psychotherapy*, xxxvii.

just laugh that they had won. But the guide drives through successfully. We arrive and are greeted.

I am now at a conference. I've signed up for one area. I am in this area, waiting for the conference to start. There are two groups meeting—like preliminary groups—groups that precede the actual conference. The program I've signed up for is also having a pre-conference session, like an introduction to the seminar. I go to the toilet. I arrive at the bathroom. There are three or four toilets sitting over holes. It is very primitive. I chose the first stool because it is cleaner and has a better seat. I sit down to defecate. I notice the toilet has two holes—one to shit in and one in front to pee in. (Journal, 1-31-01)

I called this dream "journey into the jungle." This dream kept coming back to me over and over. I figured there must something more for me in it, something that I'd missed. I decided to paint the dream. I meditated on the dream and while holding it in my mind, painted it according to the instructions given to me in the dream on painting. Below is what emerged.

Figure 3. *The Call*

This journey into the deep jungle suggested to me journeying into the deeper unconscious, into the deep realm of the earth spirit, the primitive, the place of medicine men, shamanism, the earth and the wisdom of the shadow, my own spiritual shadow, the aspects of the earth and goddess religions that live in juxtaposition to my Christian fundamentalist training and upbringing. These were all parts of my soul's expression, parts of my own unconscious, perhaps residue from an ancient time or another lifetime that had been left unattended. This painting felt like a "call" to me, the "call of nature" symbolized by the "howling wolf" and the "man coming out of the tree and woman's head." I named the painting *The Call.*

In sharing this dream with a colleague, she made the association of "going to the toilet" in the dream as "nature's call," given that we often say "nature is calling" when we have to go to the bathroom, reinforcing my own idea of the "call of nature."

As I held this dream in my mind I felt the urge to paint another painting on this dream.

Figure 4. *The Gift*

Holding the dream of "journey into the jungle" in mind I followed the procedure of painting a background, letting it dry, and then meditating or staring into the background and noticing what I saw. The first thing that I saw was the shape of a container. I then saw what appeared to be a leaf or feather coming out of the container. Behind the container I saw the slight image of the eyes of a person. I then developed these impressions and let the process move on its own.

As I developed the painting, it became clear that the object coming out of the container was a feather. It was as if this person was presenting me with a gift—a vase holding a feather. A vase symbolizes the cosmic waters, the Great Mother, the matrix, the feminine receptive principle, acceptance, fertility, and the heart.[324] In this painting it was a feather that came out of the vase, out of the Great Mother, the matrix, the feminine.

The feather symbolizes the wind, corresponding to the element of air—to the realm of the birds. The feather headdress of the Indian chief closely relates him to the demiurgic bird. The late acclaimed scholar and prolific author Jean C. Cooper says the feather symbolizes truth—which must rise—lightness, dryness, the heavens, height, speed, space, flight to other realms, the soul, and the element of wind and air. To wear feathers or a feathered headdress is to take on the power, or mana, of the bird, and puts the wearer in touch with the knowledge of the birds and with their transcendent and instinctual knowledge and magical power.

I am reminded of the dream above where I am wearing a feathered headdress as I sit with the sick lady whose energy passed through me for healing. While various traditions have their own symbolic meaning of the feather, most feature the fact that the feather represents communication with the next world.[325] For me the feather represented the shamanic path—the gifts of shamanic healing, that capacity to enter into altered states of consciousness in order to gain wisdom and healing for oneself, one's family, one's tribe, one's culture, and the world. I call this painting *The Gift*.

In 2004 my wife and I decided to take a vacation to Sedona, Arizona. Influenced by the messages in my dreams and by the images appearing in my art I decided to explore the possibility of meeting with a shaman and participating in a shamanic healing. I did an Internet

---

324 Cooper, *Illustrated Encyclopaedia*,184

325 Ibid., 65–66.

search and came across Clay Miller, a shamanic healer in the Sedona area. I contacted Clay and arranged to meet with him. In preparation for this shamanic healing experience I meditated on this idea and painted following the instruction I had been given in the dream on painting. I chose various colors and painted the background. I stared into the background and painted what I saw. Here is what emerged. I call it *Healing Hands.*

Figure 5. *Healing Hands*

Upon arriving in Sedona, I call Mr. Miller to get directions to his home. He gave me step- by-step directions and ended by saying "When you see the eagle, turn right. That is the lane back to my house." I immediately remembered this painting and the eagle in it, which I had painted in response to my meditations and reflections in preparation for this trip. I had even brought this painting with me to Sedona.

Following Mr. Miller's directions, I found the eagle and arrived at his house. Clay explained the process, stating that he used his hands to work in the energy body, clearing out energy and releasing negative energy. I lay down and he began working over me with his hands, "unwinding," he said, the dark tight energy that I was carrying in my chest area. I again remembered this painting and the hands over the male figure in the painting. Was this simply a coincidence, or was there something more going on?

Again, influenced by dreams, my paintings, and a growing interest and attraction to shamanism, in October 2005, six months after painting the man with the feather and a little over a year after my work with Clay Miller in Sedona, I decided to take an introductory weekend workshop entitled "The Way of the Shaman" with shamanic practitioner, Sandra Ingerman. In this workshop we were introduced to shamanic journeying into altered states and into the non-ordinary realms of the lower and upper worlds. From my journal:

> *Sandra has us travel to the upper world to ask for and meet a guide. Again we are asked to find a place on earth that is an opening to the upper world (e.g., a ladder, a tree, clouds, etc.). As I am waiting for something to appear I see a winged horse. I get on the winged horse and ride up, up past the clouds, up past the planets, until I see a large bright light. I keep going up and come to a canopy- like place, like a membrane or blanket of clouds. The winged horse flies through it and I come out into a place where I see a beautiful, celestial-like city, made of beautiful stone. There are streets.*

People are milling about, but they ignore me. It is like they don't see me.

I am now walking. I keep walking through this city. I come to large doors. I knock. A woman comes to the door. I say "I am looking for my guide in human form." Without saying a word she acknowledges me and invites me in. She goes to a door and through it. She returns and again without saying a word invites me in. I go into this room and there is a man with a feather (much like the man I painted recently).

I ask "Are you my guide in human form?"

He says, "Isn't that who you are looking for?"

I nod.

He says, "Trust her" referring to the lady who led me to him. The idea was that I had told her that I was looking for my guide in human form and she had led me to him.

I then asked him, "How am I to use shamanic healing methods?"

He takes the feather, walks over to the window and drops it. I watch as it gently falls down to earth. I see it land on earth.

Sandra then motions with her drumming that we are to end this journey and return. I go to find the winged horse to return like I came, but instead find myself gliding or climbing down a thread, or rope, like a cord of energy where the guide had dropped the feather. I land on earth at the spot of the feather. (Journal, 10-8-2005)

The man and the feather reminded me of my painting, *The Gift*, where the man was carrying a feather in a large bowl, as if bringing it to me. On July 26, 2007, while doing a shamanic journey, someone handed me a large feather, right up close. It was a large owl feather. In July 2009 (two years later to the month) I was leaving town to take my first week's training in shamanic healing and energy medicine with Alberto Villoldo and the Healing the Light Body School. Villoldo is a renowned medical anthropologist and psychologist and I was excited I would be training with him. As I headed to the airport, a large owl suddenly flew up from the side of the road directly in front of my car, its wings almost brushing my windshield.

The images of being given a feather both in my painting *The Gift* and in a previous shamanic journey manifested in reality at that training. The man with whom I was partnered had a large owl feather and asked if I'd be willing to use the feather to do the illumination process, an energy healing procedure. I agreed. We finished the morning session and broke for lunch. After lunch as I was walking out of the building, this man was walking in, coming toward me. He was holding the owl feather out in front of him. He extended the feather to me and said "It is yours." Again, I remembered the painting *The Gift*. I remembered the spontaneous vision of an owl feather being extended to me. And now here it was, manifesting before my eyes in what we call ordinary reality.

Mystics and sages have long believed that an interconnecting cosmic field—a web of energy—exists at the roots of all reality, and this energy both conserves and conveys information. Ever since Einstein asserted that at the most basic level everything is energy, scientists, philosophers, and theorists have been evolving the idea that everything in the universe vibrates and that everything that vibrates imparts or impacts information. The simplest definition of an energy field is information that vibrates.[326]

---

326 Dale, *Subtle Body*, 3.

Classically a field is an area in which a force exerts an influence at every point. When "information that vibrates" forms an association around a particular subject or object, an energy field is formed that vibrates with this information. This vibrating information exerts an influence.[327] Energy fields emanate from every living source, including human cells, organs, and bodies, as well as plants and animals and even our thoughts. Various scientists and researchers have hypothesized several types of energy fields.

Cell biologist Rupert Sheldrake was the first to identify morphogenetic or morphic fields. According to Sheldrake, a morphogenetic field is a subtle field of information that operates autonomously, a database of information extending in space and continuing in time, which informs people with the programs within that particular field. For example, a cardiac field becomes a heart. All living organisms from cells to people that belong to a certain group tune into the morphic field and through morphic resonance develop according to the programs within that field. These fields serve as a database as well as a mental form.

Sheldrake posits that a morphic field can be set up by the repetition of similar acts or thoughts, and therefore explains why members of a family pass down certain behaviors and even emotions. A mother's anxiety might then be carried to son or daughter via morphic fields rather than DNA. Morphic fields, being subtle in nature, are not limited to time or space. Sheldrake's philosophy also holds that past life memories could pass lifetime to lifetime through a soul's morphic field. The organizing fields of animal and human behavior, of social and cultural systems, and of the mental activity, can all be regarded as morphic fields that contain inherent memory. These memories would be nonlocal in nature and therefore not anchored in the brain or a particular life.[328]

---

327 Ibid., 91.

328 Sheldrake, The *Presence of the Past,* 155, 240, 258, 383

Ervin Laszlo, Hungarian philosopher and systems theorist—drawing from anomalies and advances in cosmology, quantum physics, biology, and consciousness studies—shows how the discovery in physics of the zero point energy field (ZPE) is also the discovery of a universal information field known as the Akashic Field or A-Field. According to Laszlo, the A-Field is not only the original source of all things that arise in time and space. It is also the constant and enduring memory of the universe and holds the record of all that has ever happened in life, on earth, and in the cosmos—and relates it to all that is *yet* to happen. Laszlo suggests that the Akashic field is like a hologram that is imprinted with all that has been or ever will be. It is essentially what helps a universe know how to become a universe, how plants know how to be plants, and so forth. It conveys all the information of life itself.[329]

Will Taegel identifies an eco-field. According to Taegel, an eco-field is a region or space configuration of nonmaterial influence vibrating with information and meaning underlying a specific location. It is a region of influence that underlies a given ecology.[330] Various eco-fields emerge out of a more profound field, itself emergent from the primordial mind. The difference between Sheldrake's morphic fields and Taegel's eco-fields is that eco-fields relate to specific physical locations whereas morphic fields relate to collectives of organisms. *But they both hold memory of the past and literally inform the present and future.*[331]

Carl Jung identified an archetypal field. According to Jung, archetypes are the essential building blocks in the psychic structure,[332]

---

329 Laszlo, *Science and the Akashic Field*, 72-77, 80, 105, 131.

330 Taegel, *Mother Tongue*, 228.

331 Ibid.

332 Jung, *Memories, Dreams and Reflections*, 161.

and are not just inactive forms, but real forces charged with specific energy.[333]

Edward Whitmont talks of the "personal shell" and the "archetypal core" of a complex. This shell can always be traced to one's personal past and explained in terms of cause and effect of one's personal history. The energetic charge of the complex—which accounts for its continuing disturbing effect even after the personal material has been understood, interpreted, and integrated—comes from the core of the complex, from the archetypal field. This is the energetic field that vibrates with the information of emotions, behaviors, and images that continue to attract those experiences that match its energy, bringing us under its spell.[334] We can no longer think in terms of human behavior as being shaped only by the individual or family, but must take seriously the reality of archetypal fields and their interactive dynamics and influences.

Psychologist Alberto Villoldo speaks of the Luminous Energy Field (LEF), an aura of energy and light that surrounds and informs our physical body. According to this construct, this field contains an archive of all of our personal and ancestral memories, all early life trauma, and even painful wounds from former lifetimes that, when activated, function like a blueprint containing instructions that compel us toward behaviors, relationships, and other experiences that mirror our emotional, psychological, and spiritual wounds.[335]

How do all these theories relate to my shamanic work and my paintings? On one hand I consider my paintings a projective experience, much like clinical psychology's Rorschach test. I paint a background of undefined content, an ambiguous scene. I then paint the images emerging from this undefined space. In painting them, amplifying

---

333 Ibid., 352.

334 Whitmont, *Symbolic Quest*, 66–67.

335 Villoldo, *Shaman, Healer, Sage*, 46–67.

them, their personal and archetypal meanings reveal unconscious forces at work in my mind. Since the mind has a tendency "to structure ambiguous scenes into personally meaningful images that symbolize underling motives and emotions,"[336] my paintings are a kind of witness that speak to my life condition, a kind of shamanic journey for healing and insight. It does seem at times that at some point in the painting experience something takes over, a kind of altered or meditative state, and I paint beyond my abilities and experience.

What has emerged over the subsequent years are paintings full of animals and shamanic themes that in retrospect seem to have guided me, along with my dreams, more fully onto the shamanic path. I came to realize that the images in my paintings, in my dreams and meditations, are more than manifestations of unconscious psychic content, more than metaphors or symbols of unconscious forces within me, more than projections of the anima. They are actual fields that exist in the energy or spirit world. They are manifestations of the energy within me that are connected to that particular energy as it exists in the energy or spirit worlds. These paintings are my relationship with these actual energetic beings, whether animal, human, plant, or rock. They are real, manifestations of subtle energy. They are the pure formless energy that is malleable to human intention and flows out into the world and affects other energy systems. This relationship with the subtle energy—as the forms in my dreams, visions, and paintings—may in fact serve as my guides and helpers or as avenues of healing.

In the workshop with Sandra Ingerman, during a healing journey that she was doing on a participant to demonstrate how to work with bringing back a person's power animal, Sandra had us imagine that we were on a boat, traveling down a river. From my journal:

---

336 Walsh, *Shamanism*, 202.

Suddenly all along the bank, coming out of the forests, were animals of all kinds, coming to watch. Suddenly I see a large black cat, like a black panther, or black jaguar. I recognize it from a dream many years ago in which a large black panther is killed. Suddenly this black cat leaped across the water from the shore right into the boat and sat down right beside me. Almost immediately, a large owl flew down from the left and sat on my shoulder. The feeling of the energy vibrating through my body was indescribable!

Later in the day while journeying with a partner where she was to find my power animal, I see the large black panther just walking around on the bank by the river. Other of my power animals are there, the owl and the rabbit. Suddenly, some kind of large animal comes up and starts licking me all over my face. I didn't know for sure if it was the black panther. I felt it licking me, its wet tongue, like it was right there. My partner tells me that the power animal that she found was a large black tiger-like cat that had left me some time ago. She said that she saw it just walking casually and peacefully along the banks of a river.

The partner had no knowledge of my previous experience with the cat, nor that I had had a dream many years ago in which a black panther had been shot. (Journal, 10-9-05, The Way of the Shaman, Sandra Ingerman, Omega Institute)

The dream to which I refer occurred in 1987. At that time I was still teaching in the small town where I lived and, as relayed in a previous chapter, struggling with whether or not to leave teaching and follow my dreams. On October 12, 1987, I dreamed:

> I *tell a woman that I can't teach anymore and that I have enrolled in a program at a university. We walk past cages with animals. It is like these cages are the spaces in the program. However, all the cages are full. There is a large black panther in one of the cages. In order for me to have space in the program, the professor has to kill the black panther, which he immediately does. He pulls out a gun and shoots it. I feel badly but it is like the professor knows what he has to do to make room for me in the training program.* (Dream Journal, 10-12-87)

The healing and training ceremony in which the black panther returned occurred eighteen years to the week of this dream. While this dream may be interpreted from several points of view given the context of my life at that time, it seems more than coincidental that the theme of the dream was about training and animals—and then I found myself in a training in which power animals and animal medicine were significant. It also seemed more than coincidental that it was a black panther that suddenly jumped to me in the shamanic journey and more than coincidental that it was a large black cat that my partner found on her journey to find my power animal. Could it be that the energy in the form of the large black cat that the professor had shot in my dream eighteen years earlier so that I could find my place in some evolving plan had returned to me on this day as confirmation of my journey? Or even stranger, could the energy of the black panther somehow have been influencing me, pulling me toward this path in some way, for some time?

In November 2010 I made my return trip from the airport. I was returning from having completed the core medicine wheel segment of this training in shamanic healing and energy medicine. I was driving on the same road I had taken to the airport to start the training. It had been on this road that a large owl had made its appearance. Now, returning on the same road, there in the middle of the road was another large owl. A large owl had greeted me on my trip to start the core training and now greeted me once again over one year later upon my return from completing the core training! This seemed to put exclamation points or quotations marks around this journey.

David Richo in *The Power of Coincidence* says that animals will appear in both waking and dream life to serve as guides or as triggers to transformation.[337] Jung points out that when we become more spiritual, an animal appears. Animals may appear in life experience and in dreams, at synchronous times, to accompany or even escort us along our path.[338] Joseph Campbell says that animals are the great shamans and teachers—messengers and personal guardians that come to bestow their warning and protection.[339] Animals will appear synchronously when we need information about our path.[340]

Carl Jung coined the term *synchronicity* to describe what he called the "acausal connecting principle" that links mind and matter. He said this underlying connectedness manifests itself through meaningful coincidences that cannot be explained by cause and effect. Jung described three types: the coinciding of a thought or feeling with an outside event, a dream, vision or premonition of something that then happens in the future, and a dream or vision that coincides with an event occurring at a distance.[341]

---

337 Richo, *The Power of Coincidence*, 137-138.

338 Ibid., 138.

339 Quoted in Richo, *The Power of Coincidence*, 138

340 Richo, *The Power of Coincidence*, 138.

341 Lundstrom, "A Wink from the Cosmos."

Synchronicities are bridges between matter and mind, manifestations of the unknown ground that underlies them both, the underlying dynamics that are common to both. The meaningful patterns found in synchronicities arise not so much from the external events but through the unfolding of their own internal significance.[342]

The synchronistic experience occurs where two kinds of reality such as inner and outer, spirit and matter, mind and body intersect and provide a deeper meaning than their separate realities provide. These events cluster together into meaningful patterns without recourse to the normal pushes and pulls of causality.[343]

While I was working on and putting together these occurrences in my life and reflecting on the idea of synchronicity and questioning again in my own mind "does synchronicity even exist (although I have experienced multiple such experiences) and can I trust such occurrences?" I met with a client, a teenage boy. He told me, "I had a dream where I was having sex with a girl. I went to school the next day and the girl I was having sex with removed a wig and I discovered that she was really a boy. I was very upset to discover that I had kissed a boy."

As we were working on this dream with its possible implications and meanings about his own developing masculinity and his attractions to a particular girl, his adult cousin (who was also in the session), suggested that he might want to tell me what he had seen on a family member's Facebook page recently. It turns out that the family member had posted a picture of himself as a cross-dresser on Facebook. Later that evening as I was continuing my research and study of my own anima projections, suddenly there popped up in my search an article entitled "The Anima and the Cross-Dresser." Is it possible that the

---

342 Peat, *Synchronicity*, 8-10.

343 Ibid.

universe heard my own questioning about the existence of synchronistic phenomena and decided to answer?

Such curious events indicate that a mutual process is unfolding out of a common ground that lies beyond the individual consciousness. The formation of patterns within the unconscious mind is accompanied by physical patterns in the outer world. These synchronistic events act as an intimation of the meaning that lies hidden within a particular life, relationship, or historical moment.[344] They open up a new approach, one that shows how mind and matter are not distinct, separate aspects of nature but arise in a deeper order of reality. Synchronicities suggest that we can renew our contact with that creative and unconditioned source that is the origin, not only of ourselves, but all of reality.[345]

I paint a horse coming out of the sea. My eye catches the word *Mercurius* in Jung's *Mysterium Coniunctionis* and I have a "feeling" there is some connection. Reading, I find Jung's reference to "the steed that is in the water is risen up" as the union of spirit and matter. A black jaguar is killed in a dream so that I have space to attend a university and years later I find myself in a weekend training on shamanic healing, and a black jaguar returns to me on a shamanic journey. I stare into the background of a painting and see a man holding a bowl with a feather as if bringing me a gift of a feather; in meditation a hand extends an owl feather to me; months later I walk out of a building at a training on shamanic healing and am met by a man holding an owl feather. He extends it to me saying "It is yours." I paint a painting of hands over a male figure with an eagle looking on and weeks later find myself going for my first shamanic healing session in Sedona, Arizona, where I am greeted by an eagle at the gate. The healer uses his hands

---

344 Ibid.

345 Ibid.

over me, working in my energy field. Years later I find myself taking training in energy medicine where hands are used to move energy.

Is to place meaning on these experiences and events as confirmation or guidance for my journey superstition and magical thinking, regression to some prerational stage of development, or some transpersonal, transrational reality—a union of spirit and matter? If so, does it transcend my current consciousness? Does it connect me to this other man living in my soul, bringing me into a relationship with the sacred masculine that lives in harmony with the earth, the feminine, the Goddess of antiquity as my unique, individual self—that "treasure hard to find" that according to the early dream was the goal of my homosexuality? Was this journey into energy medicine and shamanic healing the unfolding of my soul's longing that cried out that early morning in 1981 to sing my song—to which the unconscious had responded with the dream of the swirling rings that I had called *The Birth of the Self*?

I dream

> *I find a dog of average size. I recognize that this is a dog that I know, a dog that I own. I then see another dog that I didn't know I had. It is smaller. As I start to walk away I see a just-born puppy lying on the ground. At first I think it is dead. I then see it is alive. I pick it up. I wonder whether I can keep it alive or not. I am now in my house. Others are there. We are concerned whether this puppy will live. I ask where it is. I see it. It is lying on the piano keys. It is still alive.* (Journal, 5-12-08)

The night of this dream I had filled out the online application to register for an introductory course entitled "The Shaman's Way of Healing." I felt excited that I had finally made a decision to explore shamanic healing. I totaled up the cost of the tuition, airfare, and lodging, saw the total cost, and changed my mind. I clicked "cancel" and went to bed.

I understood this dream as my soul's response to my decision to cancel my registration to the introductory course on shamanic healing. The dog represented some instinctual energy and life in me. Finding the puppy suggested that I had found some new energy in me but this energy was on the verge of dying. Again, a dog is a protector, a guardian. He is loyal and trustworthy. The dog's loyalty to his owner teaches us to remain faithful to what is important to us in life. The puppy on the piano keys drew my attention to the piano and music. The piano had been my instrument of choice in my life as a musician in church music.

In an early dream on this journey the piano had been boxed up and delivered back to me, indicating my life in church music was finished. The puppy—this new life—lying on the piano keys confirmed once again that there was some music for me in studying shamanism. Music vibrated in this union of spirit and matter.

After reflecting on this dream, I changed my mind and attended the training I had previously been set to reject. Although this introductory training increased my interest in shamanic healing and energy medicine, I continued to question this path and whether or not this was the call of my soul. Then I dream:

> I *am with a woman, a psychoanalyst, and her husband. The woman has met a man that I know. She really wants to help this man. However, they live some distance apart. I ask the woman if she ever does meditative healing work with people—holding them in her mind while she meditates, sending healing energy and healing light to them.*

> *She is quiet and looks to her husband. Finally she says, "Are you finally going to let people know that you do this?" The man admits that he does this healing work. He says that they both do. I encourage them to do this kind of energy healing and help the man. The woman says, "A man in the psychoanalytic school has been trying to get me to change my focus and do this kind of work. Now you come along and encourage me also."*
>
> *I say, "Perhaps that is why our paths have crossed. Why I have come into your life."* (Journal, 10-12-08)

A little over one year later, on October 29, 2009, I officially started my training in shamanic healing and energy medicine.

To recognize the connection between inner and outer events, between dreams, the imagination, and what shows up in one's life is to recognize a dimension of subtle energies whose characteristics manifest in mental as well as material form. Between mind and matter are energy fields—subtle energies—that connect everything in some whole. This whole both transcends and is the ground that holds these subtle energies. These energy fields act upon us and we act upon them. It is a reciprocal relationship. In this relationship synchronicities occur and the miraculous happens.

Notes and Exercises

The psyche seeks its goals independently of external factors or the ego's desire, a process that provides a path to self-discovery, healing, personal growth and even one's destiny. The symbolic meanings of sexual dreams, fantasies and attractions may represent the soul's desire to bring alive some other part of us.

Behind any problem is formless energy that is malleable to human intention. We have the capacity to shape energy into forms. How?

When we are unable to express a thought of a feeling, the body may create a symptom to express it for us. The symptom becomes the symbol. Seeing something as a symbol allows us to get in touch with something that cannot be known in any other way.

Images in our dreams or images that we create with our intentions are connected to that particular energy as it exists in the energy or spirit worlds. Our relationships with this subtle energy as the forms in our dreams and creations may serve as guides and helpers or avenues for healing.

Synchronicity occurs when a thought or feeling coincides with an outside event, when a dream, vision or premonition of something that then happens in the future and when a dream or vision coincides with an event occurring at a distance.

The energy fields of our dreams or of the images that we create with our intentions act upon us and we act upon them It is a reciprocal relationship. In this relationship synchronicities occur and the miraculous happen.

> *Recall a dream. It can be a recent dream or a dream that you remember from a long time ago. Write the dream out in as much detail as you can. Read the dream several times.*
>
> *Create a collage that represents the dream. Look through magazines and newspapers or search the web for images to represent your dream. Choose pictures, images, even words that attract you. These pictures may or may not be the literal images of the dream. In fact, most often they are not, because the images in your dream are symbols, symbols that represent*

something else. Notice what you are drawn to, what grabs your attention, what wants to go into the collage. Use them even if they don't make logical sense to you. These pictures, images, and words become your associations to your dream; the hidden meanings in the dream. Your collage may not look anything like your dream. But the collage will represent the energy in you that is hidden in the dream.

If you prefer, you can create your collage by drawings, scribbles, doodling, painting images and shapes, and/or using various colors and textures. Read the dream, place your intention on giving form to the energy of the dream and see what shows up See what form you give the dream in your collage. This is the hidden meaning in the dream.

Hang your collage where you can see it daily. Meditate on the collage and notice what begins to show up in your life. Maybe you find yourself having insights or thinking things you never thought before. Maybe a solution to a problem comes to you. Maybe synchronicities start happening. Patience is important. Sometimes it takes days, weeks, even months for the energies captured in the creation to show up in our lives.

CHAPTER FIFTEEN

Return to Eden and the Soul's Next Manifestation

My dreams, my paintings, and an increasing awareness of certain synchronicities between my inner and outer worlds resulted in a growing interest and pull toward the study of shamanism and energy medicine. With this, I made the decision to enroll in the Healing the Light Body School of the Four Winds Society and begin training in shamanic healing. This school had been founded by psychologist and medical anthropologist Alberto Villoldo.

As I moved more and more in this direction, I noticed that my dreams on the themes of homosexuality and becoming a Jungian analyst diminished. In fact, for the most part, they stopped entirely. I found myself thrust into the world of the shaman. In this world, everything is energy, alive and connected. It vibrates with its own conscious awareness, putting wisdom, divine intelligence, and transpersonal reality back into nature and matter, back into the object—whether that object be a stone, a tree, an animal, an organ of the body, or the earth herself.

My dreams over the past several years—of seeing energy, traveling to alternate worlds, seeing into the invisible realm, seeing and interacting with spirit beings, seeing the invisible or spiritual causes of people's problems—and doing energy healing, slowly became my awakened reality. They unfolded before my eyes—not as dreams waking me in the middle of the night—but as aspects of my training in energy medicine waking me to another reality. Was this the other man in me? Was this the reality behind my same-sex attractions? Was this the "treasure hard to find" that the dream had told me was the goal of my homosexuality? Was this the meaning of the dream that told me the "healing my homosexual self would be freeing him from the parsonage?" Was this somehow the voice that on that January morning in 1978 said, "Listen to your dreams for I will speak to you through them?" Was this the bull that had been chasing me in my dreams? All I knew was that as strange as it all felt, even disorienting at times as I struggled to understand and integrate these parts of myself and my experiences, it also felt like I had come home. It felt like I had somehow found a part of myself that had been longing for me, some part of me from which I had been estranged and separated.

I dream

> *I am meditating and I see an orb. I know it is my orb. As I look closer I see a small image of me in this orb. As I look even closer I notice that I disappear, and it is all pure energy. I become aware that this orb is my soul's next manifestation.* (Journal, 10-19-08)

At the time of this dream I did not know what an orb was. My only association was the mention of orbs showing up in the photographs of Alberto Villoldo, with whom I had recently completed a weekend workshop on the energy medicine of the Americas. The idea of orbs is very controversial. Some people believe that orbs are the emanations of spirits, soul energy, what we are when we leave our bodies, spirit guides, angels, or other paranormal phenomena. Others believe they are simply light reflecting off particles of dust and water. I have no intention or desire to debate the existence or meaning of these translucent spherical masses of energy that often appear in photographs and video recordings or that are reported to be seen by psychics and others who have the capacity to see into the spirit or energetic world.

Like all images that appear in my dreams, I understand this image of the orb as a symbolic message from the unconsciousness. While it is true that I have had dreams of events and people that did in fact manifest in outer reality—not only in symbolic form but literally as dreamed—I first understand a dream by it subjective inner meaning. This dream defines the orb as my soul's next manifestation. In chapter 2, I defined soul as "the part of us that transcends our personal history, our family and ancestral patterns, transcends our beliefs, even what we might hold to be valuable and true and connects us to the Divine Spark in us that longs to fulfill its destiny." This dream suggested that the soul evolves or at least has different ways of expressing itself.

This dream also pointed to the idea that at our most basic level we are pure energy. I felt compelled to paint this dream. I began by painting two orbs, one with an image of me in it and another just pure energy. Then I came to a block, a standstill. I couldn't finish the painting. I set the canvas aside and began another painting.

I painted a background based on the dream. This time I painted the larger orb, the one that was pure energy. As is my process, I then stared into the background to see what I could see. First I saw a horse, then a human face, then a black panther. I developed these images. Then, quite surprised, I saw a fetus in the orb. I painted the fetus. I then felt drawn to add the eagle, the hummingbird, and the serpent, all important animals and symbols in the shamanic medicine traditions of the Incas in South America, the shamanic tradition in which I was being trained at the time. It is as if the horse, the black panther, the hummingbird, and the serpent, as well as the human, were awaiting the birth of the next manifestation of my soul energy. I call this painting *Anticipation*. (See figure 6.)

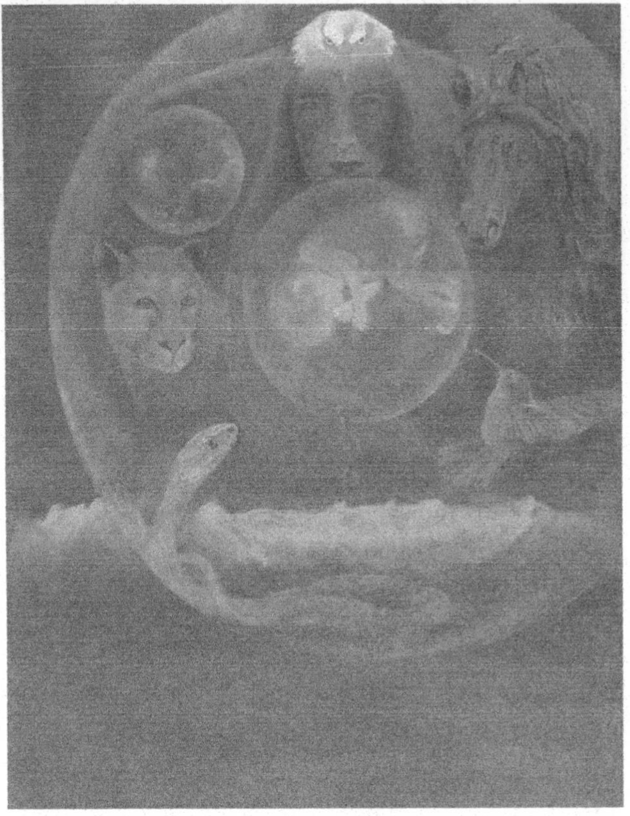

Figure 6. *Anticipation*

The first iteration of this painting sat in my office, unfinished, for three years. Then I took my shamanic training entitled "Working with the Sacred." In this training we learned how to step beyond the body and the mind and enter the domain of the soul, where the archetypal forces shape and inform our lives. We also learned how to negotiate with these forces of nature. After this training, I found myself pulling the canvas out and was able to finish the painting. As I worked on it, I saw cords of energy flowing out from the orb in the painting into everywhere, into the sky and the sea, as if impregnating or inseminating the universe with pure energy. The energy was moving. The soul's next manifestation was happening. Thus I call this painting *The Happening*. (See figure 7.)

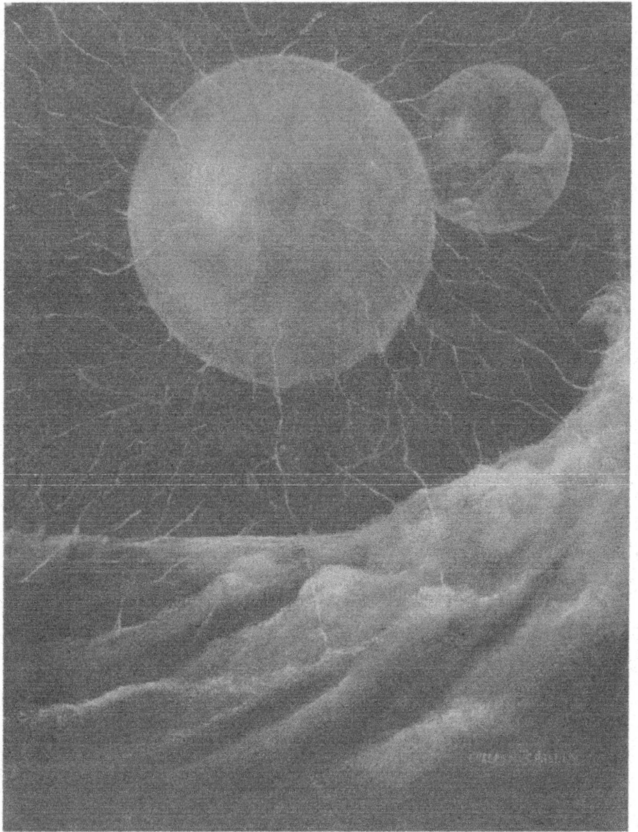

Figure 7. *The Happening*

As I continued to reflect on the orb dream and this painting over the next several months, the painting continued to evolve. It was as if the paintings reflected the emerging manifestation of this Other living in my soul. (See figures 8, 9, and 10.)

Figure 8. *The Happening Phase 2*

As I focused on the wave in the first painting, I saw a man's face emerging from the sea.

Figure 9. *The Happening Phase 3*

In *Phase 3*, I saw a man emerging from the water in the midst of two white horses. The fact that the horse motif appeared in these paintings about the orb dream suggested a connection between the painting *Steed Rising from the Sea* presented in the previous chapter as a symbol of the union of spirit and matter, and the man emerging from the sea, as my "soul's next manifestation." Perhaps this was the consciousness of "spirit in matter" that was rising in me.

Figure 10. *The Happening Phase 4*

In the next painting (*Phase 4*) the man emerged more fully from the water, flanked by the two horses. Was this the man for whom I had been searching?

I had the original orb dream one year prior to beginning my official training in shamanism and energy medicine with the Light Body School of the Four Winds. During this year I continued to study and explore various aspects of shamanism. In my prior experiences with shamanic healing I had experienced both the personal healing effects of shamanic journeying as well as my own capacity to journey. As a result of these experiences, I began to incorporate journeying into my regular meditative and spiritual practice.

As we have learned, in a shamanic journey, a man or woman goes into an altered state of consciousness and travels outside of time into invisible worlds that many call non-ordinary reality. Typically shamans use some form of percussion, usually drumming or rattling, to go into the altered state where these hidden realms are accessed.

Scientific study has found that when we are in an ordinary state of consciousness our brain waves are in a beta state. But when the shaman or shamanic practitioner listens to a rhythmic or monotonous drumbeat, the brain waves slow down. First the brain goes into an alpha state, which is a light, meditative state of consciousness. Then the brain goes into a deeper state called a theta state. In shamanic traditions it is believed that this is the state that allows a piece of the shaman's soul or luminous energy body to journey into the invisible realms of non-ordinary reality.

According to shamanic teaching, there is nothing that we can't journey about and there is no place we cannot journey to. Where we go will depend on the purpose and intention of the journey. Journeying is a way to connect with, attend to, and intervene in the energetic patterns that underlie all matter. I shared two of my early journeys in the previous chapter—a journey to the Lower World where the black panther returned to me and to the Upper World where I met a spirit guide who gave me the owl feather, detailed earlier.

One of the suggested journeys is to our personal Garden of Eden. From my journal:

> *I open sacred space, walk down a path, get on a boat, and journey down a river into a cave where I find myself in a beautiful meadow. I see Huascar, the gatekeeper to the underground, sitting by a large rock waiting for me. I*

approach him and ask him if I have permission to enter the Lower World to visit my Garden of Eden.

Huascar says, "Of course, and I will accompany you. But first we must loosen your luminous body and free it so that it can make the journey." I feel it loosening as if leaving my body, yet I am connected to it. Huascar begins walking and I follow. We come to a large tree and enter into the tree descending down through the earth via its roots. We pass through the earth layers and suddenly we are in this beautiful garden with trees, beautiful foliage, rivers, streams, flowering bushes, grasses, and every kind of animal. We journey on.

I am floating. I am energy that is me yet connected to everything. After walking some time we come to what appears like hundreds of people, dressed in black. They are standing around something. I hear the greatest joyous music coming from some place beyond them. I realize they are all standing around something, gazing at something, honoring something.

We pass through them and a path opens. We come upon the most magnificent, beautiful brilliant light that I have ever seen. It is beyond description. There is a deep opening into the earth. Out of this opening flows this amazing light and energy. The music is coming from this place also. I am invited to become one with this light and energy. At first I feel frightened. I fear that if I jump in that I will die. However, Huascar assures me that it will be okay, and together we are suddenly one with the light.

The feeling is amazing. Suddenly I realize that I am one with everything, connected to everything. I hear the words, "I am the Light of the World." The music continues—an orchestra and voices. I am floating, moving through everything all at once. These people dressed in black are really the bark of a large tree, the Tree of Life. This light is the center of the Tree of Life whose roots extend deep into the earth, where they are all one.

After several minutes of experiencing this we continue to move through the garden. I am one with everything, feeling and experiencing the trees, the leaves, the animals. Huascar indicates that it is now time to leave. I find this quite difficult.

We journey back to the river where I lie down in the water and allow the water to wash over me. I am still connected to the light, the energy, and the garden. I really have difficulty leaving. For a moment I can't remember how I got here or how to find my way back. I almost panic. I then remember the steps for returning from a shamanic journey. As I remember I pass back through the earth, past the bedrock, and return to the meadow where I had met Huascar.

I thank Huascar for accompanying me on this journey. We embrace. I then remember the boat. I board the boat and journey back to the Middle World where I get off the boat and walk back into my room. I am back in the Middle World, yet I still feel this connection to the earth. (Journal, 11-22-09)

My experience of this journey to the Garden of Eden confirmed what the ancients knew: The world is a living spiritual being. The ancient philosophers and the alchemists referred to the spiritual essence of the world as the anima mundi or the "Soul of the World," a pure ethereal spirit inhabiting all nature, the divine essence that embraces and energizes all life in the universe, the Divine Spark in matter. According to these ancient beliefs, there is no separation between matter and spirit.

The world and everything in it is alive, conscious, dynamic, interconnected, and responsive.[346]

In the biblical story of the Garden of Eden, Eve, representing the feminine principal, got Adam, the masculine principal, to eat fruit from the Tree of the Knowledge of Good and Evil. This act, which had been prohibited by God, caused Adam and Eve to be expelled from the garden, resulting in the Christian separation of spirit and matter and our separation from nature itself where spirit, mind, and man begin to be seen as superior to nature, body, and woman. The story of the Garden of Eden fundamentally underlies this separation of spirit and matter.

The Cartesian model sees reality as a dichotomy of matter (extended or spatial substance) and spirit (thinking substance, including God) creating a mind-body split. According to Cartesian dualism, the rational mind is superior to the emotional-body roots of human nature. The prime mover is God, whose directing intelligence is continually manifesting itself in the rational mind, and it is the mind, and only the mind, that has soul. This dualism removes spirit and soul from matter and the body.

Cartesian dualism assumes that the rational mind alone has the knowledge and power to know what a person should do in regards to nature while denying the ancient belief "that Nature, including human nature, contains within itself a directing intelligence (soul) which is the source of all knowledge concerning the nature of a person's being and becoming."[347] Consequently the concept of the ego has, for all practical purposes, become synonymous with the rational mind.

"*Cogito, ergo sum*: I think, therefore I am." While some have traced our modern sense of the isolated ego pitted against an alien and external world to Descartes, others prefer to see the moment of disjunction

346 Crockett, *Stone Age Wisdom*, 36-40

347 Stein, *Betrayal of Soul*, xxxvii.

in the twelfth century with the triumph of the Aristotelianism over Platonic and neo-Platonic cosmology. The defeat of that cosmology resulted in the disappearance of the anima mundi and the loss of the soul of the world.[348] Author and professor Tom Cheetham in his book *Green Man, Earth Angel* points out, "*[i]n any case it is an archetypal break—it happens in all of us sooner or later, to one degree or another. In our culture it is so much a part of us that we do not readily see it at all* [italics mine]."[349] This assumption that humanity exists as a unique entity only because of our capacity for rational thought is still the metaphysical base which prevails in much of our culture.

I agree with Robert Stein who says "When the rational mind [with its connection to God] is cut off from its connection to the body [and all matter] and is functioning autonomously, basic human needs are abused and distorted. So long as twentieth century humanity continues to approach this dilemma with the assumptions of Cartesian metaphysics [that spirit and soul reside only within the rational mind], there is no hope of reestablishing a new, harmonious and meaningful connection with basic human needs."[350]

This spirit-matter, mind-body split can be understood as the underlying archetypal cause for the conflicts that emerged in me, conflicts not only pertaining to the parsonage in which I was raised, but conflicts having to do with the culture in general and my same-sex attractions. More importantly for me was the sense that hidden within this spirit-matter or mind-body dualism was a sub-layer that could be identified as the conflict between transpersonal progression and pre-personal regression, which interprets nonrational phenomena as pre-rational or within the developmental stage of magical thinking thus relegating

348 Cheetham, *Green Man, Earth Angel*, 20.

349 Ibid.

350 Stein, *Betrayal of Soul*, xxxvii.

it to an inferior status. It is perhaps a bold statement to suggest that homosexuality and the LGBT communities in general are actually manifestations of some transpersonal energy at work in the evolution of consciousness and a more comprehensive world view than a regression to some inferior or less evolved state. It is interesting to note that in the Dagara tribe of Burkina Faso the gay person is well integrated into the community. This culture recognizes gays as having a higher vibrational level that enables them to be guardians of the gateways to the spirit world. As such they perform important and vital services for the well-being of the community.[351] (I'll expand on this idea in a later chapter.)

As my own personal journey into shamanism and energy medicine took me more and more into the nonrational realms of non-ordinary reality and transpersonal subtle energy states, I had a growing awareness that vibrating in the depths of the human psyche is a memory of the entire human race, not only our history but our future. Pieces of this memory surface spontaneously in our dreams, in our intuitions, in our inclinations, our attractions and longings, reminding us of another time. At various points in our evolution it becomes necessary to reject or simply leave behind parts of this history, parts of our individual stories.

My own story, as reflected in my dreams, suggests that it is the rejection of the pre-Christian, Earth Goddess and so-called pagan religions and matriarchal societies—the rejection of spirit in matter—that thrust me not only into the patriarchal world view, but that which stands behind my same-sex attractions—the energy of the bull of antiquity in me. The memory of this other time, my pre-Christian, pre-patriarchal history, for example, continues to vibrate in me. It is seeking

351 "Gays: Guardians of the Gates."

recognition as a way to connect me to that part of my psychic past, thereby helping to correct my one-sidedness and heal the wounds stemming from those losses and separations. It is also helping me to evolve into my future self, which is also vibrating in that psychic memory. This is all happening outside of time as we know it, all that has been and all that is yet to be—seeping into consciousness through openings in the membrane that separates these two worlds of ordinary and non-ordinary realities.

Various researchers and theorists have suggested ways to explain this phenomenon, from Barrow and Tipler's anthropic principle, philosophical implications of quantum-relativistic physics, to David Bohm's theory of holomovement, to Karl Pribram's holograph model of the brain, to Rupert Sheldrake's theory of morphogenetic fields, to Teagel's theory of eco-fields to Ervin Lazlo's Akashic field to Jung's idea of the collective unconscious.[352] It is not my intent or desire to try to prove, explain, or otherwise explore these various theories. It is my desire to provide one interpretation—my interpretation—of my story as revealed through my dreams, synchronistic events, and my journeys into the non-ordinary realities of shamanism as they revealed my soul's next manifestation.

I dream

352 Barrow and Tipler, *The Anthropic Cosmological Principle;* Goswami, *The Self-Aware Universe: How Consciousness Creates the Material Universe*; Bohm, *David Bohm's World View: New Physics and New Religion*; Pribram, *Languages of the brain: Experimental Paradoxes and Principles in Neuropsychology;* Sheldrake, A New Science of Life: The Hypothesis of Morphic Resonance; Prigogine, From Being to Becoming: Time and Complexity in the Physical Universe; Laszlo, *Science and the Akashic Field: An Integral Theory of Everything.* I also refer you to the work of Stanislav Grof, M.D. and his detailed research into this phenomenon. Also, see Grof, "Evidence for the Akashic Field from Modern Consciousness Research."

> *I go down, down, down into the unconscious, walking down a narrow stone stairs. I come into a large room with many electronic-like stations with lots of buttons and lights. It is very modern, state-of-the-art technology. We are to learn how to use this technology. It is like a chemistry or physics lab, a lab that is able to see into the cosmology of the universe, a place to learn how to read the energy fields of the universe. It is a place to acquire the ability to sense and measure vibrations, to see the imbalances in the energy fields, to turn thoughts into energy that then manifest in physical reality, into matter, a turning of Spirit into matter.*
>
> *I connect myself to the lab, to the technology. I put the headpiece on which is able to read my brain waves and my thoughts energetically. I attach electrodes to my heart, which is able to read my heart frequencies. I place my fingers on a scanner, which scans my imprints. As I sit in the chair, the chair reads my entire luminous energy body and both transmits and receives energy. Everything is energy, light beings being transmitted. In this state is telepathy, communication through means other than the senses.* (Journal, 1-2011)

One morning, two years after this dream and one year after completing the various phases of *The Happening* based on the orb dream above, I was meditating, remembering, holding, and interacting with a dream from the night before. Suddenly I was aware of the orb from the previous dream—my soul's next manifestation. I found myself holding my hands, spontaneously in a cup-like way, and the orb appeared in my hands right before my eyes. I was aware that it wanted to move into my body and around me. I felt a "quickening" in my spirit, like an excitement, as the energy moved through and around me. I had become the orb and the orb had become me. It was an exciting feeling. I continued to feel the energy in my body.

This experience came on the heels of a month of working on material related to "singing my song." I remembered the dream that I had back in 1981 of the rings spinning out in the universe, the painting of the dream. I now recognized that the colors of the paint in the center of the rings, that was then unformed, were the colors of the orb. Could it be that what I painted in the center of those rings back in the early 1980s was the beginning of the energy that had now manifested as the orb, my soul's next manifestations? Perhaps it was now time to paint the man more fully emerged from the waters, with the orb energy manifesting through and around him. I decided to make this painting more personal, more transparent, and use myself as its model. I call this painting *The Download*. (See figure 11.)

Figure 11. *The Download*

In the original painting of *The Download* the male figure was completely nude. It seemed fitting, appropriate, and even necessary that in order to be true to the intent of this painting that the male figure, the soul's next manifestation, would be nude, without attachments, as it emerged from the great waters of the sea. However, two months later I found myself feeling pulled to add a loincloth. While, on one hand, this idea may have been fueled by a need to address my discomfort about revealing a nude painting of myself to others, I discovered there is a history of symbolism attached to the loincloth that seems to have moved the evolution of this dream forward.

Originally loincloths were worn by priests and wealthy men of royalty. In the Bible, when God commanded Jeremiah who was not a priest or royalty, to purchase and wear a loincloth, it became a symbol of Jeremiah's obedience to God and the relationship between God and Israel. Gandhi's scanty loincloth was a symbol of his rejection of industry, consumerism, and materialism. In some cultures a boy's putting on the loincloth for the first time was a ceremony that marked his entrance into adulthood. The wearing of loincloths was common in indigenous cultures. No one can deny that native ways of life have taken a beating, in part from the spread of Western styles and in part because the environment is rapidly being rendered unfit to sustain a traditional indigenous life. Just as native material life adapted to these changes, the wearing of the loincloth is a small part of a psychological adaptation by mankind in which male sexuality is neither repressed nor vilified but asserted, and at the same time humanized.

Given this history of the loincloth, for me its addition to this painting symbolized my relationship with the earth, my relationships with nature and the spirit in nature, and my commitment to the shamanic path—my soul's next manifestation. It also symbolized my commitment to Spirit and living in "ayni"—living in sacred reciprocity with everything that is, recognizing and respecting the sacredness of everything. It was also a recognition and an honoring of Phallos, this other sacred masculine living in me.

In honor of the loincloth, I wrote a haika, which is a form of poetry that generally consists of three lines in which the first and last contain five syllables and the middle is made up of seven. The subject generally has to do with the natural world and is something that tends to awaken people to their sense of oneness with the Divine. Here is my haika to honor the loincloth and its symbolic meaning.

A loincloth attached
Remembers a sacred past
Nature and I one.

Again I recall the dream in the early morning in 1981 where I saw two beautiful rings in brilliant colors of red, yellow, and blue, one within the other, spinning in the universe. The dream had a felt, numinous quality. Jung speaks of the *numinosum* as an effect that seizes the human subject independently of his will, which causes an alteration of consciousness with a force not unlike a religious experience. The dream had such an effect on me—so much so that, as mentioned earlier, I felt compelled to paint it. I include it again here. (See figure 12.)

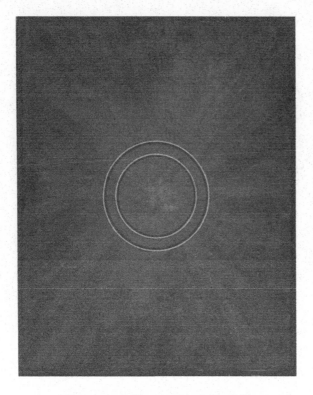

Figure 12. *The Birth of the Self*

It is as if the orb dream of the soul's next manifestation that I had in 2008 and these subsequent paintings were the continuing evolution and realization of the original dream of the spinning rings. Upon reflection I wondered if that powerful dream of the two rings was the universe's response to my soul's cry that morning to sing my song. Could it be that since that day some energetic field—such as Sheldrake's morphic field, Laszlo's Akashic field, Teagle's eco-field, or Jung's archetypal field or some other field yet to be discovered—had been pulling me toward it, toward my song?

As I look back over the last thirty-five years of my life, I see now that all of its twists and turns have been an unfolding of that call from the eco-field of my soul. In this it was calling—from its connection to other eco-fields matching its energies or morphic resonance—to bring me back into relationship with that primordial oneness—nature herself—which is none other than the ground of my own being and the longing of this other man living in my soul.

However, the full impact of this awareness was still some years away. There remained doubts, fears, and inner challenges to face, teachings to integrate, and lessons to learn.

Notes and Exercise

Through shamanic journeying we can step beyond the mind and the body and enter a place outside of time where archetypal forces shape and inform our lives. Where we go will depend on the purpose and intention of the journey.

The world is a living spiritual being where everything in it is alive, conscious, dynamic, interconnected, and responsive.

The Cartesian model sees reality as a dichotomy of matter and spirit, removing spirit and soul from matter and the body.

The ancients believed that Nature, including human nature, contains a directing intelligence which is the source of all knowledge concerning the nature of a person's being and becoming. The rejection of spirit in matter is often the source of our conflicts.

The memory of this ancient time is a call from the soul to correct our one-sidedness and heal the wounds occurring from our rejection of spirit in matter. The energy field of the soul connects us to other energy fields that match its energies and brings us back into relationship with nature herself, which is none other than our own nature.

Return to Eden Journey

Find a quiet place where you will not be disturbed. You may sit or lie down. Read through this guided meditation several times to familiarize yourself with it. Then take a few deep breaths and allow yourself to relax. In this relaxed state, read through the meditation again, allowing yourself to be carried on a journey to your sacred garden.

For another experience of this journey, you can record yourself reading this meditation and then close your eyes and play the recording, allowing your voice to guide you.

Take a few deep breaths and allow your attention to turn inward. Imagine that you are surrounded by a field of light. It may be a white light. Maybe it's a golden or a blue light. Imagine it however it comes to you. This is your luminous energy body. Now image that you are walking on the earth and you come to an opening. It might be a cave or the burrow of an animal. Maybe it's a tree with large roots. Now imagine that your luminous energy body is descending into the earth, past the roots of the trees, past the bedrock, past the great boulders, down, deep down until you come to an underground stream. When you come to the stream, lie in it and allow the cool, cleansing waters to wash over and through you. When you're ready, allow the waters to carry you down deep into the belly of the earth. The water washes you onto the shores of a sacred garden.

Feel the green moist grass. Hear the gurgling stream. Feel the cool breeze. See the forest in the distance. See the meadow before you. Walk onto the meadow to a giant boulder at the center of the meadow. Look around you. You are back in your primordial Eden. When you come to this boulder, call on the gate keeper of the domains of the soul. "You who are known by a thousand names, I call upon you. Allow me to enter your domain. Guide me as I come to discover that which will make me whole once again."

Sense the gatekeeper approaching you. This is an angelic being, a luminous being that is the protector of the soul, the protector of the region of the belly of the earth, the belly of the earth mother. Look in her or eyes. Feel yourself being welcomed. "Welcome home, my son. Welcome home, my daughter." Let the gatekeeper show you around your sacred garden, your Eden, a place you can come to anytime for healing, where you can come any time for renewal. Let him or her show you the sacred stream where you can wash away hurts, pain, any affliction you carry within you. If you want, you can lie in the stream and let its healing waters flow through you. Stay there as long as you want, releasing the pain, the hurt and wounded places that you no longer need to carry around.

Then ask the gatekeeper to show you the way to the forest, to the woods. Hear the sounds of your sacred garden. Is there music? Are there birds singing? Notice the vibration of the environment. How does it feel? Ask him or her to show you the sandy shores of the sacred river. Ask to see your sacred garden, your Garden of Eden and just notice and experience this connection to your soul, this connection to the Divine in you......(allow time to experience your inner sacred garden however it might show up).

As you prepare to leave the sacred garden, ask the gate-keeper to lead you back to the meadow where you entered and take your leave from her. Thank her for allowing you to experience your sacred garden. Walk back to where the waters brought you. Dive in the water once again. Allow the waters to take you back to the place where you rested and rest there again. Allow the waters to wash away any energies that you may not bring with you from the domains of the soul, from the lower world back into our world.

And when you are ready begin your journey up, up through the bed rock past the giant boulders, past the roots of the great trees, back up through the earth and back into your room and into your body. Take a deep breath and another. Wiggle you toes and fingers. Open your eyes. Welcome back, knowing that you can visit you Garden of Eden anytime.

CHAPTER SIXTEEN

The Matter of the Heart and the Heart of Matter

"When there is a conflict of priorities, one must follow the heart."

—From my *Swan Lake* dream

I dream

I am walking with a female psychoanalyst. I put my hand over a spot on her back at her heart area. I feel energy of a wound or illness. As I hold my hand there I begin to feel the energy moving, as if I am extracting or healing this energy. This experience intensifies. She begins to convulse. She falls to the ground as if having a seizure, eyes rolling back into her head, contorting. I become somewhat anxious, wondering if she is going to be okay. She goes back in time to where she falls off a tricycle, hits her head, and dies.

Suddenly she quiets, eyes return. She gets up and says, "I haven't felt this good after ten heart surgeries," indicating that she has heart disease or a heart condition, something I didn't know. Her husband is waiting for her in the car. She says that she is going to send people to me. I say, "I never did this before," intimating that I may not be able to do it again. I just noticed that when I put my hand on your back, I felt dark and heavy energy there and the healing just started happening." (Journal, 11-01-08)

The feeling in this dream was intense and powerful. I had this dream after doing a soul retrieval journey. In that journey I entered into what is described as the four chambers of the soul, which compares to the four chambers of the heart. In the first chamber you explore an original wound. In the second chamber you discover and renegotiate your soul's contracts that have kept you bound to repeating the events of the wounding. In the third chamber you retrieve the soul part that was lost because of the wounding, and in the fourth chamber you receive gifts that will help the recovered soul express and live its purpose.[353]

When I did this shamanic journey I did not have any particular images come to me in the various chambers. I just accepted that whatever was happening was occurring on the energetic level where everything is pure energy. Even though I wasn't aware of anything happening on the soul retrieval journey, the dream would indicate otherwise.

This was another dream about energy healing and healing the feminine. This time the healing was at the heart level. I was healing the heart of the feminine, or perhaps I was getting to the heart of the matter of the feminine. I am reminded of the *Swan Lake* dream where the lady in the dream says, "When there is a conflict of priorities, one must follow the heart."

But what does it mean to follow the heart? The lady in this dream was a psychoanalyst. She was the same psychoanalyst in the dream that

---

353 Villoldo, *Mending the Past and Healing the Future*, 48–106.

ended chapter 14, where she asked her husband if he was finally going to admit that he did energy healing. In this dream she made reference to having a heart condition. What was this heart condition? Since I accepted that dream figures represented parts of me I had to ask "What is the issue at the heart of the psychoanalyst in me?"

A psychoanalyst is someone who explores how unconscious factors contribute to problems in a person's life, believing that bringing unconscious factors into consciousness can result in the elimination of problems, contribute to healing, and move us toward greater wholeness. I have long accepted the idea that unconscious factors influence most of what a person does. My journey into Jungian psychology and my own Jungian analysis had proved that to me. Although we think that our problems are with the people or the circumstances of our lives, such problems are often reflections of the conflicts between parts of ourselves.

At the time of this dream, I was in a psychotherapy practice with a group of colleagues, two of whom were trained in Freudian-based psychoanalytic theory. One of them was the psychoanalyst in the dream; she was in training to become a psychoanalyst. My own personal journey into shamanism and energy medicine was taking me increasingly into the nonrational realms of non-ordinary reality and transpersonal subtle energy states. As a result I came up against the Freudian psychoanalytic view, represented by my colleagues, which tended to pathologize attempts to carry ascent development to its transpersonal conclusion beyond Piaget's formal operational stage of cognitive development and rational world view. These latter two constructs are widely recognized by conventional psychotherapies and mainstream science, which view such ideas as neurotic immaturities of a prerational, magical thinking stage of development. They are therefore deemed to be inferior and less developed when contrasted with elements of possible, higher stages of development such as vision-logic, psychic, subtle, causal or non-dual, suggested by some developmental researchers.[354]

As the psychoanalytic and shamanic stories, with their differing theories and assumptions, increased in their power and presence, the core conflict between these two world views collided and became activated. I felt as if my colleagues saw my journey into shamanism as invalid, regressive, and inferior and that they believed psychoanalysis to be superior. However, I did not have any concrete evidence that either of my colleagues held such classical Freudian beliefs or world views and because both were very supportive of my journey into shamanism and energy healing, I had to assume that this conflict was entirely within me and had become projected onto my colleagues, given that they carried the hook for such a projection.

As mentioned in the previous chapter, the assumption that humanity exists as a unique entity only because of our capacity for rational thought is still the metaphysical base that prevails in our culture and in much psychotherapy, perpetuating the soul-splitting effects of the Cartesian mind-body, spirit-matter dichotomy. This spirit-matter, mind-body split was the underlying archetypal cause of the conflict that emerged in me between my heterosexual and homosexual selves, between the masculine consciousness of the parsonage in which I was raised and the one emerging from the depths of my own soul.

This conflict now emerged between the psychoanalyst and the shaman in me. This most recent conflict seemed to get at the heart of the matter by throwing me headlong into a reality in which there was no such split. Spirit lived in matter, one with it. Perhaps this is what is at the heart of matter. And perhaps this is also what is at the heart

354 Walsh, "*The Spirit of Evolution.*"

of the feminine. Is this what the feminine knows? Is this what the heart knows? Is this what is vibrating in matter—there is no separation between mind and body, no separation between spirit and matter? My journey into shamanism and energy medicine had brought me face-to-face with this ancient wisdom. As I held these opposing world views, much like I held my homosexual and heterosexual selves as both being contained in some underlying whole, a journey into the Under World would provide an answer. From my journal:

> *I travel to the Underworld to visit with Huascar, the guide and guardian of the Underworld. We come to a pool of water surrounded by beautiful vegetation. I notice many hummingbirds. Huascar tells me "This is the Place of the Hummingbirds." I look into the pool, which is crystal clear. Mist rises from the pool, and Huascar tells me that the mist rising from the pool is the wisdom of the hummingbird. He instructs me to visit this place regularly and that I will learn to read the mist rising from the pool.*
>
> *Suddenly I hear these words, "Look deep within the pool that is inside you and you will find the wisdom of the universe." I'm thinking, "I don't know whether these words come from Huascar, the pool, or the hummingbirds."*
>
> *It is as if Huascar hears my thoughts and answers "It doesn't matter because they are all one. Energy of the one is continually exchanging itself with the energy of the other."*
>
> *I think "But then how does one distinguish between them?"*
>
> *Again as if hearing my thoughts, he answers "There is no distinction. It is the human mind, the ego that has the need*

to separate." As I continue to meditate on this image, I see mist rising. The mist takes various forms. (Journal, 5-6-12).

There is no separation between mind and body, no separation between spirit and matter. The energy of one is continually exchanging itself with the energy of the Other. This was the message—a message that science itself is now asserting. Everything is made up of energy and everything exchanges that energy with everything else at all times.[355]

The above dream suggested that a memory of a previous lifetime continued to vibrate in the heart. The psychoanalyst in the dream said that the energetic healing of the wound that she carried in her heart left her feeling better than ten heart surgeries had. This dream showed the effects that energy healing can have on what we carry in our hearts.

But what is it that we carry in our hearts? What is it that the heart knows? We experience our emotions, our passions, our longings, as well as our hurts and wounds—the very essence of who we are—in the chest and heart area. One only has to recall the pain of a significant loss or the excitement of falling in love to know that these events register in the heart. The dream infers that an earlier traumatic event had created a disease or condition of the heart—a condition I knew nothing about. What *was* the heart condition?

This journey began with a call to listen to my dreams and became a way to understand the meaning of my same-sex attractions. Instead of divorcing my wife and leaving my family to pursue a homosexual lifestyle, my early dreams indicated that my homosexuality was about something else—"freeing the boy from the parsonage" as a way to heal the masculine and "finding the treasure hard to find." According to most spiritual traditions the "treasure hard to find" is one's true self

355 Cameron, *A Happy Pocket Full of Money*, 26.

and the divine within. What emerged on this path was the awareness that I was actually healing a split in me between various parts of me—the split between the masculine and feminine, the split between the homosexual and the heterosexual, the split between the mind and the body, and ultimately the split in me between spirit and matter.

This mind-body, spirit-matter split can be stated in general terms as a split between the head and the heart. However, when we think of this mind-body split as a split between head and heart, there is a tendency to place thinking, rationality, and spirit with the head (mind), and to put emotion, feeling, and matter with the heart (body). To view the heart as the place solely of emotion or feeling fails to recognize the heart's connection to the energetic imprints and images vibrating in the soul.

Certainly, from a physiological point of view, the heart is simply an organ of the body—a pump so to speak—that carries blood, oxygen, and nutrition to all the cells as well as eliminating waste products. As such it is central to life. On the other hand, the heart is also a symbolic expression of that which is central to us not only as physical life but as psychological and spiritual life. In this sense the heart connects us to the life of the soul, that which brings us alive and enlivens us, even connects us to something beyond ourselves.

I have maintained throughout this book that my dreams are the expressions of my soul, their images revealing not only what is living there but what also longs for life. Many cultures and ancient traditions have long held that the heart is the seat of the soul. The dream with which I began this chapter suggested that vibrating in the heart are not only feelings and emotions but memories and images of our past and, from my own experience, images of our future. This awareness opens up another way of seeing, seeing with the heart, and seeing what is vibrating there.

James Hillman, in his discussion of the groundbreaking work of Henry Corbin —scholar, philosopher, theologian, and champion of the transformative power of the imagination and of transcendent reality in the individual—states quite clearly that the heart's characteristic action is not feeling but sight.[356] Hillman, discussing Corbin, says the thought of the heart is the thought of images.[357] The heart is the seat of the imagination. Imagination is the authentic voice of the heart. So if we speak from the heart we must speak imaginatively.[358] The heart is the place of true imagining. Hillman points out that when we personalize the heart as simply personal, confessional, subjective reflection, we drive the imagination into exile, into sexual fantasy or metaphysical conception or into objective data, none of which reside in the heart.[359]

Hillman goes on to say that the intention of the heart creates as real the figures of the imagination. The heart knows that the images we think we make up are actually presented to us as authentic creatures. Without the gift of the heart's imaginal sight we misunderstand the meaning of the images in our dreams or the persons of our imaginings and fantasies, or that which appears in a shamanic journey. We think they are subjectively real, that we made them up, figments of our imagination, apparitions—when we mean that they are *imaginatively* real. Or we think they are externally real as hallucinations when we mean they are *essentially* real. We confuse the imaginal with the subjective and internal. We mistake the essential for external and objective.[360]

Yes, the heart is an organ of feeling. But it is also the seat of the soul's imagination and our ability to see the imaginal realm. This makes

---

356 Hillman, *Thought of the Heart*, 4.

357 Ibid.

358 Ibid.

359 Ibid., 29.

360 Ibid., 6.

the imaging heart central to a spiritual or symbolic life and raises our understanding of our compulsions and desires—sexual or otherwise—to their spiritual and symbolic meaning.

Of all the images that could show up, we must ask why this image or that image. I believe that the images that show up are the ones that best describe the conditions of our soul. These images show what is vibrating there. They offer us an opportunity to interact with them and not only heal the wounds they might reveal, they also present the opportunity to bring into existence that which the soul longs to live, the wholeness that we are—the "treasure hard to find." If we are to do the healing work that they offer us, we must view them as real, for essentially they are. They describe what is fundamental and basic to the soul. They show what is living there. This is the spirit that lives in matter. This is the matter of the heart. This is what the heart knows.

Research done by the HeartMath Institute and the U.S. Army seem to support such an idea. According to their research, the heart's energy field can hold and even transfer information. In the early 1990s the U.S. Army conducted a series of experiments with human DNA. They wanted to know if and how DNA changes in response to human emotion. So they extracted DNA from donors and placed the cells in test tubes in another room of the research building. They then exposed the donors to video clips to elicit strong emotions. They showed the individuals graphic war movies, scenes of torture, erotic movies, and humorous movies. What they discovered was that at the same time the donor was experiencing the peaks and valleys of emotion while watching the video clips, the donor's DNA was experiencing the same peaks and valleys in the test tubes in another room in the building and there was no lag time (time it takes for energy to get from one place to another). It was at the same instant.

Then they wondered how far they could remove the donors' cells and still get a reaction. They moved the cells fifty miles and the results were the same. The army stopped the experiments at fifty miles but the researchers didn't. They had the donors in Los Angeles and sent the DNA cells to Phoenix, Arizona, some three hundred miles away. The results were the same. The DNA cells in the test tubes in Phoenix experienced the same peaks and valleys as the donors did in Los Angeles in response to the emotions. The conclusion is that human emotion has a measurable effect on DNA and time and distance didn't matter.[361]

Around the same time, the HeartMath Institute, one of the premier research centers of heart research, was doing research of their own on DNA. They wanted to know just how human emotions affected DNA. So they trained one group of subjects to experience strong emotions of love, compassion, care, and forgiveness and another group of subjects to experience strong emotions of anger, hate, resentment, and fear. They then measured the response of the DNA. At first when the subjects began to feel the emotions of love, compassion, forgiveness, and caring, the DNA began to relax. As they continued to experience these emotions, the DNA (which is a double intertwined helix) began to unwind. This had a positive and enhancing effect on the immune system, the endocrine system, and the hormonal systems. When the other group felt the emotions of anger, hate, resentment, and fear, the DNA twisted tighter and tighter and had a negative effect on the immune system.

The conclusion is that strong human emotions alter the shape of the DNA in either positive or negative ways. This affects the immune system in positive or negative ways.[362] The HeartMath Institute iden-

361 Ibid., 49–52.

362 Ibid., 53.

tified intention and heart coherence[363] as the critical variables in being able to wind or unwind the DNA. Other studies done by the HeartMath Institute indicate that emotional states tend to be reflected in heart rhythm patterns.[364]

The results of these studies done by the HeartMath Institute and the U.S. Army reveal that the heart's energy field not only responds to emotions, but the emotions can affect the very stuff that we are made of—our DNA. Could this dream and the findings on the heart suggest that we carry in our hearts not only the emotions of the wounds from the past but the very wounds themselves as energetic fields with their complete stories? Could it be that what we carry in our heart's energy field affects the very cells of our body in positive or negative ways?

Such findings support the Peruvian shamans' belief that our entire personal and ancestral memories vibrate in our luminous energy bodies. These imprints contain information that then predisposes us to organize our physical and emotional worlds in a particular way.[365] The dream also suggests that these old wounds can be healed through energy healing. The implications for such an energy transfer system within the body are profound. Cell biologists confirm that the heart's field permeates every cell in the body in a manner compared to information carried by radio waves. Since heart energy can also communicate

---

363 Heart coherence means that the variation in the time interval between heartbeats is concentrated into one single frequency near 0.1 HZ. While this state of coherency can be created by paced breathing of six breaths per minute, this coherence naturally emerges when people are holding intention of sustained positive emotional states without any conscious change in breathing. Rollin McCraty, Ph.D., Mike Atkinson, Dana Tomasino, and Raymond Trevor Bradley, Ph.D. "The Coherent Heart; Heart-Brain Interactions, Psychophysiological Coherence, and the Emergence of System-Wide Order," 6.

364 McCraty, et al., *Coherent Heart: Heart–Brain Interactions . . .*, 6.

365 Villoldo, *Shaman, Healer, Sage*, 46.

with the brain, it is likely that heart energy can also modulate and direct mind and body interactions.[366]

Several years prior to having the above dream about using my hands to move energy to heal the heart I was a participant in a dream group in which we used artistic creations such as painting, poetry, and the making of collages to work with our dreams and unconscious material, I had made a collage of a heart with hands and energy vibrating between them. (See figure 13.)

Figure 13. *The Path of the Heart*

366 McCraty, et al., *Coherent Heart: Heart–Brain Interactions . . .*, 6.

It is as if the unconscious material tapped into in the making of this collage several years before had now shown up in this dream and was now manifesting as my experience in shamanism and energy healing, pulling me into what might be called "the path of the heart." But I still didn't know exactly what the message of the heart was or what it meant to "follow the heart." That would all unfold over the course of the next several years.

Heart energy has traditionally been considered to be electromagnetic in nature. However, the unusual ability of heart energy to carry different frequency patterns associated with different intentions suggests a non-electromagnetic information carrier. Furthermore, the research done by the U.S. Army and the HeartMath Institute showed that human intentionality produced effects that defied conventional laws of electromagnetism with respect to their independence of space and time. The long-distance effects observed in this research indicate that coherent heart energy may be a carrier for such nonlocal effects.[367] Researchers have shown in previous studies that cells studied in vitro are responsive to the heart's field. Further studies indicate that the heart's electromagnetic field can be detected by other individuals and can produce physiologically relevant effects in a person five feet away.[368] Perhaps this "non-electromagnetic information carrier" may someday be known as the subtle energy fields that as yet cannot be measured by current technologies but have been seen and felt by the indigenous shamans for centuries.

Jungian analyst Schwartz-Salant speaks of "imaginal sight," which are words to describe the transitional phenomena that refer to another dimension of existence, "a third area whose processes can only be

---

367 Rein and McCraty, "Local and Non-Local Effects of Coherent Heart Frequencies . . .", 6.

368 McCarty, et al., "Modulation of DNA Conformation by Heart-Centered Intention."

perceived with the eye of the imagination."[369] Schwartz-Salant has written that two people can become aware of a state in which their subtle bodies are interacting. This is often felt as a change in the quality of the space between them. According to Schwartz-Salant, it is experienced as energized and more material in nature. They are at the threshold of an awareness of archetypal or transpersonal processes.[370] Perhaps this is a way to describe what the shamans speak of when they describe seeing into the spirit realm or into the realm of non-ordinary reality. It is their capacity to read what is vibrating in the energy field.

The above dream suggests that vibrating in the object—in matter, in this case the heart—is information of a spiritual or energetic nature, information of a transpersonal nature insomuch as the information transcends ego-consciousness and rational processes. The object is not just a metaphor, nor just a symbol onto which we project meaning. Nor is it a belief or a hypothesis about a spiritual realm. Rather the spirit realm is an empirical fact supported by personal experience. Hillman has suggested that the idea of withdrawing projections—the major goal of analytical practice—could become irrelevant once we recognize that much of what we call projection is an attempt by the psyche to experience things beyond ourselves as imaginal processes.[371]

Several writers (Hillman, Cheetham, Corbin, Kryder) state that we have lost the imaginal and with it we have lost the aliveness of our own souls. Tom Cheetham in his book *Green Man, Earth Angel* suggests that "all dualism of the modern world stem from the loss of the *mundus imaginales*: matter is cut off from spirit, sensation from intellect, subject from object, inner from outer, myth from history, the

---

369 Schwartz-Salant, N. *The Borderline Personality*, 101

370 Schwartz-Salant," On the subtle-body concept in clinical practice."

371 Hillman, *Hillman on Corbin*, 29–30.

individual from the divine."[372] The imaginal world is not imaginary or unreal. While the imaginary is the product of personal fantasy and is therefore subjective, the imaginal, on the other hand, gives us, as stated previously, access to a transpersonal content.

This transpersonal content has objective reality even though it may not correspond to any historical fact or physical reality. The imaginal realm or the *mundus imaginalis* exists independent of those who become aware of it. The imaginal realm possesses a truth that has a universal validity that the products of our private fantasies do not achieve.[373] Through dreams, meditations, active imagination, and shamanic journeying we have access to the imaginal realm, to the intermediate realm of the subtle bodies. We have access to the realm of real presences located between the material world of matter and the world of Spirit. Could it be that the heart connects us with the imaginal space that allows us once again to see the realities of the invisible, to see the subtle energies that carry the wisdom hidden in matter?

> *I enter the ship that carries me to the underground through a river that I access in a cave. I land in the area that I had come to know in my shamanic training as the Lower World. I wash in the stream and let it carry me until I wash up onto the land where I meet Huascar, the guardian and guide to the Underworld. I explain to Huascar that I am feeling the need to journey to the Underworld to access the wisdom that he had told Julie (my shamanic instructor with whom I had recently done some work) that I needed.*
>
> *He is happy and calls jaguar and owl, and the four of us start off through the opening into the cave area, passing*

---

372 Cheetham, *Green Man, Green Angel*, 3.

373 Naydler, "*Ancient Egypt and Modern Esotericism.*"

by the chamber of the soul. We journey on. At one point we mount horses as Huascar says that we are going deeper this time, into the deep Underworld. We journey on. Owl is flying with me. Jaguar walks at my side.

After a while I see the smoke of a fire. We come upon a group of medicine men sitting around a fire. I feel the warmth of the fire. I feel the fire in my body, in my heart and solar plexus. We greet the gathering and Huascar informs them that I have come in search of the wisdom from the Lower World. The indigenous ones look at me, like they are "scanning me." I now see what is like a computer screen showing the scan results. The scan shows two areas that need fixing.

One of the men gets up from the circle, and comes and places his hand over my heart. I think that he will put his hand in two areas—maybe the solar plexus, but he doesn't. He keeps his hand on the heart area, as if transmitting energy to my heart. I ask what the areas are that need fixing but no one provides that information. I get the awareness of "heart wisdom" since I came seeking wisdom. After several minutes, the man finishes and without saying a word, returns to the fire, and joins the group. Following Huascar's lead I place my hands together at my heart, bow, and thank them. We mount our horses and return to ordinary reality. (Journal, 2-14-13)

Once again the focus of this journey—like the dream five years before and the collage years before that—was about heart energy, healing the heart, and heart wisdom. I slowly came to understand that the images that appeared in my dreams, in my meditations, and now in my shamanic journeys were not just my imagination or some fantasy but connected me to some other realm, some other reality. I came to understand that through the images in my dreams and fantasies, the images appearing in my meditations, and now in my shamanic journeys, I had been accessing this imaginal realm, the *mundus imaginalis,* the place of "heart sight."

Ochwiay Biano, chief of the Taos Pueblo in northern New Mexico, says that the difference between the white man and the Indian is that the European thinks with his head and the Indian thinks with his heart.[374] Cheetham says that one enters into the *mundus imaginalis* through the heart, that the heart is the perceptual organ for sensing the spiritual, invisible, and energetic worlds.[375] He also asserts that wisdom is not only in the heart but also in the object.[376] We can enter into the realm of the Spirit through the *mundus imaginalis,* located in the heart as the "heart's sight." The dream above suggested that we have the capacity to enter into a spiritual realm or energetic field and not only gather information—imaginal sight—but affect healing.

One can certainly argue that such a conclusion should not be drawn on the basis of one dream, one collage, or one shamanic journey. However, my dreams as well as various synchronicities and experiences occurring during meditation and shamanic journeys over the past several years—many of which have been shared in this book—had already been moving me in that direction. Everything is energy. Everything is connected by an energetic web of subtle energies. I am a part of this web of energy, connected to everything. There is no time or distance in this energy realm. When I have a thought it immediately resonates, registers, vibrates throughout this energy web and elicits an energetic response that returns to me in the energetic realm. In fact, everything I do creates an energy imprint that causes a response in

---

374 Jung, *Memories, Dreams Reflections,* 247-48.

375 Cheetham, Green Man, Earth Angel, xiv, 70.

376 Ibid., 23.

the energy web. Every thought I have, every word I say, every action I take, every emotion I express, creates an energy imprint that vibrates through this energy web. As my journey to the place of the hummingbird had instructed, "Energy of the one is continually exchanging itself with the energy of the other." This energy manifests as images. These images connect me to the imaginal realm, which is the wisdom living in the heart. Is this the matter of the heart that is at the heart of matter?

When we split off matter from spirit or mind from body and elevate spirit and mind to a superior place over body and matter, something in us dies. We suffer a loss of connection, not only to nature but to our own souls. Slowly it became clear to me that my journey into dreams, shamanism, shamanic healing, and energy medicine was my soul's longing to reconnect me to the spirit that lives in nature, to the truth in nature, to the "directing intelligence" of my own nature, my own soul. Such "directing intelligence" knows that everything is energy or spirit—stones, trees, the human body, a lover, and everything is matter—thoughts, behaviors, attitudes, fantasies. We then, as Cheetham points out, understand soul as the embodying of spirit and as the spiritualizing process of matter.[377]

Hillman points out that words, too, burn and become flesh as we speak, wielding an invisible power over us, acting on us as complexes and releasing complexes in us.[378] The shaman sees the "matter" of words as metal darts in the luminous energy field at the level of the heart and removes them, freeing a person from the wounds of years of verbal abuse and from pattern of abusing others.

In a dream, I felt energy at the level of the heart and a woman recalled a time when she fell off her tricycle, hit her head, and died. I

---

377 Cheetham, *Green Man, Earth Angel*, xvii.

378 Hillman, *Re-visioning Psychology*, 9–10.

extracted the energy of this memory and she told me that she hadn't felt that good after ten heart surgeries.

Years later in shamanic healing work, as a client told me of a recent state of panic that she was still caught in, I saw a cord—of a state of panic related to some tragedy—reaching back into her ancestral past. As I worked on clearing this energy from the client, using my hands like I had in the dream and as trained to do in my shamanic training, she related scenes of another time where fire was destroying everything around her. She reported that her face felt hot, her lungs were burning, and she was having difficulty breathing. As I cleared out the energetic imprint of this traumatic memory, she calmed. The heat and burning subsided. She reported that the panicked feeling was gone. Delusional? Magical thinking? Or transrational, transpersonal reality—spirit in matter—and the entrance into the *mundus imaginalis*, the realm of subtle energies and subtle bodies—heart sight?

Between mind and matter exists a psychic realm of subtle bodies whose characteristics manifest in mental as well as material form.[379] When we recognize that the realm of the imagination—the heart—mediates between the physical and the spiritual then the split between them can begin to heal. Matter is no longer associated with evil. Everything becomes material. What had been seen as purely spiritual becomes the realm of subtle bodies.

Said another way, when the imaginal is given priority, the dichotomy between matter and spirit collapses. The separation between my fantasy and the image or carrier of my fantasy dissolves. The spiritual is substantial. It is not disembodied. It is not only in the Other. It is here and now.[380] I now embody this Other for which my soul had longed and which I could only see in the men in my sexual encounters. Had

---

379 Cheetham, *Green Man, Earth Angel*, 36.

380 Ibid., 109.

I projected *him* onto these men? Or perhaps *he* had presented himself to me through the images in my dreams and fantasies and them?

The cause of a person's deadness or loss of vitality is the loss of soul, both the soul of the person and the soul of the world.[381] The soul understands that psychic life is also the life of nature, the life in matter. Natural life becomes the vessel of the soul the moment we recognize that it too has an interior significance. As I discovered in my work on the *Swan Lake* dream, for modern man, myth—the life of the imaginal—is born the moment we recognize that outer images and events are carriers and therefore patterns of energy at work within the individual or collective soul. I came to recognize that this whole journey had been to embody that awareness, a reawakening, a bringing to life in me the reality of the image of the other man in me, to reclaim its meaning and its efficacy. The descent into nature, into the nature of my own soul, was for the purpose of healing this split. This was the working out of the early dreams, which said "the healing of my homosexual self was in freeing him from the parsonage" and that "homosexuality is the treasure hard to find." That healing was not about something that needed fixing or changing. Rather, it was about acceptance—embracing him and finding his meaning. It was about finding the Divine Spirit in the matter of the Other.

The matter of the heart is about this descent into matter, a returning to the wisdom, the intelligence in the object, again whether that object be a stone, a tree, an animal, a woman, a man, an organ of the body, or my own soul. Without this awareness we are left with the tragic split between spirit and matter, between mind and body, and the soul is left longing. As Cheetham points out, "We are both incomplete and disoriented because the *ground* [italics mine] of their contact

381 Ibid., 17–18.

is gone."[382] We must be willing to accept depth psychology's psyche, Corbin's *mundus imaginalis*, the anima mundi, and the shaman's world of non-ordinary reality. They allow us entrance into the imaginal space where the images express their imaginal realities. As Hillman asserts, if we are to recover the imaginal, we must first recover its organ, the heart, and the heart's way of seeing.[383]

Hillman continuing his discussion on Corbin says it is the heart that perceives the relationship between mind and body, between spirit and matter. This awareness takes place by means of the image. The image holds within itself both the qualities of the mind and spirit (consciousness) and the qualities of the body and matter (world). The image contains the interpenetration of these two worlds, and it is always and only the image that is primary to what it coordinates. This imaginal intelligence resides in the heart. Thus the heart becomes the place of the union of the two—the union of spirit and matter.[384]

I must acknowledge the wisdom of heart that the shamanic tribe of spirit walkers instilled in me during that shamanic journey. I must acknowledge the *mundus imaginalis* in which the images themselves express *their* imaginal reality, the play of *their* "light" rather than the light of consciousness that I bring to it. Each image immediately reflects its own consciousness, putting wisdom, divine intelligence, and transpersonal, transrational reality back into nature and matter, back into the object—even the object of my desire.

The messages emerging in my dreams and in my shamanic journeys began to confirm the ancient wisdom that the matter of the heart is the reality that at the heart of matter is kind of spirit or subtle energy that vibrates with information. We can interact with this energy in

---

382 Ibid., 3.

383 Hillman, *The Thought of the Heart and the Soul of the World*, 6.

384 Ibid., 7.

ways that affect healing. This is the matter of the heart. This is the heart of matter.

As the U.S. Army and the HeartMath Institute's research have suggested, an image or a thought that is held with intention within the realm of heart coherence can affect the world around us. Be it Winnicott's transitional space, the luminality that the anthropologists talk about, Schwartz-Salant's imaginal sight, or the shaman's non-ordinary reality, we can travel into this world and gather information to heal ourselves and the planet. Not only can I travel into this imaginal world and visit the spirits in matter, they visit me in spirit, coming to me in the images of my dreams, visions, and shamanic journeys. Magical? Maybe so. Transrational? Yes. And to that extent it appears magical. English author and Sufi mystic Llewellyn Vaughan-Lee concludes:

> We need the magical powers within nature in order to heal and transform the world. But awakening these powers would mean that our patriarchal institutions will lose their control, as once again the mysterious inner world will come into play, releasing forces once understood and used by the priestess and shaman . . . The science of the future will work with these forces, exploring how the different words interrelate, including how the energies of the inner can be used in the outer. The shaman and the scientist will work together, the wisdom of the priestess and wisdom of the physician renew their ancient connection." [385]

385 Vaughan-Lee, "Anima Mundi: Awakening the Soul of the World."

In a shamanic journey I tell my guide Huascar that I'd like to journey to the heart of the earth to discover what the heart of the earth knows. We journey deep into the earth. At one point I see a hole with a rope ladder. Huascar instructs that I am to climb down the ladder. I do, and I come to a whole world, a complete universe operating there, like an entire society of people going about life. I enter what is like a café and sit down at a table. An earth-type woman comes and sits down across from me.

I do not know what happens, but suddenly she gets up and walks away. As she walks away I see tears running down her cheeks. I call to her to come back and inquire as to why she is crying. Somehow I had dismissed her, had become distracted and although I had said that I had come to seek council with the heartbeat of the earth, I had ignored her.

I apologize and as I start to engage her I hear, as if vibrating all through me, the following: "Vibrating in the heart is the life of the soul. Just as clearly as you see here what is happening in the heart of the earth, your soul's life is happening in the heart—the soul's story. It is playing out there as clearly as the images you see here. You can access this life with imaginal sight. With imaginal sight we can not only access the story, we can heal the wounds that live there as well as access the life that wants to live, the life that is ours to live. This is what the heart knows."

As the reality of the imaginal world and seeing with the heart came more fully into my awareness and into my experience, a desire emerged in me to paint the original collage that I had made simply as an exercise in a dream group over ten years earlier. This was long before I knew about "imaginal sight" or *mundus imaginales,* or the shaman's way of "seeing with the heart." Of all the hundreds of images I could have chosen that day to make this collage, what had caused me to choose a heart and hands with energy vibrating between them? I suggest it was the spirit of this other man living in the depths of my soul, my soul's next manifestation.

Here is my painting of the original collage.

Figure 14. *Imaginal Sight: Seeing with the Heart*

Once we understand the spiritual and symbolic meanings of the images in our soul, we have greater choices on how we will then live.

Notes and Exercises

When we split off matter from spirit or mind from body and elevate spirit and mind to a superior place over body and matter, something in us dies. We suffer a loss of connection, not only to nature, but to our own souls.

Ancient traditions have long held that the heart is the seat of the soul. Vibrating in the heart are not only feelings and emotions, but memories and images of our past, our ancestral stories, early traumatic events, our wounds and painful places as well as images of our future.

Imagination is the authentic voice of the heart. This makes the heart central to a spiritual or symbolic life and raises our understanding of compulsions and desires—sexual or otherwise—to their spiritual or symbolic meaning.

Many have lost their imaginal sight and with it the aliveness of their own soul. Through dreams, meditations, active imagination and shamanic journeying we have access to the imaginal realm of the heart that allows us to see what is hidden there.

For modern man, the life of the imaginal is born the moment we recognize that outer images and events are carriers and therefore patterns of energy at work with us. Each image reflects is own consciousness, putting wisdom, divine intelligence, transpersonal reality back into nature and matter, back into the object, even the object of our desires.

Journey to the Heart

Find a place where you will not be disturbed. You might want to listen to some shamanic drumming or journey music.

Refer to the Resources in the back of the book for links to journey music.

Take some deep breaths and allow yourself to drift into a light trance or relaxed state. Start your music. Ask for a power animal or spirit guide to accompany you and notice what shows up. Ask the animal or spirit guide if they wish to accompany you on your journey to the heart. If you get a "yes", thank the guide and begin your journey. If you get a "no", ask to be taken to your guide. Place your intention to journey to your heart to discover what your heart knows, what is hidden there that might be useful for your healing or for your life at this time.

Imagine that you and your guide are journeying to you heart and notice what images begin to appear. Ask your guide to show you what you are holding in your heart, what is hidden there. Is it some hurt? Some pain? Some regret? Or is it some future that longs to live? If it is some hurt or wound, ask your heart what you need to do to heal. Notice what comes to you. If you remember some memory, ask how that memory can be helpful in addressing a situation in your current life. Notice what comes to you. If you notice some future that longs to live, ask how you might connect to that future and how you might manifest it in your life. Notice what questions come to you, what images show up and ask to understand their meaning. What message does your heart have for you?

As you prepare to return thank your guide for accompanying you. Thank your heart for accepting you and speaking with you. Now journey back into your room and back into your body. Wiggle your fingers and toes, take a deep breath.

Pat your heart with your hands and open your eyes. When you open your eyes, you are back in ordinary reality, wide awake and alert.

In a journal make notes on your journey and your experience or write your journey out in detail. Reflect on your journey. Let it continue to speak to you.

CHAPTER SEVENTEEN

The Return of the Green Man

I *am at a religious service, like a church service. A man who is a healer is there. This man knows what to do when there is a need for a healing. He handles it. I tell him, "You are right where you are supposed to be. It's nice to be right where you are supposed to be even though it was me that got you here." By this I mean that this man came to see me because he was attracted to me. It was his attraction to me that put him right where he is supposed to be in order to take care of a healing situation. That is what he knows. He knows how to heal.*

I reach up to kiss him. I put my arms around him. He is tall. I have to stretch up in order to kiss him. I think that he'll embrace me and kiss me, that this is a mutual attraction, a coming together. However, he is hesitant. I kiss him. (Journal, 11-29-10)

As discussed earlier, dreams often mirror back to us what is happening in the unconscious, what is happening in the matter of our own souls. Dreams of a healer, healing, and energy healing had been showing up in my dreams for some time. I believe these dreams were part of what attracted me to shamanism and energy healing. This dream said that the healer was right where he was supposed to be, which I understood to mean that I was right where I was supposed to be. According to the dream this male healer was there because he was attracted to me. Not only was he attracted to me, but I was attracted to him.

I hypothesized that this attraction to the inner masculine as healing energy is what fueled my attraction to men and is what I sought in my same-sex relationships as an attempt to heal the masculine split in me. The man's hesitance to embrace me in the dream mirrored my own ongoing hesitance to embrace both the healer in me and the integration of this other man in me. Both would heal the split between the inner man and the outer man, between the mind and the body, between spirit and matter and the split between my homosexual and heterosexual selves.

The dream ended with me stretching up to kiss this male healer. A kiss is a meaningful and highly symbolic act. Although the meaning and symbolism of a kiss varies according to the type and location of the kiss, a kiss on the lips represents a close union between two people, expressing a closeness of two hearts. Kissing on the lips symbolized the communication by one's inner spirit to unite with another's inner spirit. In other words, kissing goes deeper than the physical meeting between two people's lips. Kissing touches both the heart and the mind.[386]

Because kissing involves an act similar to breathing into someone, kissing becomes a symbol for rebirth, renewal, and transformation. We only have to think of the symbolism of the kiss in fairy tales such as *Sleeping Beauty.*[387] The "breath of new life" is delivered through the lips. Think about what happens when two people fall in love or are strongly attracted to each other. At the touch of their lips every cell in the body comes alive with new life and the soul awakens. The fact

386 "The Spiritual Origin of Kissing."

387 "The Symbolism of Kissing."

that I had to stretch up to kiss this masculine healer suggested that some stretching or expansion of consciousness or action was required to embrace the masculine healer.

Who was this other man I stretched up to kiss? Who was this healer with whom I longed to unite, into whom I longed to breathe life? Or was I longing for him to breathe life into me?

I dream

> *My wife and I are at a shamanic healing. A person hands me a note. The note says "Don't panic." The note also said "critical" and was signed "Ona." I know that Ona is involved in a healing with someone and the situation is critical. She is handing out notes to ask certain people to be in prayer, holding the space to assist energetically in the healing.*
>
> *I move up to a place and sit on the floor in order to be in the circle of people holding this space. Suddenly I start to vibrate. I vibrate so strongly that I start to fall over. A man puts his hands on my shoulders to steady me. He knows what is happening. However, the vibration becomes so strong that I start to fall over again, and he gently assists me to lie down.*
>
> *The vibration continues until I start to move. I float across the room and end up back in a corner where Ona is working with a woman who is lying on the floor. It is obvious that the woman is in serious trouble. Suddenly I start talking. I tell this woman that I am her grandmother, giving her grandmother's name. I tell her that I am from South Africa and that I have been watching over her all her life and that I have come to heal her. I then tell her other information. I speak in some other language. I then hug her and whatever her problem was, it's resolved. She sits up.*

> *At this point I wake up. My body is still tingling from the energy and my speech is slurred. My arms continued to tingle for some time. I feel overwhelming emotion, joy, and gratitude.* (Journal, 9-11-11)

Here is another dream about healing and healing the feminine. But was this only a dream? Ona is a shamanic healer with whom I had worked on multiple occasions. She was also one of the faculty in the Light Body School of the Four Winds and one of my instructors during my training in shamanic healing and energy medicine. At the time of this dream Ona was also my mentor with whom I sought supervision.

I shared this experience with her. She told me that at the exact time of this dream, she was in fact conducting a shamanic training. According to Ona, there was a lady in the training from South Africa who was in need of significant healing. Had I had a spontaneous shamanic journey while sleeping? Had I actually picked up on the healing session being conducted by Ona in another part of the world and somehow participated in the healing?

Whether this dream is describing aspects of my own unconscious with all the figures representing parts of me (which is certainly a plausible and useful understanding), or whether the dream is describing images and archetypal processes from the collective unconscious (another useful interpretation), or whether I had actually traveled to this healing session during my sleep to assist in this healing (a rationally more challenging interpretation), the dream could be adequately understood through the lens of imaginal sight as discussed in the previous chapter. These images were presented to me as real, not subjectively real but *imaginatively* real, not externally or objectively real, but *essentially* real.

To that extent, this dream and these images had a real and essential effect on my consciousness, healing the feminine in me and connecting me more directly to the healer in me. However, Ona's confirmation that she was in a healing session with a woman from South Africa that needed healing at the exact time of the dream suggested there *was* some external and objective reality to this experience also.

Imaginal sight provides for the embodying of Spirit and the spiritualization of matter. As mentioned earlier, between mind and matter exists a psychic realm of subtle energies whose characteristics manifest in mental and material form.[388] As we have stated before but bears repeating here, when we recognize that the realm of the imagination—the imaginal sight of the heart—mediates between the physical and the Spiritual then the split between them dissolves. In the physical realm Ona was participating in a healing in which she made a call for assistance from the spirit realm, a practice common to shamanism. That mental call made its way through the energetic web connecting us and showed up in my dream as images of a healing session in which I then participated.

Given the individual work I was doing at the time, I can certainly interpret this dream as mirroring my work with both the masculine, indicated by the man in the dream assisting me in the healing process, and the feminine, indicated by my being grandmother energy that assisted in the healing of the lady in the dream, representing some aspect of my own feminine energy. Ona, the shamanic healer, could symbolize the shamanic healer in me—some part of my own emerging self. However, I was at that time learning the skill of shamanic journeying, also known as astral travel or soul travel. Astral travel, soul flight, or the practice of shamanic journeying where it is believed that

---

388 Cheetham, *Green Man, Earth Angel*, 36

a piece of the soul or the luminous energy body leaves the physical body and travels to other realms and places, is often disbelieved in western science.

However, astral travel and soul flight was the subject of a dream I'd had eight months before this experience. I dream

> *I am involved in a court case, a trial. There is a woman there who knows information. When we ask her to testify, she claims immunity. Dr. Dzera is there and says something about astral travel. He says, "I would never have believed it (astral travel) possible, but I saw Linda Finch do this. It was a dark night and I saw her just take off and go zoom (flying through the sky)."*
>
> *He then puts on an astral travel suit, buckling it up at the waist. This has something to do with him being able to travel to get information regarding this case. I am getting ready to leave to go to some training. As I leave I stop by Dr. Dzera's office and get something. I am driving on the road going to the training.* (Journal, 05-29-10)

At the time of this dream I was continuing my study and training in shamanic healing. Shamanic journeying into non-ordinary reality to track or "see" phenomena on the physical, emotional, mythic, and energetic levels was a central part of this training. The doctor in this dream was a psychiatrist with whom I worked. He symbolized the rational, Western, scientific, medical model of treatment and healing. The woman named Linda in the dream was a master shaman and at the time was the dean of the Light Body School and one of my instructors.

The dream showed that the more rational, scientific, medical model part of me (the psychiatrist) was accepting the shamanic reality of astral travel (Linda) because of what he had seen. This dream showed that because of my experiences in shamanic training and actually my personal experience with shamanic journeying, the more traditional, Western medicine man in me was putting on the consciousness and the way of the shaman, symbolized by the "astral travel suit."

The previous dream where I participated in a shamanic healing, a healing that my shamanic instructor and mentor had confirmed was actually happening at the time of the dream, can also be understood as astral travel or soul flight. Part of the training and initiation into the shamanic path is to learn to send part of the soul forth intentionally on a soul flight. One of the purposes of the soul journey is to obtain information (another topic of the dream), information that can be used for healing, spiritual growth, or to work through emotional and psychological issues.

The point of this digression into astral travel or shamanic journeying is to emphasize its central role in shamanic healing. Putting these three dreams in chronological order, the dream on astral travel that came first showed the merging in me of Western psychiatric medicine and the indigenous ways of the shaman. The second dream where I kissed the male healer showed my embrace of the healer in me. The third dream showed my participation in the healing ceremony with Ona. It brought these two aspects together—astral travel and the healer—resulting in shamanic healing. But who was this healer in me?

In January of 2012 I awoke early in the morning with the urge to paint. Painting had become a way for me to interact with and bring into consciousness the images stirring in the unconscious or in the depths of my soul. I had learned to pay attention to such urges. These urges come from a place deep in my body, somewhere around the heart and solar plexus.

I proceeded to paint a background as instructed by the "painting dream" ten years earlier. As I stared into the background I saw the image of a man's head. The image reminded me of a man in a previous painting. I also kept being drawn to two other paintings, *The Call* and The *Gift,* which have already been discussed in a previous chapter. Since the image that wanted to appear on this canvas called my attention to these three men, all painted green, I wondered if "green man" had any meaning or significance. Acting on that hunch, I Googled "green man" and to my surprise I came upon a whole body of knowledge related to a concept called "the Green Man." I then realized that I had been painting a "green man" in various forms for the past nine years.

In 2003 I had painted an image of a green man. I called this painting *Emerging.* (See figure 15.)

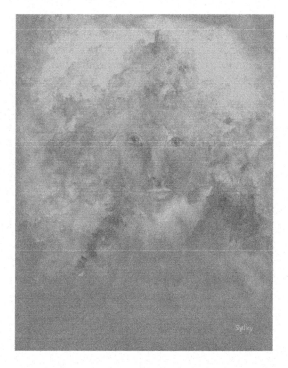

Figure 15. *Emerging*

In my search for the collage of the heart and hands discussed in the previous chapter, I discovered that the theme of the Green Man had entered my work many years before but had remained completely cut off from my consciousness. In fact, I was quite surprised to find the presence of the Green Man in a collage that I had done in response to a dream eleven years earlier, back in 2001. At that time I dreamed

> *I enter a large house that is being remodeled. My wife and a man are with me. I am wearing two shirts. I take one of the shirts off and am now in my underwear. We walk through the house, which is in various stages of remodel and repair. We go to the very last part of the house. My wife has been doing the floors—removing old tile, stripping the floors of their old finish. There is only one floor left. It is hard work. She is working on her hands and knees. The owner of the house and his female companion arrive. I walk back up through the house. I'm a little concerned about being in my underwear. The house is dark. I can't see and therefore I have to sense my way up and through the house.* (Journal, 4-15-01)

I had this dream on Easter Sunday. In the years that I had been involved in church music, serving as music director, Easter was a significant and important day in the life of the church. As music director I had often been in charge of the music on Easter, directing choirs and writing and arranging musicals celebrating Christ's death and resurrection. To have such a dream on such an important day, not only in the life of Christianity, but in my previous life in the church, going all the way back to the life in the parsonage, seemed significant to me. On that Easter Sunday and in response to this dream I wrote:

> *We go through deaths all the time. Every death resurrects into a new form. The physical (ego) resurrects as the spiritual, which is actually a transformed awareness. If we allow the resurrection power, the remodeling, the remolding, to do its work, the old transforms into the new. The statement in the dream that "I have to sense the way up and through the house" suggests another kind of seeing.* (Journal, 4-15-01)

At this time in my life I often made collages in response to a dream as a way to work with the dream and to allow the unconscious to speak to me through its images. I would hold the dream in my mind and search through magazines, choosing pictures, words, and phrases, anything that might speak to me or attract my attention or, in some cases, repel me. I took these images and shaped them into collages. Here is the collage that I did in 2001 in response to this dream.

Figure 16. The Remodel

This collage had been archived away with many other collages and paintings. In 2012, eleven years after I had completed it, it entered my life again through a seemingly unrelated event. As I searched for the collage of the heart and hands discussed in the previous chapter, I came across this collage. Several things jumped out at me that had previously escaped my attention. First, in the center is a man dressed in green. But more importantly, in the lower right corner is a reference to the Green Man. The statement under this image says "The Quest for the Green Man." For some reason I had put pictures of three tombstones in the collage. On one of the tombstones I had put a picture of John

Matthews' book, *The Quest for the Green Man.* Underneath the tombstones and the picture of the book, it said "John Matthews tracks this ancient archetype of the green and growing world through forest and woodland, folklore and ceremony, and world mythologies to produce the widest-ranging book on the Green Man to date. A colorful history aimed at reconnecting humankind to the spirit of nature."

I had no memory of placing the specific image of the Green Man into this collage. I was completely shocked and surprised by this discovery. Although I had apparently forgotten its appearance into my life until I happened upon it while searching for the heart collage, it appears that something in me had been attracted to the Green Man for some time. In light of the fact that I had the dreams on which this collage was based on Easter Sunday and that I had placed this reference to Green Man on a tombstone spoke to the idea that something that had been dead and buried in my soul now wanted to return. Apparently, it now wanted to rise from its burial ground in the depths of my unconscious, seeking resurrection. Even though I had been painting a green man for several years, I had lost awareness of this connection and certainly did not know its meaning nor its archetypal significance. Nor did I know how the Green Man was connected to my journey into shamanism and energy medicine or my soul's attempt and desire to heal the mind-body, spirit-matter split in me.

However, further investigation would reveal that long before the making of this collage and my paintings of green men, a hint of the Green Man and its transformative process had entered a dream. Of course, I didn't understand it at the time. But way back in 1978 at the beginning of this long journey, I had dreamed

> *I am riding a bicycle along the ocean. I fall off the bike and into the water. I get up and notice that I am covered in what looks like green paint. I go back home and clean up.*
>
> *I am again riding the bicycle on the beach along the ocean. Again I fall off the bike and into the ocean. Again I get up and walk out of the ocean. Once again I am green, covered in what is like green paint. I awaken with the feeling and taste of sand in my mouth.* (Journal, 1978)

Green is the color of nature and a symbol for growth, renewal, and rebirth. The color green is associated with the heart and the heart chakra. As such, green creates a balance between head and heart. This alone would have great significance and meaning for my journey. But looking back, I wonder if the Green Man had begun to make his appearance in this dream some twenty years earlier, long before I knew there was such a concept as the Green Man. Could it be that the archetype of the Green Man was behind this journey all along, pushing and pulling me to bring into consciousness this other side of the masculine—a masculine that is the spirit in nature?

Was this dream in 1978 the beginning of the man that would eventually emerge from the ocean as my soul's next manifestation, which I had painted in response to the orb dream? Was this the man that was behind my same-sex attractions?

The literature on the Green Man and its connection to the soul is an overwhelming body of knowledge with twists and turns, subtleties and paradoxes far too numerous to cover here. Suffice it to give a brief summary pertinent to my journey.

The Green Man is an archetypal figure who has appeared across many cultures for the last few thousand years. Early images of the Green Man, his face with leaves sprouting from his lips, eyes, nose, and ears, can be seen on buildings and signs all over Europe, dating back to the Middle Ages. His image is usually thought to be an anachronism of the old pagan religions.[389] He was known as Osiris in ancient Egypt, Dionysus in ancient Greece, and Bacchus in Roman times, and has been found in various forms across the Indian subcontinent.[390] Many indigenous peoples see the Green Man as a spirit of the woods, the guardian of trees and forests, the Lord of Beasts who watches over the woodland creatures. The Green Man is also related to the horned-god of antiquity and the bull itself. He is the central figure in May Day celebrations.[391]

The "Green Movement" represents in some way a contemporary resurgence of the Green Man.[392] A review of the literature on the Green Man shows that he has taken many and various forms throughout history—vegetative, animal, human, and suprahuman, and the unfolding cycle of greenness and growth. But ultimately the Green Man is the archetype representing the spiritual intelligence in nature.[393]

Andrew Rothery in his article, "The Science of the Green Man," suggests that the Green Man represents "a wide range of biological, ecological, and psychological characteristics that are inherent to Nature—renewal and rebirth, unity amongst diversity, ecological intelligence, and inter-species communication and networking."[394] Through these characteristics he communicates the underlying message of nature—the message that was given me in a shamanic journey to the Place of the Hummingbirds—there is no separation, the energy of the one is continually exchanging itself with the energy of the other. We

---

389 Kane, "Re-awakening the Green Man."

390 Rothery, "The Science of the Green Man."

391 Kane, "Re-awakening the Green Man."

392 Rothery, "*The Science of the Green Man.*"

393 Matthews, *Quest for the Green Man*, 6.

394 Rothery, "The Science of the Green Man."

are all one.[395] But is the Green Man only an image and an idea of the mind, or does he mirror some tangible aspect of planetary physiology within the earth's ecosystem?[396] And if so, what does that have to do with my journey?

A cursory review of the literature on the Green Man reveals the Green Man represents (1) our oneness with nature,[397] (2) the guardian and protector of nature,[398] (3) a spiritual or divine intelligence or essence in nature,[399] (4) a messenger revealing the relationship between man and nature,[400]' (5) the androgynous, regenerator spirit in nature,[401] (6) a Divine Spark in matter,[402] and (7) the archetypal masculine in nature as a vital resource in renewing our lost unity with the world of nature.[403]

For me the Green Man becomes a divine intelligence, a divine light, and the wisdom and consciousness in matter that both protects and reveals its spirit. To accept the Green Man is to return to the awareness of a transrational and transpersonal intelligence, a divine reality in matter, whether that matter be a stone, a tree, an animal, an organ in the body, an object of my desire, or the earth herself.

---

395 Ibid.

396 Ibid.

397 Anderson, *Green Man: The Archetype of our Oneness with the Earth, 164.*

398 Araneo. "The Archetypal, Twenty First Century Resurrection of the Ancient Image of the Green Man."

399 Cheetham, *Green Man, Earth Angel*, Anderson. *Green Man: The Archetype of Oneness with the Earth*, Araneo. "The Archetypal, Twenty First Century Resurrection of the Ancient Image of the Green Man."

400 Araneo. "The Archetypal, Twenty First Century Resurrection of the Ancient Image of the Green Man."

401 Ibid.

402 Cheetham. *Green Man, Earth Angel*, 40.

403 Anderson. *Green Man: The Archetype of our Oneness with the Earth*, Araneo. "The Archetypal Twenty First Century Resurrection of the Ancient Image of the Green Man."

"To unlock the wisdom of the Green Man is tantamount to freeing or awakening the World Soul, the anima mundi. It is not just a psychological or philosophical concept. It is a living spiritual substance within us and around us. Just as the individual soul pervades the whole human being—our body, thoughts, and feelings—the nature of the World Soul is that it is present within everything. It permeates all of Creation and is a unifying principle within the world."[404]

Jung has suggested that "an archetype will reappear in a new form to redress imbalances in society at a particular time when it is needed." Archetypes are the seeds of the psyche. If given the right opportunity, they grow and develop. For me, the Green Man was emerging from the depths of my own being as a healing substance. According to this theory, the Green Man was rising up into my present awareness in order to counterbalance a lack in my attitude toward nature. He was reminding me of the union that ought to be maintained between humanity and nature or between mind and body, between spirit and matter, and between me and my own soul.

The consciousness of the parsonage saw nature and the desires of the body as inherently evil, putting God in the heavens and the devil in the earth, including the feminine. It was this split in me, this split of spirit and matter, mind and body, the split between me and the other man living in my soul that the Green Man came to repair. The Green Man therefore pointed to a relationship between my mind or consciousness and the world of nature, a kind of nature intelligence, the light in nature and the light in my own soul. It had become clearer to me that my journey into the study of and training in shamanism, shamanic healing, and energy medicine was my soul's attempt to reconnect me

---

404 Vaughan-Lee. "Anima Mundi: Awakening the Soul of the World."

with the spiritual intelligence in nature and to the spiritual truth of my own soul.

The Green Man is a return to a recognition, of subtleties, which we have largely lost. These subtle energies connect everything in some whole that includes, and yet both transcends and is the ground, holding them all together. The energy of the Green Man first entered my dreams as a bull. This bull chased after me to awaken me to the desire behind my same-sex attractions as the longing for the divine light in nature that longed to be awakened from its slumbering in the depths of my soul. He was the one who connected me to the World Soul and compassion for all of life.

It's no wonder that I later found myself pulled toward shamanism. Images found of prehistoric shamans in animal disguise represent one of the old aspects of the Green Man as guardian of the animals.[405] Now I understand my journey into shamanism and energy medicine with greater clarity. The ways of the shaman maintain a oneness with nature and discern the intelligence and wisdom in nature, working with its spirits. The shaman *is* the Green Man who mediates between the imaginal world and the physical world. This is the reality in which the shaman lives and moves.

Again, the emergence of the Green Man in me was one more attempt by psyche to heal my fragmented self and the fragmented selves of others. For it must be emphasized that the psyche is inherently self-organizing and self-optimizing, and under supportive conditions it is also self-healing, self-actualizing, self-transcending, self-awakening, and self-liberating. Cartesian duality and the separation of mind and body, spirit and matter, resulted in the disappearance of the anima mundi, the World Soul, and with it the loss of connection to my own

405 Matthews, *Quest for the Green Man*, 14.

soul. The female deities of earth were severed from the remote and transcendent masculine gods of the heavens and relegated to the place of inferiority, devoid of spirit.

This act also pushed the masculine god of antiquity, that creative masculine spirit of the earth and nature into the unconscious, where he is waiting to be set free. Archetypically, he is the male fertility principle of the Earth Mother, her consort, bringing the greening of Spring and fruitfulness to the soil. I had encountered him in my dream as a bull chasing me up a tree, which now takes on an even more significant meaning, given the Green Man's connection to trees. Whatever his name, be it Cernunnos, the Oak King, Osiris, Dionysus, Pan, the horned god of antiquity or Green Man, he is the archetype of male mysteries and masculine power, a masculine spirit in nature, in my nature.

As such, he clearly pointed to a paradigmatic shift in my understanding of the relationship that existed between me and nature, between the masculine and the feminine, between my soul and the World Soul, and between spirit and matter. Authors such as essayist, visionary and a land-based artist, Andrew Rothery and physician Larry Dossey refer to this shift in thinking as an emergence to a "green consciousness" or a "green intelligence." This refers not just to the green world of plants and trees—the tree people and the plant people. Instead, it refers to all of nature—the stone people, the creepy crawlers, the winged, the finned, and the furred. This results in a biospherical consciousness that reflects the unity and integrity of the earth and all life, including us humans—all of us, gay, straight, bisexual, and transgendered alike—as a single ecosystem.

As mirrored in the dream with which I started this chapter, I felt uncertain about my capacity to fully engage the Green Man as healer. I felt uncertain about my capacity to sit, for example, with a kidney stone of a client and see its light or hear its wisdom, how it came to be, its message to the person who created it, and what it needs in order to be able to leave. This the Green Man knows! This is what the heart knows. This is what is at the heart of matter.

The slow dissolution of my old consciousness and my way of thinking about and seeing—not only myself but the world in general—ushered another time of transition and change. My work over the past thirty years as detailed thus far in this book had brought me face-to-face with my soul's next manifestation—a new myth. But by myth, I do not mean falsehood! A myth may or may not be based on historical facts but in essence it is truer than history or fact.[406] Michael Christensen, in *C. S. Lewis on Scripture*, says myth is an archetypal tale that portrays eternal realities. As the highest form of symbolism, myth reaches after some transcendent reality that reasoned thought cannot attain. It isn't that myth is irrational, rather it is nonrational. According to Christensen, "*Reality is infinitely greater than human rational conception* [*italics mine*]."[407]

Continuing, Christensen says that "when divine [transpersonal] truth falls on human imagination, myth is born" and "far from being less true or factual, myth puts us in touch with Reality in a more intimate way than by knowing what is merely true or factual."[408] Therefore, to regard something as myth is to acknowledge a higher truth and a deeper reality than could be otherwise expressed.[409] In my own psychoanalytic work I became aware of and convinced that for modern man myth is born when the outer images and events are recognized as

---

406 Christensen, C.S. Lewis on Scripture, 59

407 Ibid., 60.

408 Ibid.

409 Ibid., 77.

carriers and therefore *symbols of the patterns of energy at work within the individual or collective psyche.*

Any organizing myth functions in ways that may be creative or destructive, healthful or pathological. Providing a summary of the stories that explain why things are as they are organizes the diverse experiences of a community into a single story and helps to create consensus, sanctify the community, and provide a path forward.[410] This is true for the individual as well. Myths come from the same place that dreams and art come from. They bubble up from the depths of the soul. They can't be forced or construed. They can only be organized into a meaningful story. In my own life, the myth—those archetypal forces that initiated, organized, and held me in the story of the parsonage for many years—sought death and renewal, transformation and evolution. A new myth, or perhaps the remnants of an ancient myth, slowly emerged from the depths of my soul. My hunch is this is not just my myth, but a piece of a greater myth that is emerging worldwide.

As I became more aware of the likely influence of the archetype of the Green Man on my journey through the years, I decided to journey to the Green Man.

> *I journey to the Lower World for the purpose of contacting the Green Man. Green Man makes his appearance. His appearance was like a spirit emanating from all living things—from the grasses and earth, from the trees, from the plants—all vegetation, as well as from the animals, coalescing as a spiritual entity. As I go to leave, he hands me a piece of a root. As I contemplate this gift, I am instructed to plant it in my heart. Taking it in my hands, I take the root into*

---

410 Keen, "Stories We Live By: Personal Myths Guide Daily Life."

my heart chakra, breathing it in. The root of the Green Man lives in me. (Journal, 5-29-11)

I must now hold the dualities of mind and body, spirit and matter, personal and transpersonal, rational and transrational with a sense of mutual respect and honor sufficient to allow a new consciousness to emerge, one that recognizes the interconnection of all things.

This interpenetration of spirit and matter brings spirit into matter and matter into spirit with alignment and harmony; an entity that while holding the alignment and harmony is able to transcend both, forming a third thing representing the union of the two. This third thing is a manifestation of the union of the shaman with the scientist; this third thing is the Green Man.

Everything is energy (spirit). Everything is matter. It is only the mind and the illusion of time that separates them. I paint a horse coming out of the sea. My eye catches the word *Mercurius* in Jung's *Mysterium Coniunctionis* and have a "feeling" there is some connection between it and my painting. Reading, I find Jung's reference to "the steed that is in the water is risen up" as the union of spirit and matter. I dream that a man kills a black jaguar so that I can attend a university, and twenty years later find myself in a weekend training on shamanic healing where a black jaguar returns to me on a shamanic journey. I stare into the background of a painting and see a man holding a bowl with a feather as if bringing me the gift of a feather; in meditation a hand extends an owl feather to me; months later I walk out of a building at a training on shamanic healing and am met by a man extending an owl feather to me. I paint a painting of hands over a male figure, with an eagle looking on, and weeks later find myself going for my first shamanic healing session in Sedona, Arizona, where I am greeted by an eagle at the gate. In the healing session itself, the healer uses his hands over me, working in my energy field.

Years later I find myself taking training in energy medicine where hands are used to move energy. Owls show up in my dreams and paintings and owls cross my path as I travel to and from the airport, going and returning from trainings on shamanic healing and energy medicine. I dream that a woman is holding a bowl of stones, placing one in a river to heal the river. I paint the bowl of stones. A few days later I walk into my office and there is a bowl of round stones sitting on the file cabinet, almost exactly like the ones I had painted. And then sometime later I read "everyone's got to do what the shamans call 'cleaning up your river.'" I dream that I'm involved in the healing of a lady in Africa with shaman and mentor Ona Sachs, only to learn some days later that Ona was in fact involved in a healing with a lady from South Africa at the time of my dream.

Is to place meaning on these experiences and events as confirmation or guidance for my journey superstition and magical thinking, regression to some prerational stage of development? Or is it some transpersonal, transrational reality—the Return of the Green Man—archetypal masculine of a divine light and intelligence in matter renewing our lost unity with the world of nature?

As psychoanalyst or shaman, as gay, straight, bisexual, or any other label we may attach to ourselves, we must value what our journeys through our various experiences show us and say to us. Then we must accept the challenge of holding the space where opposing, powerful, and equally sovereign forces collide on their way to the transformation and healing of the soul, whether that soul be mine, yours, or the Soul of the World.

Roger Walsh, M.D., Ph, D., in his book *The World of Shamanism: New View of an Ancient Tradition* says that "[c]learly we have much to learn from what shamans do—the myths they live by, the training they undergo, the techniques they use, the crises they confront, the capacities they develop, the states of consciousness they enter, the understandings they gain, the visions they see, and the cosmic travels they make. The more we explore shamanism, the more it points to unrecognized potentials of the human body, mind, and spirit. For untold thousands of years the world of shamanism has helped, healed, and taught humankind, and it still has more to offer us."[411]

I find myself on this journey with the Green Man. Together we venture into his world of nature, into the world of the shaman, into the world of energy medicine, into the world of the healer, into the world of my own soul as indicated by the dream with which I started this chapter, my own healing and that of the world. For in healing ourselves, we heal our families. In healing our families, we heal our communities. In healing our communities, we heal the world. It begins with each individual being willing to look into the depths of his or her soul and see what is hidden there, what images long to be brought out into the light of consciousness, embraced, and held with the imaginal sight of the heart.

These images come to us. We think that we create them. We think that we make them up. But they come to us from the depths of our souls. They come to us from the World Soul. We try to think them when we should dance them, paint them, love them, befriend them, and allow them to carry us into their worlds to learn their stories—stories that will once again connect us to the subtleties of spirit that we have long forgotten—the subtleties of spirit that connect us all.

In the previous chapter I shared my awakenings to the imaginal world and to the World Soul and their connections to heart

---

411 Walsh, *World of Shamanism,* 271.

consciousness as a way of seeing the invisible world of Spirit. In this chapter I tell of the resurrection of the Green Man. I discovered that the Green Man lives in the heart. I discovered that the Green Man is the spirit at the heart of matter. I discovered that the Green Man has a relationship with nature and the feminine, the Goddess and Earth Mother. This is different from the masculine with which I'd been raised. This was the masculine that longed to live.

I came to understand that this was part of what I sought in my same-sex relationships. This was what the heart knew. This was the masculine energy that wanted to live in me. This was the masculine that I must now give expression to. It is a masculine that is one with nature and the companion of the Earth Mother—the archetypal masculine in matter as a vital life-giving force renewing our oneness with nature. Rather than a transcendent divinity that lives somewhere up in heaven, the Green Man reveals a divine light that exists in nature and connects us to the sacred masculine that lives in the matter of the soul.

I must now acknowledge the Green Man and his way of seeing with the heart. As an archetype he exerts his influence on me through my dreams, my intuitions, the visions of my meditatThe corrections and shamanic journeys, and through the imaginal realm of the soul. The more an archetype is encountered, the more functional it becomes. In order for the Green Man to ultimately be of any value it must be actualized within the psyche. While I have already shared in an earlier chapter the piece of my journey that resulted in this poem, it bears repeating here as I close this chapter: a message from the soul of the Green Man.

The Return

As the sun rises over the African jungle, a shot rings out.
Somewhere in a thatched roof, grass hut a teenage boy lies dead.
The actions of a white man come to save him from his pagan ways.
A gut-shot they call it, a bullet straight to the stomach.
A slow, agonizing painful death.
As the blood slowly drains from the stomach wound
Freeing him from animal, earth, and tree
An intellectual shell remains.
Years pass . . . and somewhere in the far reaches
of his psychic past, a memory remains
A memory of animal, earth, and tree
Slowly the blood, long encased in its earthen tomb begins to stir
Flowing up, up and upward, back into the gut-shot wound.
And with it, Animal, Earth, and Tree.

Figure 17. *The Return of the Green Man*

"I am the Green Man. I am the spirit of nature.
I bring life. I bring regeneration.
I bring abundance. I am one with Mother Earth.
I am the Green Man. I see with the heart.
I am the son, the lover, and the guardian of the Great Goddess."

Notes and Exercises

Between mind and matter exists a psychic realm of subtle energies. Subtle energies manifest as an image. Imaginal sight dissolves the split between the physical and the spiritual.

The Green Man is the archetype that represents the spiritual intelligence in nature. As such the Green Man dissolves the split between spirit and matter. To accept the Green Man is to return to the awareness that there is a divine reality in matter

The way of the Shaman maintains a oneness with nature and discerns the wisdom and intelligence in nature, working with the spirits in nature.

The psyche is inherently self-organizing and self-optimizing and, under supportive conditions, is self-healing, self-actualizing, self-transcending, self-awakening, and self-liberating.

A new myth is emerging. Myth does not mean falsehood. It may or may not be based on historical facts but in essence is truer than history or fact. Myth is the highest form of symbolism that reaches after some transcendent reality that reasoned thought cannot attain.

Images come from the depths of our souls. We try to think them when we should dance them, paint them, love them, befriend them, and allow them to carry us into their worlds to learn their stories—stories that will once again connect us to the spirit that connects us all.

Journey to the Green Man

Find a quiet place where you won't be disturbed. Put on shamanic drumming or journey music or simply take some deep breaths to the count of four. Inhale slowly, counting 1, 2, 3, 4; hold, 2, 3, 4; exhale slowly, 2, 3, 4; hold, 2, 3, 4. Repeat this routine 4 times and then just breathe naturally, allowing yourself to go deeper and deeper into relaxation.

Call in a power animal or spirit guide. Place your intention to journey to the lower world to meet the Green Man. Imagine that your luminous energy body is descending into

the earth, past the roots of the trees, past the bedrock, past the great boulders, down, deep down until you come to an underground stream. When you come to the stream, lie in it, and allow the cool, cleansing waters to wash over and through you, cleansing you. When you're ready, allow the waters to carry you down deep into the belly of the earth. Allow yourself to step into the lower world. Notice the landscape. Renew your intention to meet the Green Man.

Accompanied by your power animal or spirit guide that you invited to guide you, walk through the lower world until you meet the Green Man. Notice how he show up. Greet him. Ask him what gift he has for you. Ask what he wants from you. Notice what wants to happen in this meeting and allow it to happen if it feels safe and ok with you. This is a time to build a relationship with the Green Man. When you end this journey, thank the Green Man and begin you journey back.

Journey back to the stream Thank your guide. Lie in the stream and let the waters wash over you, cleansing you. Now begin your journey back up into your room, past the boulders, past the bedrock, past the roots of the trees and back into your room and into your body. Wiggle your toes and fingers, take a deep breath, and open your eyes, wide awake. Write out your experience with the Green Man.

CHAPTER EIGHTEEN

Homosexuality and the Two-Spirit Archetype

I dream that

> *My former lover Sam and his wife have returned. They brought with them friends, another couple. They are putting on a play. My wife is in the play. She has a table with a projection screen, and she is to roll out the table with the projection screen. There is also a second cart with a projection screen that another lady has. Sam is in the singing group. His friend is leading the group. They sing a song, "She's a strong man-woman. He's a strong woman-man." I say, "Well, praise God! Androgyny has finally come to the church."* (Journal 4-22-87)

My decision to trust the dreams that told me "the healing of your homosexual self is in freeing him from the parsonage" and "homosexuality is the treasure hard to find" as the voice of God in me resulted in a long journey into the depths of my own soul and the discovery of archetypal forces from an ancient time. The twists and turns of listening to my dreams, trusting synchronicities, following my intuition, and interacting with the spirit world through meditation and my paintings led me into the world of shamanism, the recovery of the Green Man, the discovery of the berdache or two-spirit archetype and a new understanding of my relationship to both the masculine and the feminine. I came to understand that the bull that had chased me up the tree in that early dream and that had chased me into a barn in another dream where I discovered a woman hiding behind the mask of a dog was the remnant of an ancient masculine living in the depths of my soul—a masculine that had not lost his connection to nature nor to the Great Goddess and Earth Mother. I would discover him as the shaman in me. I would discover him as the Green Man in me. I would discover him as the healer in me. I would discover him as the Divine Masculine in nature. I would discover him as the light in matter. I would discover him as the divine light in the depths of my own soul connecting me to the Earth Mother as one with her. As the dream with which I started this chapter had indicated years earlier, I would discover androgyny and my two-spirit nature.

The connection to the feminine and especially to the mother has long been a common way the West has viewed homosexuality. Multiple studies have held that one of the causes of homosexuality is an overprotective, dominating mother and the absence of the father in a boy's life. While modern brain research provides evidence that the origins of sexual orientation are far more complicated than simply the influences of parental complexes, there is evidence to suggest that the masculine and feminine archetypes as spiritual forces do set up a psychic condition whereby homosexuality emerges. Parents, to the extent that they become the carriers of archetypal forces already vibrating in the soul of a child, may assist in bringing to life the expressions of these very archetypes.

As a child I was close to my mother, identifying with her because of my natural interests in art, crafts, music, and activities typically associated with the feminine—baking, knitting, babysitting, growing plants and flowers, taking care of hurt animals, and dressing up in women's clothes. As such one could say that my ego become overly identified with the feminine, driving the more masculine characteristics into the unconscious that, as I moved into adolescence, became projected onto men with whom I longed to connect in an effort to experience the masculine—a masculine different from the one I knew in the parsonage. As my dreams began to uncover and reveal the unconscious and archetypal dynamics underlying the conflicts of my soul, I discovered other forces at work in me. I discovered that my same-sex attraction was only a small piece of a much larger story. I discovered the shaman and the Green Man and their relationship to the Earth Mother. I discovered that my identification with my mother and the feminine was only the manifestation of a much larger dynamic, one that may have been present from my birth. I discovered that not only is there the archetypal configuration of the masculine as a consort and companion of the Goddess and Earth Mother, there is also what the indigenous cultures call the berdache or two-spirit soul.

I am indebted to work of Walter Williams and his review of the anthropological studies of berdachism as well as his own extensive field study of berdaches in many American Indian and indigenous cultures as detailed in his book *The Spirit and the Flesh: Sexual Diversity in American Indian Cultures*. This chapter is not intended to be a review of berdachism. For those who might become interested in the topic, I refer you to the work of Walter Williams. Also, although there are female berdaches, my references are to male berdaches.

I am neither intending to apply nor impose the traditions of berdachism to Anglo-Americans. Such traditions clearly belong to the Native

American and other indigenous cultures as sacred and intimate parts of their tribal stories. However, what does interest me is the archetypal aspects of these traditions and how the archetype of the berdache or two-spirit may now be emerging in other cultures and societies and how that archetype may apply to my own story.

A berdache is anatomically male but does not fulfill a standard man's role in society. This person is often seen as effeminate, but a more accurate description would be androgynous. Berdaches mix together the behavior, dress, and social roles of both women and men. They often dress as women, do women's work, and care for children. They gain social prestige by their spiritual, intellectual craftwork and artistic contributions to their communities, and by their reputations for hard work and generosity. Because berdaches are not seen as men or women but as having an alternate gender that is a mixture of diverse elements, they serve as mediators between women and men as well as between the physical and spiritual worlds.[412] In fact, most important is their spiritual role as mediators between the physical and spiritual worlds, between the visible and the invisible. A relationship to the invisible or unseen world is critical to the berdache. Where the Western culture stigmatized the berdaches and wasted their spiritual power, the indigenous cultures recognized their capacity to mediate between the physical and spiritual worlds and successfully used these skills and insights for the good of the community.[413]

Berdaches often have a predisposition as a dreamer or visionary that some cultures believe connects them to the supernatural or spirit worlds. In fact berdaches often receive their call and instruction through a dream or a vision. They often assist shamans or serve as

412 Williams, *Spirit and the Flesh*, 1–2.

413 Ibid., 2–3.

shamans and medicine men.[414] Such people have a clearly recognized and accepted social status and special ceremonial roles in their communities. In their sexual lives, they generally take a nonmasculine role, either being asexual or taking the passive role in sex with men. In some situations, a berdache becomes the wife of a man, and they live together as husband and wife.[415]

Of note, because of negative connotations associated with the word *berdache* due to its linguistic roots, in the 1990s Native American anthropologists replaced it with the term *two-spirit* to refer to what was traditionally known as the berdache.[416] I have chosen to use the word *berdache* when I am referring to its long-standing historical use and to use the term *two-spirit* when speaking more about current times and the role of two-spirit people moving forward. In either case I am using the terms to refer to a person born with an androgynous spirit, as existing somewhere between the characteristics of women and men, and who possess the insights and perceptions of both. These are persons who have the perspective that others of a single gender don't or can't see.

Although berdaches may take on the dress and social roles of women and live with a man in a same-sex relationship, berdachism is ultimately a reflection of spirituality.[417] In many indigenous cultures, everything that happens is due to the spirits and the spirit world. Physical, emotional, personal, and even community health has to do with our relationships with the spirit world. Whether we know it or not, we are always interacting with the energetic world. I was told in a journey to the Place of the Hummingbird that "the energy of the one

---

414 Williams, *Spirit and the Flesh, 35-36.*

415 Ibid., 2.

416 Roscoe, "*Who Are the Native American Two Spirits?*"

417 Williams. *The Spirit and the Flesh*, 30.

is continually exchanging itself with the energy of the other." It is the respectful, reciprocal relationship with all that is that sustains and improves the health of all.

My own psycho-spiritual-physical health is dependent on the health of my soul. The health of my soul is dependent on my relationship with the spirits and the universe. My own personal journey into dreams and into the world of shamanism has revealed this to me over and over. While shamans are not necessarily berdaches, because of the berdache's spiritual connection they are often associated with shamanism and are considered to be powerful shaman or are the people from whom shamans seek advice.[418]

In Native American and indigenous cultures, families recognize the marks of a berdache early on in the life of a child. In fact, in many indigenous cultures, it is obvious from birth that a boy has the spirit of the berdache. They are often beautiful boys with effeminate voices and behaviors, avoiding rough-and-tumble play, seeking instead the play of girls. The mother often recognizes this early on and encourages the boy to participate in more traditionally feminine things such as cooking, sewing, and crafts.[419]

The day I read the description of a child born in American Indian and other indigenous societies that was recognized as having an androgynous spirit and given to things associated with the feminine who then became a berdache, I saw myself. Perhaps I wanted to see myself in that description. It gave me a context whereby to reimagine my childhood, to see it differently, to see myself differently, to feel differently, to understand myself differently, and to accept myself and my childhood. Again, the berdache is described as a non-masculine, effeminate child who likes to play with girls and girly things. He is

418 Ibid., 35–36.

419 Ibid., 40–50.

also inclined toward the arts and enjoys dressing in women's clothes. That pretty much described me as a child even into my early adolescent years. I was that child. I was non-masculine and described as effeminate, often being made fun of, called "sissy" or "a girl." I didn't care for sports or aggressive play and preferred playing with dolls and playing house with the girls in the neighborhood. I also had natural inclinations toward music and art, spending time drawing, painting, making crafts, baking cookies, knitting, and making artificial flowers and flower arrangements.

While my brothers were playing ball with the boys in the neighborhood, I was tramping through the woods, playing in the ponds, catching tadpoles and gathering up frog eggs, taking them home to watch them hatch, or bringing home a wounded bird to take care of. While I did have male friends, they were more like me—preferring art and music to sports and activities more associated with an aggressive masculinity.

In my early teens I took a liking to caring for babies and became obsessed with taking care of a newborn baby in the church, holding it during church services and then returning home with its parents so that I could care for the baby. Later, I became a babysitter as a way to earn money.

I liked wearing women's dresses even into my adolescent years. Although today I have developed a greater sense of my masculinity and have no desire to dress as a woman, I can still find that part of me, and I could take her shopping, and I know exactly how to dress her.

Along with those characteristics developed a same-sex attraction. It all seemed to fit together in a package. In same-sex relationships, like the berdache, I also preferred the passive role. So in many ways, even though I wasn't born into an Indian culture, it would appear that I exhibited many of the characteristics of a berdache. However, the culture of the Judeo-Christian evangelical parsonage in to which I was born didn't have a framework for such a child and while my non-masculine, musical, artistic, and nature-oriented attributes were not necessarily ridiculed and in many ways were even encouraged, the sexual side of this archetypal configuration was deplored and judged as morally wrong and a sin. While I made the choice not to live the same-sex attraction out in external relationships, I refused to reject it and made the choice to honor my two-spirit nature, my androgynous spirit. I found that other masculine inside me that allowed me to step more fully into the other characteristics of my two-spirit nature—the artist, the dreamer and ultimately, as my dreams would eventually reveal, the shaman and healer.

This book has been the story of my search for this other man living in my soul. As the book has revealed, I began to develop more of the masculine aspects of this two-spirit nature and to feel more balanced in the expressions of my masculine and feminine spirits. Williams points out that in his own field study and interviews with many berdaches he found a pattern that is more individual and unique and more androgynous than strictly feminine.[420]

In general, the West believes that sex is a certainty, and that one's gender identity and sex role always conforms to one's anatomical sex. Western thought tends to divide groups into dichotomies that are mutually exclusive: male and female, black and white, homosexual and heterosexual, right and wrong, good and evil. However, other world views are often more accepting of the ambiguities of life. In his study of multiple Indian cultures, Williams talks with Indian people themselves and explores how certain cultures are able to accommodate gender and sexual variation beyond the man/woman dichotomy

420 Ibid., 51.

without being threatened by it. In fact, acceptance of gender variation in the berdache tradition is typical of many native cultures' approach to life in general.[421]

Williams points out that Western psychiatrists are often more interested in finding out the cause of a boy becoming feminine or homosexual as if there is some need to change or prevent such behavior. American Indians on the other hand are more interested in the social position of such a boy. Indian parents see no need to change such a child. In fact, they take an active role in encouraging a child to become a berdache or, at the very least, accept his inclinations as a reflection of an innate spiritual character. In these cultures, gender variation is an accepted reality and families accept that this is simply who their child will be.[422]

Because of the general acceptance by the community of a berdache there is no suppression of his feminine behavior. Neither does he internalize a negative or poor self-image as is often the case in Western culture where such behaviors and inclinations are considered deviant. As a result, berdaches who value their position have fewer incidents of problems related to alcohol and suicide. As one Crow traditionalist said, "We don't waste people, the way white society does. Every person has their gift."[423]

Some anthropologists suggest that the boy who chooses to become a berdache is the boy who shies away from the pressure to develop an aggressive masculinity, fearing the masculine role of warrior in many cultures. However, Williams points out that if that were true there would be berdaches in all warlike tribes, and there are not. Another

---

421 Ibid., 3.

422 Ibid., 53.

423 Joe Medicine Crow, in Williams. *The Spirit and the Flesh*, 57.

theory for the existence of berdachism is that it is the result of too much "mothering."

This idea is based on psychodynamic theory that too much mothering causes a boy to become anxious about his masculinity and ultimately reject it. Instead of identifying with his masculine and male role, the boy identifies with mother and the feminine. In this view, berdachism is a fear of and a flight from masculinity. Williams's own field study of berdachism concludes that berdaches seem "anything but neurotic and their peaceful inclinations would be honored in many gentler cultures."[424] While in the West it has been a long-standing theory and belief that a boy's relationship to his parents—too much mother and not enough father—is the cause of gender variance including homosexuality, modern brain research and a greater understanding of gender identity has caused the basic propositions of this theory to be rejected.[425]

From the American Indian and indigenous point of view berdachism doesn't occur from outside sources such as an overprotective mother or an absent father but is a reflection of the child's inborn character or spirit.[426] To the Indians, a man is what his nature and his dreams make him. They accept him for what he is and for what he wants to be. They accept his gifts and find a place for him to serve within their society.[427]

Western homosexual and heterosexual identities are based entirely on sexual preference. There is no spiritual component associated with sexual identity in the West. For the Indian it is the character of the

---

424 Williams, *Spirit and the Flesh*, 48.

425 Bell, *Sexual Preference: Its Development in Men and Women*. Referenced in Williams, *Spirit and the Flesh*, 49.

426 Williams, *Spirit and the Flesh*, 49.

427 Ibid., 198.

person that is of prime importance. Sexuality is a part of that character.[428] Also, for the American Indian, sexual preference and gender identity are two independent variables. One can be homosexual in behavior without being gender nonconformist and without having an identity different from other men. American Indian values recognize these differences, which Western culture confuses by labeling anyone who participates in same-sex relationship as "a homosexual." By socially constructing only the berdache as different, with their partners as "normal," Indian cultures avoid categorizing people into two opposed categories based on sexual behavior."[429]

The fluidity in sexuality demonstrated by the ability of men who identify themselves as heterosexual to adapt to sex with a male is not accounted for in theories of homosexual orientation or heterosexual orientation. These men are responding to the femininity of their partner. The particular genital equipment is not crucial.[430]

Partners of berdaches are not considered homosexual. They are considered husbands. Therefore, they can leave the berdache and marry a woman. Since he was always a husband he is also suitable as a husband for a woman. For the husband of a berdache, heterosexual marriage is not ruled out any more than male marriage is ruled out for men married to women. Allowing for cultural and individual variation, the American Indian institution defines itself around gender role rather than sexual behavior.[431] This allows for a greater diversity in sexual expression. While berdaches or two-spirit men traditionally had sex

---

428 Ibid., 126.

429 Ibid., 115.

430 Ibid., 117.

431 Ibid., 122.

with men, there are reports of two-spirit males marrying a woman in order to produce and raise children.[432]

The fluidity of women's and men's role and the mixed-gender status of the berdache in American Indian societies open up other possibilities for understanding what we call homosexuality. What if instead of focusing on the sex between two men we focused on the spirit or nature of the men involved, recognizing that in the same-sex relationship they might be living out their different natures, their individual spirits, expressions of masculine, feminine, and/or androgynous spirits. Williams points out that "sexual behavior of berdache is often considered a serious reflection of their spiritual natures."[433] It might even be that there are other spiritual natures that express themselves in same-sex relationships besides what the indigenous societies call berdaches. Certainly, over the past several years, gender diversity and alternative gender expression have emerged other than the traditional male and female. Gender identity is much more fluid. Sexual attraction much more varied so that it isn't tied to a particular gender. What if we, like the American Indian and indigenous societies, begin to focus on the spirit or the nature of a person with an understanding that a person's spirit may also have an alternative sexual expression that is true to it.

For example, *the transgender* is a multifaceted term. One example of a transgendered person might be a man who is attracted to women but also identifies as a cross-dresser or as a woman. Other examples include people who consider themselves gender nonconforming, multi-gendered, androgynous, third gender, and two-spirit people. All of these definitions are inexact and vary from person to person, yet each of them includes a sense of blending or alternating the binary concepts of masculinity and femininity. We might begin to view these people

---

432 Ibid.

433 Ibid., 112.

as having particular spirits or inborn natures rather than seeing them as somehow flawed or the result of some psychological or emotional problem or the result of too much of one parent and not enough of another. Rather than forcing people to fit into the binary system of male/female and masculine/feminine, what if we evolved a system to include the spirits of such people as they are?

We must begin to open space for the multi-diversity of gender expression and allow individual spirits to make choices that are congruent with their soul. For some that may be two masculine men in a loving and sexual relationship. For others that might mean a masculine man in a relationship with an effeminate man or an androgynous male. For still others that might mean a bisexual man in a relationship with a woman. For others their same-sex behaviors may in fact be part of a larger identity with a certain spirituality that their two-spirit nature puts them in touch with—an awareness of the value and unity of all things. Each must find his or her own soul's expression. As we each find space for our soul's expression of our diverse sexualities and gender identities, hopefully the culture will begin to mirror the same and open space to embrace the diverse ways the soul expresses itself.

I suggest that pursuing and living our soul's purpose is a more important part of our self-identity than who we are sexually attracted to or who we have sex with. As a bisexual man with androgynous characteristics (more feminine when I was younger than perhaps now, as that feminine nature has seemed to have given way to a gentle man) I can feel sexual attraction to either a man or a woman.

My personal journey has brought me into agreement with the Indian view that everything that exists is spiritual. Williams, in his admittedly generalized overview of American Indian religious values, says "[e]very object—plants, rocks, water, air, the moon, animals, humans, the earth itself—has a spirit. The spirit of one thing (including a human) is not superior to the spirit of any other. Such a view promotes a sophisticated ecological awareness of the place that humans have in the larger environment. The function of religion is not to try to condemn or to change what exists, but to accept the realities of the world and to appreciate their contributions to life. Everything that exists has a purpose." [434]

In the beginning I didn't know this about my own same-sex attractions. I only knew somewhere deep inside me that my homosexuality was more than it seemed. As we have learned, in the Native American and indigenous cultures a person who is physically male might have the spirit of a female, might range somewhere between the two sexes, or might have a spirit that is distinct from either woman or man. Whatever category, this person is seen as different from men and accepted spiritually as "not man" in the community. Some cultures call this person a "man-woman" like the reference in the above dream. [435] They were believed to be born this way, with natural desires to become women and, as they grew up, they gradually became women.[436] In many indigenous cultures such boys were seen as acting out of their basic natures and made berdaches by the Great Spirit and were thus accepted as such.[437]

An androgynous spirit is more important than a person's anatomy or dress in understanding berdachism. Although berdaches are anatomically male, physical body parts are also much less important than a person's spirit or character. When the American Indian refers to the nature of a berdache, they are referring to his spiritual essence rather than names that the white man uses to denote a berdache. These

---

434 Ibid., 21. See Williams's footnote for a more detailed references on Native American religion.

435 Ibid., 26.

436 Ibid., 22.

437 Ibid., 25.

names include such terms as *hermaphrodite, transvestite, transsexual,* or *homosexual.*[438]

While in recent years there has been an increased tolerance and even increased acceptance of LGBTQ persons and other gender nonconformists in Anglo-American society, they are still met with discrimination, bigotry, and misunderstanding. Little tolerance continues to exist for gender ambiguities outside of opposites of men and women. Many gender nonconformists conclude that they only have one alternative: to make themselves into the other sex.

American Indian and other indigenous cultures provide alternative gender roles along a continuum between masculine and feminine through the tradition of berdachism.[439] Just like in the dream above that refers to a "strong-woman man" and a "strong man-woman," in indigenous cultures it is the mixture of the masculine and feminine that is important. Categories are less rigid and gender concepts more fluid. As Williams's work shows, "just as berdaches can physically move freely between the women's group and the men's group, so the lack of boundaries marks their gender status as well. They mix the attributes of both female and male, and add alternative aspects that are unique to the berdache status."[440]

As a bisexual and androgynous man born into a Judeo-Christian evangelical minister's home that neither understood my spirit nor accepted it as normal, I am eternally grateful for my dreams. From the dream of "the bull that chased me up a tree to keep me from returning to the small town in which I lived" to the dream that said "healing the homosexual is freeing him from the parsonage" to the dream that said "homosexuality is the treasure hard to find" to the dream with which I

---

438 Ibid., 71–80.

439 Ibid., 80.

440 Ibid., 81.

started this chapter that says "androgyny has come to the church" to the dream of the orb as "my soul's next manifestation," they connected me to a forgotten and primordial past and to a spirituality that embraced who I was and am at the soul level and to the call to fulfill a sacred destiny—the soul's longing.

In no way do I place myself within the time-honored and sacred tradition of the American Indian berdache. Nor do I wish to steal from the indigenous peoples a tradition that belongs to them and for which many of them have suffered more than I can comprehend. However, the knowledge of the berdache does provide me with a sense of roots, a sense of being connected to something larger than myself. It puts me in touch with an archetypal experience that I propose has a place in the greater American society.

As mentioned before, Jung has suggested that an archetype will emerge when it is needed in order to restore balance to an individual or a society. As Williams' study of berdachism notes, same-sex behavior is just one of the characteristics of the two-spirit person and is simply a part of their relationship to their spirit. Such a balance is needed today.

Certainly homosexuality exists without an association to the berdache tradition even in Indian societies, but for men who are cut off from a sense of tradition or from a sense of their own spirit, they only have their sexuality as a way to define themselves. In my own life, even though I chose to marry and raise a family, choosing not to live a homosexual life, the other characteristics of my androgynous or two-spirit nature pushed for expression. They eventually pulled me into shamanism where I could more fully live my soul's identity. As Jung has proposed, there are many homosexualities. The task and the challenge is to find out the meaning of our own.

American Indian and other indigenous societies have a place for gender diversity. Our modern American society might be able to learn something from these cultures. While berdachism is not the same as a modern gay identity, it is part of a larger homosexual question. The existence of acceptable same-sex behavior among the Indians is important for the non-Indian LGBTQ communities who are also in a struggle for social change as we work to find acceptance and our place in society. To this end the LGBTQ communities and the native peoples have a common interest and goal.[441]

Williams's field study of the berdaches across various American Indian and indigenous cultures concludes that the English language has no label that adequately describes a complex concept like berdachism. The closest synonym is *androgyny,* given that it incorporates both gender mixing and alternative gender concepts as well as implying mystical and sexual ambiguity, all of which are included in the broad expression of the berdache.[442] Rather than threatening the gender system in these societies, the berdache's androgyny is incorporated into it.[443] Berdaches seem to symbolize the original unity of humans, their differentiation into separate genders, and the potential for reunification as well. Ironically, by violating gender norms, berdachism expands the definition of what is woman and what is man.[444] While this might be an oversimplification of a very complex phenomenon, I view the berdache as having two spirits, man and woman, combined into one soul.

I came to recognize through my dreams and through my own proclivities and inclinations, interests, and talents that I am a two-spirit soul—a strong woman-man and a strong man-woman. It isn't because

441 Ibid., 205.

442 Ibid., 83.

443 Ibid., 84.

444 Ibid.

of my shy, introverted, artistic effeminate childhood, or an over-identification with mother and an absent father, or my being drawn to do work associated with women or being sexually attracted to a man or even my dreams that made me so. Although without my dreams I doubt that I would have discovered or understood the two-spirit man in me. I am the way I am as a result of all of these things; they all have had a hand in making up my androgynous nature. I now see the spiritual meaning behind all this. This is the spiritual meaning of my homosexuality. This is my soul's longing. It is this that connects me to the spirit in matter, to the spirit in the matter of my own soul, to the "treasure hard to find." This is the archetypal story of my soul.

Archetypes must have a supportive environment in which to develop and find expression. While such a supportive environment existed in many indigenous societies, that environment did not exist in the Europeans and Spanish who settled the Americas. Thus, the berdache or two-spirit archetype was driven into the unconscious where it has laid dormant, rejected or germinating until the recent rise of the LGBTQ communities and the focus on LBGTQ rights. While the current focus seems to be placed on the sexual aspect, perhaps we can open space in our culture to embrace sexual and gender diversity so that the spiritual gifts of the LGBTQ communities can find a place in the greater culture, as they did in the indigenous societies. I am in no way suggesting that we take the berdache traditions from the American Indian and indigenous cultures and try to make them ours or impose them onto modern society. I am suggesting that we make space for the archetype of the berdache, of androgyny and the two-spirit soul to find its expression in our culture as the mediator and spiritual healer it can be.

We must somehow take the wisdom not only of the American Indians but the wisdom of our own stories and open space in our worldview for the LGBTQ communities and gender diverse people if we are to recover what we have lost by our rejection of these spirits. As members of these communities we must open space in our own hearts to accept ourselves and live our gifts in ways that heal the split not only in ourselves but the split in the society at large.

While this chapter is not intended to be a study in berdachism or a call to integrate the berdache into our culture, I do wonder if many of the LGBTQ persons have a two-spirit soul, or the soul of a healer, or the soul of a shaman, or the soul of a visionary, or the soul of an artist. Having no place within the culture where such a spirit can be nurtured, valued, and given a prominent place, we have lost the gifts of so many people. Because of that, I can only imagine what LGBTQ persons have been deprived of, not only them and their families, but our society at large.

What if I hadn't listened to that call from somewhere deep within me on the January morning in 1978 that said "Listen to your dreams for I will speak to you through them?" I would have missed what was longing to come to life in me. I would have missed the bull who later connected me to the horned god of antiquity and to the Green Man and to the shaman and healer—perhaps none other than the rising up of a form of the berdache archetype in its longing to be lived, in its longing to bring balance to my own psychic system and thus to my little corner of the world.

As the Indians have integrated into the urban gay lifestyle, some identify with being both gay and berdache. While there are different styles in both traditions they see no contradiction in either role. These Indians live a combination of their tribal spirituality with the flexibility of urban life. Traditionally, in their role as berdaches they were the mediators between the masculine and the feminine and between the spirit and the physical. Because they were able to maneuver between the worlds, they were often called the "go-betweens."[445] The connection to the spirit world, and the connection between the world of women and men, is destroyed when the berdache tradition declines.[446]

One wonders what role certain members of the LGBTQ communities might play in restoring a connection to the spirit world and to the worlds of men and women because of their unique connection to these forces. I wonder what connection they might play in restoring our connection to the earth and to nature in general. As we value our own spirits, we open doors to honor the diversity of all spirits and connect to a world that transcends us, serving as the go-between between the visible and the invisible, between the spirit and the physical, between the masculine and the feminine, between ourselves and the earth.

According to many American Indian cultures, being gay connects them to their ancestors and this connection has advantages. Navajo Erna Pahe, co-chair of the Gay American Indians, says, "In our culture [and] in our gay world, anybody can do anything. We can sympathize; we can really feel how the other sex feels. [We are] the one group of people that can really understand both cultures."[447] Pahe sees this as also applying to non-Indian gay people as well, saying, "It all has to do with spirit, with restoring an awareness of our spirituality as gay people."[448]

It isn't only in the American Indian cultures that recognize special status and respected roles for individuals like berdaches. Many societies have a special gender category that is generally compatible to the berdache.[449] In Hawaii, for example, Williams found among the

---

445 Ibid., 227.

446 Ibid., 228.

447 Ibid., 251, also Roscoe, "Gay American Indians . . . ," and again in Williams, *Spirit and the Flesh*, 251.

448 Ibid.

449 Ibid., 252–275.

traditional Hawaiian *mahu* a tradition very similar to the berdache tradition. According to Williams, "They are androgynous in character, do women's work as well as men's, may dress in unisex clothing or a mixture of women's and men's clothing, are sexually active with men, and have certain special roles in traditional Hawaiian religion."[450]

While in the West, LGBTQ persons have come a long way in liberating themselves sexually, many have not yet found their spirituality. What seems common to berdaches and two-spirits across all Indian cultures is their spirituality and the spiritual role they play. It is a role that is the go-between between the invisible world of spirit and the material world of matter. Is this because of their dual natures, their two-spirit souls, the fact that they are androgynous? Is this because they live in both worlds? This is certainly a place to explore the complexities of the soul.

Williams's study of world societies regarding sex and gender roles finds that there is "quite a bit of difference between male-male sexual behavior and a homosexual identity. The many variations in sexuality worldwide are exploding our notion that humans are neatly categorized as homosexuals or heterosexuals. Institutions like the berdache are leading us also to question the categories of men and women."[451]

To explore a connection with a berdache or with the archetype of the two-spirit is to invoke its power in one's being. It is a way of altering one's polarity and aligning with oneness, a way of transcending the opposites and opening up psychic and mystical power within the soul. In these religious and ethnic traditions where berdachism was practiced, the willingness to explore this realm was not considered a perversion. Rather it was a place of honor with gifts that were seen to

---

450 Ibid., 257.

451 Ibid., 272.

benefit the community. It was a way of reaching into the realm of the spiritual unknown in order that the soul might grow.[452]

In the dream with which I started this chapter, my former lover Sam and his wife had returned and brought with them another couple. Here the masculine—the other man—that I had projected onto Sam had returned, but this time with the feminine. The other couple, symbolizing another masculine-feminine pair, made up the four—a symbol for wholeness. However, there are were two other women in the dream, my wife, representing my feminine, and another woman. They were all in a play and this play was playing out in me. The women were to "roll out the projectors."

Here we have the phenomenon of acting and projection. The psyche projects its unconscious content outside and we act out the projections. The "play" and "projectors" by the women and men may be understood as a demonstration of how the masculine and feminine roles are molded into persona, and publicly projected to get along. One man said, in reading this dream, "The man-woman, woman-man song nicely states my intuitive belief that the human genome has the capacity for masculine and/or feminine interests and expressions including sexuality," and that we are much more nature than we are nurture.[453] Perhaps the Native Americans know this. In the very least, it is nice that the native traditions have such an accepting and nurturing place for the men-women. Like my dream and my own journey, I hypothesize that many LGBTQ persons are connected to the archetypal energies associated with the berdache and two-spirit soul. I suspect these persons possess spirits of diverse gender expressions, many of them androgynous.

LGBTQ persons are awakening, becoming aware of their gifts and talents and seeking their place in society, where they can contribute

---

452 HIgherLove, "Gatekeepers and Shamanic Androgyny."

453 Private email exchange with Greg Ellis, M.D., January 18, 2016.

those gifts. The focus on the sexual orientation of these persons and the rejection of their unique spirits has driven them and their gifts into the shadows where, split off from their natures, they have struggled for acceptance and value. If we can honor these spirits with their diverse genders and sexual expressions and if we can accept their particular gifts, these men and women wishing to honor their androgynous and diverse natures, can become a symbol of the unity of the masculine and feminine and a symbol of the God and the Goddess—two spirits living in unity and harmony, co-creators in the dance of life—the soul's longing.

Notes and Exercises

The masculine and feminine archetypes as spiritual forces set up the psychic condition whereby bisexuality and other sexual expressions emerge. Not only is there a masculine archetype as a consort and companion of the Goddess and Earth Mother such as the Green Man, there is also a two-spirit archetype—a strong man-woman and a strong woman-man living in the soul.

While everyone is androgynous to some extent, certain people are more directly connected to the two-spirit archetype. The two-spirit soul is seeking to be lived in its many expressions. For some that may be within a certain spirituality that their two-spirit nature puts them in touch with—an inner healer, an inner shaman or an awareness of the value and unity of all things as a companion of the Goddess and Mother Earth, living in harmony with her.

> *Are you a two-spirit? Think back over your life, all the way back to early childhood. Write down which of these characteristics describe you: effeminate; sensitive with a*

gentle spirit; avoided rough and tumble play; didn't care much for sports; played with dolls or things associated with girls; was drawn to drawing, painting, music, or dance; liked to be out in nature, was drawn to help the animals including the birds; enjoyed things associated with the feminine such as cooking, sewing, gardening, wearing women's clothes, anything that traditionally you might associate with the feminine; felt like a girl inside.

How many things are on your list? Read through it. Allow yourself to feel and connect to those parts of you, to that part of you.

Find a place where you will not be disturbed. Take a few deep breaths and allow yourself to drift into a place of relaxation. Allow your focus to turn inward. Imagine that you are a nine-year-old boy. Now let yourself become that nine-year-old boy. Notice what it feels like to be that nine-year-old boy. What is his life like? What does he like to do? How does he spend his time? What are his interests? Who does he play with? What toys does he like?

One day his parents take him to a toy store. See yourself in the toy store. See the aisles of toys, aisles of footballs, basketballs, bows and arrows, guns. Walk through other aisles of video games, action figures. Walk through aisles of dolls, kitchens and doll houses, arts, drawing and painting. Walk all through the toy store and notice what you are attracted to, what you want to pick up and play with. Suddenly your parents call to you and tell you it is time to leave. They tell you that you can pick one thing to buy and take home. What are you drawn to? What do you want to buy? What do you take home? Is there more than one thing? Maybe you can't choose. Maybe you go home without any toy. Just notice what wants to happen. What does that nine-year -old boy want? What is his soul attracted to? What does he pick up?

Now take what you picked up and run to meet your parents. As you run out with whatever you picked up, your parents are there to welcome you.

If you were drawn to pick up something that is typically associated with the feminine or the creative side, you may be a two-spirit.

How do you feel about the nine-year-old's choice? Was it an easy choice? Did the nine-year-old hesitate? Was he drawn to one but chose the other? Was he afraid of what his parents might say or think? What other feelings did you notice? Are you a two-spirit?

CHAPTER NINETEEN

The Rest of the Story

"The years teach what the days never know."

—Ralph Waldo Emerson

Lying deep within the human soul is an unknown land, a land with its own characters, its own laws, and its own story. Somewhere in that land is a place where we put all the rejected parts of ourselves, the parts that have been wounded and hurt by others, the parts that for some reason we haven't been able to embrace or have been told can't live, even parts unknown to us—both positive and negative. All the feelings and emotions that are hard for us to feel like shame, guilt, sadness, anger, and jealousy are here. Sometimes feelings of happiness, joy, and pride, even our gifts and talents that for some reason we've been told are not acceptable or valuable, live in this land. It is a place of shelter for all that we have pushed away and disowned. This place is where we put all that doesn't fit into our lives yet are parts of us that long to live.

It is also the place where we often put Spirit—our connection to the divine light that lives in us. If we make the journey into the rejected places of the soul, we will find this divine light, lying there, just waiting for us to embrace it and bring it into our lives. It lives among the shadows of this place. It not only lives there, it accepts unconditionally all those rejected and disowned parts of the soul and holds them in love. To embrace and live this story is the longing of the soul.

This book has been primarily the revelation of my inner journey to find and live that story, the story of the other man living in my soul, a kind of psycho-spiritual memoir. While this inner journey resulted in shifts in consciousness, shifts in perceptions, and even major changes in my personal life, there was at the same time another story—the story of my family and the effects of my inner journey on their lives.

"The years have a wisdom the days know nothing of" is a paraphrase by Hilda Studebaker, a dear friend and frequent image in my dreams, of Ralph Waldo Emerson's saying that "The years teach what the days never know." At the writing of this book, I am into my seventy-fifth year. My wife and I have been married fifty-four years. For our fiftieth wedding anniversary, we took our children, their partners, and our grandchildren to Folly Beach, South Carolina, staying together in a house on the ocean to celebrate those fifty years and our lives together as a family.

The years following my revelation to my wife of my same-sex attractions and my affairs with men were a devastating and tumultuous time in our lives. As I became increasingly aware that if I were to divorce my wife and pursue a homosexual life I would end up at the end of my life knowing what I already knew intuitively and what my dreams were telling me—that my same-sex attraction was about more than being gay or bisexual. We re-affirmed our love for each other and made the commitment to our marriage, whatever that would come to mean. At the time of that decision our children were six and eight years old. During this time, our son began having nightmares for which we sought help from a therapist. In discussions with the therapist, my same-sex attractions and affairs were discussed. While the themes of my son's nightmares didn't deal directly with my homosexuality or my affairs, my wife and I did feel that he was picking up on the unrest, hurt, anger, and betrayal that we as his parents were feeling and what was vibrating in the unconscious of the family. After discussing our options with the therapist, we made the decision not to tell our children about my bisexuality or about my same-sex affairs at that time.

I understood his nightmares as evidence of how children often pick up on what is going on in their parents' lives and express it or act it out in some way. Happily, the therapist was able to help our son work through the nightmares, which stopped soon thereafter. My wife and I both worked diligently to protect our children from my indiscretions, knowing the adverse effects such revelations would have in the small conservative community in which we lived and the ramifications they would then suffer. My wife and I decided to stay together and yet we also agreed that we would revisit this decision periodically to make sure it was working for both of us.

This was the mid-seventies, just a few years after the Stonewall riots. Not only were homosexuality, gay rights, and sexual and gender diversity seen in a negative light in the community in which we lived, but the society at large held a similar view. So we focused on providing our children with the safe and secure environment that we knew all children need, and we worked hard to keep their lives as normal as possible. Today, both our son and daughter look back on those years as their "happy childhoods," and for that my wife and I are exceedingly grateful.

As I followed my journey into dreams and the story that was unfolding in the depths of my soul, my wife struggled to find her place and to make some kind of sense of what had happened, given that I had shattered her dream of our relationship. She fell into self-blame, with feelings that if she were "more of a woman" I wouldn't have these feelings or have had these affairs with men. She also felt that she was somehow "not enough" because she couldn't satisfy my same-sex need because she wasn't' a man, saying she didn't know how to compete with a man. While I was stepping into discovering myself and this other man living in me, my wife felt lost. However, we both felt a strong commitment to each other and to our relationship and our children and to what might emerge from all of it.

During the several years after coming out to my wife, as we took on the task of repairing and re-imaging our relationship, we continued to be active in the church, the community, in our children's lives, and in each other's lives. We continued to have a supportive group of friends, although only a very few of them knew of the death and rebirth process that was happening in our relationship. To the outside world our lives and the life of our family looked normal—going to work, actively involved in music and church activities, going to ball games and school activities, and visiting with friends.

Internally, however, my wife and I were often involved in tense conversations; fighting and arguing over expectations, hurt feelings, and individual needs; working hard to both manage and repair the hurt, the betrayal, the anger, and the distrust that happen when a husband is not only having affairs, but is having them with men. My wife is a remarkable woman and to her credit she somehow had the ability to hold space like a crucible for the fires of transformation that would slowly occur, encouraging me, even forcing me at times to face the truth of my own soul and own the depths of who I was.

In the process we each eventually laid bare our souls to each other, began to slowly untangle our projections and different perceptions and realities, and discovered respect, humility, acceptance, and an enduring love. This certainly didn't happen overnight. It took many years. I often say that we went through several divorces and remarriages in this process to arrive at where we are today—a loving couple who honors and accepts the best and the worst in each other.

As the images of my dreams and inner world came into conflict with the images of my outer life, I had to make changes. These changes, detailed throughout this book, not only affected me, they affected my wife and children. There had been ongoing changes in the inner worlds of both me and my wife. They included our leaving the church, closing the bookstore, and selling our home to pay off the bookstore debt. They began when our children were in middle school and high school. Since our son and daughter were active in band, sports, cheerleading, and dating, we were active supporters of their lives while continuing to work and be a part of the community. But life moved on . . . the children graduated high school. Our son went off to California to pursue his dream of becoming a model, and our daughter went off to college. It appeared that we had managed to provide an adequate container for all of us to not only get through these years but to embrace them and live them fully and successfully.

Although I didn't frame it this way at the time, my relationship to my own feminine and androgynous natures resulted in my being open, accepting, tender, caring, and sensitive to the needs of my family. As I was learning to accept my various parts and diverse interests and learning to trust and follow my own dreams, I was able to support my son's interest in music and sports. I was able to take the criticism coming my way for allowing him to be the first boy in his high school to get an earring. I drove him to Indianapolis weekly to attend the John Robert Power's Modeling School. I helped him get his first car and had ongoing discussions about girls, sex, alcohol, and drugs with him.

Our daughter's middle school and high school years were emotionally tumultuous. She suffered from severe PMS with its emotional challenges and at one point was accused by her peers as being a lesbian.

Daughters often become the carriers of the father's anima projections. Looking back I can see how she carried the unspoken same-sex issues that were rumbling around in the unconscious life of the family. These then caused her to become a target of those same-sex issues by her peers. I spent many hours sitting with her, talking to her, holding her as she struggled with the emotions associated with PMS and feelings of rejection by her peers. But even in the midst of all this, she had a good group of friends, was a cheerleader throughout high school, and reports feeling supported, valued, and loved. Certainly, being a teacher in the school our children attended, being active in many of school activities they were involved in, and teaching many of their friends threw me automatically into their lives in more ways than if I had worked elsewhere. Looking back, we all agree that those were good years.

Then 1989 rolled around. My wife, who is often the first to sense what wants to come into consciousness, sensed it was time for our children to know the story of their parents' lives for the past fifteen years. I too had been having relevant dreams. In them, I would tell our children about my bisexuality. I also had dreams wherein they already knew about my bisexuality. Of course, knowing now how the unconscious works, our children did know at some level, that something was going on. This was confirmed later when both our children told us that especially through their elementary school years when this all came to a head they felt the tension in our relationship and felt "there was always something untold" and "feared that we would divorce."

Now in college, our daughter was having difficulty in her relationships with men. She was constantly disappointed in them and always looking for something that the men she chose didn't seem to be able to give her. My wife thought that maybe she would stop looking for a man "like her father" if she knew the complete story. There were also some people in the community who knew the story, and we feared that our children were at the age now where someone might say something to them. We didn't want them to find out from someone else. So we decided it was time to tell them. But we didn't know quite how to do this. After all, it had been over fifteen years since I had revealed this part of me to their mother. As a couple, their mother and I had worked through so much and were in a much better place in our relationship. How did we bring it up now and go back through all those years? Well, as often happens when we hesitate to act, the unconscious will force things upon us.

During one of the times our daughter was hurting and angry and blaming us as somehow being the cause of her distress, my wife told her that there were things that she didn't know that might help her understand some of her pain and anger at not being able to find the man she longed for. This became known as the "secret" between her and her brother. In the weeks between this revelation and our actual disclosure, she reports that she and her brother had many conversations about the "secret," wondering what it was.

When I finally told my son about my past, he was actually relieved. He had been afraid that I had killed somebody. He didn't put being bisexual in the same category as killing someone (although I can certainly understand his reference to "killing someone" as an accurate description of what I had done to his mother.) Since it was now fifteen years in the past and not happening currently, and I assured him that I had no desire to divorce his mother and return to a homosexual life, he seemed satisfied and happy. However, he did confess later that he worried that someday I might decide to return to a homosexual life and he didn't know how he would deal with that.

My wife and son had gone to see our daughter at college where she was cheerleading for a basketball game. From the stands he yelled "I know the secret." Later that evening while sitting in our daughter's dorm room, the "secret" came up and my daughter didn't think it fair that her brother knew and she didn't. So my wife made the decision to tell her. My daughter admits that she was in shock, and felt angry, hurt, and felt betrayed. After her mother and brother left, she went to talk to friends to find solace and comfort. She told them that if I called to try to talk to her, she didn't want to talk to me. However, later that night she called me. She was still angry and hurt. I did my best to allow her to have and express her feelings. Later she told me that I had let her say what she felt and in so doing, I had honored her feelings. This was the beginning of another shift in our family dynamics—not only my own relationship with my children—but in the relationship both my wife and I had with our children.

When my daughter found out about my hidden and dual life, she reportedly went through various stages often associated with grief and loss. At first she denied it, saying she "couldn't be a child of a homosexual. How could a man as perfect as my father like to touch other men?" She didn't care that my last same-sex encounter had happened over fifteen years ago. To her it was like it was happening now. She felt betrayed. I wasn't the man she thought I was. She learned I wasn't perfect like she thought.

To my daughter's credit and perhaps to our relationship, she took the risk of telling me what she felt. If she was having a day when she hated me, she told me. If she was angry and didn't understand it, she told me. She didn't care if I hurt, for in her mind I deserved to hurt. She found it hard to hate me and love me, understand and not understand, all at the same time. At times she would take the side of her mother and say things that she thought her mother should say to me. At other times, my daughter found herself sympathizing with me but not siding with me. It was two years of anger, hurt, yelling, coming together, pulling away, holding, crying, and yes, even laughing at times.

At the end of those two years my daughter wrote, "He is no longer perfect, actually he never was, but as a father is like no other, as a friend he is the best, as a man he is exceptional, and as a husband he is coming along nicely." It would take several more years and my daughter's suicide attempt before the evolution and transformation of this family would evolve into the open, loving, accepting, tolerant, and respectful family it has become.

As I have read back through my almost forty years of journals in the writing of this book, I realized that the way I interpreted my dreams and the various synchronicities determined many of the decisions I made. These decisions set the course for both my life and the life of my family. I realized that if I had interpreted my dreams in some other fashion I would have probably made different decisions, which would have had a very different outcome for me and for my family. Most likely we would have had a very different life. To that extent, I created my life and that life affected my family and eventually influenced their lives—even to some extent who they are today.

But of all the ways I could have understood a dream or have given a certain meaning to a synchronicity, what caused me to interpret the events the way I did? Why did I interpret a dream in a certain way? Why did I see specific synchronicities? Why did I see certain images in my paintings and not others? Is there some underlying presence, some transcendent function that directs it all, influencing our way of seeing? The shamans of Peru talk about "destiny lines." They believe that each soul has certain destinies associated with it. We can fall into a destiny unconsciously and live it much like fate. We can fight against a destiny that wants to live by being in constant conflict and longing, or we can wake up to the spiritual realm of archetypal forces vibrating in our soul, cooperate with them, and co-create a destiny. I do know that looking back over my journey I see a thread that wove a particular theme into my life.

For me it was a return to earth, a return to an awareness, and the experience that everything in the world is alive, conscious, dynamic, interconnected, and responsive and that nature—including human nature and the nature of our own souls—contains within them a directing intelligence that is the source of all knowledge concerning the nature of a person's being and becoming. We are in a reciprocal relationship with these forces in a way that we can engage them and influence them, not by mastering them or forcing them or controlling them, but by merging with them and working with them as partners in a larger story. This larger story encompasses the story of the Green Man, the story of the shaman, the story of the two-spirit soul, the story of the other man, the story of the heart—the soul's longing.

As I came to the end of this book, I decided to step into the shaman in me and journey into non-ordinary reality to see if I could consult with the spirit of the berdache, to inquire if the two-spirits had any additional message for me.

> *I ask my guide, Huascar, if I may visit the two-spirit people, telling him that I want to ask them if there is any message that the two-spirits want me to share with my readers. Suddenly I am traveling deep into the Underworld through dense vegetation. I come to a clearing, like a village. Many people are milling around, working, going about various tasks. Huascar tells me that this is the place of the two-spirit people, where they live.*
>
> *I am introduced to one, an elder. I tell this two-spirit that I am writing a chapter in a book on the relationship between homosexuality and the berdache, or two-spirit, and wonder*

if there is any message that the two-spirits would like for me to include. The elder two-spirit says to me, "Tell your readers that the two-spirits are real. We exist. We are neither male nor female, yet we are able to live from the spirits of both. Having found unity and harmony within ourselves, we live in harmony with all that is. We are returning to bring harmony and balance to the earth. While the current focus in your world seems to be on sexual and gender identity, sex with its various expressions is simply an expression of the creative energy that will eventually evolve into a creative union of spirits that will live in harmony with all spirits."

With that I thank the two-spirit. As I turn to leave, the elder hands me a small branch with a leaf growing out of it. He says, "Plant this branch, feed it, water it, and nurture it. It is the future." (Journal, 1-6-16)

Notes and Exercises

Now that you have finished reading the book and completing the exercises, what is the rest of your story? What is your longing? What calls to you? What longs to live? What parts of you have you gotten in touch with that need to be embraced, accepted, and loved? Where did you feel validated and affirmed? What resonated with you? What did you learn about your own erotic longings or sexual attractions? What changes might you make to live more authentically. What will be the rest of your story?

APPENDIX

My Parents

My father was a minister of a rather narrow-minded, legalistic, fundamental, evangelical church. During my years in the parsonage, his entire life revolved around the church and "spiritual" life. Dancing, fighting, smoking, drinking, sex, anger, and aggressive actions were discouraged and considered wrong, even a "sin" in his eyes to be punished if engaged in. One time he reprimanded me from the pulpit for talking in church. In response I threw a pencil at him. He immediately had me come to the platform and spanked me in front of the congregation. He believed in a definite set of rules regarding what was right and wrong and what was considered "sinful." He enforced those beliefs by making me feel guilty or through instilling in me a fear of punishment or displeasing God and going to hell.

My father was a loud, fast-talking, old-fashioned camp-meeting type preacher who was strong on emotion and sentimentality. A great "spiritual" experience for him was, after having preached a sermon, he would invite folks to come to the altar to accept Christ, confess their sins, and receive the Holy Spirit, and indulge in a loud, crying outburst of prayer. While he asserted himself with quite a bit of aggressiveness in the pulpit espousing the "Word of God," outside of that role he was for the most part a rather passive man who disliked confrontation and conflict. In fact, he avoided confrontation as much as possible, tending to acquiesce and accommodate. Or he backed up his opinion with the teachings of the Bible or the church, to which there was no plausible argument in his eyes. He once told me that whenever he would have feelings that went against what the church or church superiors said, he would feel extremely guilty and think that he wasn't "sanctified"—meaning he wasn't filled with the Holy Spirit. If he felt that he offended someone in a way that wasn't supported by biblical or church teachings, he would become overridden with guilt and apologize, backing down. He emphasized the importance of living one's life according to God's will, which for him was defined by the Bible or at times through direct revelation. However, even that had to be verified or supported by biblical teachings. He was overly sensitive to external and internal voices of criticism and judgment and lived under fear of somehow not being good enough or of displeasing God.

My father rarely did "boy things" with me. We didn't play ball, wrestle, go camping or hunting, or play in the dirt. He didn't teach me how to live in the world of men. But to his credit he did support my music and artistic interests by making sure I practiced the piano and by attending my piano recitals and musical programs and praising my artistic creations. Sex, dirty talk, and references to bodily functions were completely off-limits. References to *passing gas* or saying words like *fart* or *butt* were not allowed.

According to my mother, early in their marriage his own view of sex was that it was for procreation only and should not be indulged in except for that purpose. Later when I was an adult, he told me that he struggled with sexual thoughts and often felt guilty around sex and sexual feelings. Whenever I would react like a boy (fight, tease, etc.), I would get reprimanded and made to feel that I had done something wrong or committed some great sin. I always had to apologize to the person I had offended—and their parents. Also, if my mother didn't want me to do something, or if I made her upset, my father would make me stop "for my mother." I can't remember one time when he stood up to my mother for me and said, "He's a boy. Let him alone. Boys are like that." It was always, "Stop, you are upsetting your mother." He could not stand for her to be upset, hurt or angry, especially with something he did or said. Therefore, he consistently gave in to her, backing down, apologizing, acquiescing, and accommodating her demands and needs. The only exception was if the topic of conversation/dispute had something to do with the church or God.

On the other hand, he over-idealized my mother, calling her "Madam Queen." As an adult looking back I now see that was probably an overcompensation for the anger he felt toward her for the way she controlled him but he couldn't own, let along express. The idealization of the feminine was probably acquired in his relationship with his own mother. He mentioned his mother often during my childhood, idealizing her and sentimentalizing her, saying she was a "real saint" who would cry out during the sermons, shout prayers, and run through the aisles of the church bursting into loud lamentations as a way to express her love for God. He had fond memories of his mother. He never spoke negatively of her and he seldom spoke of his father. One of his favorite songs was "Tell Mother I'll be There." Another one went like this: "When I was but a boy in days of childhood . . . I'd hear my mother call at set of sun. Come home, come home, it's supper time . . ." My father was very sensitive and got his feelings hurt easily. But he never told you. He just said everything was okay and then went off and prayed about it.

At his core, my father was a kind, gentle, caring, and helpful man. He was a hard worker. My childhood memories and experiences are that my father spent his days caring for and tending to the needs of his parishioners, the poor in the community, the sick, the alcoholics, and anyone else who was suffering and in need, even bringing them home at times. He took his call to preach and the ministry of the gospel of Christ and building the church and the "Kingdom of God" very seriously. On occasion we would have to shorten a family vacation or cancel a family activity so that he could return home to take care of a parishioner. To this end he was passionate, loyal, responsible, and committed, seeing himself as a servant.

My mother was an introverted, shy, quiet, anxious woman who tended toward perfectionism. She was sensitive to criticism, easily overwhelmed, and her feelings were easily hurt. She responded by crying. At the same time she was critical in a self-righteous, judgmental sort of way of those who didn't live according to her expectations or beliefs. This, however, was expressed in a hushed gossip-like way, never quite directly, often presenting one image to the public and another in private.

Like many women raising children in the 1940s and '50s she was invested in being a housewife and taking care of her husband and children. She always made sure that we had what we needed as far as physical needs were concerned. To that extent, she was reliable and dependable. Meals were always on the table, and we usually ate together as a family. The clothes were always washed, ironed, and ready to wear. The house was kept clean and orderly, even to the point that she would sometimes put newspapers down on the newly waxed kitchen floor in order to keep it clean longer. (Sometimes her need for a clean and orderly house did interfere with what my brothers and I wanted to do.)

As the wife of a minister she served the church and, in doing so, served God. She was actively involved in the various educational and musical aspects of the church, teaching Sunday school and playing piano and organ while tending to other duties of a minister's wife. These duties included calling on parishioners with my father and entertaining the church board. Like my father, the church consumed her life. The Bible, the church, and its teachings were the dominant and controlling forces in the lives of both of my parents.

My mother rarely raised her voice or disciplined us, leaving that to my father. However, although she rarely raised her voice, she was a powerful presence in the parsonage in a quiet, subtle, and manipulative way. She often controlled the atmosphere, my father, my brothers, and me with her tears. For example, when I was six years old my father took me to get a haircut. He and I decided that I would get my hair cut very short. When I got home and my mother saw my hair, she burst into tears, very upset that my dad had let me get my hair cut so short. I ran and hid behind the couch. The message I received from both my mother and my father was "don't upset your mother." Thus, I was concerned with my mother's feelings, often sacrificing my own to keep her happy.

My mother wanted her firstborn to be a girl so much so that she didn't have a boy's named picked out at my birth. As fate would have it, I was an introverted, shy, musical, artistic, and sensitive child. My mother was quite creative and spent much time sewing and making various craft projects. She disliked crowds of people and tended to withdraw into herself and her creative projects. Because of my natural tendency for the arts and music I became her companion, learning to cook, knit, draw, paint, and decorate the house— becoming in many ways the girl she had wanted. As mentioned earlier in the book, starting around the age of eight I would find any excuse I could to wear dresses, whether it was Halloween or dress-up play with my brothers and friends. This practice continued well into my teen years. While

I had male friends I didn't like playing ball or other sports, choosing rather to play house or dolls with the girls in the neighborhood.

My mother reinforced this more feminine and creative side by discouraging aggressive play and by teaching me various crafts that supported my natural interests in art and music. She also supported my interests in nature, allowing me to bring frog eggs home from my journeys to the woods and watching over them until they hatched. She allowed me to bring wounded birds home to feed, care for, and raise; I often kept them in a box in the house. She supported my interest in aquariums and fish and dogs and cats, even feeling bad and crying with me when she let one of my fish escape down the drain in the kitchen sink where she'd been cleaning the aquarium. She also cried another time when my kitten was accidently killed. It had gotten caught in the back door as my mother was emerging through it carrying a basket of clothes.

As Mother she was there to support my piano recitals, my music contests, my art contests, my band and choir concerts. Upon reflection, this support and validation for my rather shy, sensitive, introverted, and creative self set the stage for that boy to become the self-reflective, introspective, analytic, and creative man I am today— the man who sought an inner life through the study of his dreams, religion, philosophy, consciousness, and art, which provided me an avenue to a very meaningful adult life. All of this to say that in those early years in the mother-child relationship where mirroring is important I had what English pediatrician and psychoanalyst Donald Winnicott calls the "good enough mother." This probably contributed to a rather positive mother complex. And for that I am grateful.

On the other hand, my mother, being an introverted, shy, and anxious person wasn't always nurturing or caring. An experience of being loved by her was based more on what she did for us rather than what we felt from her. But that seeming indifference on her part also had its perks. Today, my brothers and I often comment on the fact that when we left the house in the morning, she often had no idea where we were going or what we were doing. We would be gone sometimes for hours, coming home to grab lunch—and then we'd be off again, exploring the world any way we wanted to.

My mother was not a strong outspoken mother but one who could make me do what she wanted. She made me not want to upset her or make her cry or otherwise feel bad. She emphasized the importance of being well behaved, keeping your clothes clean, and doing the right thing as defined by the rules of the Bible, God, and the church so as not to be an embarrassment to her as a minister's wife. As such I learned to tend to and manage her feelings and sacrifice my own desires and needs in order to keep her happy or so I wouldn't get into trouble.

ACKNOWLEDGMENTS

I wish to thank the many people who accompanied me on this journey. The late Dean Frantz, Jungian analyst, for his capacity to sit with my inner world and hold all the opposing and seemingly contradictory forces while encouraging me to trust the dreams and to allow the journey to unfold. "The dreams know the way," he would tell me. And indeed, they did! I am indebted to colleague and friend Hilda Studebaker, who first listened to my dreams and introduced me to Carl Jung by putting book by him in my mailbox at the high school where we both taught. Hilda was a frequent figure in my dreams as an inner guide, and in the real world of consensus reality, she and I spent hours discussing dreams in general. She and I also spent time reading my early writings, going over every sentence word by word to help me express exactly what I wanted to say. For all her help along the way, I am deeply grateful.

I would also like to thank my wife, Betty, for her unconditional love and belief in me, for her unwavering capacity to hold space in our relationship for this journey to unfold, and for her willingness to follow wherever it took us. My children Todd and Ruth were part of the container that held me together during this often tumultuous journey, and I am most appreciative of their support, especially given that today, as adults, they have an unwavering love and acceptance for a dad whose actions were, at times, very challenging for them. I am also indebted to Greg Ellis for the hours he spent reading the manuscript, for his encouragement that I keep writing, and for his invaluable feedback and suggestions. I also want to acknowledge the men's group that I was part of, and I thank John Nolan, Rik Spier, Reid Litwack, Dan Mosley, and Bernie Lyon for their belief in me, for their unconditional acceptance and support, and for their invaluable friendship as I shared bits and pieces of this journey with them. To Dan and Bernie for reading the manuscript. Pat Hedegard, colleague and friend, for the hours we spent discussing each chapter and for her invaluable assistance in helping me remove redundancies and unnecessary words and to get clearer on exactly what I wanted to say. My parents, Russell and Eloise Shalley, and my brothers Larry, Michael, and Jim for the invaluable childhood container of physical, psychological, and spiritual forces they provided, which set up the dynamics necessary for this life story to emerge. While much of this often seemed to be in resistance or in opposition to that container, it nevertheless became the impetus for my soul's journey. For in the ground of who they were lay the seed of who I was to become. I can now thank them for the struggles I went through, for the longing of that seed to break free from the depths of the soul and to find its life. I also want to thank my brother and psychologist, Jim Shalley, for reading the manuscript and seeing its value beyond my personal story, and for our countless hours of discussion about family and psychological dynamics.

Finally, I acknowledge the dreams themselves. Without their guidance, this journey would not have happened, nor would this book have been written. To the many allies in nonordinary reality, I thank you for your guidance and assistance.

And to synchronicity—so many synchronicities that guided my journey.

Thank you all!

For the use of copyrighted material grateful acknowledgment is made to the following:

Princeton University Press, for excerpts from the following titles:The Collected Works of C.G. Jung, ed, by G. Adler, M. Fordham, W, McGuire and H. Read, trans. By R. F. C. Hull, Bollingen Series XX, vol. 14m *Mysterium Coniunctionis* (copyright © by Bollingen Foundation and © 1970 by Princeton University Press); reprinted by permission of Princeton University Press; also, *Ariadne's Clue: A Guide to the Symbols of Humankind* by Anthony Stevens (© 1999 by Princeton University Press); reprinted by permission of Princeton University Press; also, *Psychic Energy: Its Source and Its Transformation* by Mary Esther Harding (© 1947 and 1963 by Bollingen Foundation); reprinted by permission of Princeton University Press.

Llewellyn Publications, for excerpts from *The World of Shamanism: New Views of an Ancient Tradition* by Roger Walsh, copyright © 2007 by Roger Walsh, reprinted by permission of Llewellyn Publications.

The Golden Sufi Center, for excerpts from "Anima Mundi: Awakening the Soul of the World" by Llewellyn Vaughan-Lee, *Sufi Journal*, Issue 67, Autumn 2005; copyright ©2005 by The Golden Sufi Center, http://goldensufi.org/anima-mundi-awakening-the-soul-of-the-world.

Spring Journal, for excerpt from *The Betrayal of the Soul in Psychotherapy* by Robert Stein, copyright ©1973 by Robert Stein, published by Spring Journal, Inc. and reprinted under copyright fair use law.

Beacon Press, for excerpts from *The Spirit and the Flesh: Sexual Diversity in American Indian Culture* by Walter L. Williams, copyright © 1986, 1992 by Walter L. Williams, reprinted by permission of Beacon Press.

Thames and Hudson, Inc, for excerpts from *Myth and Symbol in Ancient Egypt* by R. T. Rundle Clark, copyright © 1959, reprinted by kind permission of Thames and Hudson Ltd., London.

Northwestern University Press, for excerpt from The Feminine in Jungian Psychology and in Christian Theology by Ann Belford Ulanov, copyright © by Ann Belford Ulanov, reprinted under copyright fair use law.

RESOURCES AND RECOMMENDED READING

Books on Dreams and the Inner Life

Dream: Discovering You Inner Teacher. Clyde H. Reid. Minneapolis, Minn.: Winston Press, Inc., 1983.

Inner Work: Using Dreams and Active Imagination for Personal Growth. Robert Johnson. New York: HarperCollins Publishers, 1986.

Jungian Dream Interpretation. James Hall. Toronto: Inner City Books, 1983.

The Kingdom Within: A Study of the Inner Meanings of Jesus's Sayings. John Sanford. New York: HarperOne, 2009.

Man and His Symbols. C. G. Jung: New York and London, 1964.

The Symbolic Quest. Edward Whitmont. Princeton: Princeton University Press, 1969.

Why People Fly and Water Runs Uphill: Using Dreams to Tap the Wisdom of the Unconscious. Jeremy Taylor. New York: Warner Books, 1992.

Books on Psychology and the Soul

Archetypes Revisited: An Updated Natural History of the Self. Anthony Stevens. Toronto: Inner City Books, 2003.

The Betrayal of the Soul in Psychotherapy. Robert Stein. Woodstock, Ct.: Spring Journal, Inc., 1998.

Bringing Your Shadow Out of the Dark: Breaking Free From the Hidden Forces that Drive You. Robert Augustus Masters. Boulder, Co.: Sounds True, 2018.

The Invisible Partners. John Sanford. New York: Paulist Press, 1974.

Projection and Re-collection in Jungian Psychology: Reflections on the Soul. Maria-Louise von Franz. Peru, IL: Open Court Publishing Company, 1980.

The Return of the Goddess. Edward Whitmont. New York: Crossroad Publishing Co., 1978.

Books on Shamanism

Courageous Dreaming: How Shamans Dream the World into Being. Alberto Villoldo. New York: Hay House, Inc., 2008.

Shaman, Healer, Sage. Alberto Villoldo. New York: Harmony Books, 2000.

Shamanic Journeying: A Beginner's Guide. Sandra Ingerman. Boulder, Co.: Sounds True, 2004.

Stone Age Wisdom: The Healing Principles of Shamanism. Tom Crockett. Newport News, Va.: Bliss Press, 2010.

The World of Shamanism: New Views of an Ancient Tradition. Roger Walsh. Woodbury, Minn.: Llewellyn Publications, 2007.

Books on Earth Spirituality and the Green Man

Christianity and Nature-Based Spirituality: A Shamanic Journey through the Medicine Wheel. Lillie Rowden. Wimberly, Tex: 2nd Tier Publishing, 2014.

Green Man: The Archetype of our Oneness with the Earth. William Anderson. San Francisco: HarperCollins, 1990.

Green Man, Earth Angel: The Prophetic Tradition and the Battle for the Soul of the World. Tom Cheetham. Albany, N.Y.: State University of New York Press, 2005.

The Lost Gospel of the Earth: A Call for Renewing Nature, Spirit, and Politics. Tom Hayden. Brooklyn, N.Y.: IG Publishing, 1996, 2007.

The Path of the Green Man: Gay Men, Wicca and Living a Magical Life. Michael Thomas Ford. Toronto: Citadel; American First Edition, 2005.

The Quest for the Green Man. John Matthews. Wheaton, Ill.: Quest Books, 2001.

Books on Male Sexuality and Spirituality

Castration and Male Rage: The Phallic Wound. Eugene Monick. Toronto: Inner City Books, 1991.

Jung, Jungians, and Homosexuality. Robert H. Hopcke. Wipf & Stock Publishing, 2002.

Phallos: Sacred Image of the Masculine. Eugene Monick. Toronto: Inner City Books, 1987.

The Secret Lore of Gardening: Patterns of Male Intimacy. Graham Jackson. Toronto: Inner City Books, 1991.

Sexuality and Spirituality: A Study of Feminine/Masculine Relationship. John Moore. New York: Harper and Row Publishers, 1980.

The Spirit and the Flesh: Sexual Diversity in American Indian Culture. Walter Williams. Boston: Beacon Press, 1992.

Books on Healing

Healing of the Soul: Shamanism and Psyche. Ann Drake. Ithaca, N.Y.: Busca, Inc., 2003.

Imagery in Healing: Shamanism and Modern Medicine. Jeanne Achterberg, Boston: Shambhala Publications, Inc., 1985.

Why People Don't Heal and How They Can. Caroline Myss. New York: Harmony Books, 1997.

Discovering your Archetypes

www.archetype.com

www.culturetalk.com.

Determining your Archetypes at https://www.myss.com/free-resources/sacred-contracts-and-your-archetypes/determining-your-archetypes/

Archetypes: A Beginner's Guide to Your Inner-net. Caroline Myss. New York: Hay House, Inc., 2013.

Shamanic Journey Music

12 Minute Drumming Track with Whistles and Rattles. Sandra Ingerman. https://youtu.be/-UMH7s21ukM

Shamanic Journey—15 Minutes Solo Drumming. Michael Harner. https://youtu.be/MmQ1H4wU0zs

Shamanic Journey—30 Minutes Solo Drumming. Michael Harner. https://youtu.be/WqrBfyCQ0lQ

30 Minutes of Powerful Shamanic Drumming with Atmospheric Music. The Honest Guys. https://youtu.be/BwqH7l9xSgo

BIBLIOGRAPHY

Abrams, M. H., and G. C. Harpham. *A Glossary of Literary Terms*, ninth edition. Wadsworth Cengage Learning, 2009.

Achterberg, Jean. *Imagery in Healing: Shamanism and Modern Medicine*. Boston, MA: Shambhala Publications, Inc., 1985.

Allegro, John. *The Sacred Mushroom and the Cross*. Gnostic Media Research and Publishing, 2009.

Anderson, William. *Green Man: The Archetype of our Oneness with the earth*. San Francisco: HarperCollins, 1990.

Andrews, Ted. *Animal-Speak*. St. Paul, MN: Llewellyn Publications, 2001.

Araneo, Phyllis. "The Archetypal, Twenty First Century Resurrection of the Ancient Image of the Green Man." Journal of Futures Studies, August 2008, 13(1): 43 - 64

Balanchine, *Balanchine's New Complete Stories of the Great Ballets*. Garden City, NY: Doubleday & Company. 1968.

Barnhouse, Ruth. *Homosexuality: Symbolic Confusion*. New York: Seabury Press, 1977.

Barrow, J. D. and Tipler, F. J. *The Anthropic Cosmological Principle*, Oxford Clarendon Press, 1986.

Bell, Alan, Martin Weinber, and Sue Hammersmith. *Sexual Preference: Its Development in Men and Women*. Bloomington, Ind.: Indiana University Press, 1981.

"Biological Basis of Homosexuality." *Brain Mind Bulletin*. November 19, 1984, 1.

Bohm, David. *Wholeness and the Implicate Order*. Boston: Routledge and Kegan Paul, 1980.

Bolen, Jean Shinoda. *Gods in Everyman*. San Francisco: Harper and Row. 1989.

Cameron, David. *A Happy Pocket Full of Money*. Hampton Road Publishing Company, Inc. 2008.

Campbell, Joseph. Quoted in Richo, David. *The Power of Coincidence*. Boston: Shambhala Publications, Inc., 2007

Chalquist M.S., Ph.D., Craig, *Terrapsychology: Reengaging the Soul of Place*. Spring Journal

Books, 2007.

Cheetham, Tom. *Green Man, Earth Angel: The Prophetic Tradition and the Battle for the Soul of the World*. Albany, NY: State University of New York Press, 2005.

Christensen, Michael. *C. S. Lewis on Scripture*. Waco, TX: Word Books, 1979.

Cirlot, J. E. *A Dictionary of Symbols*. New York: Philosophical Library, 1962.

Clair, Michael. *Sexual Mysticism in Christianity*. 2009. Quoted in Suck like an Egyptian" — The Holy Grail of the Christian "Eucharist" is Founded on Ancient Semen-drinking, 1993 Rites Retrieved from zaidpub.com/.../ spermo-gnosis-or-suck-like-an-egyptian-the-holy-grail-of-t...

Clark, Robert Thomas Rundle. *Myth and Symbol in Ancient Egypt*. Thames and Hudson, Inc., 1978

Cooper, J. C. *An Illustrated Encyclopaedia of Traditional Symbols*. New York: Thames and Hudson, Inc., 1984.

Crockett, Tom. *Stone Age Wisdom: The Healing Principles of Shamanism*. Newport News, VA: Bliss Press, 2010

Dale, Cindi. *The Subtle Body: An Encyclopedia of Your Energetic Anatomy*. Boulder, CO: Sounds True, Inc., 2009.

Edinger, Edward. *The Aion Lectures*. Toronto: Inner City Books, 1996.

Edinger, Edward. *Anatomy of the Psyche*. La Salle, IL: Open Court Publishing Company, 1985.

Eliade, Mircea. *Image and Symbols*. Princeton University Press, 1961

Ellis, Greg, *Re-Membering Frankenstein: Healing the Monster in Every Man*. Bloomington, IN: AuthorHouse, 2011

Fisher, Helen, E. "*Brains Do It: Lust, Attraction and Attachment*." The Dana Foundation, 2000.

Retrieved from http://www.dana.org/Cerebrum/Default.aspx?id=39351#.

Florida Quick Facts: Ben's Guide to U.S. Government. Retrieved from www.rightsofthepeople.com/education/government_for_kids/3-5/state/

Garretmenges.wordpress.com "The Ground of All Being—High Gravity Pt. 4" (Tillich). July 29, 2013.

GodGuy.com. "The Spiritual Origin of Kissing." Retrieved from http://www.staircasepress.com.

Goswami, Amit. *The Self-Aware Universe: How Consciousness Creates the Material Universe*. Penguin Putman, Inc., 1995.

Greenberg and Pearlman. "An Integrated Approach to Dream Theory and Clinical Practice," in *in Dream* Gayle M.V. Delaney (Ed), *New Directions Interpretation*. Albany: New York University Press, 1993.

Grof M.D., Stanislav. "Evidence for the Akashic Field from Modern Consciousness Research." 2007. Retrieved from www.afterlife-library.com/.../Evidence-for-the-Akashic-Field-from-Modern-...

Guggenbuhl-Craig, Adolf. *Eros on Crutches*. Dallas, TX: Spring Publications, 1980

Haddon, Genia Pauli. "Delivery Yang-Femininity." Spring Publications (1987): 133-141.

Hall, James. *Jungian Dream Interpretation*. Toronto: Inner City Books, 1983.

Hanh, Thich Nhat, in "The Buddha Flower Opens." Kathy Butler, Common Boundary, Nov/Dec, 1989.

Hannah, Barbara. "The Archetypal Symbolism of Animals." Lecture given at the C. G. Jung Institute, Zurich, 1954–1958.

Hannah, Barbara. *The Cat, Dog and Horse Lectures, and "the Beyond."* Edited by Dean Frantz. Wilmette, IL: Chiron Publications, 1992.

Harding, Mary Esther. *Psychic Energy*. Princeton: Princeton University Press, 1973.

HigherLove. "Gatekeepers and Shamanic Androgyny." *The Mists of Avalon* (blog). April 21, 2011.

Hillman, James. *Anima*. Dallas, TX: Spring Publications, Inc., 1985

Hillman, James. *Loose Ends*. Dallas, TX: Spring Publications, 1989.

Hillman, James. *Re-visioning Psychology.* New York: Harper Collins Publishers, 1975.

Hillman, James. *The Soul's Code. New York: Random House, 1996.*

Hillman, James. *The Thought of the Heart and the Soul of the World.* Putnam, CONN.: Spring Publications, Inc., 1992..

Hoff, Bert. "Gays: Guardians of the Gates." An Interview with Malidoma Some. *M.E.N. Magazine,* September 1993.

Hopcke, Robert H. "Jung's Attitudes toward Homosexuality." *Spring.* 1987: 154–161.

Ingeborg Baldauf. "Bacabozlik: Boylove, Folksong and Literature in Central Asia." *Paedika 2* (1990): 12–31.

Ingerman, Sandra. "Shamanism: Healing of Individuals and the Planet." Retrieved from SandraIngerman.com.

Jacobi, Jolande. *Complex/Archetype/Symbol in the Psychology of C.G. Jung.* Princeton: Princeton University Press, 1959.

Johnson, Robert. *He.* New York: Harper and Row, 1974.

Jung, C. G., *Man and His Symbols.* (With M.-L. von Franz, J. L. Henderson, J. Jacobi, A. Jaffe) New York and London, 1964.

Jung, C. G. *Memories, Dreams and Reflections.* New York: Vintage Books, 1965.

Jung, C. G. *Visions.* Vol. 1, in Hannah, Barbara.

Jung, C. G. *The Collected Works of C. G. Jung.* Edited by Sir H Read, M. Fordham, G. Adler, and W. McGuire. Translated by R.F.C. Hull. Princeton: Princeton University Press (Bollingen Series XX). Volumes cited:

Vol. 5. Symbols of Transformation, 1956.

Vol. 6. Psychological Types. 1971.

Vol. 7. *Two Essays on Analytical Psychology.* 1953.

Vol. 8. On the Nature of the Psyche. 1960.

Vol. 9. Part 1. The Archetypes of the Collective Unconscious, 1970

Vol. 9, Part 2, Aion. 2nd ed. 1968.

Vol. 10. *Civilization in Transition,* 1964.

Vol. 11. Psychology and Religion: West and East, 2nd ed. 1969.

Vol. 14. *Mysterium Coniunctionis.* 1970.

Vol. 16. *Practice of Psychotherapy,* 1954.

Vol. 17. The Development of Personality. 1954.

Kane, Janet. "Re-awakening the Green Man." Jung Society of Washington. Retrieved from www.jung.org/page-18182

Kazakova, Tamara. "Coyote." *Encyclopedia Mythica.* Retrieved from www.pantheon.org.

Keen, Sam. "Stories We Live By: Personal Myths Guide Daily Life." *Psychology Today,* December 1988.

Kelsey, Morton. *God, Dreams, and Revelation.* Minneapolis, MN Augsburg Publishing, 1974

Kurtz, Ron and Hector Prestera. *The Body Reveals.* Harper Row Quicksilver Books, 1976

Laszlo, E. *The Connectivity Hypothesis: Foundations of an Integra Science of Quantum, Cosmos, Life, and Consciousness.* Stat University of New York Press, 2003.

Laszlo, E. *Science and the Akashic Field: An Integral Theory of Everythin* Rochester, Vt.: Inner Traditions, 2004.

ard, John. "Homoeroticism in Primitive Society as a Function of the Self." *Journal of Analytical Psychology,* 4.2. 1949.

ach, Maria, ed. *Standard Dictionary of Folklore, Mythology and Legend.* New York: Funk & Wagnalls, 1949

e Begins at Forty, The Phrase Finder. Retrieved from www.phrases.org.uk.

ndstrom, Meg. "A Wink from the Cosmos." *Intuition Magazine.* May 1996.

ain, Shiho. *Childhood Re-imagined.* New York: Routledge, 2008.

andal, Ananya. "Semen and Culture." Retrieved from www.news-medical.net/health/Semen-and-Culture.aspx.

atthews, John, *The Quest for the Green Man.* Wheaton, IL: Quest Books, 2001.

:Carty, Ph,D., et al. "Modulation of DNA Conformation by Heart-Centered Intention." Institute of HeartMath, 2003. Retrieved from www.aipro.info/drive/File/224.pdf

:Craty, Rollin, Ph.D., et al. "The Coherent Heart Heart-Brain Interactions, Psychophysiological Coherence and the Emergence of System-Wide Order." *Integral Review,* December 2009. Vol. 5, No. 2.

eting the Shadow. Edited by Connie Zweig and Jeremiah Abrams. Los Angeles: Jeremy P. Tarcher, Inc., 1991.

oney, John. "Differing Perspectives on Master and Johnson." *Behavioral Medicine,* June 1979.

onick, Eugene. *Castration and Male Rage: The Phallic Wound.* Toronto: Inner City Books, 1991.

onick, Eugene. *Phallos: Sacred Image of the Masculine.* Toronto: Inner City Books, 1987.

Moore, John. *Sexuality and Spirituality.* New York: Harper and R Publishers, 1980.

Myss, Carolyn. *Why People Don't Heal and How They Can.* New Yo Harmony Books, 1997.

Naydler, Jeremy. "*Ancient Egypt and Modern Esotericism.*" Rosicruc Digest No. 1, 2007.

"O Being." Recorded with Krista Tippett. NPR. October 11, 2012.

Onians, Richard B. *The Origins of European Thought.* New Yo Cambridge University Press, 1988.

Peat, David F. "*Synchronicity: The Bridge between Matter and Min* Retrieved from hhp://www.newciv.org/ISSS_Primer/seminar.ht

Peregrin. "The Penis and Male Force: A Snippet from Isis and Osir *The Magic of the Ordinary: Encounter with Mystery, Politics a Sex* (blog). March 6, 2015.

Plato. *The Dialogues of Plato.* New York: Charles Scribner's Sons, 1

Plato. *Symposium and Phaedrus.* New York: Dover Publications, 19

Pribram, K.H. *Languages of the brain: Experimental Paradoxes a Principles in Neuropsychology.* Englewood Cliffs, New Jers Prentice-Hall, Inc., 1971.

Prigogine, llya. *From Being to Becoming: Time and Complexity in Physical Universe.* W.H. Freeman & Co Ltd, 1980.

Rein and McCraty. "Local and Non-Local Effects of Coherent He Frequencies on Conformational Changes in DNA." Retrieved fr Rein and McCraty. "Local and Non-Local Effects of Coherent He Frequencies on Conformational Changes in DNA."

Richo, David. *The Power of Coincidence.* Boston: Shambh Publications, Inc., 2007.

Romer, John. *Testament: The Bible and History.* Holt, 1989.

Roscoe, Will. "Gay American Indians: Creating an Identity from Past Traditions." *The Advocate*, October 29, 1985.

Roscoe, Will. "*Who Are the Native American Two Spirits?*" *www.willsworld.org/twospiritq-a.html*

Rothery, Andrew. "The Science of the Green Man." *Journal of the International Community for*

Ecopsychology.

Reuters. "Did We Come Out of Africa? Studies Collide." *New York Times*, January 12, 2001.

Samuels, Andrew, Bani Shorter and Fred Plaut. *A Critical Dictionary of Jungian Analysis.* New York: Routledge and Kegan Paul, Inc., 1986.

Sanford, John. *Evil: The Shadow Side of Reality.* New York: The Crossroads Publishing Company, 1981.

Sanford, John. *The Invisible Partners.* New York: Paulist Press,1980.

Sanford, John. *The Man Who Wrestled with God.* New York: Paulist Press, 1974.

Savic I., H. Berglund, and P. Lindström. "Brain response to putative pheromones in homosexual men." Proceedings of the National Academy of Sciences (PNAC) (2005) 102:7356–7361.

Schwartz-Salant, N. "On the subtle-body concept in clinical practice." In N. Schwartz-Salant & M. Stein (Eds.), *The Body in Analysis.* Wilmette, IL: Chiron Publications (1986): 19-58.

Schwartz-Salant, N. *The Borderline Personality: Vision and Healing.* Chiron Publications, 1989.

Sheldrake, Rupert. *A New Science of Life: The Hypothesis of Morphi Resonance*. Park Street Press, 1981.

Sheldrake, Rupert. *The Presence of the Past: Morphic Resonance an the Memory of Nature*. New York: Vintage Books, 1988.

Snowden, Ruth. *Jung: The Key Ideas*. McGraw-Hill, 2010.

Stein, Robert. *The Betrayal of Soul in Psychotherapy*. Woodstock CONN: Spring Journal, Inc., 1998

Stevens, Anthony. *Archetypes: A Natural History of the Self*. London Routledge and Kegan Paul, LTD, 1982.

Stevens, Anthony. *Archetype Revisited: An Updated Natural History o the Self*. Toronto: Inner City Books, 2003.

Stevens, Anthony. *The Two-Million Year Old Man*. College Station Texas A&M University Press, 1993.

Stevens, Anthony. Psychological Notes: "The Penis Itself is a Phallic Symbol?" Retrieved from www.independent.co.uk/... psychological-notes-the-penis-is-itself-a-phallic.

Stevens, Anthony. *Ariadne's Clue: A Guide to the Symbols of Humankind* Princeton, N.J.: Princeton University Press, 1998.

Suck like an Egyptian" — The Holy Grail of th Christian "Eucharist" is Founded on Ancient Semen drinking, 1993 Rites Retrieved from zaidpub.com/... spermo-gnosis-or-suck-like-an-egyptian-the-holy-grail-of-t...

Swaab, Dick F. "Sexual Orientation and its Basis in Brain Structure and Function," Proceedings of the National Academy of Science (PNAC) 105, no. 30, 10273–10274.

Switzer, David K., and Shirley Switzer, *Parents of the Homosexual* Philadelphia: The Westminster Press. 1980.

egel, Will. *The Mother Tongue*. Wimberley, TX: 2nd Tier Publishing, 2012.

Paske, Bradley. *Rape and Ritual*. Toronto: Inner City Books, 1982.

esidder, Jack. *Symbols and Their Meaning*. London: Duncan Baird Publishers, 2000.

cker, Suzetta. "Christ Story Bull Page." *Christ Story Christian Bestiary*. 1997. Dec. 11, 2011. Retrieved from http://www.netnitco.net/users/legend01/bull.htm.

anov, Ann. *The Feminine in Jungian Psychology and in Christian Theology*. Evanston: Northwestern University Press, 1971.

ughan-Lee, Llewellyn. "Anima Mundi: Awakening the Soul of the World." *Sufi Journal*, Issue 67, Autumn 2005.

ughan-Lee, Lleyellyn. *The Return of the Feminine and the World Soul*. Pointe Reyes, CA: The Golden Sufi Center, 2013.

lloldo, Albert. *Mending the Past and Healing the Future with Soul Retrieval*. New York: Hay House, Inc., 2005.

lloldo, Albert. *Shaman, Healer*, Sage. New York: Harmony Books, 2000.

n Franz, Marie-Louise. (Ed.). *Aurora Consurgens: A document attributed to Thomas*

uinas on the problem of opposites in alchemy—Edited with a commentary by Marie-Louise von Franz, 2000. R. F. C. Hull & A. S. B. Glover, Trans. Toronto, Canada: Inner City. Original work published 1966.

n Franz, Marie-Louise. *Dreams: A Study of the Dreams of Jung, Descartes, Socrates, and Other Historical Figures. Boston, MA:* Shambhala, Publications, 1991.

Von Franz, Marie-Louise. *An Introduction to the Interpretation of Fair Tales*. Boston, MA: Shambhala Publications, Inc., 1973.

Von Franz, Marie-Louise. Projection and Re-collection in Jungia Psychology. La Salle: Open Court Publishing Company, 1980.

Von Franz, Marie-Louise. *Redemption Motifs in Fairy Tales*. Inne City Books, 1985.

Von Franz, Marie-Louise and Boa, Fraser. *The Way of the Drean* Boston, MA: Shambhala Publications, 1994. Also "The Way of th Dream" Documentary film series made by Fraser Boa.

Walker, Barbara. *The Woman's Encyclopedia of Myths and Secrets. Sa Francisco: Harper and Row, 1983.*

Walsh, Roger. "*The Spirit of Evolution.*" Cognitive Cultural Studie Review. UCLA, 1995. Walsh, Roger. *The World of Shamanisn New View of an Ancient Tradition*. Woodbury, MN: Llewelly Publications, 2007.

Watsky, Paul. "Anima." A lecture delivered in the fall of 2001 as segment of the San Francisco Jung Institute public program entitle Jung's Map of the Soul.

Weiss, Brian. *Many Lives, Many Masters*. New York: Simon & Schust Inc., 1988.

Wellesley, Gordon. *Sex and the Occult*. New York: Bell Publishi Company, 1973.

Wesley, John. *The Works of John Wesley Works, Volume VI*. Wesley Methodist Book Room, 1872.

Westman, Heniz. *Structure of Biblical Myths: The Ontogenesis of t Psyche*. Dallas, TX: Spring Publications, 1983.

Martes, C.J. "What is the Akashic Field?" Retrieved from www.cjmart com/cjmartes_akashicfield.asp.

Vhitmont, Edward. *The Alchemy of Healing: Psyche and Soma. Berkeley, CA: North Atlantic Books, 1993*

Vhitmont, Edward. *Return of the Goddess.* New York: Crossroad Publishing Co., 1978.

Vhitmont, Edward. *The Symbolic Quest.* Princeton, NJ: Princeton University Press, 1969.

Vilber, Ken. "Which Level of God do You Believe in?" Retrieved from www.beliefnet.com/.../which-level-of-god-do-you-believe-in.aspx

Vilkerson, Richard Catlett. *Jung, The Self and Dreamwork.* Electric Dreams 8(3). (March 2001). Retrieved from http://www.dreamgate.com/electric-dreams.

Villiams, Walter. *The Spirit and the Flesh: Sexual Diversity in American Indian Cultures.* Boston: Beacon Press, 1992.

Vink, Walter. *Unmasking the Powers.* Philadelphia: Fortress Press, 1986.

McKay, Bret and Kay. *8 Interesting (And Insane) Male Rites of Passages From Around the World*, Feb.21, 2010. Retrieved from www.artofmanliness.com/.../male-rites-of-passage-from-around-the-world/

Miclaus, Claudia. "The Symbolism of Kissing." Retrieved from www.buzzle.com/articles/the-symbolism-of-kissing.

Vynkoop, Mildred Bangs. *A Theology of Love. Kansas City, MO: Beacon Hill Press, 1972.*

Zandog 17. "Caduceus/Hermes/Aphrodite/Serpent/Androgyn." Retrieved from hobbithills.blogspot.com/.../caduceushermesaphroditeserpentandrogyn.htmlP

ABOUT THE AUTHOR

Sheldon Shalley, MA, MSW, is a psychotherapist, licensed clinical socia worker, educator, artist and shamanic practitioner. For more than thirt years he has helped people break free from destructive and unhealth patterns and move toward psychological and spiritual well-being.

Raised in an evangelical minister's home, Sheldon's desire t reconcile his traditional religious training with his non-traditiona sexuality thrust him into the study of his dreams, various spiritua traditions, philosophy, psychology and eventually shamanism an energy medicine.

Sheldon has led dream groups and shaman circles, presente workshops on understanding your dreams, sexuality and spirituality shamanism, art and energy medicine. His blog, *The Psychotherapis and the Shaman,* contains articles on the integration of psychotherapy shamanism and art as pathways to healing. An accomplished artist Sheldon regularly exhibits in the Indianapolis area and uses his art t open portals as avenues for healing.

Sheldon earned his master's degree in social work from Indian University. He lives in Noblesville, Indiana, with his wife of over 5 years, Betty. They have two children and two grandchildren. Hi personal psycho-sexual-spiritual journey and work as a psychother apist have given him direct experience with healing the emotional psychological, and spiritual wounds of human suffering. Sheldon i in private practice in Indianapolis, Indiana.

He is available for conferences, workshops, consultations, psycho-
erapy, and shamanic healing. For more information visit Integrative
ychotherapy at the Crossing at www.ip-atc.com or www.sheldonshal-
.com or contact him at sheldon@sheldonshalley.com.